# Finding the Plot

# Finding the Plot: Storytelling in Popular Fictions

Edited by

Diana Holmes, David Platten,
Loïc Artiaga and Jacques Migozzi

CAMBRIDGE
SCHOLARS
PUBLISHING

Finding the Plot: Storytelling in Popular Fictions,
Edited by Diana Holmes, David Platten, Loïc Artiaga and Jacques Migozzi

This book first published 2013

Cambridge Scholars Publishing

12 Back Chapman Street, Newcastle upon Tyne, NE6 2XX, UK

British Library Cataloguing in Publication Data
A catalogue record for this book is available from the British Library



ISBN (10): 1-4438-4238-9, ISBN (13): 978-1-4438-4238-9

# TABLE OF CONTENTS

**Part II. Story/History**



**Part III: Bending Genres**

# PREFACE

The starting point for this book was a three-day conference **Finding the Plot: On the Importance of Storytelling in Popular Fictions,** co-organised in April 2010 at the University of Leeds by the *Popular Cultures Research Network* and the *Centre de Recherches sur les Littératures Populaires et les Cultures Médiatiques*, and supported by the British Academy, the French Embassy, Society for French Studies, Association for the Study of Modern and Contemporary France, and the universities of Leeds and Limoges.

The conference itself developed out of a programme of collaboration between the two research networks that included exchange visits. Jacques Migozzi and Loïc Artiaga were speakers at two seminar/workshops in Leeds in March 2009: *Copernican Revolutions - Storytelling: le prêt-à-penser et le plaisir romanesque* and *Generic Pleasures: re-thinking genre in popular fiction*, which then gave rise to a special issue of *French Cultural Studies* on this theme in November 2010 (21/4). Diana Holmes and David Platten presented and discussed their research at LPCM seminars in Limoges in September 2009. The project of a conference on *Finding the Plot* produced a strong response, and the papers selected brought together an international group of early-career and established researchers from the existing membership of PCRN and LPCM and from well beyond. The present volume represents not a simple proceedings of the conference, but a selected and augmented series of chapters shaped to address the central issues that arose from the papers presented and, above all, from discussion.

The decision to publish the book in French and English echoes the fully bilingual nature of the conference itself. We hope that our readership will encompass the large French Studies community in the Anglophone world, and also appeal to scholars and students of literature and popular culture whose first language is French, but who also, as is increasingly the case, have a good command of English. Stories circulate across cultures and languages – *Finding the Plot*, we hope, will also connect readers and scholars from different academic traditions who share a passion for stories.

—The Editors

# INTRODUCTION

DIANA HOLMES AND DAVID PLATTEN

**1.** Good storytelling means the narrative sequencing of imaginary or real events to provoke in the audience a sense of anticipation, absorption, and a desire to follow the plot that tussles pleasurably with reluctance to reach its end. Stories provide the pleasure of imaginary travel to an elsewhere, and may even, through the coherence of narrative, enhance understanding of readers' own lives, both personal and collective. Thus effective plotting, or the skilful structuring of story into narrative, has been central to literature from (we can at least surmise) the days of oral culture, and the urgent desire to know "what happens next" has driven (and still drives) the success of the novel as a cultural form. And yet in the modern - and certainly the postmodern - era, plot has become, in Peter Brooks' words: "the element of narrative that least sets off and designs high art" (Brooks 1984, 4). What is more highly valued in the *literary* novel is formal experimentation, thematic resonance, often a self-reflexivity that interrogates the very nature of language and fiction. Plot has become associated rather with "low" or popular culture, for bestselling page-turners are acknowledged to owe their success to the craft of story-telling. In a neat and influential formulation, Barthes opposed the mere "plaisir" of consuming an accessible narrative to the "jouissance" (an untranslatable term connoting cerebral pleasure of orgasmic intensity) of engagement with the fully literary text. In France more than in Anglophone cultures, where the impact of Cultural Studies has been much greater, the hegemonic attitude to "mass" literature in general and story in particular has been one of disdain for the "easy" pleasures provided by popular fictions.

However, in France as in the international field of Franco-centric literary studies, there has been a resurgence of interest in the nature and significance of story. This has partly taken the form of renewed suspicion of storytelling as a process that subordinates and seduces the (passive) reader: Christian Salmon's forceful essay *Storytelling: La Machine à fabriquer des histoires et à formater les esprits* (2008) – translated as *Storytelling: Bewitching the Modern Mind* (2010) - defines storytelling as a manipulative strategy increasingly deployed by business and the military, among others, to sell products, ideas or a total worldview. At the same time a more positive and celebratory resurgence of interest in story has been evident in the literary world. The 2007 manifesto and subsequent book *Pour une littérature-monde* argued primarily for a polycentric vision of literature in French, rather than a binary model that divided metropolitan from "francophone" writing, but this appeal to expand the scope and readership of a national literature that (the signatories argued) had shrunk to a state of sclerotic formalism also included a call to revive the mimetic and storytelling power of the novel form, via its narrative and social engagement with "the world". Two polemical books published within a year of the manifesto, by Tzvetan Todorov and Nancy Huston (the latter a *Littérature-Monde* signatory), also defended and celebrated the novel's capacity to "represent the common world", in Todorov's words (Todorov 2007, 64), and to transport the reader, through storytelling, to a fictional universe at once reflective of and exceeding that of lived experience. In an essay which is all the more significant for its author's previous association with the structuralist and poststructuralist movements of the 1960s and 1970s, Todorov explicitly attacks the distinction (particularly powerful in France) between literature considered "high" culture and those popular fictions, such as Dumas's *The Three Musketeers* and J.K. Rowling's *Harry Potter* series, that absorb "ordinary" readers; the latter, he argued, are equally able to provide their readers with an "élargissement intérieur ( … ) l'inclusion dans notre conscience de nouvelles manières d'être" (Todorov 2007, 77). Novelist Nancy Huston, in her essay *L'Espèce fabulatrice* (2008), made the reader's suspension of disbelief, procured through effective storytelling, central to the ethics of the novel genre: "Le roman, c'est ce qui célèbre cette reconnaissance des autres en soi, et de soi dans les autres. C'est le genre humain par excellence." (186).

Meanwhile, in a more academic context, some French literary historians and theorists were already addressing the importance of story, and of its capacity to absorb the reader in imaginary worlds. Work on the nineteenth-century novel had already opened the way to reflection on those dimensions of the genre that could federate social classes and even the starkly dichotomized sexes in desire for the next episode of the *roman-feuilleton*: from text-based studies such as Québécois Marc Angenot's *Le Roman populaire. Recherches en littérature* (1975) or Michel Nathan's *Splendeurs & misères du roman populaire* (1991), to Anne-Marie Thiesse's splendid study of books and readers at the fin-de-siècle: *Le Roman du quotidien. Lecteurs et lectures populaires à la Belle Époque*

(1984). The research group *Littératures Populaires et Culture Médiatique* (LPCM), originally founded in 1997 and based at the University of Limoges, began to bring under a single umbrella much of the most interesting work on popular fictions being pursued in a francophone context, with a series of conferences and publications that united a large scale agenda of empirical research (for the popular had not hitherto excited the attention of many literary historians in France) with theoretical reflection on text, genre and reception. Exploring paths traced by, for example, Pierre Bourdieu (on the relationship between social hierarchies and cultural taste), Paul Ricoeur (on narrative identities), Michel de Certeau (on the active, participative role of the reader/spectator), and feminist theorists of the romance (on the ideological complexity of narrative pleasure), the LPCM project has shown how popular narratives encapsulate many different aspects of human interactions, interrogate relations between the real and the imaginary, and illustrate how the most straightforwardly plot-driven narratives may instigate a complex negotiation between reader and text. Recognition of the convergence between this agenda, and work on popular fiction being pursued within the Popular Cultures Research Network based in Modern Languages at the University of Leeds, led to the collaborative project from which this book emerges.

Assumptions on the distinction between "serious" and "popular" art swirl around all academic debate on artistic form, not least because, as Bourdieu's research convincingly shows, the articulation of cultural distinctions conflates taste with competence and thus has repercussions in the social and political spheres. In this regard Marc Fumaroli's despair (in *L'Etat culturel,* 1991) at the sight of young people, headphones clamped to skull, wandering around the Musée d'Orsay epitomises the prevailing attitudes towards French culture that held sway during most of the past century and persist into this. The cause of cultural conservatism in France today has been much helped by its association not just with a predictably reactionary Right, but also – and arguably still more strongly – with ardent republicanism and even the revolutionary Left. Some of the fiercest opposition to the increasing ubiquity of popular (or what the French term rather "mass") culture has come from intellectuals committed to the secular republican values of liberty and equality, such as Alain Finkielkraut and Régis Debray, and with the possible exception of the surrealists, revolutionary artists and theorists have also tended to eschew popular culture as a mere "bread and circuses" strategy that distracts the masses from recognition of their true condition. This contrasts strongly with that current in the anglophone Left that we can broadly characterize as "Cultural Studies", and that has sought to define the functions and uses of popular cultural forms starting from the premise that, to put it simply, "popular" consumers are not merely passive victims of the merchants of culture but exercise agency like their "high culture" equivalents. Popular literature has come to be taken seriously more recently in France than in the UK or the US, and the hierarchical model of culture, still strongly present but pervasively contested in the anglophone world, continues to dominate. In *La Défaite de la pensée* (1987), Finkielkraut painted a picture of genuinely intellectual French cultural values assailed from all sides by the malign forces of an international, relativist postmodernism that seeks to equate Bob Marley with Beethoven. However, the reality in the world of books and literature is that publishers, university scholars and general readers mostly subscribe, albeit tacitly in many cases, to the existence of an hegemony of literary tastes. Significantly, those who either support the intellectual validity of these hegemonic divisions or who simply perceive them as the most efficient way to market and sell new books both rely on the notion of genre, which serves to quarantine creativity and artistic endeavour so that, for example, the imaginative subterfuge of a graphic novel, which may include a significant degree of formal experimentation, is deemed worthy *within* the culture of the *bande dessinée*, but has much less of an impact beyond the confines of the genre. Sainte-Beuve's nineteenth-century appellation of "la littérature industrielle" as inimical to the creation of great art survives in this distinction of high art on the one hand and the popular genres on the other. Moreover, beyond the academy it retains a subliminal potency; crime novelist Jean-Patrick Manchette, who has been feted posthumously as a significant influence over crime and latterly literary fiction more generally, would frequently rail against reviewers who would praise "ce bon polar".

The obduracy of the serious-popular distinction has been reflected in the marked separation in French literary scholarship between the study of literature "proper" and that of what has variously been termed mass, popular, or "para" literature. The latter represents vital work, because of the scant attention paid over all to so much of the fiction absorbed and engaged with by millions of readers since the advent of mass literacy, and because the specific qualities that make a fiction popular are more than worthy of critical analysis and theorization. However, the discrete study of popular texts and genres can also paradoxically reinforce familiar hegemonic divisions in literary tastes, and thus inhibit the development of a more inclusive and nuanced perspective on a contemporary literary scene in reality characterised, in France as elsewhere, by its eclecticism. In this book, we aim to re-situate popular genres and texts not within their own distinct sphere, but as part of a literary continuum connected by the irresistible pull of being told a story. Plotting is a means of making provisional, uncertain but necessary sense of the world: here we pay due attention to the most popular of genres and texts, from the *polar* and historical romance to James Bond and the *Twilight* series, but do so alongside studies of that most apparently esoteric of literary projects, the Symbolist novel, and the fictions of acclaimed contemporary novelist Danièle Sallenave – as well as investigating how the narrative structuring of experience connects literary fiction to other modes of cultural creation such as song and gossip journalism. This decompartmentalisation (the French *décloisonnement* is neater) is echoed in the book's fusion of "French" and "English" modes of analysis – neither of these watertight, and a matter of emphasis rather than radical difference, but corresponding broadly to, on the one hand, a narratological and rigorously theoretical approach to texts and the psychology of reading (French) and, on the other, a concern with the socio-ideological implications of texts and their impact on readers (English- or at least "Cultural Studies" English). In fact the international collaboration that underpins this study is based on the substantial overlap between our practices as literary critics, but the difference of emphasis is nonetheless real, and fruitful.

There are further perspectives on popular fiction that are evoked here but not (yet) fully realized. A thorough consideration of which fictions (and which types of plot) exercise the most appeal to readers would require study of the bestseller listings. It would require a deeper understanding of how books are manufactured and promoted; there is currently a paucity of research into subjects such as the criteria observed by publishers when they make decisions on manuscripts, the politics of annual literary prizes that can transform writers' public profiles, the impact of digital tablets and the anticipated decline of paper books, and the increasingly important trend in online self-publishing. A more inclusive conception of popular literature might also challenge received ideas on what many perceive to be the primary vectors of reading pleasure, notably storytelling, verisimilitude, and empathetic characterisation. The mix of ludism, fantasy and pastiche in bestselling and durably popular novels such as Boris Vian's *L'Écume des jours* and Raymond Queneau's *Zazie dans le métro* provide a different, though not necessarily contradictory, set of reading stimuli. Different again, in the contemporary era, would be the attractions to a mass readership of the prolific Amélie Nothomb's auto-fictional tales or Michel Houllebecq's literary polemics. Our contention here though is that plot, or the absorption of the reader into an imaginary world through narrative tension and the patterning of story, is crucial to the abiding appeal of narrative fiction.

**2.** The book is organised into four sections. It opens with "Theory and Story", in which six scholars writing against the grain of a strong French critical tendency to deplore popular fictions' formal conservatism, ideological blandness and narcotic effect on readers address the nature of story and plot. Raphaël Baroni theorises how plots work from the perspective of a first reading, as opposed to the critical re-reading that more commonly forms the basis of scholarly analysis. A first reading means a sense of tension rather than a recognition of inevitable causality; we live the story forwards as in life, without knowing the dénouement, and this also offers a sense of all the potential stories evoked but whose tracks are not followed as the plot takes shape. Baroni traces the way in which the once valued "art de créer un monde et d'intéresser le lecteur" lost its "lettres de noblesse", and argues strongly for the human value of strong narratives. Jacques Migozzi sees in the recent characterisation of "storytelling" as a sinister strategy a return to paternalist assumptions about the passively manipulated reader. He argues for a model of the reader as story *player*, hence as active accomplice rather than duped victim of the author; the effects of the fictional plot and the imaginary world that the reader colludes in creating are at once cognitive, affective and ethical. Lise Dumasy, arguing from the basis of her own intense pleasure in both "literary" reading *and* the page-turning, unputdownable narratives of the late nineteenth century, disputes Barthes' stark distinction between "plaisir" and "jouissance", as she traces the continuity of a critical disparagement of popular stories based on mistrust of their power to distract, seduce and threaten a rational and productive social order. She returns, however, to the subtlety of Barthes' wider take on narrative and its pleasures. Paul Bleton interrogates what plot means from the point of view of the reader – not only the connected sequence of fictional events, but also other "distracting" but essential elements of context such as place, time, the "surface" of language. He argues that what holds together all the constitutive elements is plot, and illustrates this through analysis of a playful *roman policier*. Plot is seen as the co-creation of reader and author. The structures and techniques of storytelling, however, extend well beyond the domain of literary fiction, and Marc Lits' chapter shows how the celebrity press (in French the "presse people") has recast political leaders as protagonists in popular dramas, depicting their attributes and actions according to a logic of narrative coherence and emotional impact, rather than in terms of political debates. Popular storytelling requires a cast of rapidly identifiable characters capable of provoking an emotional response: the discourse of the celebrity press resituates politicians within this semiotic and narrative framework. David Platten closes this section with the argument that, like more "literary" texts, popular crime novels can play on the distinction between plot and narrative to elicit the creative participation of their readers. Taking as his focus Pierre Signac's 1960 *Monsieur Cauchemar*, with its unexpected fracture of the fictional illusion, he demonstrates the significance of this "landmark" text for the aesthetics of the whole genre of contemporary crime fiction.

The second section, "Story/History", illuminates the significance of plots and emplotment to period dramas and fictional settings, taking seriously the nature of readerly pleasure in stories that stage the past, whether distant or recent. Marc Guillaumie analyses the appeal of the prehistoric novel, popular since scientific exploration in the nineteenth century began to uncover evidence of a history that (by definition) left no written traces. A chain of such stories loops through different media and national cultures up to the present day, offering the emotionally resonant image of islands of human community surrounded by dark mysterious forests and terrifying monsters, and plots that often draw on powerful myths of human origins and progress. The prehistoric novel, and its cinematic avatars, offer the pleasure of fear buttressed by the reassurance of a teleological plot; they invite the reader to enjoy his or her distance from humanity's primitive origins, whilst also relishing identification with passions unconstrained by centuries of civilisation; they wear a gratifyingly educational air of being based on scientific research, but in fact, Guillaumie shows, consistently subordinate history to the narrative and ideological needs of the moment. Tim Farrant's subject is the short story and in particular the late nineteenth-century stories of Alphonse Daudet, which initially gained their popularity through a play on the folk sense of "popular", bringing tales of rural life to an increasingly urbanised audience, but then with the Franco-Prussian war of 1870 became stories of siege and suffering. In both the rural and the urban tales, an emphasis on the shared banality of the everyday overrides any concern for dramatic plot – but Farrant shows how the emphasis on the quotidian, on the plotlessness of the ordinary, carries undercurrents of anxiety that often erupted into a sharp dénouement, and paradoxically produced some of the popular "grand narratives" of the Third Republic. Brenda Hollweg also deals with the place of stories in the late nineteenth-century transition to the modern age, taking the Chicago Exposition of 1893 as a case study of the role of fictional narratives in shaping and widening the impact of great public events. The many, generically varied popular fictions that grew up around the Exposition offered vicarious experience of its excitement and newness, and also provided, both for contemporaries and for posterity, memorable narrative forms for the complex cognitive and emotional experience of this sudden encounter with multicultural, high-tech modernity. Diana Holmes pursues the theme of narrative fiction as a pleasurable structuring of historical moments. Identifying strong similarities between three bestselling historical epics published in France since World War 2 (Anne Golon's *Angélique* saga, begun in 1956, Jacques Laurent's *Caroline Chérie* [1958], and Régine Deforges' *La Bicyclette bleue* [1981]) , she argues that their mass appeal is produced by a picaresque narrative structure, by the enjoyable mix of empathy and censure provoked in (particularly female) readers by their roguish heroines, and by the pleasures of imaginary time-travel to iconic periods of history particularly well suited to the years in which each novel was published. Susan Bainbrigge shows how the collective historical traumas of a generation can be addressed through personal stories, so that a novel that tackles the putatively unspeakable horrors of the Holocaust – Philippe Grimbert's 2004 *Un secret* – could become a bestseller by offering a painful yet finally cathartic narrativisation of the central protagonist's search for an almost intolerable truth. The novel also offers a mise en abyme of its own project, for it is through storytelling, through *finding the plot* of his family's life, that the narrator reaches a degree of reconciliation with the past.

Section 3, "Bending genres", looks at the nature and significance of storytelling within different genres, from the *roman noir* to the highly literary Symbolist novel, and the popular songs of Edith Piaf - for narrative plays a crucial role in media other than the literary. Natacha Levet examines the pleasures of detective stories or *polars*, the genre that proclaims its allegiance to the "lowbrow" qualities of suspenseful storytelling and violent emotion. She demonstrates the centrality to the genre of Aristotelian tragic pleasure, composed of fear and pity: the sense of reconciliation associated with popular genres operates here only in the sense of the satisfaction of curiosity, for happy endings are largely withheld, and it is the darkness of the world that is satisfyingly echoed in *noir* plots. Loïc Artiaga shows how almost from their inception, James Bond stories were received by the public (and acknowledged by their author) to be trans-media texts, at once written and cinematic – though early critical work on Bond (for example that of Umberto Eco) remained firmly focussed on the written text. Artiaga sets both the narrative form and the reception of the Bond texts in the context of an increasingly consumerist and "Pop" culture, demonstrating a homology between textual aesthetics and social change. With Matthieu Letourneux's chapter, the relationship between medium, genre and plot structure is explored in the mass-produced and hugely popular serialised adventure stories for children that proliferated in early twentieth-century France. Necessarily repetitive due to the sheer scale of their production, their profuse narrative structure and cyclical rhythm determined by the generic needs of the serialised form as much as by authorial invention, these stories nonetheless clearly offered considerable reading pleasure, the nature of which Letourneux explores and defines. Richard Hibbitt turns to a genre strongly associated with "high" literature to pose a question central to this book's concerns: is it possible to read any narrative text without reconstituting a plot? Taking the apparently extreme example of a Symbolist novel, he establishes the unavoidable linearity of narrative form even in the most experimental and anti-realist of texts. Moreover, he attributes the relative popularity of his chosen example, Georges Rodenbach's 1892 *Bruges-la-morte*, to its hybridity that allows at once for a poetic, polyvalent reading and for a "realist" interpretation based on suspense and causality. David Looseley finds plot to be a structuring element of popular song – potentially of most pop songs, but strongly present and foregrounded in the French chanson, and exemplified here through the early songs of Edith Piaf. In Piaf's period of French stardom, before she achieved international fame, the constraints of the three-minute record become a virtue: Looseley shows how spare, economical plots are evoked and still allow for complex modes of address, characterisation and storytelling. The songs draw on popular narrative genres such as the romance and the roman noir, communicating mood and other narrative elements through melody, voice and performance as well as through the lyrics. Finally in this section, Imogen Long examines the case of the same story told in two different ways, the one in "high", avant-garde mode and the other closer to the popular genre of romance. The plot of Danièle Sallenave's 1977 novel *Le Voyage d'Amsterdam* was reworked by the author in 1986 in more "popular" form to produce *La Vie fantôme*, providing a case study in generic differences and consistencies between different 'levels' of literature and their uses of plot.

And finally "In a Spin: Storytelling in the Postmodern Era", deals with the most contemporary of popular narrative forms: globalised, cross-media texts that (possibly) elicit new forms of engagement from their readers. Anne Besson contrasts what can broadly be defined as the anglophone Cultural Studies approach, with its positive evaluation of the Internet's empowering effects on consumers of culture, with the European, and certainly French, tendency to see new media as intensifying the manipulative strategies of a consumerist culture. Agreeing with the latter camp's thesis that the current era has seen a massive return to storytelling, Besson refutes their assumption that this is a top-down, alienating phenomenon, identifying rather many signs of active, inventive consumption and creativity among fans and readers. Marc Atallah applies to the genre of contemporary science-fiction a formal, narratological analysis of the sort more commonly reserved for "high" literary forms, arguing that "critical" sci-fi's particular modes of storytelling set up for the reader a moving as well as suspenseful relationship between the hi-tech reality of 21st century living, and the futurist fictional worlds they imagine. Through a case-study analysis of Andreas Eschbach's 2003 *Le Dernier de son espèce*, Atallah shows how the science fiction genre can use stories of scientific experimentation and its effects to explore the limits of the human condition. With Malin Isaksson's chapter, the book turns to the contemporary phenomenon of fan fiction. Some readers have always taken their favourite stories as points of departure for personal invention, but new media facilitate the passage from consumer to producer of fictions, making possible the wide, free circulation of fans' own variations on or sequels to the popular canon. Malin Isaksson addresses the specific case of "femslash" or lesbian rewritings of Stephenie Meyer's internationally successful *Twilight* fictions (which comprise novels, films and on-line texts), showing how fan authors exploit the gaps or openings in the original texts to fashion alternative narratives, and asking to what extent these constitute *new* stories, not only in relation to Meyer's "canon", but also in the way that they work with and on the heteronormative genre of romance. Alexandra Ivanovitch closes this section with a richly theorised analysis of that "bestseller of bestsellers", Dan Brown's *Da Vinci Code* (2004), seeking the reasons for its massive, global popularity not in those extra-literary contextual factors (a zeitgeist of anti-Catholicism and eclectic New Age spirituality) to which many critics have turned, but rather in the text itself. The story that Dan Brown tells, she argues, follows not only the logic of the thriller, but also that of the Grail narrative, offering its readers the revelation of a fundamental narrative (that of the love between Jesus and Mary Magdalene) that works as a code to illuminate the whole of culture from high to low. One of the most popular and most critically derided novels of the contemporary era thus places the finding of the (true) plot at the heart of reading pleasure. The book closes with a brief synoptic conclusion and postscript by Jacques Migozzi, director of the LPCM and one of the French theorists who have worked to reinstate popular fiction as central to the history of French literature.

**3.** Our focus here on plots and plotting arises from an awareness that while the plot is a constituent element of all prose fiction, in much literary criticism and theory it tends to pass beneath the critical radar. On the other hand, storytelling and emplotment animate a wide variety of popular forms to such a degree that they carry a magnetic charge for the reader, as Kingsley Amis, author of *Lucky Jim*, one of the great, English, middle-brow novels, and unabashed admirer of James Bond, discovered:

> Fiction written and read primarily for escape isn't necessarily devoid of the virtues in which primarily enlightening fiction is rich, and escape fiction can have virtues much of its own as well. There's not a lot of suspense in the classics. (Amis 1965, 149).

Whether or not the classics are suspenseful, the basic question underpinning this book is: what makes us turn the page? All the contributors strive in their different ways to, in the words of Raphaël Baroni, "exhumer la force de l'intrigue" ("exhume the power of the plot") to look carefully at the "not quite yet" as well as the "now" of narrative fiction.

Critical disregard of skilful plotting as a literary quality depends in part on the belief that plot is a conservative structure, that narrative's imperative towards coherence, closure and a satisfying unknotting ("dénouement") of whatever the story has entangled make for the reader's reassurance rather than their enlightenment. The chapters here refute the notion of plot as inherently cosy, as a device that lures the reader into desire for and belief in a secure and comprehensible reality. Raphaël Baroni in his book *La Tension narrative*, as well as in this volume, argues that the experience of becoming absorbed in a suspenseful plot works not so much to divert us from existential anxiety as to intensify a sense of the random contingency of experience, "la sous-détermination du devenir et du monde" (Baroni 2007, 158), and then vicariously and provisionally to allay it. Drawing the reader into the process of literary creation, a well-crafted plot conjures up not only its own compelling thread of events, but also what Baroni terms a "network of potential stories that extends beyond textual structures" ("réseau des histoires potentielles qui s'étend au-delà des structures textuelles"). Through the experience of fictional suspense and narrative tension we play out deeper anxieties, and if these are granted imaginary resolution as the plot closes, this does not simply erase what has gone before. Moreover, as several chapters demonstrate, not all popular plots offer the security of a neatly ends-tied closure. Indeed, the commercial imperative to leave the way open to sequels, allied with a more or less conscious sense that readers desire disruption and transgression as much as they desire order, frequently leads to popular plotting that avoids any definitive resolution. And the model of "the reader" that underpins this book also contests any sense of "plot" as conspiracy, as a deliberate trick enacted on the reader by a plotting author.

Rather, the reader moves between voluntary and pleasurable immersion in the fictional world and its compelling sequencing of events, and continuing awareness of life outside, in a process that Marie-Laure Ryan nicely captures as "amphibian" (Ryan) and Ross Chambers, in his book of that name, celebrates as *Loiterature.* Plot here figures more as an appealingly mapped terrain offered for willing exploration than as a "complot" or "intrigue".

What underlies the diverse studies gathered here is the belief that today the reader is king or queen; she or he has little in common with what Jacques Migozzi terms, in the postface to this book, the "lecteur modèle" ("model reader"), the image of the reader conceived by author and/or critic. As Migozzi suggests, we might do better to refer to "reader" in the plural, to the infinite variety of human beings captured in his notion of the "lecteur ordinaire", a person who may want to leave the page to loiter for a while but will invariably return, to continue his or her journey to the centre of another's world.

## References

Amis, Kingsley. 1965. *The James Bond Dossier.* London: Jonathan Cape.

Angenot, Marc. 1975. *Le Roman populaire. Recherches en paralittérature.* Quebec: Presses Universitaires de Québec.

Baroni, Raphaël. 2007. *La Tension narrative. Suspense, curiosité et surprise*. Paris: Seuil.

Brooks, Peter. 1984. *Reading for the Plot. Design and Intention in Narrative.* Cambridge MA and London: Harvard University Press.

Chambers, Ross. 1999. *Loiterature*. Lincoln: University of Nebraska Press.

Finkielkraut, Alain. 1987. *La Défaite de la pensée*. Paris: Gallimard.

Fumaroli, Marc. 1991. *L'État culturel. Essai sur une religion moderne.* Paris: éditions de Fallois.

Huston, Nancy. 2008. *L'Espèce fabulatrice.* Paris: Actes Sud.

Le Bris, Michel et al. 2007. "Pour une "littérature-monde" en français", *Le Monde* 16.03.07.

Le Bris, M. and Jean Rouaud, eds. 2007. *Pour une littérature-monde.* Paris: Gallimard.

Nathan, Michel. 1990. *Splendeurs & misères du roman populaire.* Lyon: Presses Universitaires de Lyon.

Ryan, Marie-Laure. 2001. *Narrative as Virtual Reality.* Baltimore and London: The Johns Hopkins University Press.

Salmon, Christian. 2007. *Storytelling: La Machine à fabriquer des histoires et à formater les esprits*. Paris: la Découverte.

—. 2010. *Storytelling: Bewitching the Modern Mind*, trans. David Macey. London: Verso.

Thiesse, Anne Marie. 1984. *Le Roman du quotidien. Lecteurs et lectures populaires à la Belle Époque.* Paris: Le Chemin vert.

# PART 1:

# THEORY AND STORY

# CHAPTER ONE

# PUISSANCE DE L'INTRIGUE

RAPHAEL BARONI

## L'intrigue en puissance

L'intrigue est à la fois une forme, qui inscrit l'histoire racontée dans une configuration poétique organisée par un auteur ou un narrateur, et une indétermination de cette forme, dont dépend la force de l'intrigue, son intérêt pour le lecteur qui s'aventure dans le récit. Produire cette indétermination exige de l'auteur ou du narrateur un effort aussi important que celui qui consiste à configurer l'histoire; et pour exhumer la force de l'intrigue, qui se loge au cœur de la forme, il est nécessaire de se pencher sur la source de l'énergie du récit, sur ce qui le met en mouvement et qui permet à la configuration narrative de s'ouvrir et de se déborder. Dans la physique newtonienne, il existe deux types d'énergies fondamentales: l'énergie cinétique et l'énergie potentielle. De manière similaire, on pourrait affirmer que la force de l'intrigue consiste en la conversion de l'énergie potentielle de l'histoire, en l'énergie cinétique de la lecture, qui fait advenir cette histoire possible, qui trace une voie tortueuse parmi un réseau d'histoires alternatives. Pour dresser l'équation et mesurer la force de l'intrigue, il importerait donc de replacer au cœur de l'analyse ces deux facteurs essentiels: d'une part, le mouvement de la lecture, c'est-à-dire la progression dans le texte, et d'autre part, ce qui demeure *en puissance* dans le récit, c'est-à-dire les virtualités de l'intrigue, le réseau des histoires potentielles qui s'étend au-delà des structures textuelles. Or, pendant longtemps, ces questions ont constitué des points aveugles de la narratologie formaliste, parce que l'esthétique valorisée par la critique était celle de la relecture et que le travail de la poétique consistait à décrire les structures actualisées par les textes, et non leurs structures possibles. Ce qui intéressait les narratologues, c'était la manière dont les événements racontés se moulaient dans un inventaire de formes répertoriées, ou la façon dont le dénouement semblait inscrire la contingence des événements dans la nécessité poétique de l'intrigue.

Certes, la critique du structuralisme est périmée, mais il semble que de nombreuses approches contemporaines continuent, pour reprendre les mots de Derrida, de "faire taire la force sous la forme" de l'intrigue (1967, 44). Dans le prolongement des travaux de Paul Ricœur, il n'est pas rare que les critiques insistent sur la fonction "configurante" des récits, sans se donner la peine de mentionner leur fonction "intrigante"[1], comme si l'intrigue devait d'abord être le lieu du triomphe de la "concordance" poétique sur la "discordance" de l'événement. Par ailleurs, la linguistique textuelle en France continue de promouvoir un modèle séquentiel qui semble réduire l'intrigue à une structure prototypique de l'histoire, dans laquelle nœud et dénouement se répondent symétriquement, l'intrigue y étant définie comme l'établissement d'une chronologie et d'une causalité, alors que les rapports de tension et de successivité entre les différentes phases du récit demeurent largement sous-théorisés.

Il ne faudrait pas conclure de ce qui précède qu'une conception dynamique de l'intrigue n'aurait jamais été élaborée, ni même qu'elle aurait été entièrement occultée par la narratologie structuraliste, seulement elle a trop souvent été marginalisée, comme s'il s'agissait d'un aspect honteux de la narrativité, d'une scorie "populaire" qu'une poétique sérieuse et digne de ce nom ne serait pas autorisée à placer au cœur de ses investigations. Certes, il y eut d'heureuses exceptions, à commencer par Aristote, dont la défense des arts mimétiques passait par la valorisation de la *catharsis*, impliquant le jeu des péripéties et la production de différents effets de *pathos*: crainte, espoir, pitié, surprises liée aux brusques renversements de fortune. Claude Bremond (1973), dans sa logique du récit envisageait également les alternatives qui se présentent lorsqu'on lit le conte à l'endroit: la possibilité qu'une provocation reste sans effet ou qu'une entreprise échoue au lieu de réussir. Plus près de nous, Meir Sternberg (1978) défend depuis plus de trente ans une narratologie fonctionnaliste dont le fondement est l'analyse du suspense, de la curiosité et de la surprise, ces intérêts narratifs dont il est allé jusqu'à faire le fondement de la narrativité (1992). On peut aussi mentionner Peter Brooks qui, en associant le jeu de la tension narrative et de sa résolution avec l'approche pulsionnelle de Freud, a contribué à éclairer la fonction psychique de la mise en intrigue. Brooks affirme ainsi que l'engagement d'un lecteur qui "répond à l'intrigue" est de "nature essentiellement dynamique, comme une interaction avec un système d'énergie que le lecteur active" (1984, 111-112, m.t.[2]). James Phelan (1989), dans le

---

[1] Sur cette question, je me permets de renvoyer à Baroni (2009; 2010).
[2] m.t. = ma traduction (traduction de l'auteur).

prolongement de l'approche rhétorique initiée par Wayne C. Booth, a également défendu une définition de l'intrigue reposant sur l'analyse de "l'intérêt des lecteurs envers le récit", et il a montré que cet intérêt dépendait de la "progression" dans le texte et de la "manière dont un auteur introduit, complique et résout (ou ne parvient pas à résoudre) certaines instabilités" (Phelan 1989, 15, m.t.).

D'une manière générale, on observe par ailleurs, dans le prolongement des théories de la réception, un regain d'intérêt pour des approches qui permettent de décrire non seulement les structures cognitives qui permettent de comprendre et de mémoriser des histoires, mais également celles qui permettent d'envisager différents scénarios[3] possibles qui n'ont pas encore, et qui ne seront peut-être jamais racontés. Ainsi, Marie-Laure Ryan a-t-elle montré que la "racontabilité" des histoires dépendait de la complexité de leurs intrigues, qui dépend elle-même de l'éventail des "récits purement virtuels " qui sont "enchâssés" dans le récit effectif (Ryan 1991, 156, m.t.). Dans le prolongement de ces travaux, Jean-Marie Schaeffer souligne pour sa part que:

> La compréhension narrative apparaît ainsi comme une négociation permanente entre d'un côté des mémorisations partielles et des projections ou attentes extrapolées à partir de ces mémorisations, de l'autre le traitement d'informations nouvelles dont l'intérêt narratif dépend largement de leur déviation partielle des attentes fondées sur la mémorisation des séquences précédentes. (Schaeffer 2010, 28)

Même la sémiotique post-greimasienne a fini par se recentrer sur la question des passions et des liens entre tension et signification (Fontanille et Zilberberg 1998). Face à ces travaux convergents, comment expliquer que l'occultation de la *puissance* de l'intrigue demeure aussi tenace ? Pour éclairer ce point, il est nécessaire de souligner qu'il existe au moins deux définitions de l'intrigue, pratiquement opposées: la première, formaliste, insiste sur la création poétique d'une configuration narrative, qui inscrit l'histoire dans une totalité compréhensible; la seconde, fonctionnaliste, met l'accent sur la dynamique de la lecture intriguée et sur les dispositifs narratifs qui la sous-tendent. Force est de constater que ces deux définitions, concurrentes et partiellement contradictoires, continuent à circuler largement, au point que dans la récente *Routledge Encyclopedia of Narrative Theory*, Hilary Dannenberg affirme que:

---

[3] Evidemment, sur ce point, je renvoie aux travaux pionniers d'Umberto Eco (1985), qui préfigurent en grande partie les approches cognitives contemporaines.

> Malgré l'apparente simplicité de l'objet auquel elle se réfère, l'intrigue (*plot*) est l'un des termes les plus insaisissables de la théorie du récit. Les narratologues l'utilisent pour se référer à une variété de phénomènes différents. La plupart des définitions de base du récit buttent sur la question de la séquentialité, et les tentatives répétées de redéfinir les paramètres de l'intrigue reflètent à la fois la centralité et la complexité de la dimension temporelle du récit. (Dannenberg 2005, 435, m.t.)

Il ne s'agit pas de trancher entre des usages divergents d'un même terme, mais de constater l'existence d'un cas de polysémie engendrant de nombreux malentendus et conditionnant la portée opératoire d'un concept pourtant central pour la théorie du récit. Après avoir exposé aussi clairement que possible ces deux façons d'envisager l'intrigue, j'exposerai rapidement les raisons de la relative marginalisation de la définition fonctionnelle de l'intrigue, puis j'évoquerai quelques avantages que l'on peut malgré tout en attendre pour l'analyse des récits et pour les études littéraires.

## Définitions formelles de l'intrigue

Dans la définition formelle de l'intrigue, l'accent est mis sur la logique de l'histoire racontée. La mise en intrigue dépendrait de l'agencement des éléments de l'histoire dans une totalité: les événements racontés ne se contenteraient pas de se succéder en suivant une chronologie, mais ils s'inscriraient dans une nécessité causale ou poétique qui permettrait de les lire en sens inverse. En effet, si la chronologie des événements (ou celle de la lecture) est orientée selon un vecteur allant de l'avant en direction de l'après, en revanche, la nécessité causale ou poétique est de nature rétrograde: l'après justifie l'avant comme la fin justifie les moyens, et si tel événement est raconté, c'est *pour que* tel autre puisse advenir. Dans un univers entièrement régi par la nécessité, le temps devient ainsi une variable secondaire.

Il faut préciser qu'il peut exister différentes formes de nécessité dans l'élaboration d'une intrigue: cela peut aller de la simple relation causale jusqu'à l'élaboration d'un dispositif complexe visant la création d'un effet déterminé, en passant par la contrainte formelle imposée par un genre littéraire. Par exemple, la mort du protagoniste peut être nécessaire dans un contexte tragique alors qu'au contraire, sa survie sera attendue dans un roman d'aventure ou dans un conte merveilleux. En ce qui concerne la causalité narrative, c'est Forster qui a introduit dans *Aspects du roman*, en 1928, une différence fondamentale entre ce qu'il appelle une "histoire" (*story*) et ce qu'il désigne comme une "intrigue" (*plot*):

A) Histoire: "Le roi est mort et puis la reine est morte."
B) Intrigue: "Le roi est mort et puis la reine est morte de chagrin."

Pour Forster, dans le cas d'une simple histoire, le récit répondra à la question "et alors ?", tandis que dans le cas d'une intrigue, le récit répondra au "pourquoi ?". Ainsi que l'affirme Forster, lorsqu'une intrigue se forme, la séquence temporelle est préservée, mais elle est comme recouverte et, en quelque sorte, "occultée" (*overshadowed*) par la logique de la causalité.

Cette définition formelle de l'intrigue circule encore très largement parmi différentes communautés de chercheurs, notamment dans le monde anglo-saxon. Elle a permis à certains critiques[4] de rapprocher le travail des historiens de celui des auteurs de fiction, en soulignant que l'intelligence narrative des événements exige une forme de segmentation et de "mise en intrigue" du passé. Dans le prolongement de ces travaux, Paul Ricœur (1983) a popularisé l'idée que le rôle central de la "mise en intrigue" serait de "configurer" la temporalité, de surmonter les "discordances" de l'expérience par la création poétique d'une "concordance" racontée. Par cette opération, Ricœur affirme que la mise en intrigue inscrit l'histoire dans une totalité intelligible.[5]

Cette conception est relativement proche d'une tradition formaliste initiée par le chercheur russe Vladimir Propp en 1928. Ce dernier a cherché à abstraire les éléments invariants des contes russes, de manière à dégager une séquence de "fonctions" dont l'ordre semblait relativement prévisible, fixé par les conventions du genre. C'est en se fondant sur cette approche que les sémioticiens structuralistes, Greimas en tête, finiront par élaborer une "grammaire narrative" élémentaire, apte à décrire n'importe quel genre de récit. S'inspirant de Propp, de Greimas et de la logique narrative de Bremond, Paul Larivaille finira par donner sa forme classique au "schéma quinaire":

---

[4] Notamment Hayden White, Louis O. Mink et Paul Veyne.

[5] Dans un article récent (Baroni 2010), j'ai critiqué cette conception de la "mise en intrigue" en montrant que Ricœur lui-même a beaucoup nuancé cette thèse dans le troisième tome de *Temps et récit*.

<table>
<tr><td rowspan="2">I<br><br>AVANT<br>Etat initial<br>Equilibre<br><br>1</td><td colspan="3">II<br>PENDANT<br>Transformation (agie ou subie)<br>Processus dynamique</td><td rowspan="2">III<br><br>APRÈS<br>Etat final<br>Equilibre<br><br>5</td></tr>
<tr><td>2<br>Provocation</td><td>3<br>Action</td><td>4<br>Sanction</td></tr>
</table>

(Larivaille 1974, 387)

Si ce schéma est aujourd'hui encore aussi populaire, au moins dans la communauté francophone, c'est parce que la linguistique textuelle (Adam 1997, 54) l'a adopté pour en faire l'une des séquences prototypiques élémentaires organisant la textualité au-delà des limites de la phrase. Par ailleurs, la linguistique textuelle a fait converger ce schéma avec la réflexion sur la "causalité narrative" que l'on doit, entre autres, à Forster et à Ricœur. Jean-Michel Adam affirme ainsi que la mise en intrigue consiste en un double débordement de la chronologie par la "logique singulière du récit": d'une part à travers l'introduction d'une "problématisation par le biais de deux macro-propositions narratives – Pn2 et Pn4 – extrêmement importantes, insérées entre la situation initiale et le début du procès (Pn1) et entre le procès et la situation finale (Pn5)" (1997, 50), et d'autre part, à travers l'établissement d'une "causalité narrative", qui apparait comme l'un des attributs essentiels de la narrativité (Adam 1997, 51-56). J.-M. Adam conclut que l'"écrasement de la logique et de la temporalité est, avant tout, réalisée par la 'logique' macro-propositionnelle de la mise en intrigue dont rend compte le schéma quinaire [...] qui hiérarchise les relations, autrement simplement chronologiques et linéaires, entre cinq moments (m) de tout procès à l'intérieur d'une séquence (ou d'un texte entier)" (Adam 1997, 54).

L'opérativité du schéma quinaire et de la réflexion sur la causalité narrative n'est plus à démontrer. D'une part, cette approche permet de distinguer les *récits* proprement dits, non seulement d'autres types de séquences telles que la *description* ou l'*argumentation*, mais également de textes d'action plus élémentaires, par exemple les *relations* ou les *chroniques* (Revaz 2009, 101-137). D'autre part, ce schéma est adaptable à une grande variété de contextes, et il permet de mettre en évidence la manière dont des séquences narratives sont insérées dans des formes de textualité hétérogènes, par exemple dans des argumentations ou des explications. Enfin, cette réflexion met en évidence le rôle du discours narratif dans l'organisation logique et formelle de l'histoire racontée, c'est-à-dire dans la transformation de l'événement brut, qui devient signifiant et compréhensible lorsqu'il fait l'objet d'une "narrativisation". Cette approche renvoie ainsi à une épistémologie constructiviste visant à remettre en question le caractère mimétique de la narrativité.

Il faut toutefois noter que cette perspective engendre de nombreux angles-morts lorsqu'il s'agit de réfléchir sur le phénomène de l'intrigue tel qu'il se manifeste concrètement, c'est-à-dire sur la manière dont un lecteur empirique peut *faire l'expérience* d'une intrigue, qui se noue au cours de sa lecture et qui se dénouera, peut-être, à la fin du récit. Premièrement, l'accent est clairement mis sur le *travail poétique* de la mise en forme de l'histoire, et non sur l'*effet esthétique* visé par cette mise en intrigue[6]. Le cas d'E. A. Poe est exemplaire sur ce point: pour lui, "intrigue" est synonyme de "planification": "S'il est une chose évidente, c'est qu'un plan quelconque, digne du nom de plan, doit avoir été soigneusement préparé en vue du dénouement, avant que la plume attaque le papier" (Poe 1978, 268). Si l'intrigue est vue sur un plan rétrograde, et non progressif, c'est parce qu'il arrive que l'auteur[7] arrange son récit en fonction d'une fin planifiée à l'avance. Pareillement, Forster était d'abord un romancier et un nouvelliste avant d'être un poéticien, ce qui explique que la causalité était pour lui un travail de mise en forme narrative, et non une opération de pensée qui aurait permis à n'importe quel lecteur de combler les lacunes du récit le plus déficient. Quant aux travaux qui rapprochaient mise en intrigue et historiographie, et qui se centraient sur la segmentation et l'arrangement créatif des événements du passé, ils portaient clairement sur l'*écriture de l'histoire*, et non sur sa *lecture*. Il s'ensuit que l'intrigue, en tant que phénomène qui dépend d'un acte de lecture progressant dans le récit, n'est tout simplement pas traitée. Peut-être que certains auteurs (mais

---

[6] Dans un article à paraitre, James Morgan propose de clarifier le sens de l'intrigue en distinguant les concepts d'"emplotment", de "plot" et d'"explotment". La définition formelle de l'intrigue relèverait ainsi de l'"emplotment", du travail poétique de "mise en intrigue" des événements par un auteur ou un historien, alors que la définition fonctionnelle de l'intrigue, qui correspondrait au "plot", décrit l'intrigue du point de vue du lecteur.

[7] Ainsi que l'a montré récemment Marc Escola (2010), le caractère planifié de l'intrigue convient peut-être au genre de la nouvelle que pratique Poe, mais il est moins évident dans les romans du XVIIIe siècle. D'ailleurs, dans les séries télévisées contemporaines, des équipes de scénaristes travaillent à l'élaboration d'une histoire dont le développement demeure en grande partie imprévisible, puisqu'il dépend du succès de la fiction et des attentes des spectateurs.

pas tous !) ont déjà en vue le dénouement lorsqu'ils rédigent leurs romans ou leurs ouvrages historiques, mais les lecteurs ne peuvent avoir une première expérience de l'intrigue que dans la mesure où ce dénouement n'est que l'un des avenirs possibles du récit.

Deuxièmement, l'approche formaliste met l'accent sur la trame de l'histoire racontée, et non sur l'organisation séquentielle du récit qui raconte cette histoire. Pour le dire plus clairement, nœud (Pn2) et dénouement (Pn4) sont définis en fonction d'une sémantique du monde raconté, en tant que "complication" et "résolution" d'un conflit ou d'un manque qui affectent les personnages. Ils se succèdent donc selon un avant et un après, mais surtout pour les personnages de la *fabula* qui subissent ces événements et qui agissent pour rétablir l'équilibre de la situation initiale. Il s'ensuit que, pour le lecteur, un récit qui ne respecterait pas la chronologie des événements (ce qui est un cas évidemment très fréquent) pourrait très bien débuter par la résolution et se terminer par la complication.

Il est pourtant facile de montrer que les récits non chronologiques peuvent être tout aussi intrigants et bien noués que les récits chronologiques. Le scénario "la reine est morte de chagrin parce que… le roi est mort" est potentiellement aussi intriguant que le scénario "le roi est mort et puis… la reine est morte de chagrin". Le premier scénario devra son intérêt à la curiosité engendrée par l'événement et l'autre à son suspense, mais l'un comme l'autre ne parviendront à nouer une intrigue qu'en fonction de l'habileté du narrateur dans l'art de dilater les points de suspension de manière à augmenter les potentialités du récit: les causes et les conséquences possibles de la "mort" doivent être multipliées pour intéresser le lecteur et pour produire cette énergie cinétique propre à la lecture intriguée.

## Définition fonctionnelle de l'intrigue

Pour décrire la mise en intrigue dans les récits non chronologiques, et pour l'ancrer dans un phénomène concret qui ne peut se manifester que dans l'actualisation du texte par un lecteur, il convient donc de dissocier, au moins partiellement, les "macro-propositions" qui jouent le rôle de "nœud" et de "dénouement" de la sémantique des événements qui forment la trame de l'histoire. Si, dans certains cas, les récits se nouent en racontant une complication ou un manque et en respectant plus ou moins la suite des actions qui mènent jusqu'à une résolution, d'autres récits se nouent en présentant une situation narrative énigmatique et en scrutant le passé de l'histoire à la recherche d'une explication. Le parallélisme entre ces deux formes de narration est évident, puisque elles commencent par se nouer, qu'elles entretiennent une certaine tension pendant la lecture, et qu'elles finissent souvent par se dénouer en apportant des réponses aux questions que se posaient les lecteurs. Mais pour définir la nature de ces macro-propositions, nous devons adopter une approche fonctionnelle qui tienne compte, non de l'élaboration de la trame de l'histoire par un auteur, mais bien de son actualisation par un lecteur qui progresse dans un récit élaboré par quelqu'un d'autre.

L'intrigue ne serait qu'une partition qui nécessite un "interprète" pour être actualisée et pour engendrer les effets esthétiques par lesquels elle s'exprime. À la suite de R. Barthes, on peut associer cette partition dynamique à une forme de représentation "réticente" (1970, 75), dont la nature fondamentale consisterait à produire des dissonances narratives, c'est-à-dire à retarder l'exposition d'une information importante concernant l'histoire racontée, contribuant ainsi à induire des questionnements chez l'interprète. En suivant cette ligne fonctionnelle, on peut affirmer que le nœud du récit peut prendre deux formes principales, qui ont été décrites par de nombreux poéticiens comme étant associée à deux effets majeurs: la *curiosité* et le *suspense*. Pour ma part, je considère ces effets comme deux modalités alternatives de la *tension narrative*. Par ailleurs, j'ai associé ces deux manières de nouer une intrigue à des traitements cognitifs différenciés de la représentation de l'action, suivant que les scénarios esquissés par les interprètes prennent la forme de *pronostics* (anticipation incertaine d'un développement chronologique) ou de *diagnostics* (hypothèses visant à comprendre une situation narrative décrite de manière incomplète) (Baroni 2007, 110-120). Pronostic et diagnostic sont donc, l'un comme l'autre, des anticipations par rapport au développement séquentiel du récit, mais ils se distinguent sur le plan de l'appréhension cognitive de l'action par rapport à leur orientation temporelle au niveau de l'histoire racontée.

| | | |
|---|---|---|
| Type de réticence induite par le noeud | Représentation chronologique d'un événement instable | Représentation incomplète d'un événement |
| Type de tension narrative | Suspense | Curiosité |
| Type d'activité cognitive | Pronostic | Diagnostic |

En associant l'analyse des affects (suspense ou curiosité) et du traitement cognitif du récit (sous forme de pronostic ou de diagnostic) à des stratégies textuelles marquées par une réticence, il devient dès lors possible de refonder une véritable poétique de l'intrigue. Ces stratégies peuvent naturellement recouvrer la narration chronologique d'un conflit et de sa résolution, mais elles peuvent également impliquer la mise en scène d'une atmosphère inquiétante, diverses formes de paralipses, des restrictions de l'information passant des altérations du point de vue, des bouleversements temporels plus ou moins complexes exigeant du lecteur de recomposer la logique narrative comme un puzzle dont les pièces auraient été mélangées. Le nœud, qui peut être brutal ou progressif, correspond à la phase initiale du développement, lorsque le lecteur est amené à s'interroger sur des éléments présents, passés ou futurs de l'histoire, et le dénouement, s'il survient (il y a des récits qui demeurent en état d'ouverture), correspondra à la phase finale de la séquence, en amenant des réponses aux questions induites par le nœud, et permettant ainsi de résoudre la tension:

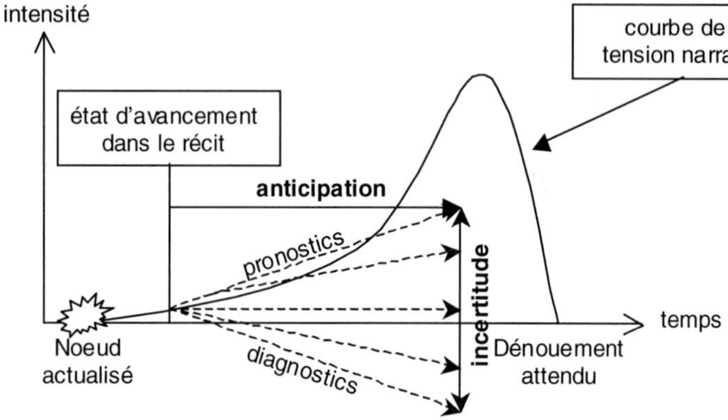


Arrivés à ce stade, nous constatons que la séquence narrative est définie non en fonction de la temporalité (ou de la logique) des événements racontés, mais en fonction de la temporalité de l'actualisation du récit par un interprète qui progresse dans l'histoire. La *puissance* de l'intrigue est ainsi corrélée aux *potentialités* (futures, présentes ou passées) de l'histoire à un moment donné de son développement, dont dépend, sur un plan pragmatique et interactionnel, la "racontabilité" de l'histoire et son intérêt. Dans le cas des récits conversationnels, les narrateurs mettent souvent en évidence ces virtualités non actualisées qui rendent l'histoire digne d'être racontée, en se servant de ce que Labov (1978) a appelé des "évaluations", par exemple des commentaires du type: "j'ai bien failli y laisser ma peau" ou bien "j'ai cru que ma dernière heure avait sonné". Dans les genres littéraires, ces potentialités induisent non seulement une intense activité cognitive de scénarisation des possibles, mais également une augmentation de l'énergie cinétique de la lecture, les interprètes progressant dans l'espoir d'obtenir des réponses aux questions qu'ils se posent.

On peut enfin postuler l'existence d'une certaine résistance du pouvoir de l'intrigue à la relecture, puisqu'il sera toujours envisageable, à chaque réitération du texte, de considérer les alternatives non actualisées par le récit, voire d'en découvrir de nouvelles. En effet, le texte travaille non seulement à raconter ce qui s'est passé, mais également à souligner ce qui aurait pu ou dû se passer. Ces virtualités ont un tel pouvoir d'attraction que certains lecteurs n'ont d'ailleurs pas hésité à transformer ces histoires virtuelles en des récits alternatifs, tel Roger Caillois qui imagine un *Ponce Pilate* qui refuse de s'en laver les mains et Nikos Kazantzakis qui offre au *Christ* une vie paisible de père de famille.

## Conclusions

Ainsi que je l'ai affirmé plus haut, il est surprenant de constater que l'analyse fonctionnelle de l'intrigue a toujours été pratiquée, même durant les périodes formalistes ou structuralistes, alors que, parallèlement, la définition formelle de la séquence narrative s'imposait comme le modèle standard de la poétique littéraire. Cette situation s'explique en partie par le fait que, jusqu'à récemment, l'applicabilité de l'approche fonctionnelle a trop souvent été limitée à des corpus d'œuvres appartenant à la paralittérature, ou à une esthétique passéiste par rapport à laquelle on postule que les fictions modernes se devraient de distancier. Ainsi, pour Tzvetan Todorov (1971), suspense et curiosité étaient des intérêts narratifs dont la pertinence se limitait à sa typologie des récits policiers, pour opposer roman à énigme et roman noir. Charles Grivel (1973), lorsqu'il a traité la question de l'intérêt romanesque, s'est fondé quant à lui sur un corpus de romans d'aventure publiés pendant une décennie du XIX$^{e}$ siècle (1870-1880), ce qui l'a conduit, lui aussi, à restreindre considérablement la portée de ses réflexions. Enfin, Roland Barthes, tout en décrivant le fonctionnement des codes proaïrétique et herméneutique dans le roman balzacien, affirmait que ces derniers limitaient "le pluriel du texte classique" et que ces "blocages" étaient "ce précisément contre quoi – ou entre quoi – s'établit le texte moderne" (1970, 33).

Evidemment, la puissance de l'intrigue est particulièrement saillante dans la littérature populaire, et dans ce contexte, il paraissait évident que le modèle formaliste devait être complété par une analyse des passions romanesques. Mais pour la "grande" littérature, ces effets de *pathos* qui s'atachent à l'intrigue avaient le défaut impardonnable d'intéresser le lecteur et, par conséquent, de passer pour des artifices "commerciaux". Ainsi, Barthes associait le suspense "aux habitudes commerciales et idéologiques de notre société qui recommande de 'jeter' l'histoire une fois qu'elle a été consommée ('dévorée'), pour que l'on puisse alors passer à une autre histoire, acheter un autre livre" (1970, 20). Johanne Villeneuve résume la nature de cette condamnation:

> Dans le domaine des études littéraires, on a longtemps rangé les "histoires à intrigue" parmi les mauvaises fréquentations. [...] Hors de l'esthétique, loin des choses sérieuses et maîtrisées, l'intrigue fait sa petite œuvre, tantôt facile, tantôt besogneuse, toujours un peu racoleuse, auprès d'un public venu s'y distraire, s'y évader ou s'y complaire. (Villeneuve 2003, xiii)

Pour définir l'échelle des valeurs littéraires, si le "style" devenait ainsi une balise fondamentale, surtout lorsque l'écriture faisait écran à l'aventure, l'art de créer un monde et d'intéresser le lecteur avait perdu ses lettres de noblesse. Ce ne sont d'ailleurs pas seulement les "récits à intrigue" qui ont alors été déclassés, mais également une certaine forme de lecture, voire une catégorie de lecteurs. Le rejet de l'intrigue est alors devenu un critère de distinction:

> L'amateur d'intrigues est un instinctif qui vous dira tout de go que *c'était bon* ou *raté*. Il ne se laissera pas entortiller dans des considérations poétiques. Certains voient en lui un pur consommateur, un entiché de mécanique, un féru de scandale, un boulimique livré vivant à la production en chaîne de la culture de masse, aveugle à la complexité des formes et sourd à l'appel de la poésie. Ainsi tournée à la caricature, l'intrigue aurait force et pouvoir d'aliénation: elle tiendrait le spectateur naïf en haleine, le rive à ses fantasmes comme à son siège. (Villeneuve 2001, 13)

W. C. Booth affirme pour sa part que "la plupart des dépréciations de l'intrigue sont basées sur l'affirmation que la vie ne fournit pas d'intrigues, et que la littérature doit être comme la vie" (Booth 1983, 57, m.t.). Mais cette idée s'applique surtout au modèle formaliste, dans la mesure où, ainsi que l'affirmait Sartre dans *La Nausée*, la vie se vit dans un sens et elle se raconte dans l'autre. Par contre, si l'on se place dans la perspective du lecteur, nous lisons les livres dans le même sens que nous vivons nos vies, orientés vers ce qui est à lire ou à venir, et les épreuves de l'existence aussi bien que les feuilletons médiatiques que nous lisons dans la presse nous rappellent chaque jour que le suspense, la curiosité et la surprise ne sont pas de purs artifices littéraires (Baroni, Pahud & Revaz 2006). On peut dès lors affirmer que la réalité elle-même se construit à la manière d'une intrigue émergeante, et qu'elle diffère au fond assez peu, au niveau de l'expérience que l'on peut en avoir, de l'histoire dans laquelle progresse un lecteur intrigué. D'ailleurs, Booth ajoutait que la critique de l'artificialité de l'intrigue devait être replacée dans son contexte historique:

> La plupart des attaques portant sur le caractère prétendument non-esthétique de l'intrigue et de l'implication émotionnelle dans les récits ont été fondées sur la redécouverte moderne de la "distance esthétique". [...] Mais ce n'est pas avant [le XX^e^] siècle que les hommes ont commencé à prendre au sérieux la possibilité que le pouvoir d'un artifice qui nous maintient à une certaine distance de la réalité pouvait être une vertu plutôt que simplement un obstacle inévitable pour un réalisme total. (Booth 1983, 121, m.t.)

Il faudrait ajouter que si l'analyse de la tension narrative semble devenue impertinente lorsqu'elle est appliquée à la littérature moderne, c'est surtout parce que cette question a été délégitimée par la critique, mais cela ne signifie pas nécessairement que les œuvres de cette période ont radicalement tourné le dos à la rhétorique de l'intrigue. Lorsque Jean Ricardou dénonçait le "totalitarisme" d'une intrigue où "tout doit concourir au dénouement" (1967, 171-172), il critiquait l'intrigue telle que la concevaient Poe ou Forster, mais nullement la dynamique inhérente aux récits qui exploitent des défigurations provisoires ou définitives de la chronologie ou de la causalité afin de créer un intense sentiment de curiosité. Les intrigues policières sont d'ailleurs l'un des prototypes architextuels qui ont le plus influencé les œuvres de la modernité, depuis *Les Gommes* jusqu'à *La Route des Flandres*, en passant par *L'Emploi du temps*. Certes, l'approche formelle et son schéma quinaire semblent peu efficaces pour analyser de tels récits, qui brisent la chronologie et qui brouillent la causalité, en revanche, le modèle fonctionnel n'a aucun mal à décrire leur dynamique[8].

Il me semble que, pour une poétique contemporaine réconciliée avec la rhétorique et qui s'intéresse enfin à l'intrication entre cognition et émotion dans l'expérience esthétique, l'approche fonctionnelle de l'intrigue est redevenue essentielle. L'intrigue est enfin sortie du laboratoire dans lequel des lecteurs professionnels l'avaient confinée, dissertant entre spécialistes sur ses méthodes de composition, sur ses structures internes ou ses défauts esthétiques, sans se préoccuper véritablement de ses usages ordinaires et de sa fonction anthropologique. À une époque où se pose, peut-être plus que jamais, la question de la survie des études littéraires, il faut rappeler que l'analyse des intérêts narratifs dans les œuvres de fiction nous offre une voie d'accès privilégiée vers ce qui constitue le cœur vivant de l'expérience de l'être dans le temps. La poétique permet ainsi de mettre au jour un jeu créatif et cathartique, qui transforme les événements racontés en un réservoir potentiellement infini d'histoires racontables.

## Références

Adam, Jean-Michel. 1997. *Les Textes, types et prototypes*. Paris: Nathan.

Baroni, Raphaël. 2010. "Ce que l'intrigue ajoute au temps. Une relecture critique de *Temps et récit* de Paul Ricœur", *Poétique*, n° 163, 361-382.

—. 2009. *L'Œuvre du temps. Poétique de la discordance narrative*. Paris: Seuil.

—. 2007. *La Tension narrative. Suspense, curiosité et surprise*. Paris: Seuil.

[8] Sur ces questions, je renvoie à Wagner (2010).

Baroni, Raphaël, Stéphanie Pahud et Françoise Revaz. 2006. "De l'intrigue littéraire à l'intrigue médiatique: le feuilleton *Swissmetal*". *A Contrario*, n° 4 (2), 123-143.
Barthes, Roland. 1970. *S/Z*. Paris: Seuil.
Booth, Wayne C. 1983. *The Rhetoric of Fiction*. Chicago: University of Chicago Press.
Bremond, Claude. 1973. *Logique du récit*. Paris: Seuil.
Brooks, Peter. 1984. *Reading for the Plot. Design and Intention in Narrative*. Cambridge & London: Harvard University Press.
Dannenberg, Hilary P. 2005. "Plot". In *The Routledge Encyclopedia of Narrative Theory*, edited by David Herman, Manfred Jahn et Marie-Laure Ryan, 435-437. London: Routledge.
Derrida, Jacques. 1967. "Force et signification", dans *L'Écriture et la différence*. Paris: Seuil.
Eco, Umberto. 1985. *Lector in fabula*. Paris: Grasset.
Escola, Marc. 2011. "Le clou de Tchekhov. Retours sur le principe de causalité régressive". Dans *La Partie et le tout*, dir. Marc Escola et al., 107-120. Bruxelles: Peeters.
Fontanille, Jacques et Claude Zilberberg. 1998. *Tension et signification*. Liège: Mardaga.
Forster, Edward Morgan. 1993 (1928). *Aspects du roman*. Paris: Christian Bourgois.
Grivel, Charles. 1973. *Production de l'intérêt romanesque*. Paris & The Hague: Mouton.
Labov, William. 1978. "La transformation du vécu à travers la syntaxe narrative". Dans *Le Parler ordinaire*, 457-503. Paris: Gallimard.
Larivaille, Paul. 1974. "L'analyse (morpho)logique du récit". *Poétique*, n° 19, 368-388.
Morgan, James. "Emplotment, Plot, and Explotment: Refining Plot Analysis of Biblical Narratives from the Reader's Perspective", manuscrit soumis à *Biblical Interpretation*.
Phelan, James. 1989. *Reading People, Reading Plots: Character, Progression, and the Interpretation of Narrative*. Chicago: University of Chicago Press.
Poe, Edgar Allan. 1978. *Histoires grotesques et sérieuses*. Paris: Gallimard.
Propp, Vladimir. 1970. *Morphologie du conte*. Paris: Seuil.
Revaz, Françoise. 2009. *Introduction à la narratologie. Action et narration*. Bruxelles: De Boeck.
Ricardou, Jean. 1967. *Problèmes du Nouveau Roman*. Paris: Seuil.
Ricœur, Paul. 1983. *Temps et récit*. Paris: Seuil.

Ryan, Marie-Laure. 1991. *Possible Worlds, Artificial Intelligence and Narrative Theory*. Bloomington, IN: Indiana University Press.
Schaeffer, Jean-Marie. 2010. "Le récit entre fait et fiction: perspectives cognitives". Dans *Devant la fiction, dans le monde*, dir. Catherine Grall et Marielle Macé. Rennes: Presses Universitaires de Rennes.
Sternberg, Meir. 1978. *Expositional Modes and Temporal Ordering in Fiction*. Baltimore & London: Johns Hopkins University Press.
—. 1992. "Telling in time (II): Chronology, Teleology, Narrativity". *Poetics Today,* n° 13, 463-541.
Todorov, Tzvetan. 1971. "Typologie du roman policier". Dans *Poétique de la Prose*. Paris: Seuil.
Villeneuve, Johanne. 2003. *Le Sens de l'intrigue*. Laval: Presses Universitaires de Laval.
Wagner, Frank. 2010. "Alain Robbe-Grillet raconte (dysnarration, *fabula*, intrigue)". Dans *Alain Robbe-Grillet. Balises pour le XXIème siècle*, dir. Roger-Michel Allemand et Christian Milat. Paris: Presses de la Sorbonne Nouvelle.

# CHAPTER TWO

# *STORYPLAYING*. LA MACHINE A FABRIQUER SES HISTOIRES ET A APAISER SON ESPRIT

JACQUES MIGOZZI

Dès son titre, fondé sur un décalquage et un décalage délibérément provocateurs, cette contribution, on l'aura compris, se propose d'adopter un point de vue très éloigné de l'essai de Christian Salmon *Storytelling. La Machine à fabriquer des histoires et à formater les esprits* (Salmon 2007). Non que cet ouvrage récent, qui a connu au sein du champ intellectuel et médiatique français un incontestable succès pendant une ou deux années – succès dont les raisons structurelles comme conjoncturelles mériteraient d'être interrogées au demeurant – ne lance des signaux d'alerte salutaires à notre vigilance civique et ne rassemble des informations dignes d'intérêt pour les chercheurs. Il est en effet important de prendre conscience d'une part que la force prescriptive du récit est sciemment mobilisée depuis une vingtaine d'années par la mercatique, par de nouveaux dispositifs managériaux, ou encore par des appareils politiques visant l'hégémonie idéologique en dominant les imaginaires de citoyens-badauds; et d'autre part que cette scénarisation omniprésente au sein du nouvel espace public symbolique narratif[1] atteint probablement aujourd'hui une ampleur et une puissance inégalée jusqu'alors dans l'histoire des sociétés humaines, et ne peut manquer vraisemblablement de modéliser partiellement les représentations des lecteurs-spectateurs-consommateurs que nous sommes tous, que nous nous en défendions ou pas. Qu'il faille aujourd'hui scruter avec attention le *soft power* du *storytelling* mobilisé par les récits circulant au sein de notre biotope médiatique n'est donc guère contestable. Mais l'essai de Salmon, héritier manifeste de l'Ecole de Francfort et de sa posture critique, postule un peu hâtivement à mes yeux, dans sa volonté militante de dénonciation, que les fictions de grande consommation distilleraient quasi immanquablement du prêt-à-penser en même temps que

---

[1] Voir Lits 2009.

du prêt-à-rêver et participeraient sur le plan systémique à la "fabrique du conformisme" ("manufacture of consentment" selon Noam Chomsky). Comme j'ai déjà eu l'occasion de le souligner en 2009 dans un précédent séminaire tenu à Leeds (Migozzi 2010), cette accusation est ancienne, bien antérieure aux analyses d'Adorno et Horkheimer sur les industries culturelles, puisque le "roman populaire" a été stigmatisé comme "opium du peuple" et "poison de l'âme" dès l'avènement du feuilleton à la fin des années 1830. Or, les apports croisés de recherches au long cours et d'ancrages disciplinaires différents aboutissent à contester ce verdict péremptoire que Jean-Pierre Esquenazi n'hésite pas à rapporter à la " posture aristocratique ou réactionnaire ou antidémocratique des intellectuels modernes vis à vis de la production culturelle [relevant] de la culture industrielle" (Esquenazi 2007, 208). Lors du cycle de rencontres internationales organisé à Limoges en 2006 et 2007 sur le thème "Idéologies et stratégies argumentatives dans les récits imprimés de grande consommation. XIXe-XXIe siècles", il a été par exemple collectivement acté que la cuirasse de monologisme dont sont couramment parés les récits imprimés de grande consommation masque une polyphonie tout aussi indéniable sur le plan argumentatif, polyphonie que le lecteur investit sur le plan éthique de sens pluriels au gré de son encyclopédie de lecteur sériel, de son ethos de classe ou de sa trajectoire[2]. Le colloque *Finding the Plot*, point de départ de ce volume, nous a conduit de même, et de manière décisive, à souligner la complexité des interactions qui se tissent entre les récits et leurs publics, ces usages ne pouvant être partiellement et partialement expliqués par le seul paradigme de la vassalisation et de la captation, comme le fait trop à mon sens Christian Salmon, aux prix d'impasses sur les recherches contemporaines portant sur la fiction, les pratiques de lecture et/ou l'étude des publics, qui pourraient contrevenir à sa posture " apocalyptique " – comme dirait Umberto Eco.

C'est dans cette optique, en inscrivant la présente contribution dans la réflexion collective capitalisée depuis une douzaine d'années par la Coordination Internationale des Chercheurs en Littératures Populaires et Culture Médiatique, que je me propose de renverser le point de vue adopté classiquement sur le *storytelling* et de porter l'accent sur ce que je me risque à nommer, par décalquage sémantique et parophonique, *storyplaying*, i.e. l'investissement et la traversée du récit par le lecteur. J'adopterai ce parti pris, tout en notant d'emblée que depuis une vingtaine d'années le dénigrement du *storytelling* cède du terrain ou en tous cas reformule plus prudemment ses soupçons, puisqu'on crédite aujourd'hui

[2] Voir Migozzi et Artiaga 2009 et 2010.

volontiers le grand public d'une lecture teintée d'ironie des fictions qui le séduisent, et qu'on ne lui dénie plus de goûter aux plaisirs plus retors du second degré et du jeu avec l'architextualité et l'intertextualité, sur lesquels tablent bon nombre de récits médiatiques contemporains. La lecture-plaisir *omnibus* n'est toutefois pas entièrement lavée du soupçon de manipuler le lecteur, puisque – pourraient objecter certains – l'instauration d'une relation foncièrement ludique – voire carnavalesque lorsque triomphe une poétique de l'hyperbole parodique – du lecteur-spectateur au récit qu'il consomme à hautes doses, ne le prémunit pas nécessairement contre l'influence de représentations qui, par leur ressassement, imprégneraient son imaginaire jusqu'à le saturer. Le seul moyen dans ces conditions de ne pas soupçonner en permanence le *storytelling* de "passer du côté obscur de la force" (narrative), c'est donc de se pencher sur la boîte noire de la réception … ce qui suppose de bousculer quelques habitudes méthodologiques des chercheurs littéraires, et d'aller au delà de la boîte à outils de la poétique textualiste.

Pour ce faire, je tisserai, sans exclusives de principe et en me montrant attentif à leurs convergences plus qu'à leur éventuelle hétérogénéité sur le plan théorique, des hypothèses portées par l'herméneutique d'un Paul Ricoeur ou la réflexion esthétique d'un Thomas Pavel, ou d'autres nourries par les acquis des sciences cognitives développées dans une perspective interactionnelle et pragmatique, comme chez Jean-Marie Schaeffer dans son ouvrage *Pourquoi la fiction?* (Schaeffer 1999) ou plus récemment Raphaël Baroni dans *La Tension narrative* (Baroni 2007). Les analyses subtiles, nourries de psychanalyse, de Michel Picard, raisonnant dès 1986 sur le *playing* toujours actif au cœur de l'immersion fictionnelle, demeurent également pour une large part très pertinentes, à condition de rompre avec l'aristocratisme foncier de cet essai pour qui les plaisirs supérieurs de "la lecture littéraire comme jeu" sont l'apanage d'une élite de connaisseurs, donc inaccessibles au grand public englué dans l'illusion (Picard 1986). En explorant les différentes facettes du *storyplaying*, il s'agira en somme de plaider pour une esthétique du jeu fictionnel, "si l'on veut bien restituer au terme d'esthétique l'amplitude de sens que lui confère l'*aisthèsis* grecque, et lui donner pour thème l'exploration des manières multiples dont une œuvre, en agissant sur un lecteur, l'*affecte*." (Ricoeur 1985, 303). Cette démarche exploratoire devrait nous amener en tous cas à ne pas réduire le jeu lectoral à une possession/dépossession du *player* par le *storytelling* et /ou au décalage ironique présenté comme consubstantiel à la postmodernité et au postmodernisme.

Jean-Marie Schaeffer, lorsqu'il raisonne sur "la fiction ludique" dans son article "De l'imagination à la fiction" (Schaeffer 2002b), distingue dans cette "attitude intentionnelle extrêmement complexe" "trois mécanismes mimétiques de base qu'elle combine, à savoir la feintise ludique, l'immersion mimétique et la modélisation analogique": par commodité démonstrative, cette tripartition servira de fil conducteur à mon investigation des tours et détours du *storyplaying*.

En définissant la fiction comme "une feintise ludique partagée", Jean-Marie Schaeffer souligne après d'autres[1] l'essentielle connivence ludique que présuppose la lecture de tout récit fictionnel, connivence active dont Coleridge avait cerné la bonne volonté fondamentale par sa célèbre formule "willing suspension of disbelief". Le *storyplaying* suscité par le *storytelling* combine par conséquent en permanence, selon des dosages éminemment variables entre lecteurs, mais aussi entre moments de lecture chez un même lecteur, distanciation *et* participation, immersion *et* dégagement, fièvre de l'introjection psycho-affective *et* nonchalance à la Hoggart. Tout lecteur donc se dédouble – que ce dédoublement demeure infra-conscient ou soit au contraire perçu et savouré comme tel – et oscille, pour reprendre des termes anglo-saxons mobilisés par Michel Picard, entre *playing*, qui lui fait goûter les délices de l'identification consentie et temporaire, et *game*, qui lui fait savourer en connaisseur averti le jeu des codes et avec les codes. Ce phénomène semble particulièrement avéré, à suivre par exemple les analyses de Paul Bleton, dans le compagnonnage de lecteurs sériels avec des récits "formulaires" – selon la terminologie de Cawelti – puisque l'architextualité y est de toute évidence posée par le récit et appréhendée par le lecteur comme un terrain de jeu(x).[2] Autrement formulé, pour employer cette fois la typologie des instances lectorales développée par Vincent Jouve en prolongeant les analyses de Michel Picard (Jouve 1992), tout lecteur doit se voir reconnaître la dignité de "lectant jouant" et ne pas être présumé embobiné par le texte, au point de se cantonner au "lu" et au "lisant"[3] comme l'a longtemps prétendu la légende noire du lecteur populaire décervelé et berné.

Pour autant, en reconnaissant ainsi la présence latente d'un plaisir savouré au second ou au troisième degrés[4] au coeur de toute lecture, nous sommes loin d'avoir cerné l'essentiel de la force anthropologique du *storyplaying*, car cette expérience complexe n'est pas réductible à une

---

[1] On saluera entre autres l'allégresse et le brio avec lequels Jean-Claude Vareille dans son dernier ouvrage défendit cette thèse: voir Vareille 1994.

[2] Voir Bleton 1999.

[3] J'ai défendu cette thèse dans le chapitre 6 de mon essai *Boulevards du populaire* (Migozzi 2005).

[4] Voir Dufays 1994.

partie de cache-cache formaliste avec le texte et que la littérature ne nous touche et ne nous intéresse au sens fort qu'en suscitant des émotions. Raphaël Baroni, dans son remarquable essai sur *La Tension narrative*, a ainsi éclairé le rôle essentiel des "fonctions thymiques" du récit[5] que sont le "suspense", la "curiosité" et le "rappel" (ou "suspens paradoxal"), permettant de comprendre pourquoi les fictions dites populaires suscitent l'adhésion: c'est que leur fidélité aux fonctions fondamentales du récit classique et à son noyau irradiant de tension dramatique leur permet précisément de procurer avec prodigalité des émotions éphémères, lors même que ces émotions, aussi salutaires qu'apparemment "gratuites", sont souvent dévalorisées dans le champ littéraire par les critiques qui dénoncent leur exploitation commerciale. Mais les analyses de Baroni éclairent aussi du même mouvement un point tout aussi essentiel: la *forme* même du *storyplaying* est décisive sur le plan psychique pour ce qu'elle peut avoir de rassérénant. S'interrogeant sur le rappel ou "suspense paradoxal" (le lecteur connaît déjà la fin, mais éprouve néanmoins une émotion anticipatrice), Baroni remarque par exemple: "Le récit présenterait dans l'expérience de la répétition une *forme* impérissable; or, cette *forme*, capable de ressurgir identique à elle-même à chaque réactualisation, s'opposerait, comme le suggérait déjà Gerrig, à l'expérience quotidienne de l'irréversibilité de l'événement" (Baroni 2007, 291). Elargissant son propos, il insiste alors en conclusion sur la puissance réconfortante de la mise en intrigue, "précisément parce que la narrativité représente la seule médiation symbolique capable de représenter l'ineffable, de créer un espace à l'intérieur duquel l'indétermination du futur et du monde s'inscrit dans l'harmonie et l'intelligibilité d'un discours. " (Baroni 2007, 406). On retrouve ici bien sûr la thèse capitale de Paul Ricoeur patiemment élaborée et démontrée tout au long de la somme de *Temps et récit*, selon laquelle le récit est planche de salut contre l'aporétique du temps vécu, et qu'il permet de donner sens parce que forme à la temporalité. Anne Besson, lorsqu'elle raisonne sur les cycles et séries dans la littérature de genre marque dans une même optique le rôle foncièrement rassurant de cette forme narrative puisque "le cycle donne à lire une succession de volumes chronologiquement liés, distincts et pourtant harmonieusement fondus en un ensemble unique, une histoire unique; une succession de moments prenant place dans une temporalité maîtrisée; une continuité du discontinu

[5] "La 'thymie' (du grec *tumos* qui signifie 'cœur, affectivité' est une humeur, une disposition affective de base. En psychologie, la régulation de l'humeur se définit par une 'fonction thymique'.[…] Nous nous servirons de cette expression pour désigner des effets poétiques de nature 'affective' ou 'passionnelle'" (Baroni 2007, 20).

dont la promesse est qu'elle peut se poursuivre à l'infini et dessiner une complétude toujours plus satisfaisante." (Besson 2004, 208-12).

Si le récit fictionnel a pu être crédité à bon droit d'une fonction consolatoire, 'est donc probablement entre autres raisons[6] parce qu'il nous permet par la répétition d'une forme narrative stable de jouir d'un sentiment de maîtrise face à un réel souvent vécu comme dysphorique. A tout prendre, le *storyplaying* s'apparenterait par ses protocoles aux rituels par lesquels le petit enfant observé par Piaget conjurait et apprivoisait l'absence de la Mère en lançant au loin puis en ramenant à lui sa bobine, ou encore ceux des enfants scrutés par Winnicott régulant leur relation au monde en se situant dans une "aire transitionnelle". Pourquoi en revanche faudrait-il qualifier péjorativement, comme le fait Umberto Eco, cette "joie de la consolation [qui] répond à des exigences profondes, sinon de notre esprit du moins de notre système nerveux" de "plaisir régressif du retour à l'attendu" ou de "fastes de la paresse infantile" goûtant l'apaisement par "une orgie de redondance" (Eco 1993, 19 et 61) ? Comme le fait remarquer Daniel Couégnas dans sa contribution sur les enjeux du dénouement romanesque lors du récent colloque "Littérature et consolation", c'est peut-être parce que Eco, tout en soulignant de manière pionnière le bonheur combinatoire que procure la narrativité populaire fondée sur la répétition, "s'attache beaucoup au 'signifié' et simplifie à l'excès la complexité de l'acte de lecture, réduit aux mécanismes de l'illusion référentielle et de l'identification", ce qui le conduirait à minimiser l'importance esthétique – au sens ricoeurien du terme rappelé en introduction – du rituel de "complétude, finition, fermeture" que constitue le dénouement (Couégnas 2012).

Le storyplaying donc rassurerait le lecteur par sa forme réglée, dispensatrice de "healing", si l'on préfère cette notion empruntée à l'anglais (et à Marvin Gaye) à celle de "consolation" trop lestée de son sémantisme religieux originel. N'en tirons toutefois pas des conclusions schématiques sur la sensation de maîtrise qu'il procure au lecteur: Raphaël Baroni insiste en effet dans *L'Œuvre du temps*, en s'écartant de Ricoeur et surtout de sa vulgate pour réarticuler les 3 stades de la *mimèsis*, sur le rôle essentiel de la discordance au cœur de la narrativité intrinsèque à l'agir et au pâtir humains (mimèsis I), et souligne que la "*mimèsis II intrigante* [par opposition à la *Mimèsis II configurante*] serait le propre des récits (généralement fictionnels) qui jouent à ressembler aux histoires actuelles que l'on rencontre au stade de la *mimésis I*" (Baroni 2009, 89).

---

[6] Voir Migozzi 2012.

Défions-nous du même coup du biais possible d'une "posture poétique" face au texte, qui tendrait à spatialiser abusivement la configuration de l'œuvre par un point de vue rétrospectif, et qui ce faisant écraserait la temporalité de toute première lecture, nierait le rythme et la tension inhérents à une "lecture à l'endroit". Bref, retrouvons la dynamique passionnelle et passionnante du récit.

La forme du récit, réglée et régulatrice, n'est en effet foncièrement délectable que parce qu'elle autorise et décante l'expression des émotions et des pulsions. Longtemps considérée par l'appareil scolaire et universitaire comme une forme primitive et infantile de lecture, l'implication émotionnelle du lecteur *par* le *récit* et *dans l'histoire* est en effet capitale et se manifeste le plus souvent par ce qu'il est convenu d'appeler l'"identification" au personnage – même si cette notion pourrait prêter à débat dès lors qu'on l'interpréterait comme un oubli de soi et/ ou des conditions du jeu lectoral. Qu'elle soit avouée ou inavouable, assumée ou latente, qu'elle procède par "admiration", "compassion" ou "association", la projection psychique sur l'écran désirable du personnage permet au lecteur de se faire son cinéma intérieur et de donner figures à ses fantasmes, sans que cette décharge pulsionnelle soit socialement compromettante ou risquée. Il s'agit donc bien pour reprendre une formule heureuse de Michel Picard, de "traiter par homéopathie le danger", ce qui relève des "fonctions endotéliques" de la fiction, que Jean-Marie Schaeffer définit comme des "fonctions compensatoires par rapport à des modélisations cognitives qui nous frustrent, nous mettent dans un état de stress ou encore nous font souffrir" (Schaeffer 2002b). A l'instar des "visions du monde" "qui essaient tant bien que mal à trouver un compromis entre l'indésirable et l'inévitable ainsi qu'entre le désirable et l'impossible", la fiction romanesque permettrait ainsi "de stabiliser ou de dynamiser notre univers mental" mais, par son caractère fictionnel même, pourrait exercer sa fonction compensatoire et positive "sans que nous ayons à la payer par une contamination de nos interactions 'sérieuses' avec la réalité."

Convenons toutefois que cette incontestable puissance consolatoire de la fiction romanesque, et particulièrement pour nombre de genres dits de grande consommation (polar, thriller, aventure, espionnage, horreur, porno …) repose souvent sur un pacte d'écriture et "un contrat de lecture" – au sens que prêtent à ce terme Alain-Michel Boyer et après lui Daniel Couégnas – placés sous le signe de la duplicité et de l'ambivalence, valeurs cardinales du *storyplaying*. Dans son essai de synthèse sur le roman d'aventures, Matthieu Letourneux rappelle ainsi le double sens irréductible de toute *catharsis*, car c'est bien de cela au fond qu'il s'agit:

> Selon qu'on met davantage l'accent sur le premier ou sur le second moment de la catharsis, on tend à privilégier le plaisir de l'émotion et le processus de purgation (l'une des traductions du terme), d'élimination des passions par leur spectacle, ou à mettre l'accent sur la compréhension critique des passions, l'accès à un sens supérieur, le travail de purification (autre traduction du terme). (Letourneux 2010, 391)

Il peut alors souligner le "paradoxe central du roman d'aventures, qui joue à tous les niveaux du texte":

> En un sens, le roman paraît condamner les valeurs de sauvagerie, à travers un discours moral, un dispositif actantiel manichéen, et une mise à distance de l'univers de l'aventure (dépaysement et esthétique du romanesque); à l'inverse, le cœur du texte consiste en la mise en scène de cet univers sauvage à travers une succession de mésaventures violentes, la figuration d'un espace de liberté à la fois cruel, sans lois et infiniment plus riche que l'espace réel du quotidien dans lequel le héros peut entièrement laisser s'exprimer son libre-arbitre." (Letourneux 2010, 10)

Deux lectures sont donc toujours du même coup possibles de la sauvagerie dans le roman d'aventures: d'une part, la libération symbolique des pulsions, d'autre part, le dépassement de ces pulsions; et cette ambiguïté est tout à la fois consubstantielle au genre, fondé sur la mise en récit et en scène de la violence transgressive, et décisive dans son succès durable. Au risque d'être accusé d'extrapolation, risquons-nous à généraliser cette thèse: lorsque le lecteur s'encanaille avec de mauvais genres aux charmes équivoques, sa lecture cathartique ne lui fait-elle pas goûter aux délices de "la mauvaise foi", puisqu' "à l'insu de son plein gré" il choisit sciemment de se leurrer lui-même? Cette proposition fait consonance en tous cas avec les analyses de Jean-Marie Schaeffer lorsqu'il raisonne sur "le romanesque" et son "rôle important dans notre économie mentale", puisque, note-t-il, "le romanesque trouve des points d'accroche psychologiques largement partagés au delà des différences culturelles" (Schaeffer 2002a,13): distinguant donc, au sein de cette catégorie littéraire articulée à un éthos existentiel, deux grandes tendances, un romanesque blanc , "optimiste ou heureux (ce qui est le cas du romanesque grec privilégié par Pavel"), et un romanesque noir, malheureux ou pessimiste. Schaeffer note leur fréquent mixage: "On a souvent noté la tendance par exemple dans le roman grec à détailler les aventures des héros et à s'attarder sur les outrages qu'ils subissent. En fait cela montre qu'il est rare que le romanesque blanc lui-même se passe entièrement de toute incursion dans le romanesque". Et de poursuivre: "notre méchanceté – qui n'est pas moins 'humaine' que notre bonté – a elle aussi besoin de nourritures fictionnelles." (Schaeffer 2002a, 9 et 10)

Nous ne touchons pas encore pour autant au fin mot de l'histoire en matière de plaisirs du *storyplaying*. En rester là pourrait de fait cautionner une approche classiquement réductrice des fictions populaires, qui les confine à la satisfaction standardisée et pauvrement sublimée d'émotions naïves ou de fantasmes omnibus. Or il convient d'affirmer la fonction cognitive trop méconnue des fictions de grande consommation, dont Jean-Pierre Esquenazi dans son dernier ouvrage a judicieusement marqué l'efficience dans nos représentations mentales (Esquenazi 2009)[7]. Jean-Marie Schaeffer a pour sa part fortement insisté sur ce point en soulignant la fonction de "modélisation analogique" de la fiction: "Ainsi, un modèle fictionnel est susceptible non seulement d'être un modèle *de* la réalité, mais aussi un modèle *contre* la réalité, et cela parce que dans tous les cas il est un modèle *pour* la réalité (au sens où il est appelé à être projeté sur cette réalité, leur superposition ayant le statut d'un palimpseste)." (Schaeffer 2002b, 9).

Si l'on admet avec Thomas Pavel que la fonction cognitive de toute fiction découle non de sa "dimension référentielle" mais de sa "portée inférentielle", il paraît fallacieux de refuser aux fictions de grande consommation l'appartenance à cet "art de l'éloignement" qui permet au lecteur de penser le monde grâce au détour de la fabulation:

> Le mouvement des pulsions, des maximes, des biens et des valeurs fondatrices qui anime les personnages captive et entraîne également le moi fictif du spectateur. Si ce dernier saisit l'action de cette œuvre, ce n'est pas simplement parce qu'il perçoit les évènements qui la composent et en déchiffre les enjeux, mais parce que ces enjeux deviennent d'une certaine manière les siens. Par le biais du moi fictif, je me laisse volontiers impliquer dans les complexités de l'intrigue et, par là même, dans la charpente axiologique de l'œuvre. (Pavel 2003, 7-9)

Qu'il en ait conscience ou pas, le *storyplayer* serait par conséquent engagé sur le plan éthique et sa lecture-plaisir l'entraînerait vers l'inévitable "perplexité morale" sécrétée par toute fiction, a fortiori par les genres (par exemple le macro genre du policier, ou celui évoqué supra du roman d'aventure) thématisant une inquiétude essentielle sur les normes et les valeurs. Une telle thèse trouve son écho dans le chapitre X "Pourquoi le roman" de *L'Espèce fabulatrice* de Nancy Huston et un contrepoint stimulant dans le volet conclusif de l'article de Schaeffer sur le

[7] "L'imaginaire est dans la réalité; en outre il contribue à la former, à la déformer et à la reconstituer ensuite." (Esquenazi 2009, 193).

romanesque: posant l'hypothèse que celui-ci est "la traduction d'un désir d'harmonie ou de toute-puissance", et que le romanesque blanc relève plutôt de la modélisation axiologique et le romanesque noir de la modélisation pulsionnelle, Schaeffer suggère que "le romanesque construit des passages à la limite dans le domaine de la modélisation axiologique et affective". "Comment serait le monde si le bien et le mal étaient nettement séparés et si le bien pouvait vaincre? mais aussi: comment serait le monde si je pouvais exercer de la manière la plus 'pure' ma propre volonté de puissance ? Dans les deux cas, nous avons affaire à des modélisations qui nous proposent des univers hautement désirables bien qu'antagonistes." (Schaeffer 2002a). En bref, l'expérience imaginaire du storyplaying peut confronter le lecteur aux ambivalences et tensions inhérentes à son identité, le manichéisme massif des représentations ne pouvant entraver le jeu lectoral.

La lecture-plaisir de fictions visant avec franchise le divertissement de leur(s) lecteur(s) ne saurait donc se réduire à un jeu gratuit ou immanquablement mystificateur, mais peut au contraire jouer un rôle de médiation symbolique, puisqu'elle offre au *storyplayer* l'occasion de *réfléchir* à sa vie par le truchement d'un récit-miroir où le lecteur/la lectrice peut se mirer (*se réfléchir*) imaginairement. A l'issue de longues enquêtes les chercheuses féministes de la "seconde génération" des *gender studies* ont ainsi été conduites à réviser des jugements péremptoires antérieurs, fondés sur une répudiation de principe de la féminité traditionnelle et conventionnelle et de ses genres fictionnels propres. Qu'elles aient travaillé sur le *soap opera*, la série *Dallas* ou les romans sériels de la multinationale Harlequin, Charlotte Brundson, Ian Ang, Janice Radway ou Julia Bettinotti ont toutes souligné "le mélange de détachement et d'attachement envers leurs objets qui caractérise ces publics […] [qui] construisent en même temps leur vision des œuvres et aussi la forme d'intimité qu'ils veulent entretenir avec elles." L'évasion par la fiction n'est plus dès lors à appréhender comme un subterfuge aliénant mais comme "l'aménagement d'un lieu et d'un temps à part du courant quotidien", qui permet "d'une part d'éviter une confrontation déplaisante entre ces publics et les difficultés de leur existence, d'autre part […] [de] compose[r] un biais grâce auquel ces dernières peuvent être représentées et réfléchies." (Esquenazi 2007, 185-7)

Dans *La Vérité de la fiction*, Esquenazi en arrive à proposer la notion théorique de "paraphrase" pour désigner cette relation spéculaire et cognitivement constructrice que le *storyplayer* – pour le dire selon mon propre parti pris terminologique – établit avec la fiction qu'il habite et peut-être métabolise. C'est à des conclusions homologues *mutatis mutandis* qu'aboutit le travail d'Erik Neveu et d'Annie Collovald sur les lecteurs français contemporains passionnés de polar (Collovald et Neveu, 2004). "Lire du noir" n'est de fait pas seulement distraction pour ces amateurs-connaisseurs mais lecture de savoir – construisant un point de vue critique et inquisitorial, foncièrement politique, sur un monde opaque – et même plus encore pour certains: lecture de salut, à laquelle l'individu recourt lors de cassures dans sa "trajectoire" sociale et existentielle. Last but not least, le *storyplayer* n'est pas nécessairement seul pour penser-rêver sa vie en se mirant dans le prisme fictionnel: Radway comme d'autres chercheurs constate que la lecture est aussi une pratique socialisante[8] et que les échanges et discussions qui prolongent la lecture intime et solitaire sont déterminants pour faire du *storyplaying* un espace de négociation du sens de la vie.

Le *storyplaying* qui se déploie par le truchement des fictions dites populaires n'a donc rien, dans sa complexité de médiation symbolique, d'un parcours interprétatif contraint et aliénant, dominé à tout coup par les injonctions d'un *storytelling* omnipotent. Il faut par conséquent s'inscrire en faux contre la résurgence sous de nouveaux oripeaux d'une rengaine ancienne et objectivement anti-démocratique, selon laquelle la lecture d'évasion / de détente / de plaisir enfermait le lecteur dans une illusion régressive, "que le lecteur soumet[tait] ses attentes à celles que le texte développe,[qu'] il s'irréalis[ait] lui-même à la mesure de l'irréalité du monde fictif vers lequel il émigre". Si l'on dépasse cette vision dépréciative décrétée a priori et ex abrupto et si l'on observe ce que le texte fait au lecteur et ce que le lecteur fait au texte et avec le texte, on s'avise – pour reprendre toujours à dessein les mots de Ricoeur – "que le lecteur incorpore – consciemment ou inconsciemment, peu importe – les enseignements de ses lectures à sa vision du monde, afin d'en augmenter la lisibilité préalable" et que dans ces conditions "la lecture est pour lui autre chose qu'un *lieu* où il s'arrête; elle est un *milieu* qu'il traverse." (Ricoeur 1985, 327-8)

Le *storyplaying* relève fondamentalement sur le plan anthropologique de la dynamique constructive et protectrice du jeu, dans lequel nous nous engageons au sens fort du terme. La fiction nous pousse à fabriquer des histoires, nos histoires, en jouant et rejouant la discordance vécue pour la dépasser et en jouir. Elle nous apporte donc un "apaisement"[9] inestimable,

---

[8] Voir sur ce point Artiaga 2008, 134-5.

[9] Le terme d'"apaisement" semble tous comptes faits plus pertinent et moins tendancieux que celui de "consolation" pour désigner cet effet tout à la fois roboratif et rassérénant du *storyplaying*, car "consolation" s'inscrit d'une part dans un horizon sémantique et idéologique chrétien, d'autre part a été assimilé à un

en digne héritière laïcisée du mythe, dont Yves Citton rappelle judicieusement qu'il est foncièrement "thelktêrious muthous", "l'*enchantement* qui apaise les peines et les dieux." (Citton 2010, 89).

## Références

Artiaga, Loïc. 2008. "Lu, critiqué, consommé: le roman populaire et ses lecteurs." In *Le Roman populaire en France (1836-1960). Des premiers feuilletons aux adaptations télévisuelles*, dir. Loïc Artiaga. Paris: Editions Autrement, Collection Mémoires/Culture.

Baroni, Raphaël. 2007. *La Tension narrative. Suspense, curiosité et surprise*. Paris: Seuil, Poétique.

—. 2009. "Histoires vécues, fictions, récits factuels". In *L'Œuvre du temps*. Paris: Seuil, Poétique.

Besson, Anne. 2004. *D'Asimov à Tolkien. Cycles et séries dans la littérature de genre*. Paris: CNRS éditions.

Bleton, Paul. 1999. *Ça se lit comme un roman policier*. Québec: Nota Bene, Etudes culturelles.

Citton, Yves. 2010. *Mythocratie. Storytelling et imaginaire de gauche*. Paris: Editions Amsterdam.

Couégnas, Daniel. 2012. "Dénouement et consolation". In *Littérature et consolation*, dir. Emmanuelle Poulain-Gautret. Arras: Presses Universitaires de l'Université d'Artois.

Dufays, Jean-Louis. 1994. *Stéréotype et lecture*. Liège: Pierre Mardaga éditeur, collection φ.

Eco, Umberto. 1993. *De Superman au surhomme*. Trans. Myriem Bouzaher. Paris: Grasset.

Esquenazi, Jean-Pierre. 2007. *Sociologie des œuvres. De la production à l'interprétation*. Paris: Armand Colin.

—. 2009. *La Vérité de la fiction. Comment peut-on croire que les récits de fiction nous parlent sérieusement de la réalité ?* Paris: Hermès/Lavoisier.

Jouve, Vincent. 1992. *L'Effet-personnage dans le roman*. Paris: PUF, Écriture.

Letourneux, Matthieu. 2010. *Le Roman d'aventure*. Limoges: PULIM, coll. Médiatextes.

Lits, Marc. 2009. "La médiatisation du politique ou le passage d'un espace public délibératif à un espace public symbolique narratif". In " Récits

---

subterfuge aliénant dans la tradition marxisante et gramscienne se défiant de "l'espoir et la consolation" procurés par le roman populaire.

journalistiques et culture médiatique ", dir. Jacques Migozzi et Loïc Artiaga. *A contrario* 12, http://www2.unil.ch/acontrario
Migozzi, Jacques. 2005. *Boulevards du populaire*. Limoges: PULIM, coll. Médiatextes.
—. 2010. "Storytelling: opium du peuple et/ou plaisirs du texte". In "Story-Telling in Contemporary French Fiction: le 'prêt-à-penser' and Reading Pleasure", ed. Diana Holmes and David Platten. *French Cultural Studies*, 21 (4), 247-55.
—. 2012. "Les 'artifices de la consolation': illusions et vertus du jeu Romanesque". In *Littérature et consolation*, dir. Emmanuelle Poulain-Gautret. Arras: Presses Universitaires de l'Université d'Artois.
Migozzi, Jacques et Artiaga, Loïc, dirs. 2009. "Récits journalistiques et culture médiatique", *A contrario* 12, http://www2.unil.ch/acontrario
—. 2010. "Roman populaire et idéologie", Belphégor IX, 1 (février), http://etc.dal.ca/belphegor/vol9_no1/fr/main_fr.html
Pavel, Thomas. 2003. "Fiction et perplexité morale", juin, http://www.fabula.org
Picard, Michel. 1986. *La Littérature comme jeu*. Paris: Editions de Minuit, coll. Critique.
Ricoeur, Paul. 1985. *Temps et récit 3. Le Temps raconté*. Paris: Seuil, coll. Points Essais.
Salmon, Christian. 2007. *Storytelling, La Machine à fabriquer des histoires et à formater les esprits*. Paris: La Découverte.
Schaeffer, Jean-Marie. 1999. *Pourquoi la fiction?*. Paris: Seuil, Poétique.
—. 2002 a. "Le romanesque", http://www.vox-poetica.org
—. 2002 b. "De l'imagination à la fiction", Vox Poetica, http://www.vox-poetica.org
Vareille, Jean-Claude. 1994. *Le Roman Populaire Français (1789-1914) -- Idéologies et Pratiques*. Limoges/Québec: PULIM/Nuit Blanche Editeur, Littératures en marge.

# CHAPTER THREE

# L'ENJEU DU PLAISIR DANS LA RECEPTION CRITIQUE DU ROMAN POPULAIRE AU XIXE SIECLE

LISE DUMASY

Lorsque j'ai lu pour la première fois *Le Plaisir du texte* de Roland Barthes (Barthes 2000 [1973]), dans ma belle jeunesse, j'en suis ressortie troublée. Alors que j'adhérais, en effet, à nombre de ses analyses, la division (voire l'opposition, parfois) que faisait Barthes, entre d'une part une "jouissance" esthète, informée, haut de gamme, réservée aux lectures "aristocrates" et que ne pouvait provoquer que la nouveauté absolue des textes de la modernité, et d'autre part un "plaisir" du texte plus banal, quoique non négligeable, expérience commune, pour ainsi dire détachée du langage, et procurée par le texte "classique", particulièrement romanesque – cette division donc, entre plaisir et jouissance du texte, ne me persuadait guère, et pour tout dire me paraissait éminemment suspecte. Elle ne me semblait guère correspondre à mon expérience de lectrice forcenée, lisant pêle-mêle *Les Trois Mousquetaires*, *Les Misérables* et *Le Grand Meaulnes*, Balzac, Flaubert et Féval, Racine, Beckett et les Jalna, Duras et Agatha Christie…et ne trouvant plaisir aux textes romanesques de la modernité que si quelque chose en eux, pas si différent, me semblait-il, de ce que je trouvais dans les autres, me poussait à tourner les pages jusqu'au bout. A bien y réfléchir, c'est sans doute ce trouble et cette réticence à suivre pleinement dans ses analyses un auteur que j'admirais le plus souvent, qui m'orienta, dans le choix de mon sujet d'étude, vers le roman populaire (particulièrement le grand texte narratif du XIX$^{e}$ siècle); son écriture, sa lecture, sa réception et son inscription dans la vie littéraire, sociale, politique, symbolique de son époque. Je choisis le XIX$^{e}$ siècle et le roman, parce que justement y faire jouer cette distinction m'y semblait des plus problématiques. Et, comme de toutes les explorations qui nous tiennent à cœur, de cette exploration je ne suis guère sortie.

C'est pourquoi je souhaite reprendre à nouveaux frais cette réflexion sur le *plaisir* suscité par la lecture du texte romanesque populaire, en l'abordant par un biais que j'ai déjà exploré précédemment dans un article (Quéffelec 1986) ainsi que dans ma *Querelle du Roman Feuilleton*, mais que je vais essayer d'approfondir: celui du rapport ambigu, et majoritairement hostile, que la réception critique entretient avec le roman feuilleton populaire en France, dans ce XIX$^{e}$ siècle qui vit en même temps l'expansion du capitalisme industriel et commercial, et la mise en place progressive de notre moderne et bourgeoise démocratie à travers l'exténuation de la Révolution.

Rappelons en quelques mots que le roman feuilleton, introduit dans les quotidiens français en 1836 (d'abord dans *La Presse* et *Le Siècle*, puis progressivement étendu à tous), connut dès 1838-1839 ses premiers grands succès, puis une expansion spectaculaire tout au long du XIX$^{e}$ siècle: toute la production romanesque du siècle, à quelques exceptions près, y passe. L'engouement du public fut immédiat, *toutes classes confondues* (on y reviendra), et le *rejet* exprimé par la critique tout aussi immédiat, sur un triple front: *moral* (le roman feuilleton est immoral ou amoral au regard de la morale bourgeoise – bon sens, raison, mesure, "réalisme" accompagné du gazage des sujets trop choquants, comme le corps, le sexe, la mort); *esthétique* (classicisme contre romantisme, caste critique et esthètes contre foule); *politique* (parole romanesque de l'imagination, refoulée au nom de la parole politique de la raison – toutes deux s'affrontant dans le champ du journal, jusque là essentiellement politique).

L'ensemble de ces critiques (revues, journaux, livres, discours dans les assemblées politiques) mettent en jeu de manière récurrente, voire obsessionnelle, un réseau de notions liées entre elles par l'isotopie du *plaisir* (intérêt, curiosité, avidité, ardeur; sensation, émotion, imagination; oisiveté, passer le temps, occuper le temps; délassement, amusement, divertissement, distraction, loisir) ou encore de couples opposés (plaisir/instruction, divertissement/pensée, imagination/raison, merveilleux/vraisemblance, aventure/peinture de mœurs). En explorant ces réseaux, les images et les arguments qui les portent, je voudrais retracer ce qui se dit, explicitement ou implicitement, du *plaisir de lire* que tous reconnaissent lié au roman feuilleton – romantique, populaire, et donc à la force du récit et de l'intrigue.

Notons tout d'abord que la question de la lecture, et plus précisément de la *lecture romanesque* et du plaisir qu'elle procure, commence à préoccuper de façon récurrente les critiques à partir de la deuxième moitié du XVIII$^{e}$ siècle, qui est aussi, et ce n'est pas une simple coïncidence, le moment où le roman se développe en s'imposant sur la scène littéraire européenne (Richardson, Fielding, Crébillon, Prévost, Lesage, Rousseau avec *La Nouvelle Héloïse*…). Nathalie Ferrand le note dans son ouvrage sur *Livre et lecture dans le roman français du XVIII^e^ siècle* (Ferrand 2002), l'expérience de lecture passionne auteurs et critiques, à partir des années 1760. Les traités sur la lecture explosent: en France, L.S. Mercier, *Discours sur la lecture*, 1764, Boilloud-Mermet, *Essai sur la lecture,* 1765; en Italie, Giambattista Roberti, *Del leggere: libri de Metafisica e divertimento*, 1769; en Allemagne, J.A. Bergk, *Die Kunst Bücher zu lesen*, 1799, etc. La lecture est aussi très souvent représentée dans le roman, qui explore les conditions et effets du plaisir de lire. Si certains auteurs de traités font l'éloge unilatéral de l'activité de lecture, tel Boilloud-Mermet: "O! Lecture, présent du ciel, plaisir pur, délicieux, tranquille et durable (…) que le repentir ne suit jamais" (Ferrand 2002, 122-123), les contemporains ne sont pas unanimes, et L.S. Mercier s'inquiète en des termes déjà proches de ceux que nous retrouverons chez les critiques du roman feuilleton: devant la situation actuelle, il s'effraye de l'abondance des livres de "pur agreement", de pur plaisir donc, abondance qui "annonce une pauvreté réelle; si un livre était véritablement agréable, se verrait-il, dès l'instant même de sa naissance, éclipsé par un autre, qui est effacé à son tour".[1] Mercier se plaint ainsi de l'hégémonie du plaisir qui instrumentalise le livre et qui fait qu'on se soucie peu, sur le fond, de ce qu'on lit – qu'importe le flacon pourvu qu'on ait l'ivresse… On se condamne alors à la succession, à la série des livres qui font s'enchaîner les plaisirs.

Mercier dresse ensuite le triste portrait de celui qui ne lit que pour son agrément et ainsi altère son être même. En voici le début: "Si [la lecture] est l'aliment d'une curiosité vaine ou l'amusement d'une oisive imagination, elle peut à notre insu changer notre caractère naturel; ce mal est très grand car on n'est jamais bien que soi-même" (Ferrand 2002, 269). Parmi ces lectures dénaturantes le futur romancier qu'est Mercier n'hésite pas à placer les ouvrages de fiction, son idée étant que la lecture de fiction, au lieu de stimuler la sensibilité l'épuise, l'affaiblit, et qu'à force de pleurer sur des malheurs imaginaires, on devient incapable de s'émouvoir à bon escient. Mercier incite donc le lecteur de romans (comme le feront tant d'autres après lui au XIX^e^ siècle) à remplacer le plaisir du roman par celui de la charité.

D'autres déjà, particulièrement des romanciers, tiennent à différencier entre eux les romans, et opposent au roman d'aventures,

[1] Mercier, "Discours sur la lecture" dans *Eloges et discours philosophiques*. 1764. Amsterdam: chez E. Van Harrevelt, cité par Ferrand 2002, 245.

lecture vaine, l'instructif roman de mœurs (comme le fera la critique du XIX$^{e}$ siècle, mais pour se plaindre que le roman de mœurs n'existe plus). Ainsi Crébillon fils (Crébillon 1977 [1736-8], 27-28) oppose un programme "réaliste" du roman ("Comme la Comédie, le tableau de la vie humaine, [où on] censurera les vices et les ridicules") aux romans d'aventures, pleins de

> situations ténébreuses et forcées, de héros dont les caractères et aventures sont toujours hors du vraisemblable (…) [Dans un roman à programme "réaliste"], le lecteur n'y trouverait plus à la vérité ces événements extraordinaires et tragiques, qui enlèvent l'imagination et déchirent le cœur; plus de héros qui ne passât les mers que pour y être à point nommé pris des Turcs, plus d'aventure dans le sérail, de sultane soustraite à la vigilance des eunuques par quelque tour d'adresse surprenant; plus de morts imprévues et infiniment moins de souterrains (…) L'homme enfin verrait l'homme tel qu'il est; on l'éblouirait moins, mais on l'instruirait davantage.

A l'instar de romanciers comme Crébillon ou Diderot, Madame de Staël exprime sa préférence pour le "roman de mœurs", le roman "vraisemblable" - qu'elle estime encore largement à venir – dans son *Essai sur les fictions* (Staël 1861 [1795], 62-72). Elle exprime toutefois un avis nuancé sur les dangers des fictions "merveilleuses", et tout en liant l'imagination à l'enfance et au peuple, elle souligne sa persistance chez l'adulte, ainsi que la porosité éventuelle des frontières entre "peuple" et "philosophe" dans la communion romanesque; ainsi est-elle amenée à aborder la question de la *confusion des publics* dans la lecture romanesque, question qui, nous y reviendrons, se posera de façon aiguë au XIX$^{e}$ siècle.

Distinguant trois genres de fiction, les fictions "merveilleuses et allégoriques", les fictions "historiques" et les fictions "vraisemblables", Madame de Staël écrit à propos des premières:

> La fiction merveilleuse cause un plaisir très promptement épuisé; il faut que les hommes se fassent enfants pour aimer ces tableaux hors de la nature, pour se laisser émouvoir par les sentiments de terreur et de curiosité dont le vrai n'est pas l'origine; il faut que les philosophes se fassent peuple pour vouloir saisir des pensées utiles à travers le voile de l'allégorie (…) On a dit que les yeux étaient toujours enfants; c'est à l'imagination que ce mot s'applique; s'amuser est tout ce qu'elle exige (…) Elle sert à tromper la vie, à dérober le temps; elle peut donner au jour les rêves de la nuit. (Staël 1861 [1795], 63)

Que devient cette problématique dès lors que les premiers grands succès du roman feuilleton viennent porter sur la place publique, par le biais du journal, et du jugement de l'opinion publique qu'il instaure, la question du "plaisir de lire"?

Notons d'abord que la plupart des critiques – tous en fait - reconnaissent le phénomène, au demeurant difficilement niable: le roman feuilleton fait vendre le journal. Les abonnements se multiplient, parfois dans des proportions extrêmes, et le public achète le journal *pour* le roman feuilleton. Les critiques doivent donc reconnaître, fût-ce dans la mauvaise foi et la mauvaise humeur, que le roman feuilleton plaît. Ainsi Louis Reybaud, dans *Le Constitutionnel* du 15 juin 1840, écrit-il:

> Il y a engouement, succès d'émotion, succès de larmes (…) On ne saurait refuser à cette suite de publications des qualités réelles de composition et d'intérêt dramatique. Le style pèche souvent (…) La morale y reçoit plus d'une atteinte et s'y prête à plus d'un accommodement. Cependant l'ensemble plaît, séduit, attache. (Dumasy 1999, 57)

De son côté Cuvillier-Fleury, dans le *Journal des Débats* du 14 juin 1842 fait état de "la passion furieuse du public pour le roman qui est le seul goût littéraire de l'époque" et, mi-figue mi-raisin, interpelle ainsi les écrivains: "Conteurs, nos beaux conteurs, donnez-nous des contes, bons ou mauvais, niais ou sublimes, vertueux ou sataniques, avec ou sans style; mais donnez-nous des contes: car nous ne savons lire autre chose " (Dumasy 1999, 65-66). Et à l'autre bout du siècle, Maurice Talmeyr, dans un article de la *Revue des Deux Mondes* du premier septembre 1903 fait la même constatation.

Cet attrait universel du roman feuilleton, le *plaisir* qu'on y prend, constaté, avéré, est en général dans le même mouvement *dévalorisé* par le discours critique, à l'aide d'un arsenal de stratégies argumentatives, que l'on retrouve combinées dans la plupart des articles critiques. Ce sont ces stratégies argumentatives que nous allons maintenant étudier. Elles sont au nombre de trois, qui lient le *plaisir* 1) au *désoeuvrement* 2) au *dérèglement* 3) au *désordre.*

1) Le plaisir pris à la lecture du roman (populaire, feuilleton, "contemporain") est condamnable parce qu'il s'agit d'une perte de temps, d'une dépense d'énergie improductive: c'est le thème du *désoeuvrement*, opposé à l'*œuvre* (travail et pensée), de la *distraction* opposée à l'*étude.* Ainsi selon Sainte-Beuve en 1839, les auteurs contemporains "remplissent un désoeuvrement, ils n'occupent pas une pensée. On les accepte comme une distraction, on ne les reconnaît pas comme une étude" (Dumasy 1999, 46). De même Gustave Planche affirme-t-il, dans "Le roman en France à la fin de 1853" paru dans la *Revue des Deux Mondes* du 15 décembre de

cette année: "Essaierai-je d'analyser les interminables récits qui aident les désoeuvrés à tuer le temps ? (…) Uniquement occupés d'amuser le public, ils [les auteurs] ne souhaitent rien de plus et se moquent de toutes les poétiques (…) Pourvu qu'ils tiennent la curiosité en haleine, leur ambition est satisfaite."

L'*amusement*, lié à l'*oisiveté* ou au *loisir* (souvent confondus dans un même anathème dans la mesure où la lecture "amusante" n'occupe pas utilement le loisir), est toujours condamné comme vide et improductif. C'est en quelque sorte du temps pris sur l'universel temps de la production. A propos de Balzac, Louis Reybaud, dans *Le Constitutionnel* du 15 juin 1840, juge ainsi que "le monde des oisifs et des femmes émancipées lui appartient; on l'y accepte à titre de distraction, et il s'y glisse comme enseignement" (Dumasy 1999, 60). Et, partant du cas d'Eugène Sue, Cuvillier-Fleury estime plus généralement que, pour la "nation positive" qu'est devenue la France, "le roman n'est plus, comme on le disait autrefois, l'expression de la société, mais l'instrument souple et vibrant dont quelques hommes d'esprit se servent pour amuser ses loisirs" (Dumasy 1999, 78).

2) Le plaisir pris à la lecture de ces romans est condamnable parce qu'il est lié à l'*excès*, au *dérèglement* des sens, des sentiments, de l'imagination, et derrière ce dérèglement plane, jamais bien loin, l'ombre de l'*ébranlement révolutionnaire*, fantasmé comme source et/ou aboutissement possible de ce dérèglement. Ainsi Louis Reybaud, dans le premier article de "Revue littéraire. Œuvres de M. de Balzac" du *Constitutionnel* du 8 mai 1840 écrit: "Les voies révolutionnaires conduisent vite et loin; on s'abandonne aisément à leurs émotions vertigineuses (…) La révolte plaît par sa nouveauté, son bruit, son désordre." (Dumasy 1999, 50). Et dans le deuxième article du même titre déjà cité (Dumasy 1999, 58), il poursuit, introduisant un thème de grande portée, celui de la monstruosité: "L'idéal de M. de Balzac est dans l'exagération des monstruosités exceptionnelles que peut offrir la société."

L'excès, assimilable à la perte de l'équilibre, et producteur de monstruosité, est en effet, pour ces critiques, partout: dans la curiosité excitée, dans les émotions, dans l'imagination et l'invention. De toute cette thématique, Chapuys-Montlaville se fait, du haut de la tribune du parlement orléaniste, le relais permanent et intransigeant. Dans un discours prononcé à la Chambre des Députés le 6 avril 1847 (publié dans le *Moniteur Universel* du 7 avril) il tonne littéralement contre les défauts qu'il attribue à la littérature populaire et feuilletonesque:

> L'intention morale n'apparaît nulle part, les faits sont vulgaires, passionnés, violents, le langage est hardi, cynique, les auteurs ne se soumettent, pour l'invention ou le style, à aucune règle (...) Ces industriels littéraires n'ont pour but et pour objet que d'exciter la curiosité, de tenir l'abonné en haleine et de mettre en émoi toutes les mauvaises passions. (Dumasy 1999, 107-8)

Les conséquences de ce genre d'analyse suivent tout naturellement. Dans un discours précédent fait à la Chambre, le 13 juin 1843 (*Moniteur Universel* du 14 juin 1843), Chapuys-Montlaville avertit déjà solennellement contre les dangers moraux (et politiques...) du dérèglement littéraire qu'il dénonce:

> Les œuvres d'une imagination sans règle et sans mesure sont accueillies avec une faveur marquée. Il semble qu'on se plaît à augmenter, par de déplorables entraînements, les dispositions de notre peuple à se laisser séduire et emporter par les élans de l'imagination, principal, brillant mais dangereux attribut (quand il n'est pas réglé par le jugement) de notre nature française. (Dumasy 1999, 82)

On se doute que ce genre de frayeur orléaniste allait avoir une belle postérité. Ainsi, en plein Second Empire, le critique Alfred Nettement retrouve une inspiration que n'aurait pas reniée Chapuys-Montlaville (d'ailleurs rallié entre temps à l'Empire). Dans *Le Roman Contemporain* (Nettement 1864), Nettement écrit ainsi, à propos des triomphes retentissants de l'inoffensif Ponson du Terrail, que "les lecteurs délicats" ne se plaisent pas à ces romans "qui leur causent à peu près l'épouvante qu'une émeute dans la rue cause aux hommes d'ordre" (tout en rajoutant avec une sorte d'amer humour: "Mais combien y a-t-il de lecteurs délicats? A peu près autant que de gens qui s'abstiennent du cigare").

Bref, comme en plus la lecture du roman feuilleton est souvent comparée à une "pâture" ou à une "pitance" (alliant les sèmes d'ingestion et de bestialité), la notion du "plaisir de lire" en vient à se combiner à celles de l'addiction, de l'illusion et de la déchéance pour susciter l'image de la *drogue*. Ici encore, Chapuys-Montlaville, dès son discours à la Chambre du 13 juin 1843, fournit une argumentation archétypale:

> Au lieu de vivre tout simplement suivant la vieille mode du genre humain sur le sol, au milieu des joies et des labeurs alternatifs de la vie réelle, on vit dans le monde idéal, on se berce d'illusions, on se repaît de chimères; chacun, après avoir bu à cette coupe parfumée, remplie des liqueurs les plus enivrantes, perd le sentiment et le goût de la réalité; les effets de ce redoutable opium se révèlent bientôt. (Dumasy 1999, 82)

Là encore, Alfred Nettement, dans ses *Etudes critiques sur le feuilleton roman*, se révèle un fidèle continuateur de cette thèse:

> Il ne s'agit plus de faire une œuvre d'art, une œuvre littéraire; il s'agit de remplir chaque jour d'une liqueur capiteuse la coupe que le journal tend au romancier pour la porter aux lèvres du public qu'il faut enivrer. (Nettement 1846 [huitième lettre])

Toutefois l'image la plus prégnante de ce dérèglement des sens et des mœurs dont la critique fait grief au roman feuilleton est sans doute celle de la *prostitution*. La prostitution, dont Peter Brooks a montré de manière magistrale le "rôle particulier et exemplaire" qu'elle jouait dans le "narrable du XIX$^{e}$ siècle" (Brooks 1992 (1984), 143-70), la prostitution donc est également l'image centrale et cardinale par laquelle la critique du XIX$^{e}$ siècle appréhende le roman feuilleton: cette image se retrouve en effet pour définir tous les aspects de roman – que ce soit la *production,* le *produit* ou la *réception*.

Du point de vue de la *production*, l'image qui s'impose est celle du proxénétisme – de la "muse vénale". Par exemple Gaschon de Molènes, dans sa "Revue littéraire" publiée dans *La Revue des Deux Mondes* du 15 mars 1842, s'exprime de la sorte sur Alexandre Dumas:

> Je croirais volontiers que M. Dumas traite sa muse comme certains maris traitent leurs femmes quand elles ont des galanteries lucratives. Pourvu qu'elles rendent compte de leurs bénéfices, ils ne s'inquiètent pas des jugements que l'on peut porter sur leurs fredaines. (Dumasy 1999, 189)

Le *produit*, quant à lui, est selon les critiques marqué par une fascination, que la plupart d'entre eux jugent excessive, pour les courtisanes, repenties ou non (que ce soit chez Sue, chez Balzac, chez Soulié ou bien d'autres), ainsi que par un goût racoleur pour les tableaux licencieux (notamment chez Dumas). Ainsi Gaschon de Molènes, dans un article de la *Revue des Deux Mondes* du 15 juin 1843, reproche-t-il à Balzac son "curieux amour de détails de l'existence intime jusqu'à en être quelquefois honteux" (Dumasy 1999, 226), tandis que Sainte-Beuve, quinze jours plus tard, dans "Quelques vérités sur la situation en littérature" (article de la *Revue des Deux Mondes* du 1$^{er}$ juillet 1843), remarque: "Il y a un fonds de De Sade masqué, mais non point méconnaissable, dans les inspirations de deux ou trois de nos romanciers les plus accrédités: cela gagne et chatouille bien des simples".

Mais l'attaque porte de façon encore plus systématique sur la *réception*: le plaisir pris à la lecture du roman, plaisir que l'on assouvit honteusement contre de l'argent, est implicitement assimilé aux jouissances illégitimes de la prostitution. Non seulement l'œuvre-prostituée, comme on l'a vu, "met en émoi les mauvaises passions" (Chapuys-Montlaville, discours du 6 avril 1847), mais encore, tout comme les excès de la luxure, elle ne fait qu' "amortir sous les extravagances de l'imagination la virilité de notre jeunesse française" (discours du 13 juin 1843, Dumasy 1999, 83). L'horreur devant le plaisir "illégitime" de la lecture des romans feuilletons est d'autant plus forte que la puissance de ce plaisir est conçue comme irrésistible, comme brisant la résistance de la saine volonté; cette conviction se retrouve ainsi exprimée sous la plume d'Evariste, dans *La Mode* du 25 novembre 1844:

> Le goût de ces écrits frivoles qui ne s'adressent qu'à la curiosité s'est répandu partout (...) On se défend, vis-à-vis des autres et vis-à-vis de soi-même, du plaisir qu'on y trouve et de l'intérêt qu'on y prend; mais le fait est qu'on y prend l'intérêt le plus vif et qu'on y trouve un plaisir extrême (...) Qu'est-ce donc que cette littérature qu'on déguste en secret et qu'on se défend d'admirer, comme un vice dont on jouit et que l'on cache?

Et en 1880 encore, Arthur de Grandeffe, dans *Ce qu'on lit*, reprend le thème, à propos de *La Maîtresse du mari*, de X. de Montépin (avec une très belle illustration de la figure du déni qui accompagne fréquemment ces représentations):

> Ces divertissements sont les mouches cantharides du marquis de Sade. On lit avidement et pour peu qu'on ait quelque vergogne, on est écoeuré et on jette au loin le livre qui sera relevé par un autre et lu par lui avec non moins d'avidité. (Grandeffe 1880)

Si, comme le pense Peter Brooks, la source énergétique et dynamique des *Mystères de Paris*, comme des romans de Balzac et, de manière plus globale, des romans populaires du XIX^e^ siècle fascinés par toutes les formes de déviance, si cette source donc se trouve dans le nœud entre sexualité, argent et narration ou *storytelling* (Brooks 1992, 163), alors on peut dire que le discours critique du XIX^e^ siècle ne se trompait guère sur la dynamique libidinale qui orientait l'intérêt des lecteurs, mais qu'il ne pouvait guère la reconnaître qu'en la rejetant.

3) Dernier reproche adressé au texte de plaisir, ou au plaisir du texte (narratif): celui-ci est source de *désordre*. Ce désordre est tout d'abord psychologique, conséquence naturelle du dérèglement analysé au point précédent. Ce dérèglement en effet, en faisant rêver de chimères, en nourrissant le fantasme, *dégoûte du réel*. Comme le dit Chapuys-Montlaville, dans son discours du 14 mars 1845: "L'illusion tue la réalité,

enfante dans la pensée un monde merveilleux qui dégoûte du réel." (Dumasy 1999, 99).

Mais surtout ce désordre est d'ordre sociologique, parce qu'il *subvertit les limites des classes et des rôles sociaux*. Dans la formule "tout le monde lit le roman feuilleton", que l'on entend répéter à satiété et sur tous les tons du début à la fin du siècle, il faut moins entendre une extension quantitative (quoique celle-ci en effet se fasse continûment tout au long du XIX$^{e}$ siècle) que la constatation, le plus souvent dépitée, d'une *confusion* des publics dans la lecture du roman populaire, d'un effacement des hiérarchies politiques, culturelles et sociales[2]. Desnoyers, dans un article du *Siècle* daté du 29 septembre 1847, constate ainsi que, en ce qui concerne le roman feuilleton, "on ne travaille plus pour un public d'élite, on travaille pour tout le monde" (Dumasy 1999, 145). Et Zola lui-même, dans *Le Salut Public* du 11 septembre 1866, affirme: "Ce ne sont pas seulement les pauvres intelligences qui se nourrissent de ces romans vides et banals. Je connais des gens honnêtes et instruits qui en font leur nourriture quotidienne." (Zola 1952-5, 617).

De façon plus directe, voire corporatiste, les critiques ne sont pas sans remarquer que le plaisir pris à la lecture du roman populaire via le feuilleton constitue directement *l'opinion publique* comme juge – et donc les destitue de leur pouvoir de guide. De plus, la *parole romanesque* vient également faire concurrence, au sein même du journal, à la *parole politique*; la presse politique recule devant le journalisme commercial, et l'on en vient à s'abonner au journal pour son feuilleton, et non plus pour soutenir son orientation (voir à ce sujet tous les discours de Chapuys-Montlaville). C'est là, pour le discours critique, fortement dépendant en général de l'orientation politique de l'individualisme libéral, un scandale qui n'est qu'une manifestation de plus de la crainte, mille fois exprimée tout au long du XIX$^{e}$ siècle, de l'engloutissement de toute individualité et de toute différence dans une vaste indifférenciation (l'"égalisation") décrite comme "démocratique" (en fait liée au jeu du marché capitaliste).

Aussi voit-on que, à peine cette constatation de la confusion, de l'indifférenciation des publics est-elle posée, elle est immédiatement combattue et battue en brèche, d'un côté par le déni pur et simple, d'un autre côté par une série d'oppositions et de différenciations visant à restaurer, au sein de ce public massifié, les hiérarchies d'un ordre rassurant.

---

[2] V. l'article de Gobineau reproduit dans Dumasy 1999, particulièrement p. 88.

Le déni est fort bien exprimé, dans toute son ambiguïté, par Charles de Rémusat, dans "De l'esprit littéraire sous la Restauration et depuis 1830", *Revue des Deux Mondes*, 30 avril 1847:

> L'opinion n'est pas favorable à la littérature actuelle: on la goûte sans l'estimer, et il est de mode d'en dire grand mal et de ne pouvoir s'en passer (...) Souvent aussi on critique par hypocrisie, et l'on rougit d'avouer ce qui a su plaire. (Dumasy 1999, 251)

Quant au rétablissement de différenciations rassurantes, il est à l'œuvre dans presque tout le discours critique. Ces différenciations reposent elles-mêmes sur toute une série d'oppositions plus ou moins convenues, qui fournissent l'outillage notionnel permettant de briser l'indifférenciation honnie:

- Opposition des *familles* (pour lesquelles, selon Reybaud, devrait écrire Balzac) aux *oisifs*, aux *femmes émancipées* ou aux *femmes de mœurs suspectes* (lesquelles composeraient, toujours selon Reybaud, le lectorat balzacien habituel (Dumasy 1999, 60-1).
- Opposition des *barbares* aux esprits *cultivés* (Gobineau), des hommes *sensés et délicats* aux esprits *incultes et grossiers* (Nettement).
- Opposition des enfants, et du Peuple (ou encore du Peuple comme enfant), à l'homme adulte et individuel (Gobineau, Evariste, *La Mode* du 5 juillet 1844).
- Opposition, enfin, de la femme à l'homme. Il est à noter toutefois que cette distinction des genres ne se développe guère de façon massive dans le discours critique avant les années 1860, du moins explicitement (car implicitement on a toute raison de penser que passion, sensation, imagination, frivolité et oisiveté sont connotées au féminin; d'ailleurs tout le discours médical du siècle tend à cette connotation[3]). Zola en fera explicitement le thème essentiel de sa critique, surtout après 1870.

C'est donc petit à petit, et non d'emblée, souterrainement et implicitement avant de devenir explicite, que s'ordonne le tableau idéologique d'un lectorat du roman populaire limité à la triade (aux termes fondamentalement équivalents) *femme – enfant – peuple.* Cette triade forme un sujet de lecture défini par l'intimité et par le primat de l'imagination, de la sensation et de l'émotion; un tel sujet se distingue

---

[3] Voir à ce sujet Quéffelec 1986.

d'un sujet politique, public, faisant preuve de raison, de jugement et de pensée, de l'*homme mûr*, officiellement imperméable aux séductions du plaisir romanesque. On remarquera que c'est surtout après 1848, et encore plus après 1870, que ce topos du primat "féminin" et, indissociablement, "populaire" et "enfantin" de la lecture romanesque s'imposera de façon massive dans le discours critique. On peut y lire l'effet de l'opposition de plus en plus forte entre les classes, provoquée par les répressions de juin 1848 et de la Commune, ainsi que des atteintes irréparables portées, dès 1848, à la fiction de l'union du Peuple sur laquelle reposaient l'élan et la dynamique du récit romantique.

Face à ce déferlement de critiques assassines, le roman-feuilleton trouve-t-il des défenseurs ? Quelques voix s'élèvent en effet en défense du roman feuilleton et du plaisir qu'il procure; nous renvoyons pour plus de détail notre lecteur aux articles d'Alexandre Weill, journaliste de la fouriériste *Démocratie pacifique*, et aussi à ceux de Louis Desnoyers, rédacteur en chef littéraire du *Siècle* et auteur de romans pour enfants, en avril et septembre 1847,[4] qui sont des réponses aux attaques de Chapuys-Montlaville, ou encore de Cuvillier-Fleury et de Gobineau, tous repris dans *La Querelle du roman-feuilleton*. Nous en résumerons ici brièvement l'argumentation. La défense se fait sur trois lignes principales:

1. La reconnaissance de qualités littéraires: facultés d'observation (chez Balzac surtout), quoique gâtées par l'exagération, le recours au mélodrame et à l'aventure; plus souvent, et plus systématiquement, reconnaissance de qualités d'imagination, d'invention et de composition, toutes celles, donc, qui font les bonnes intrigues.
2. La reconnaissance d'une valeur didactique, acculturante, pour un peuple encore "enfant", et qui ne saurait accéder à un enseignement sans passer par une sorte de vulgarisation dont le roman-feuilleton serait porteur.
3. La reconnaissance d'une fonction de consolation, liée à l'exotisme. L'argumentation est en gros la suivante: à une société ennuyeuse et ennuyée d'elle-même, terne, morne, non idéalisable, telle que la société bourgeoise, il faut des fictions exotiques et consolantes, qui aillent chercher dans les royaumes de la fantaisie de quoi peupler les rêves et les fantasmes qui fassent supporter la réalité. Cette

[4] A. Weil, "La politique et la littérature. Le feuilleton et la Chambre", dans *La Démocratie pacifique*, 11 avril 1847 (Dumasy 1999, 117-120); Louis Desnoyers "Un peu d'histoire à propos de roman", dans *Le Siècle*, 5, 28 et 29 septembre 1847 (Dumasy 121-154).

> argumentation s'accompagne souvent de l'affirmation du droit de tous au plaisir, opposé à l'ennui distillé par la société bourgeoise. On notera qu'une telle argumentation repose sur une analyse diamétralement opposée à celle de Chapuys-Montlaville, par exemple quant au potentiel révolutionnaire de telles rêveries consolantes…

La question du plaisir du texte, on le voit, est toujours posée en rapport avec celle de la *valeur* (esthétique, mais surtout *éthique*) des œuvres: le *plaisir* ne s'admet que s'il y a par ailleurs *progrès moral* attaché à la lecture de l'œuvre. Le plaisir se trouve ainsi légitimé par la promotion de valeurs morales, celles produites, bien évidemment, par l'idéologie de la bourgeoisie dominante. Par ailleurs importe aussi la *valeur esthétique*: le "style" justifie le plaisir par la distinction que donnent la possession et l'exercice du jugement esthétique. Selon l'appartenance du critique plutôt à la sphère bourgeoise ou plutôt à la caste (interne mais décalée) de la critique culturelle professionnelle, l'accent est mis sur l'éthique ou sur l'esthétique – et souvent sur les deux à la fois.

Or, dans le cas du roman feuilleton, ce qui pose problème, de façon très majoritaire, c'est que le plaisir est constaté, mais que les critiques ne reconnaissent l'œuvre, ni comme opérateur de progrès moral, ni comme accomplissement esthétique. Dès lors, le *plaisir* apparaît comme injustifiable, voire comme dangereux et condamnable: il n'est plus qu'une dépense gratuite d'énergie (c'est le thème de la *perte de temps*), et, comme toute dépense qui ne rapporte rien qu'elle-même, est, dans le contexte d'une société bourgeoise privilégiant l'épargne comme mode d'accumulation du capital, perçue comme un irrationnel *gaspillage*. Dans un certain nombre de cas, il arrive aussi que la morale du roman (car il n'existe guère de fable sans morale…) ne soit pas acceptée comme telle par la critique – parce que, par exemple, elle attire l'attention sur les inégalités sociales, sur les racines sociologiques de la criminalité, sur les désastres engendrés par la pauvreté, etc.: il n'y a plus alors simplement absence de légitimité du plaisir, mais dénonciation de la perversité liée à la lecture de ce qui est perçu directement comme thèses subversives et immorales. Cette dernière situation est la plus courante dans les débuts du roman feuilleton, avant 1848; à partir du Second Empire, le triomphe du conformisme idéologique dans le contenu explicite des romans populaires fait disparaître le danger politique direct, et la critique peut se contenter de la déligitimation du genre.

L'affirmation massive et le déni tout aussi massif dont, tout au long du XIXe siècle, le plaisir romanesque a fait l'objet de la part des représentants de la bourgeoisie (porteurs de l'ordre esthétique et politique), me semblent manifester la fascination/répulsion pour des fictions dans lesquelles les dits bourgeois désirent et en même temps craignent de se mirer; et cela exprime aussi, sans doute, la perception de la nature fondamentalement anarchiste d'un tel plaisir, qui subvertit les codes et les hiérarchies culturelles et échappe au contrôle de la "raison" politique. Ce qui nous ramène à Barthes, avec qui finalement nous nous retrouverons d'accord. Car, dans ce texte lui-même plein de contradictions qu'est *Le Plaisir du texte*, et au-delà de ses propres réserves esthètes et de ses distinctions discutables entre "jouissance" et "plaisir" du texte, Roland Barthes est sans doute un de ceux qui ont le mieux perçu la nature de ce plaisir. Dans *Le Plaisir du texte*, il exprime ainsi sa rêverie d'une

> Société des Amis du texte: ses membres n'auraient rien en commun (car il n'y a pas forcément accord sur les textes du plaisir) sinon leurs ennemis: casse-pieds de toutes sortes, qui décrètent la forclusion du texte et de son plaisir, soit par conformisme culturel, soit par rationalisme intransigeant (…), soit par moralisme politique, soit par critique du signifiant (Barthes 2000 [1973], 93).

Et de conclure un peu plus loin:

> Même si nous replaçons le plaisir du texte dans le champ de sa théorie et non dans celui de sa sociologie (…) c'est bien une aliénation politique qui est en cause: la forclusion du plaisir (et plus encore de la jouissance) dans une société travaillée par deux morales: l'une, majoritaire, de la platitude, l'autre, groupusculaire, de la rigueur (politique et/ou scientifique). On dirait que l'idée de plaisir ne flatte plus personne. Notre société paraît à la fois rassise et violente; de toute manière frigide. (114-15)

On ne saurait mieux dire, et j'espère que l'analyse menée ci-dessus aura contribué à en expliciter les raisons, en explorant sur un champ précis (celui du roman-feuilleton du XIXe siècle et de sa réception) ce qui se joue autour du plaisir du texte, en l'occurrence, narratif.

## Références

Barthes, Roland 2000 [1973]. *Le Plaisir du texte.* Paris: Seuil.

Brooks, Peter. 1992 (1984). *Reading for the Plot: Design and Intention in Narrative.* Harvard University Press.

Crébillon fils 1977 [1736-8]. Préface aux *Egarements du cœur et de l'esprit.* Paris: Gallimard Folio.

Cuvillier-Fleury, Alfred-Auguste. 1842. "M. Eugène Sue, Le Morne-au--diable ou l'Aventurier", *Journal des Débats*, 14 juin 1842. In Dumasy 1999, 65-79.

Dumasy, Lise, ed. 1999. *La Querelle du roman-feuilleton. Littérature, presse et politique, un débat précurseur (1836-1848)*. Grenoble: Ellug.

Ferrand, Nathalie. 2002. *Livre et lecture dans le roman français du XVIII<sup>e</sup> siècle*. Paris: PUF, coll « écriture ».

Grandeffe, Arthur-Raoul de Guilloteau. 1880. Paris: A. Chaix.

Nettement, Alfred. 1846. *Etudes critiques sur le feuilleton-roman*, tome 2. Paris: Perrodil.

—. 1864. *Le Roman Contemporain.* Paris: Lecoffre.

Queffélec, Lise. 1986. "Le lecteur du roman comme lectrice: stratégies romanesques et stratégies critiques sous la Monarchie de Juillet", in *Romantisme* 53, troisième trimestre, 9-21.

Sainte-Beuve, Charles. 1839. "De la littérature industrielle", *Revue des Deux Mondes*, 1er septembre. In Dumasy 1999, 25-43.

Staël, Germaine de. 1861 [1795]. *Essai sur les fictions.* Genève: Slatkine.

Zola, Émile. 1952-5. *Œuvres complètes*, t.10. Paris: Le Club français du livre.

# CHAPTER FOUR

# INTRIGUE, AS-TU DU CŒUR? LECTURE, PLAISIR CRIMINEL

PAUL BLETON

## L'intrigue reconnue ou construite?

La lecture ordinaire: l'invitation qui nous est faite de rendre au plaisir émanant de l'intrigue une certaine dignité théorique s'appuie sur cette pratique culturelle. Ici, cette lecture ordinaire semble largement surdéterminée par son objet, le roman populaire. Je précise que ce dernier se définit moins par son public que par la culture imprimée dont il relève: il s'agit de la fiction romanesque en régime médiatique. Née à mi-chemin du livre et du journal, elle s'est autonomisée du journal au point de devenir une industrie culturelle à part entière. Angenot (1989) montrait qu'un demi-siècle après la rencontre de la fiction romanesque et du journal, le récit avait enlevé à l'argumentatif sa position hégémonique dans le discours social, autant dans les fictions que dans les textes non-fictionnels. Non seulement le roman mimétique avait-il alors tendu à devenir la forme narrative de référence par rapport à quoi toutes les autres allaient devoir se définir mais il s'était aussi imposé comme cadre interprétatif universel, sorte d'*épistémè*. Ce modèle culturel, le *romanesque général*, allait s'adresser à tout le monde et articuler la lisibilité des personnages par leur typicité, la lisibilité de l'univers construit par le discours, le "droit de retrait méditatif et droit de glose" du narrateur/observateur et la double rationalité de l'événement: celle, fonctionnelle, de l'enchaînement des causes et des effets; et celle, interprétative, de la relation indicielle du perceptible physionomique, comportemental, avec le type sous-jacent.[1] Le plaisir de lecture spécifique dérivé d'une telle configuration se serait donc fondé sur une sorte de platonisme cognitif: on lisait pour reconnaître, pour

[1] Ce qui anticipe la conception du *storytelling* de Salmon (2007) qui, il est vrai, a chez lui un champ d'application plus restreint: marketing, management, et communication politique.

trouver de quoi se conforter dans le prévisible, quelles que soient les inquiétudes suscitées par l'invention fictionnelle, quelle que soit la vision du monde faisant communier auteur et lecteur – du pessimisme cynique à la concorde consolatrice. La culture médiatique contemporaine doit encore beaucoup au romanesque général; il ne serait guère judicieux de contourner l'idée de platonisme cognitif en parlant de la lecture du roman populaire d'aujourd'hui. Mais occupe-t-il toujours la même place prééminente?

Quelles que soient les réticences que des lecteurs ou des critiques manifestent sur la qualité d'un tel plaisir, le sens commun le sait indéniable. Malgré les admonestations francfortiennes, parler d'aliénation n'épuise certainement pas la longue permanence de ce goût pour la répétition. Rétif plaisir, il s'enracine dans un sol psychique bien plus fondamental, bien plus archaïque que celui de la lecture sérielle, cette prédilection pour un auteur, un genre, un personnage ou type de personnage. Le retour du même ne se réduit pas au seul ressassement; il obéit aussi à une paradoxale logique de la constitution de l'objet mise à jour par Winnicott (1965): l'enfant doit créer pour lui un objet qui est déjà là (le sein de la mère). Fondement de toute série éponyme, ancrage de tout héros increvable, c'est aussi lui qui *a posteriori* fait juger de tel roman comme une histoire typique de son genre ou de son auteur. Voici dès lors appariée la dyade du marché: puisque, une fois sorti de la toute petite enfance, le lecteur ne se satisfait plus de se faire raconter toujours la même histoire, qu'il attend ne retrouver la répétition qu'à travers les bigarrures de la diversité, la sérialisation de la fiction constitue la réponse de l'industrie culturelle à cette quête du plaisir pour le lecteur – culture médiatique en général et littérature populaire en particulier sont prodigues d'intrigues. Le dynamisme de la quête s'enrichit à chaque lecture, se sédimente en encyclopédie, s'institue en pratique culturelle. Évidence de l'intrigue: tout lecteur a l'intuition que la surface prolixe du roman est commandée en sous-main par une histoire, cet enchaînement temporel et causal d'événements fictifs advenant aux personnages ou déclenchés par eux. Pas immédiatement accessible mais objectivable, l'intrigue se trouverait dans le texte, sous le texte. Il en serait la simplification, dans trois directions: elle s'obtiendrait en débarrassant le récit des anecdotes secondaires (excentriques, superficielles, dilatoires, ancillaires, c'est-à-dire les "motifs libres" de Tomachevski (1965) par opposition aux "motifs associés" qui constituent la concaténation fabulaire), des oripeaux de la narration (qui voit? qui raconte?) et de l'épaisseur linguistique traversée par le lecteur pour parvenir à l'histoire. Elle en est aussi bien la sublimation, au sens alchimique: ce dont il se souviendra. En regard de l'intrigue, le plaisir de lecture consisterait en un pli: sur la face extérieure, que le lecteur ait vécu par procuration cet enchaînement d'événements plus ou moins éloignés de sa vie propre, qu'il se soit senti aspiré par l'action, impliqué par les personnages dans leur pâtir et leur agir dont la pertinence conforterait ou élargirait son expérience et, sur la face intérieure, selon la logique winnicottienne, que le lecteur doive créer pour lui-même une histoire qui est déjà là. Et le plaisir propre à la lecture sérielle siègerait dans l'assurance que, autant de fois fût-elle renouvelée, cette expérience a la structure d'un entonnoir: tout comme l'infinie diversité des histoires, des configurations situationnelles et des surprises qu'elles ménagent se réduit en un nombre important mais fini d'intrigues (la lecture de roman, c'est alors passer de la devanture à l'ossature), ces intrigues se réduisent à leur tour aux quelques usages que le lecteur peut en faire. Comme le souvenir acheté par un touriste ou la photo de famille, pour le lecteur l'intrigue ferait office de rappel du plaisir ressenti dans l'acte de lecture.

Toutefois cette évidence de l'intrigue n'empêche pas d'en distinguer l'ombre portée; tout autant qu'une chose, apparentée au roman lu mais évanescente tant qu'elle n'a pas été verbalisée, l'intrigue est elle-même le résultat d'une *opération cognitive*. Moins essence que pratique, l'intrigue impose d'immédiatement tenir compte des agents et des moments possibles de cette opération: affaire de lecteur menée parallèlement à la lecture du roman et dans son for intérieur? Ou affaire d'informateur, de prescripteur, d'analyste, menée rétrospectivement et transformant le livre lu en référent d'un énoncé? Issues d'un même modèle, le roman d'où elles sont tirées, ces formes diverses de l'intrigue n'en sont pas moins distinctes.[2]

Tout d'abord, l'intrigue se constitue lors d'un des moments cognitivement *top-to-bottom* dans le for intérieur du lecteur. Au moment où il entreprend sa lecture, si le lecteur de roman policier s'attend à quelque chose d'à la fois flou et contraignant en fonction de la carte de visite du roman (son titre, le graphisme ou l'illustration de sa couverture), du genre de la fiction (explicitement ou implicitement exhibé par le roman,

---

[2] Avant d'entrer dans le détail de ces différentes constructions de l'intrigue, je précise que c'est du roman policier que seront tirés tous mes exemples, sans regard pour la variété des qualités mais en essayant d'en diversifier les sources dans l'histoire du genre en France, à cause de la place éminente de l'intrigue dans l'horizon d'attente – forte anticipation de l'énigme à résoudre et de la bien connue structure préalable de l'enquête qui, pour le lectorat, définissent largement le genre, même si, outre la tête, ce dernier ne néglige pas de faire vibrer le cœur et les tripes.

adéquatement ou pas supposé par le lecteur), de la signature de l'auteur (si le lecteur en connaît l'œuvre antérieure), de l'univers de référence évoqué (comme le théâtre aujourd'hui dans les arènes de Nîmes ou la Florence de Pic de la Mirandole[3]), le lecteur sériel reconnaît aussi quelque chose dans le cas où il a affaire à un programme. Si dans le cas du chapelet des arrondissements parisiens de Léo Malet il y est aidé par un faux-titre général, "Les Nouveaux mystères de Paris", en cas de *fabula* conventionnelle c'est son encyclopédie de lecteur qui peut éventuellement lui suggérer un air de famille, voire sa désignation, comme le mystère en chambre close.[4] Du côté du lecteur, l'intrigue résulte donc d'une opération d'extraction cognitive qui aboutit à une représentation miniaturisée du récit, plus ou moins drastiquement et fidèlement simplifiée.

Mais l'intrigue n'est pas seulement ce que le lecteur reconnaît dans son for intérieur; elle s'objectivise, se verbalise. Outre les variations liées à la relation à son modèle (quel degré d'allègement le récit subit-il? des éléments de la narration sont-ils mentionnés? lesquels?), cette représentation simplifiée peut aller de l'oral à l'imprimé. Forme orale, elle va de l'échange informel consistant à inciter ou décourager l'interlocuteur à lire le livre, ou visant à entrer en relation avec sa voisine de siège en avion, jusqu'à l'enquête interrogeant auteurs ou lecteurs. En cas de forme imprimée, elle varie en fonction des auteurs de ces représentations simplifiées, romanciers, éditeurs, critiques, lecteurs. Si elles s'adressent bien tous à de futurs lecteurs, chacune de ces formes objectivées définit l'usage spécifique de sa représentation miniaturisée du récit. Représentation miniaturisée du récit, l'intrigue gît-elle dans le simple synopsis selon l'auteur lorsqu'elle précède la rédaction du roman: texte généralement pas public, Baudou et Schléret (1984) n'en fournissent pas moins un exemple en citant une correspondance personnelle de Jean-François Coatmeur qui leur synthétise son roman *Chantage pour une ombre* (1963):

> Un flic, en retraite, venu à Douarnenez s'incliner sur la tombe de son ami défunt, croit deviner que le suicide officiel n'en est pas un et enquête… Ça se passe pendant le Carnaval. (Baudou et Schléret, 1984, 123)

Sans doute diffère-t-elle d'un prière-d'insérer en 4$^{e}$-de-couverture, écrit apostérioriquement par l'auteur ou son éditeur, adressé au chaland pour le

---

[3] Je pense au roman policier de Barjavel (1985), à celui policier et historique de Deschodt et Lattès (2004).

[4] Le lecteur peut ainsi toujours rapporter à un roman typique et exemplaire de cette *fabula* conventionnelle, comme Leroux (1907), d'autres bien moins connus, comme Verdier (2003).

transformer en acheteur puis en lecteur. D'ailleurs, les prière-d'insérer ont beau tous être doublement surdéterminés, en amont donner une idée du contenu et en aval convaincre le lecteur, ils n'en utilisent pas moins de nombreuses stratégies discursives – résumé, questions, échantillon[5]... En complément à cette fonction publicitaire, l'éditeur doit aussi prévoir. Prévoir par exemple que les destinataires puissent être plus des utilisateurs que des lecteurs, prévoir de futurs classificateurs comme les bibliothécaires, prévoir que, dans une fiche, le prière-d'insérer peut accompagner les adresses bibliographiques, sous sa forme originale ou non. Voire anticiper que le lecteur ait connaissance d'une autre forme médiatique du roman, différente de l'œuvre originale; ainsi par prudence, le Livre de Poche ajoute un *nota bene* au long prière-d'insérer introduisant la réédition de Claude Néron (1968) postérieure à la sortie et au succès de son adaptation filmique par Claude Sautet en 1971:

> Il est utile de préciser au lecteur que, dans le film, le personnage de Lily, incarné par Romy Schneider, prenait une plus grande importance. Par voie de conséquence, les rapports entre Max et Lily avaient un autre caractère. Ils ne sont pas les mêmes dans le livre.

Ici, pour l'acte de lecture se pose la question de savoir dans quel ordre le lecteur prend connaissance du roman et de son résumé, ces deux représentations d'une même histoire; paradoxalement, l'intrigue en tant que représentation simplifiée peut interférer avec l'acte de lecture du roman lui-même. Ensuite se pose la même question en fonction de la coexistence d'adaptations avec l'œuvre originale, c'est-à-dire de représentations différentes d'une même histoire, quoique celles-ci sans miniaturisation ni défictionnalisation.

---

[5] Trois exemples: "Marcus Aper est sur le point d'accepter d'être nommé juge à Gergovie quand Floris, le patron d'une grande officine industrielle de vaisselle en terre cuite de Millau, vient le supplier de le défendre contre l'accusation de meurtre qui l'oppose à son ancien potier, dont la fille a disparu [...]" (de Leseleuc, 1993). "Pourquoi Hervé est-il dans le box des accusés? Qui a-t-il tué? Pourquoi a-t-il tué? A-t-il seulement tué quelqu'un? Trois femmes sont à l'origine du drame qu'il vit [...]" (Thomas, 1976). "Découvrir que le meurtre que vous n'avez jamais eu le courage d'accomplir est là, devant vous, décrit au détail près. Le découvrir à Florence, sur une fresque du XVe siècle. Une fresque de Paolo Uccello. Que faire? Peut-être prendre le train de nuit pour Paris, attendre dans un parking souterrain et y assassiner l'homme de la fresque par la masse et par le feu. C'est ce que fit Nec. Ensuite il rencontra Béa. Tout le reste était déjà écrit. Il n'y avait plus qu'à suivre avec son doigt. Jusqu'au bout du canal" (Picouly, 1992).

Miniaturisation? On comprend que le prière-d'insérer qui annonce en quelques phrases l'histoire à venir se garde bien d'en trop révéler. L'expérience auprès de lecteurs à qui est demandé de rapporter l'intrigue d'un roman montre plutôt qu'ils recourent spontanément à une miniaturisation, à une sélection plus ou moins habile d'éléments saillants avec, parfois, un souci de faire paraître la cohérence des enchaînements. Défictionnalisation? Dans le prière-d'insérer de *Max et les ferrailleurs*, l'avertissement sur les rapports entre Max et Lily positionne le futur lecteur à l'extérieur de la fiction, révèle ces relations sous le jour d'une construction romanesque. De la même manière, cette correspondance de Pierre Darcis avec Baudou et Schléret exhibe la distance de l'auteur devant son propre roman, dessinant ainsi une place d'où son lecteur pourrait lui aussi la voir.[6]

Version portative du roman, ainsi obtenue par simplification, miniaturisation et défictionnalisation, l'intrigue occupe donc trois positions par rapport à l'acte de lecture. Dans deux d'entre elles, l'intrigue est actualisable, sinon toujours actualisée, car communicationnelle, visant un destinataire. Sont bien des sous-produits de l'acte de lecture le prière-d'insérer, en amont, du moins celui qui ne se contente pas de titiller mais qui annonce, résume, présente l'histoire à venir pour amorcer la curiosité ou l'inquiétude, et, en aval, le résumé apostériorique que le lecteur peut être amené à faire de sa lecture, pour en parler dans la conversation, pour répondre à une question, une demande, une enquête, etc. On ne peut en revanche accéder à la troisième position, l'intrigue comme moment de la construction du sens, voire comme style de lecture, que par une démarche phénoménologique.

## L'intrigue: intrication et intégration

Sans chercher à reprendre les riches analyses de Ricœur (1983, 1984 et 1985), notamment leurs distinctions entre *préfiguration*, *configuration* et *refiguration*, voyons plutôt ce qu'il en est de la place de l'intrigue dans la compréhension du roman lors de tel acte de lecture particulier. *Treize reste raide*: avant d'entreprendre la lecture de Merle (1997), signataire

[6] "L'intrigue se déroule dans l'Indre. Un peintre non figuratif, qui possède deux maisons au bord du fleuve, loue l'une d'elles à une Américaine, auteur de romans policiers. Le même jour, il repêche dans la rivière une jeune femme mystérieuse qui se prétend poursuivie par l'homme qu'elle vient d'épouser. La romancière s'efforce d'appliquer à des faits réels ses qualités de déduction, tandis que le peintre trouve le fin mot de l'imbroglio devant un chevalet à l'aide d'une estompe et d'un fusain..." (Baudou et Schléret, 1984, 148).

vraisemblablement inconnu du lecteur sériel puisqu'il s'agit d'un premier roman policier de cet auteur, si le lecteur n'est pas bouliste le titre lui-même est énigmatique. Rapidement résolue par le prière-d'insérer, cette énigme ne sert que d'apéritif à une autre servant d'intrigue-squelette au corps de la fiction: qui tue tous ces pépés marseillais et pourquoi ?

"L'enterrement monte vers le cimetière *quillé** en bordure du plateau […]", Merle (1997, 7): dès la première phrase, la lecture est censée au moins ralentir devant cet adjectif morphologiquement familier mais lexicalement étranger au français, juste le temps d'apercevoir en note infrapaginale qu'un glossaire en fin de volume "fournira quelques éclaircissements, si besoin est, sur les termes ou expressions en italiques" (Merle, 1997, 7). S'il n'est pas familier du dialecte marseillais, il sait maintenant avoir à choisir un style de lecture allegro qui n'ira consulter le glossaire qu'en cas de trop forte opacité de la phrase (un seul mot incompris ne vaut peut-être pas une telle interruption) et un style de lecture plus méticuleux, plus curieux de la langue mais plus lent, et plus tolérant aux interruptions de l'effet d'immersion. En fait, face à de tels grumeaux sur la surface verbale, il a plutôt le choix entre trois styles de lecture, chacune vectrice d'une forme de plaisir: confrontée à la nébulosité lexicale, la lecture allegro compte sur le courant d'air pour disperser les mots qui s'interposeraient à la compréhension de l'histoire; la lecture plus méticuleuse se délecte d'un autre type d'immersion, moins assujettie à l'enchaînement des actions que sensible au monde représenté et aux phrases le représentant; entre les deux enfin, un style de lecture hybride, légèrement décalé, rêveur peut-être, se laisse porter par l'intrigue tout en goûtant l'authenticité d'une diglossie vivante, exempte d'exotisme,[7] suppose dans les phrases représentant ce monde qu'elles en sont elles-mêmes issues, entend peut-être le fantôme d'une parlure, d'un accent.

Mimétique, le roman parle du monde; or ce qu'il en dit freine l'avancement de l'action. L'intrigue de *Treize reste raide* est ponctuée de discussions entre protagonistes sur la situation sociopolitique de la ville de Marseille. Ainsi, lors de leur premier échange, Meiffret l'armateur et Laurent Laugier le journaliste à travers qui nous prenons connaissance de l'histoire, se placent sur un observatoire cognitif pour parler de leur ville; même si l'on entrevoit bien les réticences de Laugier, ce sont les deux grands registres de compréhension de Meiffret que la narration expose: le contexte historique des actuelles contradictions de Marseille entre

---

[7] Merle est aussi historien, notamment des pratiques linguistiques provençales et franco-provençales, et connaisseur de la renaissance littéraire du provençal au XIXe siècle. Trois autres devaient succéder à *Treize reste raide* chez des éditeurs plus petits mais plus en phase avec son militantisme régional.

communautarisme et repli identitaire frontiste et la conception vitaliste nietzschéenne qu'il y voit à l'œuvre. Le lecteur accepte (ou pas) de tels ralentissements en se doutant que l'histoire et la sociologie de Marseille doivent avoir leur pertinence: à la fois dans le déroulement spécifique de l'intrigue, même s'il ne la distingue pas encore (attente du plaisir associé à ce qui viendra donner rétrospectivement sa cohérence à tout le roman), et dans le regard binoculaire porté sur Marseille, corpusculaire pour l'historique et le sociopolitique mais aussi ondulatoire pour la vibration affective particulière inspirée par la ville au héros et à l'auteur (plaisir immédiat de l'immersion dans un monde affectant les trois *âmes* aritotéliciennes du lecteur). Pour éviter la simple juxtaposition des deux registres, l'avancement de l'action et l'immersion dans le monde, Merle veille à ce que cette échappée vers le monde lors de la première rencontre entre Meiffret et Laugier ne se définisse pas exclusivement par sa fonction référentielle, ses enseignements sociopolitiques; elle se trouve fermement enclose par l'acte de langage rectionnel qui réunit l'armateur et le journaliste – le premier propose au second de travailler pour la boîte de communication qu'il veut fonder et, presque jusqu'aux toutes dernières pages, leur relation qui ne sera pas parvenu à devenir contractuelle semble la structure encadrante de l'intrigue.

En contradiction avec les velléités d'écriture de Laurent, le héros, et le ton auto-ironisant de leur présentation, Véro, sa maîtresse, "le pousse à une intrigue style Navarro tendance B.H.L. avec plein de Blacks et des Beurs en crise, la drogue, les cités [...] Y a des types très lancés qui se sont mis au polar. Même Julia Kristeva..." (Merle, 1997, 17). Même si des occurrences d'autoréférentialité s'avéreront récurrentes dans le roman – depuis belle lurette ce registre n'est plus réservé aux belles-lettres, il est même de plus en plus fréquent dans le polar contemporain et fait partie de l'horizon d'attente et suscite un plaisir spécifique – l'acte de lecture tend à plutôt les verser à l'*éthos* du héros-narrateur qu'à y voir un élément de l'intrigue. S'en doutant, l'auteur ne se fera pas faute d'en tirer parti pour inventer une fin inattendue, qui, avec une subtile brusquerie, rabat sur l'intrigue cet apparent divertissement – cruelle surprise, affect foudroyant, la chute a une soudaineté qui laisse la lecture doublement orpheline, le roman fini mais sans détente.[8]

[8] Ainsi, après une torride rencontre entre Laurent, victorieux pour avoir réussi à démêler les fils d'une affaire dont le nœud initial datait des années 30, et la séduisante veuve de celui qui semblait l'ultime cause de ces embrouilles sanglantes, leur premier accouplement débouche sur cette ultime catastrophe:
Il ouvre les yeux et voit le silencieux braqué devant lui.
– Laure, vous plaisantez ou quoi ?

Certes, la lecture comprend l'action parce que "la composition de l'intrigue est enracinée dans une *pré-compréhension du monde de l'action*: de ses structures intelligibles, de ses ressources symboliques et de son caractère temporel" (Ricœur, 1983, 17); ce qui incite Gervais (1990) à proposer d'entendre plutôt le processus que le résultat dans le mot *enchaînement*, de comprendre l'intrigue en priorité par la manière dont chaque roman enchaîne une situation narrative à la suivante: non seulement par l'évidente concaténation chronologique mais aussi par l'agent, par le lieu, par la dyade moyen-but. *Intrigue* ici vaut aussi bien pour un roman que pour un scénario de BD ou de jeux de rôles. Mais l'intrigue a aussi une fonction compositionnelle, plus spécifiquement romanesque: on vient de la voir épisser des brins apparemment centrifuges (digressions mimétiques, autoréférentialité, ironie). Elle peut tout aussi bien, par exemple, fabriquer des effets de boucle.[9] Nécessaire, la pré-compréhension du monde de l'action s'avère ne pas être suffisante ici, et la concomitante réduction à l'intrigue lors de l'acte de lecture dans un style de lecture allegro ne pas pouvoir éviter les délectables ou cruels leurres machinés par l'auteur. Complémentaires, certes, ces deux dimensions de l'intrigue n'en sont pas moins distinctes.

À la lecture de romans policiers, on peut sans doute distinguer l'art de l'intrigue de ceux, (subordonnées?) du traitement du temps et de l'espace fictionnels, mais peut-être pas toujours facilement. En fait ce bref survol incite à reconsidérer l'évidence de l'intrigue. Celle-ci serait non seulement ce qui enchaîne une situation narrative à la suivante par la chronologie, l'agent, le lieu, la dyade moyen-but, compréhensible pour le lecteur parce qu'il pourrait y projeter une préalable pré-compréhension du monde de l'action, mais elle serait aussi ce qui réussit à harnacher les forces centrifuges du temps et de l'espace que l'histoire du genre semble rendre

---

Elle sourit dans un signe enfantin de dénégation.
– Laure, déconne pas, je voudrais être un héros récurrent.
– Laurent, c'est ça le vrai contrat.
Et elle appuie sur la détente (Merle, 1997, 236).

[9] Ainsi, miroir asymétrique de la *motivation* prospective et du *mobile* rétrospectif, alors que le lecteur n'est que progressivement admis dans l'intimité de la motivation du journaliste tout au long de l'intrigue et que c'est en tâtonnant avec lui qu'il avance dans l'enquête, ce n'est qu'à proximité du dénouement et en deux phrases que lui est enfin révélé le mobile de l'armateur multiplement meurtrier:

– […] Au fait, les Treize, pourquoi il vous en voulait comme ça, Meiffret? Qu'est-ce que vous lui aviez fait?

– Nous, rien. Il s'est juste pris une vraie rouste. Mais après on l'a passé à l'équipage d'un cargo italien, des Somaliens. Ils l'ont enculé toute la nuit. (Merle, 1997, 233).

de plus en plus innovatrices, de plus en plus rusées. L'intrigue serait non seulement une forme résultant d'une opération d'extraction mais aussi la résultante de forces antagonistes, se manifestant à tour de rôle durant l'acte de lecture et tiraillant la compréhension dans différentes directions.

## L'intrigue: duplication ou complexités polarisées

La phase du roman de détection avait fermement tiré le genre du côté du jeu donnant ainsi sa physionomie narrative au roman policier mais ouvrant aussi la voie à des scénarios sans narration (fiction par dossier de Wheatley (1938), sites en ligne comme jeu-detective.com), voire sans lecture (*murder-parties* comme outils d'animation au service de la performance en entreprise)... La fiction d'énigme criminelle en tant que jeu a prouvé être progressivement capable de se débarrasser de ses oripeaux romanesques, même si la culture médiatique continue à tirer des nutriments de ce sol ancien. La phase du roman noir avait tout aussi fermement ramené le genre vers la formule régnante, le roman mimétique, et sa dominante, l'immersion du lecteur dans l'univers fictionnel. Même si l'immersion s'obtient d'autant plus aisément que les romanciers rendent poreuse la séparation entre faits et fiction en jouant de la proximité du polar avec la nouvelle journalistique dans la culture médiatique, en profitant de ce que détectives et journalistes se partagent la forme de l'enquête, immersion et intrigue n'en sont pas moins dans un rapport ambivalent. Par l'entremise de la curiosité du lecteur, la fiction subit l'appel centrifuge du monde où elle pourrait se disperser. Et, si l'on en croit l'hypothèse de Raabe (1995) sur la lecture sérielle – pour le lecteur accro à une collection, celle-ci fonctionne comme la partie d'un jeu dont chaque roman lu serait un coup – le risque s'accroit d'autant qu'un même genre (il y suffit d'une énigme criminelle et d'une enquête) l'entraine vers d'insolites quartiers du monde, peu connus, hétérogènes – aussi bien collectionneurs de petits soldats de plomb chez David (1949), turpitudes feutrées de la grande bourgeoisie bordelaise chez Vigne (1987) que grandes manœuvres des compagnies pétrolières américaines pour s'approprier les ressources du sous-sol de la République de Sakha-Yakoutie chez Pellerin (2000).

Par ailleurs, la dimension du jeu n'est pas simplement résiduelle dans le roman noir, pas cantonnée à la seule structure énigme-enquête; elle affecte bien d'autres registres de la lecture. Dans Fonteneau (1992, 1993), la focalisation s'effectue respectivement à travers un couteau et une marche d'escalier! Les allusions intradiégétiques au genre constituent un *topos* attendu.[10] De manière moins régionale, certains romans sont entièrement informés par un intertexte, parfois relevant des Belles-lettres, parfois de l'histoire du genre. Jean Kéry se spécialisait dans les pastiches.[11] Les romans de Montbrun (1994, 1998, 2001 et 2006) côtoient Réouven (1980) et les parodies de Viard et Zacharias (1966, 1966, 1967, 1968). Derrière le pseudonyme de la première se cache une prof d'études littéraires spécialiste de Proust, bonne connaisseuse aussi de Marguerite Yourcenar, Colette et Pablo Neruda: impénitent, son héros récurrent le commissaire Foucheroux est amené à enquêter sur des meurtres commis dans la maison de tante Léonie où le petit Marcel passait ses vacances, à Petite Plaisance, dans la villa-musée Yourcenar sur l'île des Monts-Déserts au large du Maine, au Musée Colette de Saint-Sauveur-en-Puisaye et dans la villa accueillant des artistes à Isla Negra au sud de Valparaiso à côté de la maison du poète chilien. Le second entremêle avec jubilation tradition biblique et meurtres en chambre close, poisons et contrepoisons, Sarah devenant veuve sept fois lors de ses banquets de noces et démon Asmodée, traduction "fidèle" du prophète Daniel ayant jadis fait office d'enquêteur et anachronismes allègrement détraqués. Par réfraction déformante, les deux parodistes font apparaître les histoires respectives de l'*Illiade*, *Hamlet*,[12] *Lorenzaccio* et *Don Quichotte*... Quant à lui, le lecteur des romans de Patrick Pécherot (2001) n'a pas de gros effort herméneutique à fournir pour reconnaître Léo Malet dans le détective Nestor dit Pipette – à cause de la célèbre pipe à tête de taureau.[13]

Dès la phase du roman de détection, le crime n'apparaissait que comme la face exotérique d'une énigme; l'enquêteur s'instituait vicaire d'une double présupposition – une explication du crime apostériorique et rationnelle est possible et cette explication est un récit. Comme l'intrigue de son enquête (racontée par la fiction) est la tâtonnante reconstruction de l'intrigue qui avait mené au crime et que le roman le montre en herméneute capable d'expliquer les enchaînements, le lecteur en prend peut-être la leçon, se fait étudiant en herméneutique criminelle… et en lecture. Modèle de lecture par duplication, donc: l'intrigue au sens 1, celle

[10] Fussent-elles ironiques comme dans ce passage où Véro conseillait Laurent dans *Treize reste raide*.

[11] Dans des volumes de Tallandier présentant deux titres chacun, Kéry (1952, 1953 et 1953) pastichent Maurice Leblanc, Georges Simenon, Émile Gaboriau, Conan Doyle, Peter Cheyney...

[12] Roman adapté à la télévision par Dayan (1980) pour Antenne 2.

[13] Les deux titres suivants de la série prendront un peu plus de distance par rapport au modèle, mais c'est ce premier hommage qui aura été récompensé par le Grand Prix de la littérature policière en 2002.

qui est en amont du récit (l'intention criminelle, le complot malveillant ou le funeste concours de circonstances), impose à l'enquêteur de régressivement la reconstituer dans ses phases et leurs enchaînements (intrigue au sens 2, celle qui résume le roman) et de l'exposer dans un récit de vérité, intradiégétique, manifestant l'*adequatio rei intellectus*, l'assujettissement de la quête de vérité à l'exposé de la vérité et la superposition de la parole adéquate à ce que le roman avait tenu caché au lecteur – avant le récit, en dehors des focalisations, dans les silences de la narration. Tel serait du moins le type de jeu compétitif qu'aurait voulu imposer le roman de détection, réalisant plus complètement que d'autres genres populaires les potentialités du romanesque général, transformant parfois en leurres pour le lecteur typicité, cohérences, place en retrait du narrateur, interprétation du sens d'un événement en fonction d'un récit y conduisant ou d'un type le surdéterminant. Romans policiers lus pour se distraire mais qui tout aussi bien tentent de distraire la sagacité du lecteur. Eisenzweig (1986) a fort justement souligné qu'il s'agissait d'un jeu à dés pipés. En s'éloignant de cette lecture-telle-qu'elle-devrait-être, le roman policier ultérieur a libéré l'acte de lecture, non sans que chaque roman, plus ou moins joueur, tente de reprendre barre sur lui par d'autres moyens. Certes les fictions peuvent être des institutrices; sans doute en les lisant apprend-on sur l'Histoire, sur la société, sur nous-mêmes; mais plus systématiquement que d'autres genres populaires, dans le roman policier la velléité pédagogique le cède à la proposition de jeu, jeu qui à la fois prétend plus ou moins clairement avoir des règles mais aussi tolère tout autant l'inattention du lecteur et l'omission des pages mal prometteuse sautées[14] que la mauvaise foi du romancier, voire ses ruses qui tiennent compte de la vraisemblable désinvolture de son lecteur… Fictions institutrices mais prévisibles et lestes, organisées et aventureuses, pensives et perverses. Leur leçon s'avère donc souvent ambiguë quant au contenu, à l'histoire et à sa morale, et ambivalente quant aux principes et procédures d'interprétation – le roman policier s'est bien complexifié depuis les 65-centimes Fayard d'avant 1914 et leur modèle paralittéraire.

Si l'on n'est plus emprisonné par la lecture-telle-qu'elle-devrait-être, on peut observer les leçons d'interprétation offertes par le genre et considérer la lecture-telle-qu'elle-est devant ces leçons. Le lecteur sériel dispose donc d'un critère d'évaluation permettant d'apprécier ses lectures: le degré d'intégration que l'intrigue fait subir aux éléments constitutifs de la fiction. L'intrigue émane-t-elle du monde ou se contente-t-elle de s'y

[14] Je rejoins ici la conception de la lecture proposée par Pennac (1992), double connaisseur en tant qu'enseignant et auteur de polars.

surimposer? Émane-t-elle du jeu ou se contente-t-elle de s'y superposer? Le roman policier a son histoire, et pour les auteurs la nécessaire répétition (signatures et personnages récurrents, types d'intrigues et *fabulæ* préfabriquées, lois du genre et de chacune de ses grandes familles) n'en doit pas moins composer avec la tout aussi nécessaire innovation. Du coup, pour son lecteur la simplification consistant à parvenir à l'intrigue après avoir écarté langage et narration peut à son tour se voir happée par cette double recherche d'immersion et de jeu. Tout en relevant toujours de la lecture ordinaire et de la fiction populaire, le roman policier s'est diversifié et complexifié; sa diversification et sa complexification l'entraînent à tenter des formules métafictionnelles qui pour autant n'oublient pas leur fondement, l'intrigue. Qu'on pense notamment à ces romans qui promeuvent comme ressorts de l'intrigue diversité sociolectale et idiolectale des narrateurs et des personnages,[15] mise en scène explicite des circuits communicationnels auxquels recourt la fiction,[16] ambivalence générique,[17] intertextualité déjantée[18] et lecture ordinaire pervertie en piège,[18] c'est-à-dire à ceux qui jouent sur les éléments narratologiques ou pragmatiques de la fiction pour accroître le degré d'intégration de l'intrigue.

On le voit, le roman policier peut bien avoir initialement tenté d'imposer à son lectorat une conception de l'intrigue, sorte de jeu compétitif entre romancier et lecteur, des contraintes propres à l'écriture

---

[15] Avec des titres aussi différents que la célèbre trilogie d'Izzo (1995, 1996 et 1998), l'ironie grinçante d'A.D.G. (1973), le décalage entre l'auteur et le sociolecte dans Marie et Joseph (1989) et dans Salva (1975), les turgescences stylistiques de San-Antonio.

[16] Narration de Lamblin (1951) qui multiplie des véhicules narratifs hétéroclites, inconsistances pragmatiques assujetties à la mauvaise foi narrative de Boileau-Narcejac (1961), pièges dans lesquels tombent les lecteurs de Philippe (2003) ou Rozenfarb (2003) à cause du style du narrateur induisant une fausse image, orientant la lecture, double perversion d'actes de communication chez Monteilhet (1963) – la confession, par un acte d'écoute séculier, clandestin et révélateur des méfaits de la modernité (un sociologue vraisemblablement disciple de l'école de Chicago enregistrait les confessions de tous les paroissiens), puis perversion de cette intention scientifique par la philosophe qui met la main sur les bandes après la disparition du sociologue et utilise le chantage comme arme de moralisation des turpitudes multiples et croisées de la population de cette petite ville.

[17] Comme la fiction policière de Magnan (1992) qui dissimule jusqu'à la fin son vrai genre, son juste interprétant: le fantastique.

[18] Comme chez Viard et Zacharias (1966, 1966, 1967, 1968) ou Réouven (1980).

[18] Comme dans le jeu trompeur et artificieux de Siniac (1988) qui machine un subtil court-circuit.

(narratologiques, langagières), l'aimantation du réel social subi par la fiction et le dynamisme propre de l'évolution du genre ont progressivement complexifié cette règle du jeu. À cause de la recherche d'immersion, dans l'acte de lecture réel, l'intrigue va bien au-delà de l'extraction inversée de celle inventée par le romancier: non pas duplication mais complexités polarisées, elle sert aussi au lecteur de romans policiers de critère d'appréciation pour son plaisir de lecture, mesurant le degré d'intégration que l'intrigue fait subir aux éléments constitutifs de la fiction.

## En avoir le cœur net...

Structuralisme des formalistes russes, étude cognitive de la lecture, analyse du discours social... chacune avec ses objectifs propres, des approches aussi différentes ont depuis longtemps pris au sérieux l'intérêt de l'intrigue. Il faut toutefois passer du côté de l'acte de lecture pour entrevoir la principale polarisation dans la diversité des conceptions de l'intrigue proposée dans la littérature critique. Soit l'on comprend l'intrigue comme un élément caractéristique du récit, l'interface structurale qui, dans le roman, relie entre elles des situations narratives (par le temps, l'agent, le lieu, la dyade moyen-but) et leur fait contribuer en faisceau à construire le thème de la fiction. Soit l'on comprend l'intrigue comme une co-construction du lecteur, dans son esprit (lors de l'acte de lecture, lorsqu'il tente de comprendre où le récit l'entraîne) ou de manière plus ou moins explicitement verbalisée après l'acte de lecture (lorsqu'il tente de se formuler ou de formuler à autrui ce qu'il a compris de ce qu'il a lu). Il semble difficile de tenir l'intrigue pour le principal plaisir de la lecture ordinaire sans articuler intrigue comme caractéristique du récit et intrigue comme supputation de l'acte de lecture, ni sans préserver leurs dissemblances.

"Ça se lit comme un roman policier": si l'on en croit le figement de l'expression, passée dans la langue comme une locution, ce genre populaire, de manière plus emblématique que d'autres, affiche justement se fonder sur l'intrigue et promettre la lune au lecteur, "tu ne pourras pas décrocher de l'histoire avant la fin, quelle que soit l'heure du repas, des obligations, de l'endormissement...". Autant partir de ça pour en avoir le cœur net sur cette question de l'intrigue. Aussitôt sourd un scepticisme – malgré son évidence, la notion d'intrigue est-elle si consistante qu'on n'ait plus à l'examiner? – qui incite à préférer commencer par parcourir les différents usages de l'intrigue faits par auteur, lecteur, éditeur que de commencer par la définir, à préférer, au moins pour un temps, sa possible hétérogénéité au maintien du flou conceptuel. Le risque est d'autant moins grand que, entre la compréhension en-deçà du roman, par pré-compréhension du monde de l'action, et, au-delà du roman, la lisibilité (facilitation de la compréhension) du romanesque général, la leçon fournie par le genre à ses lecteurs ne manque pas de pertinence. L'articulation de l'intrigue dans le récit et de l'intrigue dans l'acte de lecture s'effectue par sa fonction compositionnelle de force centripète qui harnache les nombreuses forces centrifuges travaillant le roman en tant qu'être de langage, discours (lui-même composé de discours composites), récit, genre, et fiction.

Dans Bleton (1999), je proposais de centrer la réflexion sur la lecture de genres populaires à l'aide d'un modèle incluant la reconnaissance comme compétence cognitive cardinale (héritage du romanesque général et du modèle paralittéraire), la symétrie de l'offre et la demande (de l'industrie paralittéraire et de son lectorat) mais aussi l'extensivité sérielle de l'acte de lecture et la constitution résultante d'une encyclopédie spécialisée chez chaque lecteur. Comme ce modèle de la lecture sérielle insiste sur les opérations mentales mises en œuvre pour comprendre une histoire (le lecteur n'est pas un simple réceptacle, ni la lecture le renversement en miroir de la conception de la fiction par le romancier), relativement fidèle jusqu'ici aux conceptions de Couégnas (1992) et Angenot, il s'en distingue de deux manières. D'une part, en faisant la part belle aux effets en retour sur l'acte de lecture de sauts qualitatifs résultant de la capitalisation d'une encyclopédie spécialisée, il souffle d'explorer ce niveau d'une telle encyclopédie spécialisée, celui définissant la lecture sérielle, avant de sauter à celui d'une *épistémè* plus ou moins consciente; peut-être pas lettré, le lecteur sériel n'en devient pas moins un fin connaisseur de son auteur ou de son genre favoris. D'autre part, à la configuration de base il articule plusieurs variations, hétérodoxes mais déterminantes puisqu'elles ont influencé l'évolution des genres populaires, comme la promotion d'opérations mentales plus ouvertes que celle de seule reconnaissance, notamment l'immersion, la rêverie, le jeu. Alors? Comment comprendre ce rappel de la diversité et de la complexité des configurations du roman policier par rapport aux conceptions de Couégnas et Angenot? Bricolage d'anomaliste plutôt que plan d'analogiste? Reflet de la dilatation continue du genre? Cet engrènement du vieux fond de reconnaissance (morts violentes, énigmes, enquêtes) avec les entraînements fournis par les jeux incluant le lecteur et avec les échappements obtenus par son immersion dans l'action et dans le monde en vient à proposer une horlogerie de montres molles, à cause du panachage de plaisirs de lecture assassins, d'intrigues qui auraient du cœur et de la cervelle.

## Références

A.D.G. [Alain Fournier]. 1973. *Berry Story*. Paris: Gallimard, "Série noire", n° 1586.

Angenot, Marc.1975. *Le Roman populaire. Recherches en paralittérature.* Montréal: Presses de l'Université du Québec.

Barjavel, René. 1985. *La Peau de César*. Paris: Mercure de France, "Crime parfait".

Couégnas, Daniel. 1992. *Introduction à la paralittérature*. Paris: Seuil, "Poétique".

David, Henri. 1949. *Jeux de plomb*. Paris: Librairie des Champs-Élysées, "Le Masque", n° 367.

Dayan, Josée. 1980. *L'Embrumé*, d'après Henri Viard et Bernard Zacharias, avec Patrick Bouchitey, Antenne 2.

Deschodt, Éric et Jean-Claude Lattès. 2004. *Marguerite et les enragés: meurtre à Florence*. Paris: Seuil.

Eisenzweig, Uri. 1986. *Le Récit impossible: forme et sens du roman policier*. Paris: Bourgois.

Fonteneau, Pascale. 1992. *Confidences sur l'escalier*. Paris: Gallimard, "Série noire", n° 2294.

—. 1993. *États de lame*, Paris: Gallimard, "Série noire", n° 2325.

Gervais, Bertrand. 1990. *Récits et actions. Pour une théorie de la lecture.* Longueuil: Le Préambule, "L'Univers des discours".

Kéry, Jean [Jean-Marie le Covec de Kéryvallon]. 1952. *Monsieur Frémond disparu*, suivi de *Le Dernier dossier de M. Lecoq*. Paris: Tallandier.

—. 1953. *Chantage*, suivi de *Le Muet*. Paris: Tallandier.

—. 1953. *Un Béguin de plus*, suivi de *La Disparition de Mary Crawl.* Paris: Tallandier.

Lamblin, Pierre. 1951. *La Concierge n'est plus dans l'escalier*. Paris: Éditions des deux mondes.

Leroux, Gaston. 1907. *Le Mystère de la chambre jaune*. Paris: Lafitte.

Leseleuc, Anne de. 1993. *Marcus Aper chez les Rutènes*. Paris: U.G.E. 10/18, "Grands détectives", n° 2384.

Magnan, Pierre. 1992. *Les Secrets de Laviolette*. Paris: Denoël.

Marie et Joseph [Corinne Bouchard et Pierre Mezinski]. 1990. *Le Piège au jardinet*. Paris: Gallimard, "Série Noire", n°2235.

Merle, René. 1997. *Treize reste raide*. Paris: Gallimard, "Série Noire", n° 2471.

Montbrun, Estelle [Élyane Dezon-Jones]. 1994. *Meurtre chez Tante Léonie*. Paris: Viviane Hamy.

—. 1998. *Meurtre à Petite Plaisance*. Paris: Viviane Hamy.
—. 2001. *Meurtre chez Colette*. Paris: Viviane Hamy.
—. 2006. *Meurtre à Isla Negra*. Paris: Viviane Hamy.
Néron, Claude. 1968. *Max et les ferrailleurs*. Paris: Grasset.
Pécherot, Patrick. 2001. *Les Brouillards de la Butte*. Paris: Gallimard, "Série noire", n° 2606.
Pellerin, Marc-Alfred. 2000. *N'oublie pas d'avoir peur*. Paris: Gallimard, "Série Noire", n° 2586.
Pennac, Daniel. 1992. *Comme un roman*. Paris: Gallimard.
Philippe, Cécile. 2003. *Salut Lulu!* Paris: Gallimard, "Série noire", n°2681.
Picouly, Daniel. 1992. *Nec*. Paris: Gallimard, "Série noire", n° 2297.
Réouven, René [René Sussan]. 1980. *Tobie or not Tobie*. Paris: Denoël.
Ricœur, Paul. 1983. *Temps et récit*. Paris: Seuil.
—. 1984. *La Configuration dans le récit de fiction*. Paris: Seuil.
— 1985. *Le Temps raconté*, Paris: Seuil.
Rozenfarb, Michèle. 2003. *L'Homme encerclé*. Paris: Gallimard.
Salva, Pierre. 1975. *Le Diable dans la sacristie*. Paris: Librairie des Champs-Élysées.
Tomachevski, Boris. 1965. « Thématique », *Théorie de la littérature*, (sous la dir. de Tzvetan Todorov). Paris: Seuil.
Thomas, Louis C. 1976. *Pour le meilleur et pour le pire*. Paris: Éditions OPTA.
Verdier, David. 2003. *L'Homme qui expliquait l'impossible*. Châteauroux: La Bouinotte.
Viard, Henri et Bernard, Zacharias. 1966. *Le Roi des Mirmidous*. Paris: Gallimard, "Série noire", n° 1018.
—. 1966. *L'Embrumé*. Paris: Gallimard, "Série Noire", n° 1075.
—. 1967. *Le Mytheux*. Paris: Gallimard, "Série noire", n° 1110.
—. 1968. *L'Aristocloche*. Paris: Gallimard, "Série noire", n° 1222.
Vigne, Jean-Claude. 1987. *Embrouilles*. Paris: Librairie Séguier.
Winnicott, Donald W. 1965. "De la communication et de la non-communication", *The Maturational Processes and the Facilitating Environment. Studies in the Theory of Emotional Development*. New York: International Universities Press.

# CHAPTER FIVE

# FICTIONNALISATION ET *STORYTELLING* DANS LA PRESSE TABLOID: LE CAS DU PERSONNEL POLITIQUE

MARC LITS

Depuis Richard Hoggart, la presse tabloïd fait partie intégrante des productions narratives consommées par les usagers dits populaires, et on ne peut plus dissocier fiction littéraire et médias fictionnalisants en termes d'usages. Les médias imprimés ont toujours proposé les histoires de célébrités présentées comme les héros heureux ou tragiques de nos modernes contes de fées, qu'ils soient acteurs de cinéma ou princesses (de Galles ou de Monaco). Désormais, les hommes et les femmes politiques sont aussi présents dans ces magazines, au même titre que les personnages du *show business*, et mis en scène dans des formes qui contribuent à transformer la nature du débat politique médiatisé. Ces politiques ne sont plus présentés au départ de leur programme, mais dans une mise en récit et en fiction qui utilise tous les ingrédients du *storytelling* pour construire des personnages proches. C'est leur vie privée, leurs amours, leurs émotions qui créent la proximité avec le public, dans des décors mis en scène, des séquences narratives construites, des images proposées, des histoires racontées. La contamination avec la fiction est omniprésente, et la mise en récit a remplacé la mise en débat. Au-delà des enjeux narratifs et médiatiques, cela pose aussi la question de la transformation du politique sous l'emprise du *storytelling* construit par des *spin doctors*. Éric Maigret a ainsi montré combien l'hyperprésident Sarkozy s'est "lentement et systématiquement construit par le biais de récits de vie, de photographies saisissantes et de formules chocs" (Maigret 2008, 13). Le conseiller du président français, Henri Guaino, déclarait dans *Le Monde*, en juillet 2007, que "la politique, c'est écrire une histoire partagée par ceux qui la font et ceux à qui elle est destinée. On ne transforme pas un pays sans être capable d'écrire et de raconter une histoire" (Salmon 2007, 200). Plus récemment, lors de la campagne électorale anglaise de 2010, David Cameron n'a pas hésité à évoquer le drame de son enfant pour adoucir une image jugée trop rigide.

## "People" et politique

Il faut donc s'interroger sur l'arrivée de nouveaux personnages dans les pages "people", ou sur le traitement "people" de personnages publics autrefois épargnés par cette approche.[1] Les hommes politiques ont désormais endossé l'habit de la personne publique, du "people", en utilisant les recettes déjà proposées par Jacques Pilhan, le conseiller en communication des présidents Mitterrand et Chirac, décrites dans un entretien dès 1995, bien avant le succès des ouvrages consacrés au *storytelling*:

> Les citoyens vivent les hommes publics comme des personnages de feuilleton. La règle de base de l'écriture d'un feuilleton télé est d'attribuer aux personnages un caractère simple et constant auquel vous devez vous tenir. L'image d'un homme public obéit à la même règle. Les citoyens lui attribuent, consciemment ou inconsciemment, un caractère (Pilhan 1995, 11).

Tous sont touchés par cette contamination du people. Le supplément *Victor* du quotidien *Le Soir* du 29 octobre 2005 n'hésite pas à titrer un dossier sur Olivier Besancenot, le leader de la Ligue communiste révolutionnaire, "Le people du peuple". Il est loin le temps où Habermas centrait son concept d'espace public sur la raison, où l'argumentation primait sur la persuasion ou la séduction. Mais aujourd'hui, privé et public interfèrent de plus en plus, de même que persuasion et argumentation,

---

[1] Dans le monde anglophone, le terme de tabloïd renvoie non seulement à un format de journal, mais aussi à un type de contenu, axé sur le sensationnel, les crimes, les vedettes du *show business*, tout ce qui relève des "*human interest stories*". En français, le terme "tabloïd" n'est guère utilisé pour désigner ces magazines et quotidiens, qui sont rassemblés sous l'étiquette "presse people". Quand on utilisera le terme "people" dans cet article, il n'a donc aucun lien avec la traduction littérale du terme en anglais, il renvoie soit à un certain type de journal à sensation (les "tabloïds", selon la terminologie anglophone), soit au traitement particulier fait de certaines personnalités, pour lesquelles on va surtout porter attention à leur vie personnelle (amours, fêtes, loisirs…), dans les rubriques qualifiées de "people". Ces personnalités du *show business* seront aussi, par extension, rassemblées sous le terme générique "people". Nous emploierons désormais ce terme, rentré dans le langage courant en français, sans guillemets.

rationnel et non-rationnel, culture d'élite et culture populaire. La dimension publique de la production des messages et la dimension privée de leur consommation s'entrecroisent de plus en plus.

Ce nouvel espace public a partie liée avec l'émergence forte du divertissement, de la marchandisation de l'information, de la spectacularisation, dont la presse people serait la quintessence. Désormais, presque tout peut être dit et montré dans l'espace public, y compris ce qui relève du privé, de l'affectif, de l'émotionnel. Ce qu'a bien compris ce grand communicateur qu'est Nicolas Sarkozy. Tout projet politique doit intégrer, dès le départ, une stratégie de communication dans laquelle la présence médiatique, y compris dans la presse people, sera déterminante. Dès lors, l'homme politique acceptera souvent les propositions qui lui sont faites de mettre en scène sa vie privée, s'il pense par là toucher un public qui s'est distancié de la politique, qui s'en méfie. Patrick Charaudeau a rappelé qu'une carrière politique se joue désormais autant sur une image qu'un programme: "Ce qui est en jeu est la captation du public. Bien plus importantes sont alors les stratégies de persuasion et de séduction" (Charaudeau 2008, 7). Éric Maigret va encore plus loin - mais on ne le suivra pas sur ce point - en avançant que Sarkozy n'est pas seulement bon dans les médias, il est devenu "un média à lui tout seul, qui plus est un média grand public" (Maigret 2008, 15).

On passe donc, aujourd'hui, du modèle délibératif à la mise en spectacle de personnages politiques. En termes de genres télévisuels, cela pourrait se résumer par le passage du débat au *talk show*, voire à la téléréalité. En presse écrite, cela se traduit par le développement d'approches people dans le traitement de l'information au sein même de la presse de référence. La politique a changé, le personnage politique doit donc construire son image dans d'autres lieux et sous d'autres formes.

## Presse people et personnage

Il faut d'abord revenir sur le fonctionnement narratif de la presse people et l'importance occupée par le personnage dans cette matrice. Longtemps méprisé par les théoriciens structuralistes du récit, le personnage est revenu en force avec le déclin des analyses textuelles d'inspiration structurale. On s'accorde désormais à considérer le personnage comme l'un des moteurs de toute organisation narrative, au point que ce personnage devient le principal incitant à la lecture. Lire un texte narratif, c'est aller à la rencontre d'une figure héroïque pour partager, d'une manière ou d'une autre, son destin. Et pas seulement pour les midinettes abusées par des romans sentimentaux ou des gazettes à deux sous fabriqués pour renforcer leur aliénation sociale.

Les travaux d'Yves Reuter ou de Vincent Jouve ont fait de l'étude du personnage un des lieux privilégiés d'entrée dans le texte littéraire. Mais si l'on accepte que le personnage est constitutif du type narratif, quelles que soient ses manifestations discursives, on conviendra qu'il est aussi un élément central du récit médiatique, et tout particulièrement dans la presse people, ou dans les traitements journalistiques qui en imitent les procédés. En effet, ce n'est pas par hasard que la rubrique people de *Paris Match* s'est longtemps appelée "Les gens", et désormais "People". Il est significatif aussi que le slogan du magazine, "Le poids des mots, le choc des photos" ait été remplacé par "La vie est une histoire vraie". Ce qui est central dans ces pages, ce sont moins les actions dont ces acteurs seraient les protagonistes, puisque celles-ci sont souvent d'un intérêt limité, mais la personnalité des intervenants. Ce qui compte dans la rubrique people, et en cela son intitulé est d'une rare pertinence, ce sont bien les personnes dont on y parle, les personnages qui y sont construits par le récit médiatique.

La culture médiatique se caractérise centralement par le primat qu'elle accorde à la récitation d'histoires et la dimension narrative qu'elle privilégie dans toute restitution événementielle. Daniel Couégnas consacrait déjà un des chapitres de son étude sur la paralittérature à "la narrativité dominante" (Couégnas 1992). Les productions de masse se caractérisent par une hypertrophie de la fonction narrative. C'est le cas dès que se développe une presse à bon marché. Quand Émile de Girardin lance son quotidien *La Presse* en 1836, il fonde le succès de ce nouveau type de journal sur deux choix stratégiques: un coût d'abonnement divisé par deux par rapport à ses concurrents (grâce à l'introduction de la publicité); et l'introduction du roman-feuilleton (cette première narration sérialisée qui marque bien les débuts de l'ère médiatique).

La presse people du XXIe siècle n'a qu'à emprunter ce chemin narratif tout tracé et à l'agrandir, entre autres par un recours généralisé à la photographie, en générant une série d'effets induits: l'importance accordée aux personnages médiatiques, réels mais construits en recourant à des stéréotypes narratifs; le primat accordé à l'émotion, voire à la sensation, sur la rationalité; la réception fondée sur l'identification ou la projection plutôt que le recul critique… Ce qui induit des logiques d'appropriation plus fortes, faisant du lecteur un acteur potentiel de cet univers tendant au fictionnel, du moins par procuration, dans sa proximité artificielle avec les personnages people qu'il côtoie semaine après semaine. Cela l'installe dans une position narcissique, puisque ce qu'il découvre, dans ces feuilletons mêlant splendeur et déchéance, c'est une part de son être, comme l'avance Jean Bellemin-Noël, quand il parle des contes de fées, qui présentent quelques analogies avec la presse people, du moins dans leur usage:

> Ce qui me touche, c'est l'évocation de mes problèmes hors de moi, où ils trouvent un cadre: j'y reconnais une autre dimension, une dimension d'Autre. Voilà des rêves qu'on partage au lieu de les inventer chacun pour soi. Et des rêves mis en mots, avec lesquels on peut jouer à volonté, à satiété, en restant éveillé. Ils donnent le droit de faire mourir ou souffrir tel ou tel, de se mettre à telle ou telle place d'ordinaire jalousement interdite (Bellemin-Noël 1983, 14).

## La Scène médiatique people

En partant de ce constat, l'analyse de l'effet-personnage permet de saisir le fonctionnement narratif des personnes réelles présentées dans la presse people, essentiellement saisies à travers le prisme voyeuriste du "lu", où le "désir de voir, de connaître, conduit très vite dans des territoires défendus" (Jouve 1992, 90). La perception que le lecteur peut avoir de ces personnes conditionne de manière centrale la consommation de ces articles. Les trois fonctions que Reuter attribue au personnage se retrouvent aisément dans la scène médiatique people. Il lui assigne d'abord un rôle de marqueur typologique, puisque le personnage "différencie le récit des autres types de textes (descriptif, argumentatif, etc.) et contribue à spécifier des sous-catégories narratives (les genres)" (Glaudes et Reuter 1998, 16). Cela permet d'identifier les rôles de cette scène: la vedette du show-biz, l'aristocratie, mais aussi, depuis quelques années, les personnalités politiques.

Si le personnage sert à distinguer le type narratif des autres types discursifs, il permet aussi d'identifier le sous-genre narratif dans lequel s'investit le lecteur. Ici, le doute n'est pas permis, tous ces personnages, sans exception, appartiennent aux mêmes groupes sociaux, réunis par la fortune, la naissance ou l'activité liée au monde du spectacle dans des espaces spécifiques liés à la fête et au divertissement, réservés à un public privilégié. Le personnage people, ainsi identifié, permet de distinguer ce type de récit médiatique des autres lieux d'information, et sert de marqueur typologique du genre people.

Il y a donc bien des personnages spécifiques de la scène people, qui appartiennent à des groupes sociaux aisément identifiables par tout un chacun, et qui apparaissent aussi de manière privilégiée dans la presse people. En outre, ces personnages sont saisis dans des mises en scène propres à leur caractère people (accent sur la vie privée, et tout particulièrement la relation amoureuse, attributs positifs, place prépondérante de l'émotion…). Dès lors, si le personnage est aussi un organisateur textuel, deuxième trait retenu par Glaudes et Reuter, on verra que le personnage people, c'est-à-dire tel qu'il est mis en récit dans la presse du même nom, appelle certains types de scénarios, souvent stéréotypés et organisés de manière feuilletonnesque. Puisque ce type de magazines n'a pas pour priorité la présentation d'informations nouvelles relatives à des événements significatifs, il peut se démarquer des faits réellement attestés et construire des scénarios dont la trame narrative utilise de manière récurrente les mêmes scènes stéréotypées. Ainsi, lorsqu'ils intègrent des figures issues de la sphère politique, comme cela se pratique de plus en plus couramment, ces journaux ne doivent pas les inscrire dans un scénario portant sur la gestion par ces personnages de la chose publique (campagne électorale, conflits internationaux, questions sociales et économiques…), mais ils déportent ces actants politiques vers des thématiques et des scénarios qui relèvent de la scène people: naissance heureuse (photos de Ségolène Royal prises à la maternité pour *Paris Match*), amours multiples (Nicolas Sarkozy avec Cecilia, puis avec Carla Bruni), séjours de vacances sur des plages ensoleillées (de Villepin, Royal, Sarkozy), mais aussi séparations douloureuses (Royal tout comme Sarkozy). La couverture de *VSD*, à la mi-août 2006, propose à la fois « Charlène à Monaco », la nouvelle conquête du prince Albert, et un "Duel au soleil", avec un photo-montage de Ségolène Royal et Nicolas Sarkozy, tous deux en maillot de bain sur la plage.

Quand Sarkozy est élu président en mai 2007, pour *Paris Match*, il réalise "le rêve d'une vie". Le terme n'est guère éloigné de celui employé par Barack Obama dans le titre d'un de ses ouvrages, *Dreams from my father*. Mais les drames aussi forgent le personnage. Ainsi, lors des élections anglaises de 2010, David Cameron évoque la mort de son fils de six ans, atteint d'une maladie grave, dans le *talk show* "ITV1's Tonight Spotlight on the Leaders". Dans tous ces cas de figure, quand une nouvelle catégorie de personnages entre dans les pages people, elle doit prendre les attributs du genre. Ce fut le cas avec les grands entrepreneurs, c'est désormais vrai pour les politiques. Ils ne peuvent plus parler politique, ils doivent entrer dans un nouveau système sémiotique et narratif, qui privilégie les thématiques relatives à la vie privée, aux drames humains, en sélectionnant les événements porteurs de *human interest*, comme disent les découpages en rubriques américains. Et ce type d'événement doit être scénarisé selon des modèles canoniques: la rencontre coup de foudre, les amours contrariées, la fin tragique, la scène de tromperie ou de rupture, en privilégiant quelques procédés narratifs constitutifs du genre: le suspense, le rebondissement, le secret dévoilé. Le traitement journalistique people des amours et morts princières a ainsi toujours suivi les modèles des contes et légendes, comme si la continuité des figures (de Cendrillon à Diana) facilitait les filiations narratives. Ainsi, sur les douze unes que *Paris Match* consacre à Nicolas Sarkozy depuis son élection de 2007, neuf sont centrées sur sa vie amoureuse, une sur sa famille, et deux à son travail de président.

Si *Point de vue* et *Royals* s'intéressent aux drames humains des dynasties européennes, ils sacralisent aussi les gouvernants issus des élections, mais selon la même trame. "Nicolas Sarkozy & Carla Bruni. Ils vont se dire OUI. En Jordanie avec Aurélien, le fils de Carla, le bonheur tout simplement. Dans un mois à peine, on les dit même unis pour le meilleur...", éditorialise *Point de vue* le 8 janvier 2008, après une couverture titrée "Leur coup de foudre pour la vie". Et les magazines people les suivent. Puisque la couverture de *Paris Match*, le 3 janvier, montre "Les amoureux du Nil. Baisers, fous rires, gestes tendres. L'album de leurs vacances", tandis que celle de *Gala*, du 9 janvier, montre "Carla si fière de la bague de Nicolas... Pour les fêtes, elle lui a offert une montre, il l'a couverte de bijoux; c'est l'heure des fiançailles!" L'emploi même des prénoms, outre la proximité qu'il veut créer avec le lecteur, atteste du glissement du président de la République dans une autre galerie de personnages, puisqu'il a changé de rôle, en glissant de la rubrique politique aux pages people. On parle de Nicolas (Sarkozy) de la même manière que de son ami Johnny (Hallyday). Ce tutoiement gagne d'ailleurs la sphère politique elle-même, puisque lors de la rencontre entre les présidents français et américain en avril 2010, les deux hommes s'appelaient par leur prénom devant les journalistes, pour témoigner de leurs convergences de vues.

Il y a donc une stratégie relationnelle mise en œuvre par les intéressés eux-mêmes. C'est ainsi que Nicolas Sarkozy "a développé des techniques empruntées aux médias de divertissement comme l'humour, la proximité avec les journalistes, critiqués et choyés, ou la recherche du scandale qui, depuis une dizaine d'années, renforce la notoriété au lieu de détruire les carrières, effet surprenant du nouveau régime de médiatisation, celui de la visibilité indispensable" (Maigret 2008, 33).

## Personnage et identification

Ce type de glissement est aussi dû à la troisième fonction affectée au personnage par Glaudes et Reuter: "Le personnage est, pour les scripteurs et les lecteurs, un lieu d'investissement de leur expérience psychologique et sociale" (Glaudes et Reuter 1998, 16). Le personnage people devient, presque par essence, une figure d'identification ou de projection pour les lecteurs. Pour Vincent Jouve, le personnage romanesque n'est ni complètement réel, ni complètement irréel: il en va de même pour le personnage people, mais en sens inverse. Johnny Hallyday, Britney Spears, la famille princière de Monaco, tout comme Ségolène Royal ou Nicolas Sarkozy sont des personnes réelles, mais saisies quasiment comme des personnages de fiction, des créatures de papier, et surtout d'images saisies à la dérobée. S'il est peu discutable que le président Sarkozy existe et a une vie dans la réalité, il faut cependant admettre que la quasi-totalité des téléspectateurs et lecteurs de journaux ne le découvre que par les récits de presse qui le présentent à l'attention de l'opinion. Ils n'en connaissent, et n'en connaîtront jamais que ce qu'en disent les médias. Et ceux-ci construisent le personnage selon des critères de vraisemblabilité.

La figure de François Mitterrand a été présentée comme un héros de roman. *Paris Match*, le 10 novembre 1994, "lève le voile sur le dernier mystère de la vie romanesque du président" quand il relate "le bouleversant récit d'une double vie". L'écriture narrative, recourant aux stéréotypes et aux référents fictionnels, est également employée pour le portrait "Qui est vraiment Ségolène Royal?" rédigé dans *Gala* par Daniel Bernard en 2006. L'accroche en est significative:

> Elle nous est devenue tellement familière qu'on l'appelle affectueusement "Ségo". Avec son sourire de Mona Lisa, elle séduit peu à peu des Français de tout bord. Enfance, couple, vie familiale, patrimoine. On vous dit tout sur cette femme forgée par ses blessures intimes.

Le portrait est d'ailleurs complété par le thème astrologique de cette Balance "dotée de charme", titré "Les astres lui veulent du bien". Née sous une bonne étoile donc, la jeune femme s'est construite seule, pour devenir "une mère référence", la compagne aimante d'un autre battant politique, une femme engagée, une battante… Une nouvelle héroïne pour un public en attente de figures à admirer.

Cette logique de construction médiatique des personnages people, qui pourrait apparaître choquante, s'explique si l'on accepte que l'information, ici, ne réside pas dans l'événement, mais dans sa mise en récit. Dès lors, son critère de pertinence n'est plus de l'ordre de la vérité mais du vraisemblable. Et notre rapport aux grandes figures médiatiques ne fonctionne guère différemment de celui que nous entretenons avec les héros de fiction. Les personnalités présentées dans les médias servent aussi, et peut-être d'abord, de surfaces d'investissement, avec lesquelles nous établissons des rapports de type affectif (lorsque nous maîtrisons la relation établie) ou pulsionnel (quand nous succombons à l'illusion référentielle).

Si le personnage, dit Vincent Jouve, assure la cohérence textuelle, sur base de *frames* (le *frame* est une structure de données qui sert à représenter une situation stéréotypée), ce qui permet l'anticipation par référence à des situations stéréotypées, celui-ci fonctionne aussi comme lieu d'investissement pulsionnel. Dès lors, le code affectif prime le marquage idéologique (le désir est un vecteur de sympathie privilégié, et le plus sympathique est celui qui s'ouvre le plus au lecteur). Cela explique pourquoi le terme "désir" est récemment entré dans le discours politique, puisque le site Web de la candidate Royal s'appelait "Désirs d'avenir". Le lecteur de la presse people active moins sa capacité de rationalisation, d'interprétation critique (le "lectant") que des formes d'investissement plus affectives (le "lisant"), voire pulsionnelles (le "lu"). L'objectif de la presse people est bien de créer un effet immédiat, intense (Lits 1999), ce qui est le propre de la sensation (là où le sentiment s'inscrit dans la durée). Effet qui n'est bien sûr pas dénué d'intentions mercantiles, puisque ce type de magazine s'achète davantage au numéro que par abonnement, dans une pulsion créée par le choc photographique de la couverture. Ce n'est donc pas tellement le contenu informationnel qui doit attirer le lecteur que l'effet de réception marqué, passant par les stratégies de la révélation, de l'émotionnel, de l'intrusion dans la vie privée. Le lecteur de la presse people est confronté à ses propres pulsions, qui se retrouvent de manière quasi archétypale dans tous ces articles, et peuvent servir à expliquer la fascination des lecteurs pour ce type de magazine.

Si le personnage est mort, il n'est pour autant pas impossible d'encore accéder à son intimité. "Mitterrand. Ce qu'il confiait à son psy…" annonce la Une de *Gala* le 23 novembre 2005. Ainsi, "un psychoroman plein de petits secrets" confiés au psychanalyste Ali Magoudi sera lui aussi révélé au lecteur, comme un "formidable thriller psychanalytique". On y apprend ainsi que Mitterrand "voyait en Thatcher l'image de sa mère", on évoque "sa situation conjugale complexe", "l'amour fusionnel qu'il entretenait avec Mazarine, son unique fille", voire "ses rapports avec Dieu".

## Humaniser les politiques

Cette professionnalisation des acteurs politiques qui ont appris à maîtriser leur communication, cette personnalisation qui peut aller jusqu'à l'exhibition de leur vie privée se manifeste aussi dans les médias audiovisuels. L'homme politique s'est adapté, il sort du cadre jugé étriqué des émissions politiques, et accepte (voire sollicite) les invitations dans des programmes de divertissement. L'interviewer n'est plus un journaliste mais un animateur, qui cherche à produire un spectacle attractif, en évitant la polémique, les débats de fond, au profit d'une mise en avant de la personnalité de l'invité. C'est l'homme (ou la femme) qu'on veut donner à voir, et à aimer, non le programme du parti qu'il représente. Mais la personne publique peut aussi, dès ce moment, être saisie comme un people, sans même l'avoir sollicité. À ce moment, c'est moins leur programme que les politiques proposent à des citoyens que leur image qu'ils tentent de vendre à des consommateurs (Sennett 1979). Le people aurait ainsi contaminé l'expression politique.

L'argument des tenants de l'ouverture maximale à la dimension privée tient en deux points: les hommes politiques sont des personnages publics; montrer leurs aspects plus privés les humanise. Cela les oblige aussi à sortir de la langue de bois et à adopter un "parler vrai". Mais ce type de traitement repose la question du rôle et de l'image de l'homme politique dans la cité. La figure en majesté n'a plus lieu d'être, ni le discours de célébration. Ce qui est en jeu, c'est la transformation du système politique classique remplacé progressivement par une démocratie de l'opinion ou du public. *Gala* deviendrait ainsi un concurrent du *Monde* dans la fabrication d'un espace public de moins en moins délibératif. La couverture médiatique du politique montre que les modèles journalistiques, mais aussi les types discursifs utilisés, que ce soit le narratif, le dialogue ou l'argumentatif, sont en train de se transformer. Et qu'avec eux se transforment les rapports au politique. Quand les candidats à l'élection présidentielle française avancent comme argument premier leur plastique avantageuse, leur foulée sportive sur une plage à la mode, il y a lieu de s'interroger sur ces modifications de la communication politique. Mais il faut interroger ces évolutions sans a priori, sans stigmatisation.

Le constat semble pessimiste, en ce qu'il annoncerait la fin d'un modèle opératoire pour expliquer le rôle classique des médias dans la construction d'un espace public communément partagé. C'est un constat à dresser avec la même prudence qui conduit Georges Balandier, dans *Le Pouvoir sur scènes*, à refuser de croire à la fin du politique:

> Selon certains, le politique s'est totalement dissous dans le médiatique; ce serait donc la fin du politique [...] et, parallèlement, s'accomplirait sous les effets de la surmodernité la fin du social, l'effacement des relations structurées et des groupements établis dans la durée. [...] Selon d'autres, au contraire, la télévision publique permet l'avènement de la "démocratie de masse". [...] Chacune de ces théories opposées pratique l'oubli d'une donnée permanente: le politique ne disparaît pas, il change de forme; il ne

disparaît pas parce qu'il est indissociable du tragique toujours présent, en tout temps, dans toutes les sociétés (Balandier 1992, 169).

Si le politique ne disparaîtra pas, le journalistique et le médiatique non plus. Ce qui n'empêche que le paysage médiatique est amené à se recomposer autrement. De même que la presse écrite doit réinventer ses modes d'intervention sous la pression de la télévision, d'Internet, de l'arrivée de la presse gratuite, elle doit aussi prendre en compte la contamination de l'information people, plus ou moins assumée. En ce sens, un examen plus approfondi de la construction des personnages people, dans la presse du même type et dans la presse d'information généraliste, permet de mieux comprendre le sens de ces transformations, ce qu'elles disent des changements de société, des rapports sociaux.

## Politique et populaire

Si les politiques voient leur style se modifier sous l'influence de la presse people, ils sont aussi amenés à glisser dans des logiques d'intervention qui les rapprochent des modes d'expression relevant des catégories du populaire, et ne sont donc jamais loin non plus du populisme. Jan Baetens identifie trois traits spécifiques de la culture populaire:

> La culture populaire semble refuser tout ce qui touche de près ou de loin à la distance: c'est une culture qui exige la participation, (…) c'est une culture qui insiste non seulement sur le corps, mais aussi et surtout sur le plaisir, (…) le grand écart entre la pauvreté apparente des objets que produit ou affectionne la culture populaire et la grande densité des significations dont ces objets se trouvent revêtus (Baetens 2005, 72).

Ces trois traits semblent antithétiques du fonctionnement politique qui prône la réflexion et la critique plutôt que l'adhésion béate, qui privilégie les échanges intellectuels et se méfie toujours de la corporalité et de la jouissance, qui se projette dans des objets symboliques fortement marqués, comme en témoigne le goût des chefs d'État pour l'érection de grandes bibliothèques et de musées. Mais c'était le cas dans les modèles politiques classiques que des dirigeants actuels mettent à mal. Nicolas Sarkozy affiche plus de sympathie pour Johnny Hallyday que pour *La Princesse de Clèves*. Il se sent proche du monde du spectacle, il apprécie le contact direct avec les gens, par le toucher, mais aussi par la parole directe (allant jusqu'aux invectives). Il affiche son goût pour les programmes télévisés plutôt que pour les arts légitimés. Dès lors, les trois traits qui seraient spécifiques de la culture populaire peuvent très bien s'appliquer à l'analyse de ses interventions sociales. Là où les présidents précédents affichaient leur goût pour la littérature, en publiant des anthologies de poésie (Pompidou, qui sera imité plus tard par de Villepin), en participant à des émissions littéraires comme "Apostrophes " (Mitterrand et Giscard d'Estaing), en publiant des essais et des mémoires (de Gaulle ou Mitterrand), voire des romans (Giscard d'Estaing), en entrant même à l'Académie française (Giscard), l'actuel chef de l'État préfère fréquenter les salles de spectacle de variétés et côtoyer les vedettes du *show business*. Il s'inscrit ainsi très clairement dans une culture populaire, à la fois par goût personnel, et par volonté de proximité avec un public populaire.

Cela peut sembler bénéfique, en termes de popularité, et donc de résultats électoraux, d'autant plus que le people est plutôt rassembleur. Celui-ci joue dans le registre du privé, de l'affectif, en privilégiant le consensus, le glamour, l'admiration, comme en témoignent les émissions télévisées et les magazines spécialisés dans les "*royalties*". Tout le monde s'aime (sauf les couples en instance de séparation), tout le monde est merveilleux, alors que le champ politique apparaît comme un terrain de luttes fratricides, entre adversaires politiques, mais aussi entre les différentes factions d'un même parti. Le gain semble donc indiscutable, quand les amours du président occupent les unes des journaux, plutôt que les dissensions politiques ou les annonces de mesures d'austérité. Mais il est aussi fragile, comme le montre la fin de mandat difficile du président Sarkozy. Le réel ne peut être aussi facilement évacué, les enjeux politiques, les conflits sociaux reviennent toujours sur le devant de la scène. Le *storytelling* peut donc se vendre comme une nouvelle mode de marketing politique, aux frontières du populisme, mais au moment où les sociologues en font l'analyse, il semble déjà dépassé comme modèle de gestion des affaires de l'État. Comme le disait Balandier, le politique ne disparaît jamais, et le *storytelling* n'a sûrement pas réussi à l'occulter.

Mais le *storytelling* peut aussi emprunter de nouvelles formes, plus complexes. Pour revenir à l'exemple du président Sarkozy, sa stratégie de fin de mandat a sans doute été plus subtile. Le *storytelling* n'a pas été entièrement abandonné, il est plutôt pris en charge par les réseaux sociaux, sur lesquels des proches peuvent toujours alimenter le *buzz*, tandis que le discours officiel assure la légitimité de la fonction. Ainsi, il est possible de développer deux stratégies en parallèle: la communication explicite reprend les traits des campagnes classiques tandis que le *storytelling* est devenu viral, ce qui relève d'une stratégie plus complexe qu'il n'y paraît, adaptée à différents types de publics et de formes de contacts. Le *storytelling* ne serait donc peut-être pas dépassé, mais il se nicherait dans des formes de communication hypermédiatiques. Aujourd'hui, tous les journaux proposent de pleines pages sur l'usage de Twitter par le personnel politique en campagne, ils invitent aussi leurs lecteurs à *chatter* avec les candidats, et relayent les déclarations pseudo-intimes qu'ils ont déposées sur leur page Facebook.

À l'heure où les réseaux sociaux deviennent un lieu central pour toucher de nouveaux publics, souvent peu intéressés par la politique, c'est à travers ces nouveaux outils de communication que se construisent (ou se déconstruisent) des images politiques. L'exemple récent du *tweet* envoyé par la nouvelle campagne du président Hollande, récemment élu, à la candidate aux élections législatives Ségolène Royal (et ex-compagne du président) montre bien que ces réseaux sociaux renforcent la perméabilité entre les dimensions publique et privée des personnalités politiques. Ces réseaux sociaux jouent même un rôle nouveau, dans la mesure où ils peuvent très rapidement dévoiler et faire circuler des images défavorables à l'*ethos* construit par le candidat. Vidéos datant de la jeunesse, images de prestations maladroites oubliées de tous, séquences les tournant en ridicule, par exemple parce qu'ils ont fait une chute, voire détournements satiriques de leurs propos et de leur attitude: tous ces matériaux audiovisuels contribuent à construire une contre-image du candidat sur laquelle il n'a aucune prise, et face à laquelle toute dénégation ou toute condamnation ne ferait que renforcer son impact et sa circulation.

Ces nouveaux usages, qu'ils soient contrôlés par les politiques et leurs conseillers, ou qu'ils circulent sur internet sans leur contrôle, par des détournements d'images, des parodies ou des scènes de vie privée volées, révèlent tous la même chose: les personnages politiques restent les éléments moteurs du discours politique médiatisé, mais ils contribuent aussi à construire, à travers leur mise en scène publique, une certaine représentation du politique, et donc de nouvelles formes de relation entre les citoyens et les politiques. Celles-ci sont davantage fondées sur la relation directe (ou pseudo-directe) qui s'établit avec une personne perçue proche, sur l'histoire que raconte cette personne, sur l'incarnation qu'elle réalise d'un programme jugé abstrait. La mise en intrigue, au sens ricœurien du terme, devient le passage obligé d'un projet politique qui doit être diffusé sous la forme d'un grand récit médiatique mettant en scène un acteur politique qui va l'incarner aux yeux du public, en jouant un rôle qui refuse la distance, qui privilégie le contact, y compris dans l'exhibition de traits privés. L'intrigue politique, ce n'est plus le fait de comploteurs cherchant à renverser des adversaires, c'est devenu l'art de raconter en histoires imagées, incarnées par une figure forte, le projet de société d'un parti.

## Références

Baetens, Jan. "La culture populaire n'existe pas, ou les ambiguïtés des *cultural studies*." *Hermès*, 42 (2005): 70-77.

Balandier, Georges. 1992. *Le Pouvoir sur scènes*. Paris: Balland.

Bellemin-Noël, Jean. 1983. *Les Contes et leurs fantasmes*. Paris: Presses Universitaires de France.

Charaudeau, Patrick. 2008. *Entre populisme et peopolisme. Comment Sarkozy a gagné!* Paris: Vuibert.

Couégnas, Daniel. 1992. *Introduction à la paralittérature*. Paris: Seuil.

Glaudes, Pierre et Reuter, Yves. 1998. *Le Personnage*. Paris: Paris, Presses Universitaires de France.

Jouve, Vincent. 1992. *L'Effet-personnage dans le roman*. Paris: Presses Universitaires de France.

Lits, Marc (ed.). 1997. "Le récit médiatique", *Recherches en communication* 7.

—. 1999. "La sensation", *Médiatiques* 16.

—. 2005."De la culture populaire à la culture médiatique. Marchandisation et mondialisation", *Recherches Sociologiques*, 2-3: 77-98.

—. 2008. *Du récit au récit médiatique*. Bruxelles: De Boeck.

Maigret, Éric and Macé, Éric. 2005. *Penser les médiacultures. Nouvelles pratiques et nouvelles approches de la représentation du monde*. Paris: A. Colin.

Maigret, Éric. 2008. *L'Hyperprésident*. Paris: A. Colin.

Migozzi, Jacques. 2010. "*Storytelling*: opium du peuple et / ou plaisirs du texte?", *French Cultural Studies*, 21(4): 247-55.

Pilhan, Jacques (entretien avec). 2005. "L'écriture médiatique", *Le Débat* 87: 2-24.

Salmon, Christian. 2007. *Storytelling. La machine à fabriquer des histoires et à formater les esprits*. Paris: La Découverte.

—. 2009. *Storytelling saison 1: chroniques du monde*. Paris: La Découverte.

Sennett, Richard. 1979. *Les Tyrannies de l'intimité*. Paris: Seuil.

# CHAPTER SIX

# ON THE ART OF PLOTTING, AND THE READER AS CO-CONSPIRATOR: PIERRE SIGNAC'S *MONSIEUR CAUCHEMAR* (1960)

DAVID PLATTEN

Still the coolest of popular literatures, crime fiction is exalted. The imagination and craft of the practitioner is routinely admired, and by virtue of its thematic elasticity and the cultural authority afforded to its major figures - Manchette in France, Ellroy in the States, Mankell in Sweden - the genre has periodically interested the higher brow. However, the strength of the assumption that by dint of its generic status crime fiction will always be differentiated from the literary mainstream, implying that it exists in its own cultural universe, has ensured that a considered critical discourse has yet to mature. The signs are now more positive. Ideas relating to story, plot, character, and authorial intent, which were seen by much literary theory as prejudicial to serious thinking about literature, have resurfaced. These aspects are sometimes suggested as modes of cognition that help to determine how narrative fiction is read. It is not possible within the confines of this study to venture far into the debate over literary cognition that is currently live in at least two distinct fields of intellectual endeavour: literary studies (broadly defined) and the philosophy of aesthetics. However, this chapter, which will explore how a seminal work of French crime fiction - Pierre Signac's *Monsieur Cauchemar* (1960) - foregrounds the nature of the reader's engagement with the novel, implicitly acknowledges the growing importance to literary criticism and theory of recent work in aesthetics.

## Stories of consequence

Before alighting upon *Monsieur Cauchemar*, some thoughts on the cultural and technical ramifications of stories and storytelling, and of plots and plot-making would seem apposite. Storytelling, or narrativity, has often been juxtaposed with ideology. In 1936 Walter Benjamin lamented the prospective extinction of a species he describes as "tribes of storytellers" (Benjamin 1999, 84), nomads who would bring enlightenment to the people of the places they visited by relating their experiences in the form of stories. Contrastingly, Christian Salmon, in his analysis of storytelling in contemporary western culture, shows how strategists in the spheres of economics, politics, religion and science have flicked an epistemological switch, by opting for narrative modes and particularly for the invention of stories to communicate their messages at the expense of the discourse of reason and logic. Seventy years on, the neutral dispenser of knowledge and wisdom that Benjamin would have retrieved from antiquity in order to challenge totalitarian dogma has evolved into a Rapunzel figure, a hired hand weaving stories like thread to promote the interests of corporate America. Once primarily associated with the creative arts, storytelling now permeates western culture; in Salmon's words: "L'empire a confisqué le récit", a conglomerate of commercial and political interests in the West has staged "cet incroyable hold-up sur l'imaginaire" (Salmon 2007, 20).

The purpose of comparing Benjamin with Salmon was not to erect a false binary but to show that both thinkers, though operative in very different historical contexts, occupy polar positions on the subject of storytelling. Since the dawn of time, stories have been used as vehicles for the dissemination of religious or political messages, the modern news media constantly search for the best stories, advertisers encrypt their messages in stories told in increasingly sophisticated ways, and scientists have become more adept at transforming data into narrative paradigms, allowing non-specialists to apprehend as a story-board complex ideas or processes that would otherwise lie over the horizons of their intellectual competence. Moreover, the infant child's uncanny responsiveness to the storyteller has encouraged educationalists to argue that the human being is genetically primed to process information on the external environment in narrative form. Still, however pervasive this narrative principle may be and however receptive we may be to it, storytelling is but one of many ways of making sense of the world. Like his spiritual ancestors from the Frankfurt School, Salmon underestimates the capacity of the consumer-citizen for critical judgment. The consumer may open a window on this kaleidoscope of stories and be momentarily dazzled, but he or she has learned to step back and analyse narrative by applying precisely those attitudes of logic and sceptical reasoning that the seductive story supposedly overrides. So, in the world of politics the era of the spin doctor, or political storyteller, has proved to be short-lived. And with the advent of social media, especially Twitter and Facebook, which are essentially fora for metacritical debate, the consumer has turned critic.

Salmon's argument echoes the ideas of Hannah Arendt and Paul Ricœur on 'lived' or 'narrative' identities. Ricœur's notion that human identity is intrinsically narrative seems prescient when we consider the taste in recent decades for biography, autobiography and other variants of life writing.[1] Stories are the primary means by which we learn about other people. They are also a possible means by which we reflect on the self, but again not the only one, given that our sense of self is always heavily infused with the present. Narrative exists in a temporal mode and it is in its relation to time that it is fundamentally distinguished from ideology. The former belongs to the past; it consists of the sequencing or organisation of a series of events performed by a more or less tangible agent. As such, the existence of any narrative implies both the communication of meaning and, importantly in so far as this chapter is concerned, the *intention* to communicate meaning. However, the narrative properties of ideologies are often attenuated. The construction of an ideology may have been informed by stories but ideologies are more like buildings; once constructed they tend to last longer in the same form and thus have a greater purchase on the present. Let us draw an analogy between Ricoeur's narrative identity, the sense of a singular, human life demarcated through time, and the set of social dispositions governing our interactions with the external environment that Pierre Bourdieu termed the *habitus*. The former, reassuringly, identifies the subject as the primary creator of identity, whereas for the latter individual identities are socially determined. Yet, to articulate one's narrative identity would seem to be a valedictory act; we

---

[1] Ricœur argues that, just like the narratives of history, our personal life stories are multi-layered and frequently subject to verification and re-interpretation: "La psychanalyse constitue à cet égard un laboratoire particulièrement instructif pour une enquête proprement philosophique sur la notion d'identité narrative. On y voit en effet comment l'histoire d'une vie se constitue par une suite de rectifications appliquées à des récits préalables, de la même façon que l'histoire d'un peuple, d'une collectivité, d'une institution procède de la suite des corrections que chaque nouvel historien apporte aux descriptions et aux explications de ses prédécesseurs, et, de proche en proche, aux légendes qui ont précédé ce travail proprement historique" (Ricœur 1985, 444).

prefer to think of ourselves as political, social and moral beings with individuated tastes and desires, subject to the vicissitudes of time of course, but existing fully within the present. This is also predominantly how we think of character, both in the real world and, more emphatically, in narrative fiction.

Storytelling, or creating narratives, is of course fundamental to the art of the novel, though some novelists set greater store by telling stories than others. An ingenious story more or less defines the genre of detective fiction, such that in discussion of the detective novel the word "plot" will often be substituted for "story". With regard to traditional crime stories, in which the solving of the crime restores order to society, fully grasping the plot is associated with coherence and stability; in the vernacular, "to lose the plot" suggests some sort of mental disorder. E. M. Forster's distinction between "story" and "plot" underscores this idea of unity and well-being:

> Let us define a plot. We have defined a story as a narrative of events arranged in their time-sequence. A plot is also a narrative of events, the emphasis falling on causality. "The king died and then the queen died" is a story. "The king died, and then the queen died of grief" is a plot. The time-sequence is preserved, but the sense of causality overshadows it [...] Consider the death of the queen. If it is in a story we say: "And then?" If it is in a plot we ask: "Why?" (Forster 1927, 87)

Plot-lines change the character of the story, providing causal as well as temporal connections and thereby enhancing narrative coherence. A significant degree of plotting will result both in a compacted narrative with its beginning, middle, and end emboldened and possibly in a corresponding intensification of the reading experience. This stoking of a greater emotional engagement on the part of the reader might be construed as a positive feature of conspicuous plotting. However, where events are tightly linked by cause and effect as well as ordered in temporal sequence, and the internal narrative coherence is thus reinforced, scope for the reader's creative input will be limited. The instantaneous excitement of the page-turner may leave an after-taste of perceptual claustrophobia, the quick fix will lengthen to a gloomy addiction, and the plot-driven narrative will lose its lustre. As Barthes surmises in his erotics of reading: "...toute l'excitation se réfugie dans l'espoir de voir le sexe (rêve de collégien) ou de connaître la fin de l'histoire (satisfaction romanesque)" (Barthes 1973, 20).

Forster's commentary is less partial. In capturing the distinction between "story" and "plot", he establishes the premise that plots are stories of consequence, meaning that they give a strong indication of the author's intention. What does not necessarily follow is that the reader, given a clearer idea of what an author may have wanted to communicate, will automatically abrogate his or her own critical judgment. All artistic undertakings are at root statements of intent yet, read in different times and at different places, the most didactic of narratives, such as the fable or folk tale, can acquire an extraordinary degree of interpretive diversity. Plot-driven narratives may not offer smorgasbords for the kind of intellectual contemplation encouraged for example by the great works of literary modernism; however, by way of compensation they can provide the trigger for an imaginative involvement on the part of the reader, the nature of which interests philosophers of aesthetics as much as literary critics. As we shall see, crime fiction, with its heavy plotting, can offer the wildest of literary adventures.

There is one further aspect to this emphasis on plotting, which concerns the extent to which it bears on the discipline of writing. In a radio interview in 1999, Daniel Pennac, whose novels dominated sales of French fiction over the second period of the Mitterrand presidency, revealed that, before starting to write, he would design his plots on a huge canvas laid out on the floor of his office. Pennac's need was for something to curb his own rapacious wordplay and imaginative deviance, which, he felt, was jeopardising the realisation of the novel. Writing crime novels is (or was), for Pennac, literally a *mise en intrigue*. In the case of Signac and *Monsieur Cauchemar*, the *mise en intrigue*, or emplotment, is more like a *mise en scène*.

## *Monsieur Cauchemar*: the secret of the plot, or the plot of the secret?

Pierre Signac's *Monsieur Cauchemar* is a hidden gem, widely touted by connoisseurs but difficult to find. The author, who amended his pen name to 'Pierre Siniac' (by which he will henceforth be referred to in this chapter), went on to produce a number of highly regarded works - notably *Les Monte-en-l'air sont là!* (1970), *Reflets changeants sur mare de sang* (1980), *Femmes blafardes* (1981) and *Le Mystère de la sombre zone* (1999) - as well as a series of novels starring Luj Inferman and La Cloducque, two misfits modelled on the characters Sam Jaffé and Sterling Hayden in John Huston's 1950 film *The Asphalt Jungle*.

First published as a novel in 1960, *Monsieur Cauchemar* has spawned - and this is perhaps indicative of its cult status - two graphic adaptations: one of the same title produced in 1987 by André Benn; and the other a Tardi-Siniac collaboration entitled *Le Secret de l'Étrangleur*, which was published in 1992 and reissued in 2006, three years after Siniac's death.[2] The *bandes dessinées* are mostly faithful to the plot of the novel that inspires them, a plot which can only be described as skeletal.[3]

The reader is firstly alerted to the importance of the setting, which amounts to three environmental factors: the biting cold of February nights in Paris; an unusual period of weather during which the city at night is enveloped in a thick fog or 'pea-souper' as such fogs used to be known in London during the 1940s and 1950s; and a police force that has gone on strike leaving the streets at night deserted. Notions of causality and motive are immediately diminished, for this triple coincidence offers a once-in-a-lifetime opportunity for a murderer, or serial killer in contemporary parlance - Siniac uses the term "assassin" - to execute a series of manœuvres that have been long in the planning. What then happens in the novel may be appropriately represented as a short, one-act play:

Scene 1: a person scurrying home at night gradually becomes aware through the sound of footsteps echoing his own as he stops and starts that he is being followed;

Scene 2: after a furious chase the intended victim is caught and, as he is being strangled, lets out a blood-curdling scream;

Scene 3: people in a nearby café or pub hear the scream and rush out to find the intended victim who, having survived the attack, is rubbing his tender neck. He reassures everyone that he is OK and that the danger has passed, "A présent, il ne m'arrivera plus rien. C'est fini" (MC, 32);

Scene 4: some time later the body of the intended victim is found in a location not far from the original attack. He has been strangled.

The event becomes a ritual as it is played out on four separate occasions, leaving the reader with four different victims none of whom are known personally to the killer. This ritualistic sequence of analagous procedures and actions is all that remains of what in conventional detective stories would pass for a plot.

The novel flouts generic conventions in a number of respects. Changes in the narrative point of view follow no discernable pattern, as it shifts regularly from assailant to victim to observer. Hence the panic and fear of the victim, who realises that he is being stalked and begins to run, is transmuted into the fear of the methodical strangler that he will fail to achieve his objective, as, huffing and puffing, he struggles to catch up. According to Todorov's classification or "typologie" of the crime novel,

---

[2] All future references to the text of the novel *Monsieur Cauchemar* will be indicated by the abbreviation MC.

[3] The Benn-Siniac version transposes the action from Paris to London, since, in the popular imagination, the latter is more associated with fog.

*Monsieur Cauchemar* cannot be "un roman à suspense", as the reader is not drawn to identify in any more than a casual way with the perspective of each victim. Neither is it a "roman d'énigme", as we find out who is doing it, or rather who appears to be doing it, within the first twenty pages. The strangler is Valentin Esbirol, the owner of the book shop. Moreover, the crimes appear to be motiveless. When Esbirol is asked by the errant schoolboy Francinet, whom he has befriended and who becomes his willing accomplice, why he strangles people, he replies, "Parce qu'il y a du brouillard ... et pas de policiers" (MC, 92). There is little in the way of psychological profiling. Interestingly, Benn the illustrator of one of the graphic adaptations of the novel whitens out the lenses of M. Cauchemar's spectacles, portraying visually the reader's limited access to his mind. Nearly all the characters in the novel are what E. M. Forster would describe as "flat". Indeed some border on village stereotypes. The reader is introduced to the burly butcher with forearms like joints of ham, the gangster's widow who has married the police inspector who sent her first husband to the guillotine, and the precocious schoolboy whose humdrum life contrasts with the excitement and adventure he finds in the books he steals from Esbirol's shop.

As is often the case with Siniac's work, the crime serves up an intellectual conundrum. Why, when having screamed and fought successfully during Phase 1 of the attack, does the victim resign himself to his fate in Phase 2 without so much as a dying gurgle? Esbirol knows that this will be the key to his success. Running through the preparations for his first murder, he reflects that, "La seconde fois, la victime se laisserait tuer par persuasion" (MC, 28). Later he boasts to Francinet that he has discovered the perfect crime, "j'ai trouvé le moyen de tuer mes 'clients' avec leur consentement" (MC, 92). Secondly, and this is also a Siniac trait, though perhaps more marked in *Monsieur Cauchemar* than in his other fictions, interest is concentrated on the staging of the event, as a narrative phenomenon rather than a textual occurrence.

The series of murders is contained within a set time frame, the duration of the foggy spell and/or the police officers' strike. Each killing is described as if it were a singular event, with all the minor variations on the previous iteration detailed, so this is not, as one might have expected, a narrative of diminishing returns in which the same processes are abridged ever more briefly. The four victims are all distinguished by, indeed selected for, their silhouettes or accoutrements that will render them perceptible in the fog: a theatre actor, who quirkily returns home in his stage costume; a blind man with his clacking white stick; a barge-dweller with his boater and swishing waders; and a hunch-backed, white-bearded newspaper seller. The accent is on perception, or to be precise on the visual supported by the auditory. As Jerry Fodor has shown, in order to recognise objects we rely fundamentally on the alignment of certain spatial features that are already banked in our memories;[4] Esbirol embarks on reconnaissance missions prior to each attack in order to identify the victim and track his movements. The spatial features unique to each introduce one element of difference in these narratives of sameness. However, there is a perpetual oscillation between sameness and difference in the successive narrations. Each of the four individuated, spatially-defined victims makes the same mistake, which is to assume that the attack on their person - Phase 1 of the process - is a singular event. Like Proust, Siniac evokes a strong sense of habit and routine. Life is a series of repetitions, not only for the mainstream of society but also for those existing at its margins, be they actors in a theatre like Malinguet, the first victim, addicts like Esméralda, the alcoholic *chiffonnière*, who finds a blood-stained newspaper with the "Monsieur Cauchemar" headline cut out of it, or Esbirol himself, a compulsive killer. No logical reason exists for the victims to suppose that having survived one attack, they will not be attacked again, in fact quite the contrary. They ought to expect Phase 2, but they don't. As elsewhere in his fiction, Siniac insists on the normalisation of violent crime. The actions of "Monsieur Cauchemar" are rapidly assimilated to the discourse of the everyday, discussed in shops and cafés and anticipated by the screaming headlines of the local press.

The other element of difference concerns the increasing involvement in the perpetration of the crimes of the truant schoolboy Francinet, only this aspect of the novel is framed within a different context. *Monsieur Cauchemar* exhibits a literary self-consciousness, which does not divert the reader into esoteric worlds far removed from the fog and the darkness of the strangler but is instead anchored to the experience of one character, whose relationship to books and particularly to works of crime fiction reanimates the plot, by providing it with much needed momentum.

Francinet is an avid reader of crime, mystery, and adventure stories. His "soif de mystère et d'émotion" (MC, 44), a thirst not slaked in the safe environment of the family home where he is banned from reading

[4] Fodor conceives of reality as a series of inputs that are processed by the mind, which, in itself, has an inbuilt "modularity" or perceptual mechanism, akin to Chomsky's theory of generative grammar. So, although an organism generally sees what is there and not what it wants or expects to be there, the perception of novelty depends on "bottom-to-top perceptual mechanisms" (Fodor 1983, 68). Or, as he succinctly puts it, "You can't hear speech as noise *even if you would prefer to...*" (Ibid, 53).

unsuitable literature, causes him to miss school on a regular basis and attracts him instead to Esbirol's bookshop: “Mais comment résister à l'attrait de toutes les merveilleuses histoires qui dormaient dans ces tas de papier!” (MC, 42), his inner voice exclaims. Admiring Francinet's passion for the subject, Esbirol tolerates his light-fingered approach to browsing, remarking “Il finira flic, assassin... ou auteur de romans policiers” (MC, 42).

This then is a crime novel, in which one of the main characters is a keen reader of crime fiction, a passion which inevitably results in him taking on the mantle of putative investigator. Viewed in this light, Francinet personifies Wolfgang Iser's concept of the “ideal reader”. He is confronted with what Iser terms “la discontinuité narrative”, the impasse in the plot created by the repetitive series of murders and especially by the intellectual conundrum, our not-knowing the secret of the strangler. Prompted by an acute curiosity to discover the secret thereby solving the conundrum, Francinet plays an increasingly central role in determining the course of events, in a manner which approximates to - indeed could be said to dramatise - Iser's theoretical account of the reader's participation in the novel: “La discontinuité du récit fait que le lecteur est amené à produire lui-même ce qui rend vivante l'action décrite: il se met à vivre avec les personnages et subit avec eux les événements dans lesquels ils sont impliqués” (Iser 1976, 333).

Francinet's role evolves from that of precocious reader of crime fiction - novels by Agatha Christie and William Irish as well as the adventures of Sax Rohmer's notorious villain, Dr Fu-Manchu - to strangler's accomplice, taking him from interested bystander to the heart of the action. Thus Siniac specifically highlights the affective dimension of popular fiction, the implication being that writers of popular fiction or storytellers should always aim for the complete appropriation of their reader's imagination. In a press interview, New York-based crime novelist Harlan Coben declared: “J'écris des livres d'immersion [...] Lorsqu'un lecteur lit un livre, c'est un univers entier qui prend vie” (Coben 2010, 8). In *Monsieur Cauchemar* Siniac deploys his schoolboy *ingénu* to draw his reader into his imaginary world. The paths of literature and of Monsieur Cauchemar run in parallel before converging in the character of Francinet. Excited by Esbirol's revelation, Francinet expresses his hope that there will be more murders via literary analogies: “Si seulement, pensa l'enfant, il pouvait s'agir d'une série de crimes ... comme dans *Six hommes morts* ou *Dix petits nègres*” (MC, 50). Within a fairly short space of time Esbirol has persuaded him to cross the threshold and accompany him, in order to witness his literary fantasies transformed into reality: “Non, crois-moi”, he says, “... Tu vivras un véritable roman criminel et tu me verras assassiner un passant" (MC, 72). Literary fiction is about to become lived experience.

Gregory Currie has written of how consumers of fiction (novels, films, or televison series) engage with stories by aligning their mental processes with the minds of characters represented on screen or in print. This kind of imaginary simulation best describes, according to Currie, what happens when we read novels or watch films. However, it falls short of total immersion; Currie insists that the consumer's mind runs "off-line", disconnected from its normal sensory inputs and behavioural outputs (Currie 1995, 144). In the case of Francinet, Currie's distinction is abolished. The imaginary book-world of the schoolboy seeps out and into Francinet's "behavioural outputs". He finds himself huddled in the shadows of a doorway, a wide-eyed, trembling onlooker as Esbirol accomplishes his dastardly deed, and then literally racing to discover the secret of the strangler that lies in the pages of a forbidden text, Esbirol's own unpublished opus, entitled *Le Secret de l'Etrangleur*. And the real reader, you and I, begins to worry about Francinet and what will become of him. Then something extraordinary happens.

## The reader hypnotised?

On Page 161 Siniac intervenes in his own novel, exposing the so-called mimetic illusion deemed indispensable to all popular fictions and infringing the "contract" between author and reader which is implied in all detective or crime narratives:

### Entracte

> Nous avons pensé ajouter quelque intérêt à ce récit (tout en innovant une formule que d'autres écrivains policiers pourraient appliquer dans certaines de leurs œuvres) en proposant au lecteur trois dénouements différents.
>
> Voici ces trois fins.
>
> L'AUTEUR

This authorial intervention a la Laurence Sterne offers three different endings: "Fin qui pourra laisser le lecteur sur sa faim"; "Happy end"; "Explications rationnelles de faits apparemment inexplicables".

The temptation is to read it as a postmodern conceit in keeping with a novel which toys with questions of readership, and with an inventive writer who pushes against the boundaries of the genre. But the argument is not congruous. Crime fictions demand narrative unity above all else. In contrast to John Fowles' *The French Lieutenant's Woman* or Italo Calvino's *If on a winter's night a traveller*, both of which resist narrative closure, Umberto Eco's *The Name of the Rose*, which supplies, in the guise of a detective fiction, a guided tour through the history of knowledge in the west, has one climactic ending. In the case of the inconclusiveness of *Monsieur Cauchemar*, the splintering or trifurcation of the plot may not necessarily deny the reader the satisfaction of an ending. Here personified by Francinet, the reader is implicated in the plot but (also like Francinet) she or he is a reader of crime fiction. Signac's authorial intervention breaks the spell of the fiction thereby reaffirming his or her role as, to borrow a term used by Jacques Migozzi, the *storyplayer*, no longer Francinet the frightened schoolboy but Francinet the avid reader of crime novels, ready at this climactic moment to play his part in "la dynamique constructive et protectrice du jeu" (Migozzi 2010, 254).

In the field of the philosophy of aesthetics there has been much reflection on intersections between the categories of fictional narrative, character and reader. For example, Ismay Barwell suggests that narratives without conclusions are simply not meaningful, though he concedes that many narrative performances rely on the contributions of readers and watchers in order to bring them to conclusions (Carroll 2009, 58). In a scintillating essay Currie promotes the epistemological status of narrative, describing it as "able to represent richly individuated temporal and causal connections between motivation, decision and circumstance in ways that other representational forms cannot match" (Carroll 2009, 63). This vitality, he argues, is largely determined by character delineation. As the key vectors for their maker's intent, characters are, to Currie's way of thinking, the "inner source of action" (Carroll 2009, 61) within narratives. Since they are devised to express intention, fictional characters also may seem to evince richer, more rounded personalities than their real-life counterparts. Although in life our knowledge of the other is provisional, in fiction the reader enjoys a privileged relationship with those he or she meets. Writing specifically on detective fiction, Alvin H. Goldman astutely observes that, in striving to solve the mystery, the reader is often required to imagine him or herself as characters with whom he or she may not naturally identify.[5] In *Monsieur Cauchemar* the identification between reader and character is mutually exclusive; the reader of the crime novel is equated with the character who reads crime novels.

Excepting Francinet, Siniac maintains a detachment from the characters in his novel. In his book *The Uses of Literacy* (1957), which warns of the imminent rise of mass culture in Britain, Richard Hoggart sees popular fictions as existing in an ironic relation to the lives of those who consume them. Of course the model here is Emma Bovary, who tries to adapt her life to her fantasies gleaned from the pages of romance fictions. In *Monsieur Cauchemar* the relationship of the sensationalist crime story to the adventures of Francinet is also depicted in ironic mode; for example, at one point Esbirol imitates Francinet's parents as he pretends to chide his young protégé for reading "trop de romans policiers". However, Siniac reserves his "bovarisme" for another character, who is presented in glorious counterpoint to the *polar*-loving schoolboy. In a delicious sub-plot, Francinet's stepfather Inspecteur Budé stumbles across a prime piece of evidence, a blood-stained newspaper with the "MONSIEUR CAUCHEMAR" headline cut out of it. Budé, a pompous, judgemental man takes it upon himself to investigate the case of Monsieur Cauchemar. He whittles down the suspects to three customers who would have bought faux filets wrapped in newspaper on the previous Tuesday morning from the local butcher's. And the most likely of these suspects is Esbirol. However, forewarned by Francinet, Esbirol is able to prove his "innocence" and cleverly removes himself from the frame. Standing in the doorway of the butcher's shop, a crestfallen Budé, whose has just seen his great chance of making a name for himself evaporate, is captured in a sublime sentence, studded with Flaubertian commas, which brings the curtain down on his involvement in the story: "Et l'inspecteur, sur le pas de la porte du 'Paradis du Bœuf', regarda, navré, la longue perspective de la rue" (MC, 129).

When Siniac makes his surprising proposition, he is confident that his reader will not be marooned like Budé, looking broken-hearted down a long, empty road. It is, of course, the terrified Francinet who is recuperated. The three endings signify the return of the plot, or rather the manifestation of three phantom plots, what Pierre Bayard calls "une réserve d'hypothèses" (Bayard 1998, 47), the invisible, virtual narrative

[5] Goldman argues that the detective genres incline readers to inhabit the personalities of characters with whom they would not normally associate: "What is most engaging to our imaginations and most broadening of our horizons is to be able to identify with or think like characters very different from us" (Goldman 2011, 267).

streams running beneath the text of the classic *roman policier*. If the reader is jolted from the foggy streets of his or her hypnosis, this is firstly to make the point that going beyond immersion into a state of hypnosis can be dangerous - the secret of the strangler could be Esbirol's ability to hypnotise his victims - and secondly to remind him or her that the reader of crime fiction will always be required to exercise his or her critical judgment.[6] Siniac's intervention heralds a type of literary ingenuity that, as he and others subsequently discovered, the crime genres can accommodate. It also places a trust in his reader, that he or she will make the right choice of ending and eventually find the plot.

## Works cited

Barthes, Roland. 1973. *Le Plaisir du texte*. Paris: Seuil.
Bayard, Pierre. 1998. *Qui a tué Roger Ackroyd?* Paris: Minuit.
Benn-Siniac. 1987. *Monsieur Cauchemar*. Grenoble: Glénat.
Benjamin, Walter. 1999 (1937). *Illuminations*. London: Pimlico.
Carroll, Noel (ed). 2009. *The Poetics, Aesthetics, and Philosophy of Narrative*. Oxford: Wiley-Blackwell.
Coben, Harlan. 2010. *Le Monde*, 19 mars, 2010: 8.
Currie, Gregory. 1995. *Image and Mind: Film, Philosophy and Cognitive Science*. Cambridge: Cambridge University Press.
Fodor, Jerry. 1983. *The Modularity of Mind*. Cambridge Mass./ London: M.I.T Press.
Forster, E. M. 2000 (1927). *Aspects of the Novel*. London: Penguin.
Goldman, Alvin H. 2011, "The Appeal of the Mystery", *The Journal of Aesthetics and Art Criticism* 69.3: 261-272.
Iser, Wolfgang. 1976. *L'Acte de lecture. Théorie de l'effet esthétique*. Bruxelles: Pierre Mardaga.
Migozzi, Jacques. 2010. "Storytelling: opium du peuple et/ ou plaisirs du texte?", *French Cultural Studies* 21 (4), 254.
Ricœur, Paul. 1985. *Temps et Récit 3: le temps raconté*.Paris: Seuil.
Salmon, Christian. 2007. *Storytelling, la machine à fabriquer des histoires et à formater les esprits*. Paris: La Découverte.
Signac, Pierre. 1960. *Monsieur Cauchemar*. Paris: Denoel.
Tardi-Siniac. 1992. *Le Secret de l'étrangleur*. Paris: Editions du Masque.
Todorov, Tzvetan. 1971. *Poétique de la prose*. Paris: Seuil.

---

[6] This invitation to the reader to exercise his or her judgement is made explicit in the Tardi-Siniac adaptation, where the three endings are sealed. In order to reveal them, the reader must have recourse to a paper knife.

# PART II:

# STORY/HISTORY

# CHAPTER SEVEN

# LES NOMADES DE LA PREHISTOIRE: PERSONNAGES, RECITS, IMAGES ET LECTEURS

MARC GUILLAUMIE

En hommage à Nancy Huston, nous voudrions ici examiner cette capacité propre à notre espèce: celle de créer, et surtout de répéter des histoires. Car c'est ainsi seulement qu'elles deviennent fabulae, des fables au sens où on parlait autrefois de "la Fable grecque", la mythologie.

Les romans préhistoriques stricto sensu (RP) seront ici les récits qui racontent une histoire censée se dérouler dans la Préhistoire, par opposition aux voyages dans le temps et aux histoires de mondes perdus (Guillaumie 2006, 23-27). Ils représentent une production ininterrompue depuis qu'il existe des sciences de la préhistoire. Ils comptent quelques best-sellers diffusés à des millions d'exemplaires, comme *La Guerre du feu* (Rosny 1911) ou la série étasunienne *Earth's Children* (Auel 1980-2011). D'après les éditeurs, *The Clan of the Cave Bear* (Auel 1980) aurait été le premier roman dont la première publication a dépassé le million d'exemplaires. Si l'on pense aussi aux films[1] et bandes dessinées[2] à grand succès, alors on voit que ce minuscule domaine a son importance: Roger Lécureux, qui n'a pas fait que Rahan, aurait été le scénariste de bande dessinée le plus productif de tous les temps! La vulgarisation scientifique aussi, a toujours eu recours à la fiction et au

---

[1] Don Chaffey, *One Million Years B.C.*, Great Britain, Hammer Films, 1966. Scénario Michael Carreras. Avec Raquel Welch et John Richardson.
Jean-Jacques Annaud, *La Guerre du feu/Quest for Fire*, France et Canada, AMLF, 1981. Scénario Gérard Brach "d'après Rosny Aîné collection Rouge et or" [*sic*]. Avec Everett Mc Gill et Ron Perlman. Conseillers: Anthony Burgess, Desmond Morris.

[2] Roger Lécureux et André Chéret, *Tout Rahan*, 22 albums, Soleil, 1998-2000. Réédition de "Rahan fils des âges farouches", série parue entre 1974 et 1988 dans *Pif* et *Rahan*.

récit. Enfin, songeons aux jeux, aux détournements parodiques ou publicitaires.

En dépit des références scientifiques qu'il affiche, le RP met en scène un monde qui est presque inconnu. Les rares traces matérielles recueillies par les savants ne peuvent que suggérer des hypothèses sur les univers sociaux et mentaux disparus. Le récit concerne une période qui, par définition, n'a pas laissé de récit: le romancier est contraint d'inventer. Cela ne signifie pas qu'il est libre. L'ignorance de ce qu'a pu être la Préhistoire réelle oblige le créateur à puiser (pour être compris, édité) dans les idées reçues sur une Préhistoire désirable ou idéologiquement utile au moment où il crée. Il y a donc d'un récit à l'autre circulation d'images, de situations narratives, de figures conformes à l'air du temps.

Depuis vingt ans, quelques universitaires s'intéressent à ce petit genre (Stoczkowski 1994, Lysøe 1994, Cohen 1999) et des livres lui sont même consacrés (Ducros 2000, Bulliard 2001, Benhaïm 2004). Mais il reste peu exploré; c'est encore un genre naïf et sûr de lui: ainsi le romancier Marc Klapczynski (Klapczynski 2004) rejette la plupart des idées que nous énonçons. Selon lui, le RP s'appuie essentiellement sur des savoirs, qu'il se contente de romancer;[3] mais Élie Berthet disait la même chose au XIXè siècle (Berthet 1884, 8); pourtant les RP de Berthet illustrent, aux yeux du lecteur d'aujourd'hui, bien davantage l'idéologie que les sciences de son temps.

Nous allons voir que dans le RP la combinatoire des aventures est limitée; que le "vrai" qu'il énonce concerne davantage l'imaginaire que les sciences, et bien davantage notre époque que la Préhistoire; enfin que le RP, dans son activité (af)fabulatrice, recycle d'un support à l'autre, d'un genre à l'autre et d'un siècle à l'autre les mêmes récits et les mêmes images.

# I. Plaisirs de l'image et du texte

## L'aventure, mais le sérieux

Il est un plaisir du conteur ou de l'artiste, et de son lecteur (ou spectateur) que nous voudrions d'abord souligner. Conscient que la fiction préhistorique est essentiellement une fabulation (préparée souvent par une documentation sérieuse), le méticuleux et talentueux auteur de bandes

---

[3] Propos tenus au festival "Écrire la Préhistoire ", 18-19 août 2008, parc de la Préhistoire de Tarascon-sur-Ariège.

dessinées Emmanuel Roudier[4] nous a confié que c'était moins la mise en scène des aventures qui l'intéressait, que la peinture des paysages. De même, que serait le western sans les paysages? Ce sont bien les paysages étranges et les ciels dramatiques des illustrations de *La Guerre du feu* dans la collection "Rouge et or" qui non seulement donnent le ton du récit, mais fascinent, et font tomber l'enfant lecteur dans l'histoire.

Le héros de RP s'aventure sur des savanes inconnues. Entraînant le lecteur à sa suite, il pénètre les jungles et remonte les fleuves: il s'approche de quelque mystérieux Cœur des ténèbres, et les plaisirs troubles de l'identification au héros dans une situation angoissante sont provoqués chez ce lecteur, qui n'a pas choisi par hasard cette période obscure.

Comme dans les romans de chevalerie, l'espace dans le RP est composé d'îlots humains cernés par la forêt. Domaine des monstres, elle est hantée par des fauves géants, par des tribus inconnues. C'est le lieu de toutes les découvertes (géographiques, amoureuses) et de tous les dangers: le lieu de l'épreuve.

Il y a curieusement peu de science de la préhistoire dans le roman préhistorique. *La Guerre du feu*, par exemple, ne décrit pas la taille des silex: on ne voit cela ni dans le roman de 1911, ni dans le film de 1981 qui dispose pourtant de conseils "scientifiques". En revanche, le sérieux s'impose dans de nombreux passages consacrés à la géologie, la botanique, la zoologie – bien que souvent imaginaires ou extrapolées. Ici le RP ressemble aux romans du capitaine Mayne Reid: le plaisir de la découverte de terres inconnues s'accroît, pour le lecteur, du plaisir supposé sérieux que procure la vulgarisation scientifique.

## La peur, mais la distance

Les images qui accompagnent le RP (illustrations, couvertures) ou qui mettent en scène une Préhistoire fictive (gravures, films) sont dominées par le gigantisme et l'étrangeté, elles suggèrent la violence et souvent la dévoration. Ainsi les amusantes illustrations d'un livre de fiction savante (Boitard 1861) montrent, avant même qu'existent vraiment les sciences de la préhistoire (mais la paléontologie était déjà ancienne) des fauves issus d'une hypertrophie de nos gentils animaux familiers: un matou préhistorique terrasse un éléphant, un caniche dévore un lion. Les

[4] Emmanuel Roudier, *Vo'Hounâ*, 3 albums, Soleil, 2002-2004; *Neandertal*, 3 albums, Delcourt, 2007-2009; *La Guerre du feu*, 3 albums à paraître, Delcourt 2012.

anachronismes comiques ne sont pas l'apanage du XIXè siècle: en témoignent les innombrables combats de Rahan contre des dinosaures. La Préhistoire, c'est le gigantisme, l'étrangeté, la violence. Ainsi les mammouths, du XIXè au XXIè siècle, sont dans la fiction toujours surdimensionnés.

Ce plaisir de la peur s'accompagne du plaisir d'être rassuré: la Préhistoire est une époque révolue. A cette distance temporelle protectrice s'ajoute une distance spatiale quand les monstres passent devant les héros sans les voir, scène récurrente dans le RP. Les images des volcans d'Auvergne en activité le montrent bien aussi: il s'agit de provoquer chez le spectateur une inquiétude passagère, sans gravité. Et si ces volcans se réveillaient? Mais non, ils sont éteints.

On ne peut s'empêcher de soupçonner l'auteur (et le lecteur que nous sommes) d'une fascination infantile ou morbide, de la recherche d'un plaisir régressif. Le RP est animé d'un double mouvement, il obéit à deux impulsions contradictoires: orienté vers une fin heureuse, progressiste et globalement "de gauche", il suscite pourtant ces délectations troubles qui naissent des évocations malsaines: meurtres, viols, éviscérations sont toujours condamnés, mais toujours présents chez les vieux auteurs "farouches" ... comme chez notre contemporaine, la bien-pensante Jean Auel.

## L'imaginaire, mais la vérité scientifique

Les intrigues dans le RP s'inspirent de l'idéologie du moment: à l'époque des conquêtes coloniales, Rosny mettait en scène des gestes épiques qu'il pimentait de quelques viols inter-raciaux; aujourd'hui que le discours social condamne la violence raciste ou machiste, la supposée "féministe" (Rigaud 1991, 10-11) Jean Auel met en scène une société plus apaisée… mais elle non plus, ne peut éviter de montrer des viols inter-raciaux. Ces deux visions opposées de la Préhistoire ont peu de fondement en science, et doivent l'essentiel au discours social dominant. Leurs étonnants points communs (les viols) viennent des nécessités narratives: comment montrer dans un récit qu'une société imaginaire est bonne, si l'on ne montre pas les pratiques mauvaises qu'elle interdit ?

Pourtant, jamais le RP ne renonce à ses références savantes. Que ce soient des notes en bas de pages dans le premier RP de Rosny *Vamireh* (1891), des déclarations liminaires chez Élie Berthet, ou aujourd'hui des préfaces rédigées par un préhistorien télégénique (Coppens 1990), la caution scientifique est sollicitée explicitement ou non pour tous les RP.

Étrange storytelling romanesque, qui se prétend dépendant des sciences, et se voudrait presque non littéraire!

**Finding the plot, I**: Dans le RP, qui est souvent un roman d'aventures, il existe un nombre limité de rapports possibles pour constituer l'intrigue. Ils sont réductibles à la fonction centrale d'appropriation ou de prédation (conquête d'un abri, d'un territoire, d'une femme, d'une technique, d'une proie) et susceptibles de se combiner par enchâssement, réciprocité, causalité, etc.: par exemple dans *La Guerre du feu*, les Oulhamr tuent des chacals pour en utiliser les peaux, afin d'approcher les Kzamms sans éveiller leur odorat et de dérober leur feu; mais les Kzamms veulent manger les Oulhamr. Ici le feu symbolise toutes les techniques, et permet au romancier de contourner la difficulté repérée par Jack London dès 1906: comment le RP peut-il montrer, pendant la vie d'un personnage fictif, une évolution technique qui fut très probablement millénaire? Ces contraintes narratives font que l'on rencontre souvent des similitudes: il y a des "Hommes du Feu" féroces chez Jack London (London 1907) comme dans *Le Félin géant* (Rosny 1919).

## II. Destinataires et contenus

### Notre Europe et notre monde

Le RP semble suivre respectueusement les découvertes scientifiques sur le terrain: au XIXè siècle il montrait la vallée de la Vézère; aujourd'hui il montre aussi les bords du lac Turkana. Ce respect n'est qu'apparent. En réalité, le RP met les sciences au service de ce qu'il a à montrer, lui, et qui ne relève pas des sciences. Ainsi Élie Berthet met en scène au fil de ses quatre RP l'évolution du site de la future ville de Paris, où presque rien n'avait été alors découvert. En montrant des lieux familiers ainsi transfigurés, le romancier veut provoquer l'étonnement et ne se soucie guère des sciences. Madame Stanislas Meunier dans son RP bardé de références (souvent trompeuses) fait faire à son héros un tour du monde, prétexte à un exposé des découvertes dans tous les pays. Mais cet exposé est orienté, ses références implicites sont celles de la France revancharde: quand le héros quitte son pays et traverse le Rhin, il rencontre des géants blonds féroces (Meunier 1893). Ernest d'Hervilly, dans son RP destiné aux enfants, multiplie les admonestations sous prétexte de science: ainsi, il ne faut pas que les petits lecteurs ressemblent aux hommes préhistoriques, dont l'auteur sait de science sûre qu'ils étaient très sales! (Hervilly 1887). Cette amusante pseudo-science n'est pas réservée au XIXè siècle. Anthony

Burgess, qui a inventé des langues pour le film de Annaud, explique comment parlaient les Oulhamr (Ulams dans le film): "[…] on sait qu'ils ne pratiquaient pas une langue à clicks, ni une langue tonale comme le chinois"[5]. C'est de nous que parle le RP, et non pas des préhistoriques. C'est à nous qu'il s'adresse, pour nous donner des leçons. Il ne se réfère au passé que pour mieux parler de notre présent, et même du futur vers lequel nous devrions tendre.

## Ton histoire, ô lecteur !

Burgess insiste sur la leçon universelle que contient *La Guerre du feu*: le vrai sujet du film, c'est la solitude de l'homme. Les premières images, saisissantes, montrent la lueur d'un feu lointain, dans l'effrayante forêt nocturne. On pense aux gravures d'Émile Bayard pour le livre de Louis Figuier (Figuier 1876, 51): "Une caverne pendant la nuit, à l'époque du grand ours et du mammouth"; ou à celles de Manuel Orazi pour la première parution de *La Guerre* en feuilletons en 1909: "Parmi les pierres géantes et les grands arbres". Plus amusante, une image du livre de Camille Flammarion qui montre des animaux disparus répugnants et en partie imaginaires a pour légende: "Tous ces êtres qui ont précédé l'homme et qui sortent aujourd'hui de leurs tombeaux [grâce à la paléontologie] ne semblent-ils pas des monstres? Pourtant ils sont rattachés à nous par des liens originels." (Flammarion 1886, 97). Rapprochons-la de cet extrait du Sottisier de Bouvard et Pécuchet cité par Claudine Cohen (Cohen 1999, 206):

> Un préhistorique
> Ciel atroce – loups – cabanes sur pilotis – grotte.
> Portrait de l'homme – ours.
> Il viole une femme
> Il tue un homme pour la violer
> Mange l'homme, - et comme la femme en veut un morceau, il la tue, mange et s'endort tranquille.
> C'est ton aïeul, ô Parisien du XIXè siècle.

Parfois, avec moins d'humour mais avec une force saisissante, Edmond Haraucourt prend soudain à partie le lecteur de son roman:

> Je n'invente rien: j'essaye de me rappeler. Vous aussi vous vous souvenez, mais vous ne le savez pas. Écoutez, qu'on vous aide. Vous portez, dans vos

---

[5] *La Guerre du feu*, photos, chronologie de la réalisation, interviews: plaquette s.l.n.d., édition AMLF.

> nerfs et dans votre sang, l'imprescriptible survivance de ce que vous fûtes jadis, en la personne des plus lointains aïeux.

Haraucourt explique le présent par la Préhistoire: "Les violations de la règle, que nous désignons sous le nom de crimes et de vices, ne sont que les réminiscences d'un temps où l'égoïsme animal avait tous les droits." (Haraucourt 1914, 41, 225).

## La Préhistoire est toujours latente en Europe…

Ray Nyst explique, dans la longue "Introduction documentaire" de son RP (Nyst 1909), que si la pression de la civilisation se relâchait, alors les troupeaux redeviendraient sauvage; le lion remonterait vers le nord… Ce frisson délicieux, auquel Rosny dans ses écrits théoriques ne répugne pas de se livrer aussi, est sans doute la marque d'une époque inquiète: la vieille Europe conquérante se sentait pourtant menacée, elle peinait à soutenir "le fardeau de l'homme blanc", et le thème de la dégénérescence obsédait les auteurs de RP comme les autres écrivains, les médecins et les anthropologues. Mais ce frisson est aussi (car ici rien n'est univoque) la marque d'une vitalité violente, d'un esprit d'enfance: ce retour possible du lion évoqué par Nyst (lui-même chasseur de fauves) est presque désiré par cet écrivain qui, comme Rosny, déplore les ravages de la civilisation, destructrice de la vie sauvage.

## …et vivante en nous !

Dans la limite de nos lectures, il nous a semblé que la Préhistoire était souvent plus sombre ou plus risible chez les écrivains de langue anglaise. Plusieurs héros de Jack London entrent en Préhistoire après une régression terrifiante. Certains auteurs anglophones semblent marqués par une répugnance masquée par l'humour: Kipling met en scène des hommes préhistoriques comiques dans *Just so Stories* (1902), comme le fait London dans *The Strength of the Strong* (1908). Pensons aussi à Desmond Morris (autre conseiller de Annaud) qui dans son livre de vulgarisation *The Naked Ape* (1967) avait insisté sur les similitudes un peu répugnantes entre le comportement humain et celui des grands singes, multipliant les allusions croustillantes sous couvert de franc-parler éthologique. En France et en-dehors du RP, on trouve chez les romanciers des allusions explicites à l'abominable violence préhistorique: les crises de fureur de Jacques Lantier ont leurs origines dans la Préhistoire (Zola 1977 [1890], 86, 228, 416, 419).

**Finding the plot, II**: La lecture du RP est donc aussi une opération de décodage, de repérage des indices somatiques et culturels de l'évolution humaine, de reconnaissance de ce qu'il faut penser. Pour cela, le lecteur dispose des connaissances courantes de son temps: quelques éléments tirés des théories des aliénistes et des criminologues permettaient au lecteur ou au spectateur du XIXè siècle de comprendre ce que suggérait, dans un RP ou sur une image, telle structure crânienne. Aujourd'hui, la Vulgate des idées reçues ayant changé, le lecteur a à relever des indices différents: par exemple le (supposé) respect de la Nature qu'avaient les préhistoriques, chez Jean Auel. L'Autre vit encore en nous: le roman peut avoir une tonalité effrayante, voire fantastique. Le romancier s'aventure avec ivresse dans des temps presque inconnus, tout en prétendant effrontément s'en remettre aux sciences. Le lecteur ou le spectateur subit avec délices cette fascination.

Dans beaucoup d'images contemporaines, les préhistoriques tournent vers le spectateur un regard pensif. Ces humains fictifs sont notre miroir; silencieusement, ils nous interrogent sur ce que nous avons fait des promesses de l'espèce humaine. Chacun sait bien que l'image ment, de ce "mentir vrai" qui est propre à la fiction (les "reconstitutions" savantes sont ici aussi menteuses que les fictions; davantage même, puisqu'elles ne se présentent pas comme fictives). Pourtant le spectateur bascule dans cette image vertigineuse pour dialoguer avec son double.

## III. Une littérature populaire?

### Lectures au tournant du siècle

Dans les RP de la fin du XIXè siècle et du début du XXè, la distraction agrémente l'instruction: c'est le cas dans le RP de Hervilly déjà évoqué. Il propose au jeune lecteur des leçons morales et sociales: les paysans sont plus proches que nous du préhistorique; et certains sauvages "tout à fait primitifs" d'aujourd'hui, eux, sont encore des hommes préhistoriques. Dans la revue *Je sais tout*, qui publia en feuilletons *La Guerre du feu* en 1909, le roman voisine avec la vulgarisation scientifique et des reportages sur le bagne, l'exploration de l'Afrique, les grandes chasses, la répression des révoltes coloniales et la surveillance policière des bas-fonds. Cette imprégnation préalable à l'acte de lecture du RP prédéterminait sans doute le sens du roman-feuilleton. Les images établissent aussi un parallèle entre Préhistoire et actualité: un "pilou-pilou de Canaques" s'organise exactement comme les farouches danses des cannibales préhistoriques; un criminel célèbre présente des traits néandertaliens... "Si la géographie ça sert à faire la guerre, alors l'anthropologie, ça sert à faire la chasse à l'homme" (Chamayou 2010). Tous ces récits ou images tirés des sciences, de l'actualité, des idées reçues et de la fiction montrent bien l'activité de lecture comme construction du monde, selon le mot de Paul Ricoeur cité par Jacques Migozzi.

## Adaptations et relectures

Nomades, les images et les récits passent d'un support à un autre, d'un domaine à un autre. Nous avons vu qu'à la fin du XIXè siècle, les images étaient capables de migration des sciences ou de l'actualité vers la fiction, et réciproquement. Ces migrations d'images et de récits ont lieu aussi de cette époque vers la nôtre. Ainsi par exemple la main tenant un silex: elle apparaît dans un livre du préhistorien Gabriel de Mortillet, où elle a une fonction explicative, illustrant l'idée que certains outils n'étaient pas emmanchés. On retrouve cette main dans le RP d'Élie Berthet, où elle illustre sans explication une autre époque et un autre sujet. Aujourd'hui, revisitée par un designer, elle sert d'emblème au musée de Tautavel. Le combat contre l'ours est un autre exemple de ces images nomades: il est montré par de nombreux graveurs du XIXè siècle, par le peintre Franz Roubal dans les années 1930, et aujourd'hui dans des "reconstitutions" et dans de multiples bandes dessinées. Le fauve se tient debout au seuil de la grotte; il a saisi ou il a abattu un chasseur; mais un autre va porter le coup décisif. Scène dramatique dont personne ne peut témoigner qu'elle ait eu lieu un jour, mais dont les détails sont fixés dans l'imaginaire depuis le XIXè siècle.

Le récit lui aussi est nomade. Par exemple, quand *La Guerre du feu* est-elle devenue un livre pour enfants? Elle ne l'était certainement pas pour les lecteurs de *Je sais tout* (juillet 1909) ni pour ceux de la première édition en volume (Fasquelle 1911). La mention "roman des âges farouches" apparaît plus tard (Plon-Nourrit 1927, Nelson 1951, Gedalge 1952, Dauphin 1952, GP "Rouge et or" 1959) et disparaît ensuite. C'est dans ces années que le texte semble le moins respecté, puisqu'un éditeur (Gedalge) opère des coupures non signalées. Les illustrations de couverture révèlent des erreurs de lecture (Plon-Nourrit, Dauphin) ou une lecture qui met en valeur les grands coups de massue (Nelson). A partir des années suivantes, une reconnaissance nouvelle apparaît: il existe des éditions soignées (Fasquelle 1960, Club français du livre 1963), des éditions préfacées par des préhistoriens (Fasquelle, Hachette 1980 "Le livre de poche", Hachette "Jeunesse" 1994) ou par des littéraires (*Romans préhistoriques*, Laffont "Bouquins" 1985). Il y a désormais deux circuits distincts: certaines éditions sont destinées aux adolescents et aux enfants (MDI "Jeunesse" 1964, Hachette "Jeunesse", Nathan "Aventure" 1994) et *La Guerre du feu* est proposée en classe de Cinquième dans les années 1990; mais d'autres éditions sont destinées à des lecteurs adultes, désireux de connaître la Préhistoire ou feignant d'en être désireux (Fasquelle, Club français du livre), ou encore peut-être ironiques, avides de savourer le charme suranné de ce roman vieillot (Laffont "Bouquins"). Les célèbres adaptations en bande dessinée par Pellos (1976) et au cinéma par Annaud (1981) ont peut-être marqué ce tournant. Ainsi ce roman aux enjeux évolutionnistes très complexes, écrit dans une langue précieuse, a glissé vers les bibliothèques des collèges avant de revenir par un tout autre biais parmi les lectures savantes.

*La Guerre du feu* est mentionnée comme lecture d'enfance par certains préhistoriens: elle est à l'origine de leur vocation. En particulier, l'édition "Rouge et or" illustrée par Jean Chièze a marqué de nombreux lecteurs.

## Dénigrements, parodies et reprises

Un autre plaisir pervers de lecteur est la dénonciation rituelle des idées reçues sur la Préhistoire, et la condamnation subséquente des romans comme *La Guerre du feu*: c'est-à-dire, nous l'avons vu, les romans dont l'idéologie est jugée simpliste, parce qu'elle ne correspond plus aux idées les plus simplistes de notre époque. L'accusation de simplisme est ancienne, et Rosny ou London, qui en sont victimes aujourd'hui, la dirigèrent jadis vers d'autres auteurs qui les avaient précédés. La parodie, l'humour, la gauloiserie et la farce sont depuis longtemps aussi des ressources offertes au scénariste soucieux de se distinguer de ses prédécesseurs, ou de montrer qu'il n'adhère pas entièrement au message idéologique de la fiction. Ainsi Matthieu Bonhomme parodie, dans les premières vignettes de sa belle bande dessinée.[6] un tableau de Zdenek Burian si célèbre qu'il a été plagié sans scrupule depuis les années 1950 dans des revues de vulgarisation, sur des timbres-poste, etc. Un peu plus loin, Bonhomme détourne une des scènes de *La Guerre du feu*  le héros court vers un troupeau de mammouths pour échapper à ses ennemis; l'alliance avec les puissants mammouths va retourner la situation! Mais les mammouths de Bonhomme se contentent de barrir, agacés. Pourtant, l'adhésion au registre épique reste puissante. Le héros prométhéen, porteur de lumière et père de toutes les techniques (le préhistorique brandissant une torche) apparaît dans les gravures de Manuel Orazi (1909), dans les

[6] Matthieu Bonhomme, *L'Âge de raison*, 1 album, Carabas, 2002.

images finales du film de Annaud, dans de multiples vignettes de Rahan, et dans le film de vulgarisation *L'Odyssée de l'espèce*[7] (2002). Nulle solution de continuité entre roman, film et bande dessinée, entre vulgarisation et fiction, entre XIXè et XXIè siècles. Dans *L'Odyssée de l'espèce*, l'histoire de Lucy démarque un roman déjà ancien de Pierre Pelot, illustré par l'auteur de bandes dessinées Liberatore (Pelot 1990).

**Finding the plot, III**: Le récit préhistorique se veut storytelling global de l'humanité, "roman de l'homme" comme titrait un vulgarisateur, ou encore "odyssée de l'espèce". Les auteurs rêvent parfois de concurrencer la Genèse, dont souvent ils suggèrent une relecture selon eux plus conforme aux sciences. Certains savants s'aventurent sur ce douteux terrain et proposent, qui une explication géologique du Déluge, qui une origine neurologique du Mal. Avec aplomb, le RP et une large part de la vulgarisation scientifique revisitent les mythes. Ils ne se limitent pas aux mythes chrétiens: le temps où les bêtes parlaient, l'Âge d'or, les figures de Gaïa et d'Orphée leur sont familières aussi. L'Odyssée est convoquée, comme on l'a vu. Même l'épopée romaine a été discrètement démarquée.[8] "Finding", c'est ici surtout retrouvailles. Les sciences cherchent, la fiction préhistorique ressasse: par les réinterprétations, les adaptations, les parodies, elle retrace sans cesse les voies anciennes par où étaient passés les auteurs du XIXè siècle. Ce ressassement inlassable des mêmes canevas, des mêmes situations, des mêmes types héroïques, évoque le plaisir qu'ont les enfants à écouter les contes. D'ailleurs les ténèbres et la dévoration, constitutifs du RP bien davantage que les sciences, ont beaucoup à voir avec les peurs enfantines.

## Conclusion

Ainsi le RP, la fiction et la vulgarisation préhistoriques, du XIXè siècle jusqu'à nos jours, offrent un nombre limité de combinaisons narratives et de figures. Loin d'avoir pour vocation d'exposer les découvertes ou de refléter la vie préhistorique, ces récits sont orientés vers nous, lecteurs. Récit des origines qui explique et justifie le présent, qui donne des directives, le RP correspond à ce que Mircea Eliade appelle un mythe. Il n'y manque pas même la croyance: c'est ici, ici seulement, que

---

[7] Jacques Malaterre, *L'Odyssée de l'espèce*, France, France 3 éditions, 2002. Scénario Jacques Dubuisson et Michel Fessler, direction scientifique Yves Coppens.

[8] Dans *La Guerre du feu*, Naoh triomphe des trois "Velus" grâce à la tactique d'Horace contre les Curiaces.

le RP a besoin des sciences auxquelles il feint de se soumettre, avec une modestie ostentatoire. Georges Dumézil associe en outre le récit mythique à des rites. Dans le cas de la fiction préhistorique, le rite c'est le spectacle: spectacle et récit associés sont appris ou vus à l'école, répétés à la maison, vus au cinéma, revus à la télévision, réadaptés sans cesse aux modes du moment et aux nécessités idéologiques.

Pastichant *Il superuomo di massa* d'Umberto Eco, nous résumerons ainsi l'intrigue de tout RP: le passé, la bestialité, le monde sauvage jouent; l'espèce humaine joue et gagne. Reprise inlassable du même "grand récit" sur le même canevas, le RP s'adapte cependant à l'air du temps avec plasticité. Au temps des conquêtes coloniales et de la lutte contre les calotins, il mettait en scène des cannibales et des sorciers pervers. Au temps des inquiétudes écologiques, des revendications féministes, du respect des peuples "premiers" et des nouvelles spiritualités, il met en scène de sages chamanes respectueuses de la nature. Mais sous ces oripeaux divers, toujours on retrouve ces grandes figures nomades de la Préhistoire que sont Hercule, Prométhée, Caïn, la Dame aux bêtes...

## Références


Auel, Jean M. 1980. *The Clan of the Cave Bear*. New York: Crown.

—. 1982. *The Valley of Horses*. New York: Crown.

—. 1985. *The Mammoth Hunters*. New York: Crown.

—. 1990. *The Plains of Passage*. New York: Crown.

—. 2002. *The Shelters of Stone*. New York: Crown.

—. 2011. *The Land of Painted Caves*. New York: Crown.

Benhaïm, André et Lantelme, Michel (dirs.). 2004. *Écrivains de la préhistoire*. Toulouse: PUM.

Berthet, Élie. 1884 [1876]. *Paris avant l'histoire*. Paris: Furne Combet et Boivin.

Boitard, Pierre. 1861. *Études antédiluviennes: Paris avant les hommes, l'homme fossile, etc.* [sic]. Paris: Passard.

Bulliard, Mélanie. 2001. *L'Enjeu des origines: les romans préhistoriques de J.-H. Rosny Aîné*. Lausanne: Archipel.

Chamayou, Grégoire. 2010. *Les Chasses à l'homme*. Paris: La Fabrique.

Cohen, Claudine. 1999. *L'Homme des origines: savoirs et fictions en préhistoire*. Paris: Seuil.

Coppens, Yves. 1990. "La première histoire d'amour du monde" dans Pelot, 1990.

Ducros, Albert et Jacqueline (dirs.). 2000. *L'Homme préhistorique: images et imaginaire*. Paris: L'Harmattan.

Figuier, Louis, 1876 [1870]. *L'Homme primitif.* Paris: Hachette.
Flammarion, Camille, 1886. *Le Monde avant la création de l'homme.* Paris: Marpon et Flammarion.
Guillaumie, Marc, 2006. *Le Roman préhistorique: essai de définition d'un genre, essai d'histoire d'un mythe.* Limoges, PULIM.
Haraucourt, Edmond, 1988 [1914]. *Daâh le premier homme.* Paris: Arléa.
Hervilly, Ernest d'. 1887. *Aventures d'un petit garçon préhistorique en France.* Paris: Librairie mondaine.
Huston, Nancy. 2008. *L'Espèce fabulatrice.* Paris: Actes Sud/Lemeac.
Klapczynski, Marc. 2004. *Aô l'homme ancien.* Anglet: Aubéron.
London, Jack. 1907. *Before Adam.* London, New York: Macmillan.
Lysøe, Éric, 1994. "La Guerre du feu, une vision épique de l'évolution" dans Rosny Aîné, 1911.
Meunier, Madame Stanislas, s. d. [1893]. *Misère et grandeur de l'humanité primitive.* Paris: Picard et Kaan.
Nyst, Ray, 1909. *La Caverne: histoire pittoresque d'une famille humaine de vingt-neuf personnes, filles et garçons, petits et grands, à l'époque des luxuriantes forêts tertiaires et des saisons clémentes dans l'Europe centrale.* Paris: Baillière.
Pelot, Pierre. 1990. *Le Rêve de Lucy.* Paris: Seuil.
Rigaud, Jean-Philippe. 1991. "Préface" in Jean M. Auel, *Les Enfants de la Terre.* Paris: Presses de la Cité.
Rosny Aîné, J.-H. 1911. *La Guerre du feu.* Paris: Fasquelle.
—. 1919. *Le Félin géant.* Paris: Plon-Nourrit.
Stoczkowski, Wiktor. 1994. *Anthropologie naïve, anthropologie savante: de l'origine de l'homme, de l'imagination et des idées reçues.* Paris: éditions du CNRS.
Zola, Émile. 1977 [1890]. *La Bête humaine.* Paris: Gallimard.

# CHAPTER EIGHT

# CAN A TALE BE TELLING WITHOUT A PLOT? DAUDET AND THE PERILS OF THE POPULAR

TIM FARRANT

## I: The popular, plots and control

This chapter tackles two main themes: first, the search for the plot, in Daudet's *Lettres de mon Moulin* (1869) and the *Contes du lundi* (1873), and in the emergent Grand Narrative of Third Republic France; second, the relationship between those narratives and the popular, as it verges on the populist – even if the latter term did not yet exist.[1]

There is no doubt that the popular, and the popular story, in the sense of the actual or supposed folk-tale, becomes increasingly topical in France by the 1860s. Sand's *Légendes rustiques* appeared in 1858; La Villemarqué's rediscovered, if not entirely authentic, Breton folk-tales, begun in 1839, culminated in 1860; Champfleury's *De la littérature populaire en France: La Légende du Bonhomme misère* in 1861;[2] Zola's 1864 *Contes à Ninon* and Sand's *Contes d'une grand-mère* (1873 and 1876) are more properly literary offspring of the phenomenon.[3] The vogue for the popular is indissociable from regionalism, from folk-

---

[1] *Populeir* dates from the twelfth century, unlike *populiste* (1907) and *populisme* (1912) (*Le Nouveau Petit Robert*).

[2] Villemarqué's first collection of Breton ballads, the *Barzas* [sic] *Breiz*, appeared in 1839, *Contes populaires des anciens Bretons* in 1842, and *Les Romans de la table ronde et les contes des anciens Bretons* in 1860. Champfleury's *De la littérature populaire en France. Recherches et variations sur la légende du Bonhomme Misère* came out in 1861 (having been preceded by collecting, and publishing on, popular images and artefacts: Asfour 2001, 61); Luzel's *Contes et récits populaires des Bretons Armoricains* appeared in 1869, his *Contes bretons* in 1870, his *Traditions orales des Bretons Armoricains* in 1874, and his *Contes populaires de la Basse Bretagne* in 1887.

[3] For a wider contextualization, see Ponton 1991.

narrative, the stories of the people;[4] but in this period, the popular begins to acquire a sense we would more readily recognize, of written as opposed to oral or spoken narrative or tales, widely disseminated and read.[5] Regionalism had been pioneered by Fabre d'Olivet's semi-authentic spotlighting of Occitan in his 1803 verse dialect-collection *Le Troubadour, poesies occitaniques du XIIIe siècle*, and pre-eminently exemplified by *le Félibrige* (launched in 1854), and by its most famous exponent, Daudet's friend Mistral.

In some ways, this burgeoning interest in the popular looks like a development, or even re-run, of the Romantic quest for storytelling authenticity which threads the century from Chateaubriand's *René* (1802) to Maupassant via Barbey's *Les Diaboliques* (1874). It is marked by the replication of popular and / or viva voce narrating contexts in frame stories depicting a tale's relation to a fictional audience. Mérimée's *La Partie de trictrac* (1830) and *Carmen* (1846) are examples, but even novel-length works like Balzac's *Le Médecin de campagne* or Sand's *Mauprat* are frame stories, in the case of *Mauprat* an attempted imitation of peasant *Veillées*, evenings of storytelling and dancing (Lyons 1983).[6] Such narratives seem like symptoms of the anxiety about the loss of oral storytelling voiced by Benjamin ("Der Erzähler", Benjamin 1977), about the novel as fodder for the solitary reader who may seek, but cannot give, counsel. For Peter Brooks, they are a "war against the situation of any text in the modern world" and "a protest against the decontextualization of discourse", seen as inferior to the storyteller, and audiences, in live, *viva voce* interaction. (Brooks 1994, 81, 85).

There is no doubt something in this. The burgeoning interest in the popular, especially the popular story, was doubtless a corollary of the ongoing rise of the novel, with the story, indeed history itself, the very identity of the nation, seen as under threat. As *Le Barzhaz Breizh*'s preface puts it, "On sent battre là le coeur d'une noble race; les poètes nationaux lui ont donné une voix" (La Villemarqué, 1997, 36). La Villemarqué's was only the most prominent attempt to salvage something from the rising tide

---

[4] "*Régionalisme* (1875); de *régional* (1534; rare avant 1848): tendance à conserver ou à favoriser certains traits d'une région, d'une province. – intérêt particulier porté à une région dans une œuvre littéraire; fait de langue propre à une région; système administratif donnant aux régions, aux provinces, une certaine autonomie; voir *décentralisation. Décentralisation* (n.f., 1829; de *décentraliser:* action de décentraliser; son résultat" (*Le Nouveau Petit Robert*).

[5] See Farrant 2009.

[6] See Lyons 1983, 102-114.

of urbanization and print culture (Williams 2007, 41-44).[7] Not that these were undesirable; but the idea that they were lay arguably behind La Villemarqué's (and Mistral's) enterprises,[8] suggesting that beyond this academic interest in the popular lay more than a post-Rousseauesque nostalgia for some narrative state of nature – something closer, perhaps, to a more authoritarian conception of the General Will. Because as soon as the traditions of the people became the subject of antiquarian, scholarly or academic interest, they could not remain "only" academic: they inevitably became part of the discourse and preoccupation of the ruling elite, as a subject of political as well as intellectual concern, and a potential means of social analysis and control. From the *Académie celtique*, founded in 1804,[9] to Champfleury's apparently innocent enterprises in *De la littérature populaire* (1861), to the reactionary revivalism of *Le Félibrige*, supported on occasion by the *Académie française* and the government, the popular becomes corrupted, instrumentalized, turned into an agency of the state. Nisard's 1852 *Commission sur les livres populaires*[10] is an early Second-Empire attempt to take control of the popular, much as are, in the realm of the novel, attempts to regulate the *roman-feuilleton*, from Nettement (*Etudes sur le feuilleton-roman*, 1845-6) and the Second Empire onwards.[11] In this respect, *pace* Brooks and Benjamin, stories and novels were very much in the same boat.

Except when it came to the plot. Because novels, unlike stories, had lost the plot, or rather, had it docked, in 1850, by the *Amendement Riancey*, which imposed duty of one centime on every newspaper publishing a feuilleton as a means of restraining the subversive ideas supposedly spread by serialization; a measure aimed also at incipient Realism; thereby at the popular in the sense of writing that is widely read.[12] It negated that central constituent of Realism, *le romanesque*,

---

[7] Williams 2007, 41-44. The 1833 education act began to bite only in the 1860s when print media (contemporary novels distributed via *colportage*, the 1863 founding and rise of *Le Petit Journal*) began to supplant traditional print media: Price 1987, 143-4, 177-8).

[8] Notably Mistral's: Ponton 1991, 69, 71.

[9] The *Académie celtique* was founded in 1804 in order to discover the authenticand true remains of France; its remit was revised in 1813, when it was renamed the *Société des Antiquaires de France* to include Roman remains and again under Charles X in 1829 when its primary focus became what would subsequently be known as "Nos ancêtres les Gaulois." But its ideologically unifying purpose was constant: it persists today as the *Société nationale des Antiquaires*.

[10] Nisard 1854.

[11] See also Fortoul 1853, and de Certeau 1980, ch. 3.

[12] Nerval, 1989-93, 2 1314; Claudin, 1850, and Dunn, 1983.

identified by Nerval in the 1852 *Nuits d'octobre* (Nerval 1993, 3 314) as well as, potentially, the movement's subversive power. The *Amendement* targetted particularly the era's most successful novelist, and now *député*, Eugène Sue; for whom the *feuilleton* was, in the absence of proper suffrage, "la représentation poétique du peuple."[13]

So the ongoing rise of the novel needs perhaps to be taken with a pinch of salt. Sue's style was hardly cramped by Riancey, and neither were many others; but Nerval's *Les Faux Saulniers* is an ironic example of a novel *en creux*, of what could happen by slavishly obeying (at least apparently) the letter of the law: it is a novel so constrained by regulation that it is virtually content-free. *Madame Bovary*, on the other hand, is more cunning, exploiting the semiotic possibilities of being economical with the truth. The *fiacre* scene, for example, where Emma and her lover Léon are driven around Rouen by a "fureur de la locomotion" on a journey seen only from outside, and whose true nature we can only infer, gave prosecutors some paradoxical problems during the famous trial of Flaubert's novel. The latter's innocence was deftly suggested by comparison with *La Double Méprise*, a novel published nearly twenty-five years earlier by Prosper Mérimée (now a Senator), in which seduction in a carriage is much more explicitly shown.[14] Stories, conversely, escaped such legal strictures, on account of brevity and perceived inconsequentiality; their authors were arguably able to exploit the demand for documentary reportage, accuracy in fact and verisimilitude in fiction apparent in the series of tales of real life produced by Champfleury in the fifties (*Contes domestiques*, 1852), with their subversive echo of Dickens's *Household Words*.[15]

[13] Cf. Lyon-Caen, 2008; Brix, 1999, 95 n.3; Fonyì, 1999, 67 n.5. Nerval's *boutades* against the *Amendement Riancey*, launched in 1850, were repeated in *Les Illuminés* in 1852. Nerval 1989-1993, 2 1313-1327.

[14] "Plaidoirie" in Flaubert 1979, 399-401. Cf. La Capra 1982; Strauss 2002, 826-33.

[15] Dickens stresses the imagination's power, says that "no mere utilitarian spirit, no iron binding of the mind to grim realities" will appear within it: "in all familiar things, even in those which are repellent on the surface, there is romance enough, if we will find it out" (Dickens, 1850). Though Dickens's periodical carries consciousness-raising social criticism as well as narrative, Champfleury, makes a similarly wide-ranging claim for realism in the dedication of the *Contes domestiques* (Lecou, 1852).

## II: Zola and Daudet

In this context, then, young authors, Zola, Daudet, southerners from Aix and Nîmes, could appear as authentic *voix du terroir*, standing outside the academic and institutional system, representing something both traditional and real.[16] Zola exploits a range of fairy-tale and contemporary modes in the *Contes à Ninon*, but never loses sight of narrative; Daudet finds his plot by losing it, by presenting his first series of stories as letters – the *Lettres de mon Moulin* (1869). Zola keeps his narrative driver but only pays lip-service to the provincial: Provence is an Arcadia to which he vows to return but which his stories never actually revisit, mentioning it again only in the preface to the second edition of *Contes à Ninon* (1874 – none of his tales has a Provençal setting[17]); Daudet invokes Provence constantly (though from just outside – Nîmes, capital of the Gard); they are the work of a Provençal *malade de Paris*, who has purged the unhappier aspects of his provincial childhood in *Le Petit Chose*,[18] and who now seeks solitude and solace in his mill. If Paris equals sickness, action, frenzy, Provence means indolence, inaction, losing the plot (i.e. organized action). The *Lettres* begin with the mill's purchase, its bill of sale, and leave us in no doubt that it is a ruin, totally incapable of fulfilling its purpose of milling wheat. But the mill's loss is Daudet's gain: it is also a refuge from and rejection of the modern world, a *Thébaïde raffinée* but *à rebours*, going with rather than against nature, celebrating a *plaisir de vivre* associated with Provence: the lazy days in *Les Vieux* or the idyllic visit to "le poète Mistral."

Yet the *plot/plotlessness, action /inaction* dyad is more complex; these evocations of *paresse* are, of course, nothing of the sort. The *Lettres* are the product of intense industry; the *Moulin* is a *Moulin à paroles*. For all their supposedly innocent, indolent authenticity, the literary is at the centre of the *Lettres* – literally, and nowhere more so, than in *Le Poète Mistral* half-way through. Daudet's account of a visit to his friend and leader of the Occitan *Félibrige* movement makes plain the importance of the literary

---

[16] See Minogue and Pollard 2008.

[17] Indeed, many *Nouveaux contes à Ninon* are striking in lacking a specified setting: it is either undefinedly rural, as in *Les Fraises*, or Parisian by default (*Le Grand Michu*, *Les Epaules de la Marquise*). Zola's very lack of specificity lends his work a symbolic, transcendent quality often absent in Daudet's.

[18] *Le Petit Chose*, after an initially quixotic account of the protagonist-narrator, Daniel Eyssette's, background and upbringing, settles down into a picaresque account of his early experiences as a *pion* in a college in Sarlande – a representative *roman d'apprentissage*.

– but of the literary as a full engagement with life. In this story, Daudet reads his friend's latest poem, *Calendau* (1867); but the real point, we take it, is to see him, and then go out and enjoy the *fête*. But it's all, of course, a plot. *Calendau* is a heroizing of a Provençal fisherman, a small narrative writ large; the literary is at the centre of life, as is storytelling of popular, even populist, ideology. Not only do the *Lettres*, *mine de rien*, multifariously exploit the literary;[19] at their centre is an *hantise* about futility, about the possibility of not being popular, of not finding an audience, a plot, a *raison d'être*. Whilst the *Lettres* aspire to a transcendence of time and space, draw on myriad genres, proffer a fiction of Provençal authenticity and community to pit against Parisian modernity and fragmentation, this transcendence is menaced by a void; would-be Provençal plenitude is undercut by a threatening anarchy. The vessel is resonant, but empty: "ce sont les tonneaux vides qui chantent le mieux" (*L'Elixir du Révérend Père Gaucher*, Daudet 1986 I, 368).

Nowhere is this clearer than in the collection's emblematic story of a mill, *Le Secret de Maître Cornille*. This tale of a miller who apparently defies the incursions of modernity, seemingly keeping his own mill thriving when every other has been driven out by steam, in fact surviving only by villagers humouring him in delivering imaginary sacks of corn (actually, rubble), is an imagining of Daudet's own potential failure, of the fate which awaits both the windmill and the *Moulin à paroles*: "Les ailes viraient toujours, mais la meule tournait à vide" (Daudet 1986 1258). The miller pays others and himself the coin of word – raising, but also questioning, the project of popular renewal, renovation, through language, through Provençal, *le Félibrige*, which is at the centre of the *Lettres* – in *Le Poète Mistral*'s project of popular cultural renovation through

---

[19] The *Lettres de mon Moulin* use the literary, the tale, to engage life trans-historically, traditionally, and transcendently, via a whole variety of genres. Even ostensibly genuine letters are only nominally so; there is no sense of correspondence or continuity; Daudet reminisces as much as he reports, often drawing on storytelling tropes: tale told in a stagecoach (*La Diligence de Beaucaire*) which here becomes a *conte gaulois*, half-anticipating *Boule de suif*, half-echoing *L'Elixir du Révérend Père Gaucher* which like *Le Curé de Cucugnan*, *Les Trois Messes basses* and *La Mule du pape* recalls Renaissance *contes*, Verville or Des Périers; the deserted house story (*L'Arlésienne*, reflecting Balzac's *Grande Bretèche*); the animal-fable-come-*conte moral* (*La Chèvre de M. Séguin*, *La Mule du pape*, *Le Sous-préfet aux champs*, second of the *Ballades en prose*); the sea-story (*La Phare des sanguinaires*, *L'Agonie de la Sémillante*, *Les Douaniers*), the *conte fantastique* (*La Légende de l'homme à la cervelle d'or*); the *fantaisie* (*Les Etoiles*, *Les Oranges*), the *etude de moeurs* (*Le Portefeuille de Bixiou*, *En Camargue*, *Nostalgies de caserne*).

language; in the Provençal terms littering the text; and in the words Daudet uses to pay us. The peasants in Cornille's story console him with their imaginary sacks of corn, but the reprieve is only temporary: when he dies, so does the mill. The past cannot contain the future: "le temps des moulins à vent était passé comme celui des coches sur le Rhône, des parlements et des jacquettes à grandes fleurs;" modernity, compromise, the idyll's ruination is inevitable. *Le Secret de Maître Cornille* seems to crystallize an anxiety about the popular not just restricted to plot: an ironic reflection on Mistral's project of making Provençal a literary language, and an *hantise* about Daudet's own potential irrelevance, about the inevitable compromise of needing to sell copy.[20] In the final letter, *Nostalgies de caserne*, a soldier on leave from Paris, a drummer, cannot resist practising in Provence. In a closing, almost Baudelairian reflection, Daudet is reminded of his own servitude: "Si tu as la nostalgie de ta caserne, est-ce que, moi, je n'ai pas la nostalgie de la mienne? Mon Paris me poursuit jusqu'ici comme le tien. Tu joues du tambour sous les pins, toi ! Moi, j'y fais de la copie… Ah ! les bons Provençaux que nous faisons ! (…) Ah ! Paris ! Paris!... Toujours Paris!"

## III: Contes du Lundi

These *hantises* – the *hantise* of the other (Paris), the fear of venal / commercial compromise, an awareness of the paradoxical (literary / not literary) status of the popular, lies at the heart of the *Contes du lundi* (1873). This collection, so called because many of its pieces were first published in newspapers on a Monday, incorporates most of the articles from an earlier series, and volume, the *Lettres à un absent* (1871). The *Contes du lundi* themselves have a pendant, the story-collection published under the title of its first novella, *Robert Helmont*, as *Robert Helmont. Etudes et paysages*, in 1874, itself soon overshadowed by the definitive edition of the *Contes* the following year.

In this involuted history, the key division is between the *Lettres de mon Moulin* and the *Contes du lundi*, between pre- and post-1870 / 1871, between the Second Empire, and the Siege of Paris, Commune and emergent Republic. For if Zola's *Contes à Ninon* are missives to an intimate, and the *Lettres de mon Moulin* provincial bread cast on Parisian

[20] See *La Légende de l'homme à cervelle d'or*, who is fleeced by all he meets and is ultimately condemned to die: "Il y a par le monde de pauvres gens qui sont condamnés à vivre de leur cerveau, et paient en bel or fin, avec leur moelle et leur substance, les moindres choses de la vie. C'est pour eux une douleur de chaque jour; et puis, quand ils sont las de souffrir:" (Daudet 1986, I, 328).

(as well as rural) waters, the intervening series, the *Lettres à un absent*, mostly published in *Le Soir* between February and September 1871, are sent from beleaguered Paris into a void. They have an implicit narratee but no explicit correspondent, and are as mechanical as the weekly *Contes du lundi*. The novella *Robert Helmont*, conceived in spring 1871 but not composed in earnest until two years later (Daudet 1986 11638-9), is a diary which simply peters out – a fictional journal soon followed by myriad tales of vehement patriotism; a loss not just of audience but of plot. The *Contes du lundi* are the cold turkey, the hangover, of the Second Empire; and like all hangovers they come with violence and stridency in the assertion of a voice, in getting anyone who will to listen.

Banality is the watchword of these *contes*; it is in this sense that they lose, but eventually find, a plot. The *Contes du lundi* are *banal* in a sense stricter perhaps than for any other contemporary writer, in the original (1247) understanding of the term: "qui appartient au ban, circonscription du suzerain," and from which derives, the second, more common, modern meaning, "qui est extrêmement commun, sans originalité" (Rey and Rey-Debove, 2005). The *Contes du lundi* are banal in treating almost solely Paris at its most circumscribed during the Siege and the Commune (1870-71), in the absence of allegiance to any movement, in their weekly appearance (first in *L'Événement*, then *Le Soir*) as part of the regular fare of the *jour*-nal.[21] Some years ahead of Maupassant's *Chroniques* (published from 1876-7 onwards, and for which banality was also a danger[22]), Daudet's *Lettres à un absent* and *Contes du lundi* do something less obtrusive but ultimately more central to the nation's mythic life: evoke the trivial and everyday, the writer's existence, but also everyman's, and everywoman's, circumscribed by Siege and Commune.[23] The banal subject-matter voices impotence, constraint and deprivation, the impossibility of looking, still less moving, beyond Paris. It gives readers experiences otherwise unavailable, yet tells Parisians what they already know: cold comfort maybe, but nonetheless consolation through narrative of collective (if negative) identity, and hence a renovation, in printed form, of the fundamental life-affirming purpose of the *conte* (even, perhaps

[21] "Prière quotidienne du Français moderne," as it became in this period (Duby 2003, 781). Reading *Le Petit Journal* is ritualistic in Coppée's *Une idylle pendant le siège* (Coppée 1874: 59, 120).

[22] Patrick Kechichian 2008, 15: "La banalité guette, et aussi la vacuité. La régularité peut devenir une contrainte. Et bientôt plus personne ne vous lit."

[23] Many of these *Lettres* and *Contes* are mainly *études de moeurs*, panoramic literature, evocations of daily life on the 1840s, Balzacian, proto-realist model.

especially, if the tale told is unhappy).[24] As Daudet says in "Aux avant-postes", "Tout cela est haché, heurté, bâclé sur le genou, déchiqueté comme un éclat d'obus" (Daudet 1986, I 613), chopped-up bits of experience, *Tableaux parisiens*, as Daudet initially called the third series, echoing *Les Fleurs du mal*'s eponymous second section, but also *Le Spleen de Paris*'s dedication to Arsène Houssaye: "Nous pouvons couper où nous voulons, moi ma rêverie, vous le manuscrit, le lecteur sa lecture (…) Enlevez un vertèbre, et les deux morceaux de cette tortueuse fantaisie se rejoindront sans peine. Hachez-la en de nombreux fragments, et vous verrez que chacun peut exister à part" (Baudelaire 1975, 1 275). Each of Daudet's pieces is thus supposedly authentic but not transcendent, certainly not in the Baudelairian sense of suggesting any unity in the urban or explicit manipulation of form. Indeed, the very circumstances of the Siege militate against any imposition of highly dramatized plot with its implication of pattern and progression.

Yet if most of the *Contes* are studies of manners and diary-pieces, relating ordinary life in a way redolent of Zola (in *Nouveaux contes à Ninon*: *Le Chômeur*, *Le Forgeron*), the element which is *haché* goes beyond plotlessness, fragmentation and banality to bring a sting in the tale. In *Un teneur de livres*, for example, extensive evocation of the book-keeper's mundane life (buying apples for his lunch, loving his office-comforts), the cliché of his workplace, the morgue (nowhere's deader), his own dispassionate attitude to his calling, is suddenly subverted by the discovery of the pathetic victim, a young *ouvrière* almost starving to death. The carapace of banality, the numbness of compassion-fatigue, is suddenly punctured, perhaps less by plot than by the *rond de cuir*'s sudden perception of the girl's innocence and vulnerability.

This pattern is followed in other *Contes du lundi*, life gliding along quite happily until some undercutting disruption reveals the brutal, irrepressible forces beneath the everyday, the undermining abjection of human nature tested to and by the limits: *Les Petits Patés*, where a bourgeois's desire for pies literally crushes all other concerns as he rides roughshod over others to get them, or conversely some good deed in a naughty world: the Imperial standard-bearer who refuses to acquiesce to his treasonous superiors in *Le Porte-drapeau*. Daudet takes one of the folktale's fundamental premises, an initially stable situation which is soon upset,[25] and extends and reverses it, distending "plotless" banality over

[24] Cf. Coppée's similarly popular *Une idylle pendant le siège*. But Coppée, unlike Daudet, implies no political solution, only spiritual retreat, and was ultimately to follow a more aggressively right-wing path.

[25] Propp 1973 36, 50; functions I and IX; cf. appendix I, 146-9.

most of the narrative, then puncturing it by a final disruption. But some of his stories do not even puncture. *Mon vieux képi* spins out the narrator's fond meditations about the cap he wore as a *Garde national* in the last days of the Second Empire, and ends with his just throwing it away. The old tale, it seems to say, is told; the new one has not yet begun.

Yet, for all their apparent plotlessness, the *Contes du lundi* are very much *the* tales of the Siege and Commune, anecdotes and *témoignages* which would feed into the Third Republic's Grand Narratives, become part of its emergent national myth. They did so by entertaining, perhaps less by imposing pattern, order, or readily-legible form on raw experience than by being continuous with it, making points about it – points which puncture the apparently innocuous and steady status quo. The newspaper and first book publications of the *Lettres à un absent* foreground the political: in each case the first pieces (*La Reddition*, *Les Dictateurs*, *Une Champignonnière de grands hommes*) are explicitly polemical, critical of Republicans and the new régime, like some of the last (*Les Tricoteuses*, *Le Naufrage*, *Un an de trouble*: Daudet 1986 1 1383-6). From 18 July 1871, the series which had been appearing in *Le Soir* under the rubric *Lettres à un absent* now appears in that paper under the heading *Contes du lundi*, heralding the collection which would be immortalized in book form in 1873, and from the very first pieces – for posterity amongst the most famous (*Le Siège de Berlin*, 18 July; *L'Enfant espion*, 25 July) – there is a change. These stories are more overarching, more symbolic: in *Le Siège de Berlin* a dying first-Empire general (another head-in-sand-burying Maître Cornille) is protected from the awful truth of the siege of Paris by dispatches on an imaginary, but victorious, siege of Berlin. The virtual, the transcendent, starts to be more important than the everyday banal, and to acquire an emblematic political significance.

This evolution is pursued in the first book version of the *Contes du lundi* (Lemerre, 1873), and confirmed by the final one still generally read today (Charpentier, 1875). In Lemerre, *La Partie de billard* opens, offering a clearly-legible contrast between the battle outside, and a general's determination to ignore it until he has finished his billiard game. He wins the game but loses the war: a satire of French military self-indulgence found later in Maupassant's *Le Lit 29* (Maupassant 1884 and 1885). In Charpentier, it is *La Dernière Classe* which opens, and which, perhaps in consequence, becomes Daudet's most famous story. For the move from Lemerre (publisher of the Parnassians and in due course of Symbolist writers) to Charpentier (publisher of the Naturalists, Maupassant and notably Zola) after initial refusal of the *Lettres à un absent* by Hetzel, the most popular and pedagogic publisher of mid-nineteenth-century France, signals an occupation of the territory of the popular via the symbolic, a transcendence of cultural and political opposites (Symbolism/Naturalism, Lemerre/Charpentier) and the agent of Daudet's consecration as perhaps the most politically-influential storyteller of nineteenth-century France.

It is an influence which is exerted via myth – the myths which end all three *Contes du lundi*-related series – the *Pétroleuses* which conclude the *Lettres à un absent*, with its historical invocation of the *Tricoteuses*; the *Fées de France*, at the end of the first section (*Fantaisies et caprices*) of the 1875 *Contes du lundi*; *Wood'stown* at the end of the *Contes du lundi*'s sequel, *Robert Helmont*. *Les Fées de France* is a striking example of what might be called "myth-fulfilment," a rejection of inconvenient political and social realities by means of an apparently victorious transcendent subjectivism worthy of *Les Dons des fées*, no. 20 of Baudelaire's *Le Spleen de Paris*. Baudelaire's fairies bestow an apparently useless '*Don de plaire*' on an avid (and hence indignant) shopkeeper's child, having given much more practical (and venal) gifts to others (Baudelaire, 1975, 1 307). Daudet's French fairy is the last of her kind, driven out by modernity:

> Mais le siècle a marché. Les chemins de fer sont venus. On a creusé les tunnels, comblé les étangs, et fait tant de coupes d'arbres, que bientôt nous n'avons plus su où nous mettre. Les paysans n'ont plus cru à nous. (…) nous venons de voir ce que c'est qu'un pays qui n'a plus de fées. Nous avons vu tous ces paysans repus et ricaneurs ouvrir leurs huches aux Prussiens et leur indiquer les routes. Voilà ! Robin ne croyait plus aux sortilèges; mais il ne croyait pas davantage à la patrie. Ah ! si nous avions été là, nous autres [fées], de tous ces Allemands qui sont entrés en France, pas un seul ne serait sorti vivant. (…) C'est comme cela qu'on fait la guerre nationale, la guerre sainte. Mais hélas ! dans les pays qui ne croient plus, dans les pays qui n'ont plus de fées, cette guerre-là n'est pas possible. (Daudet 1986, I, 711).

Daudet's disillusioned fairy, dragged before the magistrates for having been a *pétroleuse*, is condemned as mad, a traditional fate of the dissident. Her *plaidoyer* both offers a hope of transcendence, an imaginary refuge from modernity with its *incrédulité* (albeit in fictional form), yet also shows how it is doomed to fail (Compare *La Vision du juge de Colmar*, *Le Pape est mort*, *Le Perdreau rouge*). Other tales relate how myth-pursuit is doomed not to lead to fulfillment: in *La Partie de billard* the field-marshal wins his game but loses the battle; in *Le Siège de Berlin*, the Napoleonic hero colonel Jouve is told that Berlin, not Paris, is under siege, and drops dead when the truth is revealed. These illusions are part of a national delusion, a collective losing of the plot. Like *Mon vieux képi*, *Le Concert de la huitième*, and perhaps in the *Lettres de mon Moulin* themselves, nostalgia may be attractive, but the way backwards is no way forwards, the past cannot offer an answer. The last piece, *L'Empereur aveugle*, confirms that the Emperor has indeed no clothes.

And yet it is this mythic, symbolic and national terrain which the *Contes du lundi* ultimately occupy. Their very heterogeneity ensures their reach, their widespread popular appeal (as it did for the *Lettres de mon Moulin*), whilst their progressive downplaying of explicitly political or anti-republican sentiment (in the Lemerre edition, *Les Dictateurs* and *La Reddition*, for example, are removed) attuned them more to the increasingly well-established Third Republic. Out of their very banality came transcendence. Losing one plot means finding another – mankind cannot live without narrative – even if that new plot is pernicious or a lie. Nowhere more is this truer than in the first and most famous tale, *La Dernière Classe*. This story, of a *lorrain* schoolteacher giving his last lesson in French before Lorraine became German, was internalized, becoming a kind of would-be national Grand Narrative despite, or doubtless because of, its brevity.[26] The dejection of defeat gives rise to the defiance of insubordination; Daudet's schoolteacher chalking on his blackboard *Vive la France*. Yet the tale's vigorous self-affirmation derives only by anathematizing the other – from an inflation of the provincial self-affirmation already seen in the *Lettres de mon Moulin*, and a proto-fascistic fetishizing yet ultimate denigration of politics, as *Robert Helmont*'s epilogue makes clear. Citing Heine, it declares: "En France, il n'y a plus de nation, il n'y a que des partis". (Daudet 1986, 1 928)

What an insult, readers must have thought, a German writer seeing the truth about France; what a paradoxical incentive to action; what an effective stiffening of national resolve. Self-affirmation by caricaturing others and denigrating enemies / insulting politics is a tempting get-out from unpalatable realities, seeming to find the plot by dint of sequels: *La Dernière Classe* rewrites its own fiction as the history of the future, anticipating / imagining a France triumphant still to come; no wonder the story was an early favourite in school anthologies,[27] embodying the

---

[26] "On lit, on connaît par coeur *La Dernière Classe* d'Alphonse Daudet. Des complaintes sont chantées aux carrefours ou aux foires, telles que celles du *Maître d'école* alsacien: La patrouille allemande passe;/ Baissez la voix, mes chers petits; / Un jour, la langue du pays / Nous la parlerons dans l'Alsace." The army would be reorganized and conscription introduced from 1872: Pichois 1979, 2 22). The factual foundations of the story's popular Gallic patriotism, and its effectiveness in exciting it in Alsacians more interested in independence are, however, dubious: Harp 1998, 127-133.

[27] Guiney 2004, 221.

identity and resilience of the nation. Yet such populism can be a fast-track to fascism, as within five decades a reversed Franco-German polarity (not to mention the trajectory of Daudet's son Léon) would show. The four years of Daudet's career from the *Lettres de mon moulin* to the *Contes du Lundi* see him losing the plot, and then finding it. The over-confidence of his Provençal letters, already emblematized by maître Cornille's mill *tournant à vide*, is deflated by 1870 and punctured by stories which make points more than construct causation in *Lettres à un absent* and the *Contes du lundi*. It is telling, even prophetic, that in *La Dernière Classe*, Lorraine should supplant Provence as the defining province, the one on which distinctive identity will be founded, having foundered. For Barrès, in *Les Déracinés* (1897), would make it an emblem of dispossession which would be writ large in the subsequent history of France, of Germany, and beyond. But finding that plot was also losing it, and a way to neither *plaisir*, nor *jouissance*.

## Works cited

Asfour, Amal. 2001. *Champfleury: Meaning in the Popular Arts in Nineteenth-Century France*. Frankfurt, New York: Peter Lang.

Balzac, Honoré de. 1832. *La Grande Bretèche* in *Le Conseil*, *Scènes de la vie privée,* « seconde édition », Paris: Mame et Delaunay-Vallée.

—. 1833. *Le Médecin de campagne*. Paris: Mame and Delaunay-Vallée.

Barbey d'Aurevilly, Jules. 1874. *Les Diaboliques*. Paris: E. Dentu.

Baudelaire, Charles-Pierre. 1975. *Œuvres complètes*, edited by Claude Pichois. Paris: Gallimard-Pléiade, 2 vols.

Benjamin, Walter. 1977. 'Der Erzähler.' In *Illuminationen. Ausgewählte Schriften 1*, Frankfurt am Main: Suhrkamp, 385-410.

Brix, Michel. 1999. *Le Romantisme français: esthétique platonicienne et modernité littéraire*. Louvain, Paris: Peeters, Société des études classiques.

Brooks, Peter. 1994. *Psychoanalysis and Storytelling*. Cambridge (Mass.) and Oxford: Blackwell.

Carruthers, Janice, and McCusker, Maeve. 2009. *The Conte: Oral and Written Dynamics*. Oxford, Bern, Berlin, Bruxelles, Frankfurt am Main, New York, Vienna: Peter Lang.

Champfleury. 1852. *Contes domestiques*. Paris: Lecou.

—. 1861. *De la littérature populaire en France: recherches sur les origines et les variations de la légende du bonhomme Misère*. Paris: Poulet-Malassis et De Broise.

Chateaubriand, François-René de. 1802. *René*, in *Génie du Christianisme ou Beautés de la Religion Chrétienne*. Paris: Migneret, 5 vols, vol. 2, 163-216.
Claudin, Gustave.1850. *Le Timbre Riancey*. Paris: Dumisseray.
Coppée, François. 1874. *Une idylle pendant le siège*. Paris: Lemerre.
Daudet, Alphonse. 1868. *Le Petit Chose*. Paris: Hetzel.
—. 1869. *Lettres de mon Moulin*. Paris: Hetzel.
—. 1871. *Lettres à un absent*. Paris: Lemerre.
—. 1873. *Contes du lundi*. Paris: Lemerre.
—. 1874. *Robert Helmont. Etudes et paysages*. Paris: Dent.
—. 1875. *Contes du lundi*. Paris: Charpentier.
—. 1986-94. *Oeuvres*, edited by Roger Ripoll. 3 vols. Paris: Gallimard-Pléiade.
De Certeau, Michel. 1980. *La Culture au pluriel: la beauté du mort*. Paris: Bourgois.
Dickens, Charles 1850. *Household Words*, 30 March.
Duby, Georges. 2003. *Histoire de la France des origines à nos jours*. Paris: Larousse.
Dunn, Suzanne. 1983-4. 'Transgression and the *Amendment Riancey*', *Nineteenth Century French Studies*, Fall-Winter, 12.1, 86-95.
Fabre d'Olivet, Antoine. 1803. *Le Troubadour, poésies occitaniques du XIIIe siècle, traduites et publiées par Fabre d'Olivet*. Paris: Henrichs, Imp. Valade.
Flaubert, Gustave. 1979. *Madame Bovary*, edited by Jacques Suffel. Paris: Garnier Flammarion.
Fonyì, Antonia. 1999. *Prosper Mérimée écrivain, archéologue, historien*. Geneva: Droz.
Fortoul, Hippolyte. 1853. *Ministère de l'Instruction publique et des cultes. Instructions relative aux poésies populaires de la France. Décret du 13 décembre 1852*. Paris: Imprimerie Nationale.
Guiney, Mortimer. 2004. *Teaching the Cult of Literature in the French Third Republic*. Basingstoke: Palgrave Macmillan.
La Capra, Dominick. 1982. *Madame Bovary on Trial*. Ithaca: Cornell University Press.
La Villemarqué, Théodore Hersart de. 1839. *Barzas* [sic] *Breiz, Chants populaires de la Bretagne, recueillis et publiés avec une traduction française, des éclaircissements, des notes et les mélodies originales*, Paris: Charpentier.
—. 1997. *Le Barzhaz Breizh. Trésor de la littérature orale de la Bretagne*. Spézet: Coop Breizh.

—. 1842. *Contes populaires des anciens Bretons, précédées d'un Essai sur l'origine des épopées chevaleresques de la Table ronde, par Th. de la Villemarqué*. Paris: Coquebert.
—. 1860. *Les Romans de la table ronde et les contes des anciens Bretons*, par le Vte Hersart de la Villemarqué, 3e édition. Paris: Didier.
Luzel, François-Marie.1869. *Contes et récits populaires des Bretons Armoricains, par F.-M. Luzel*. Nantes: Forest et Grimaud.
—. 1870. *Contes bretons, recueillis et traduits par F.-M. Luzel*. Quimperlé, E. Clairet.
—. 1870. *Traditions orales des Bretons Armoricains, Légendes chrétiennes, par M. F.-M. Luzel*, Saint-Brieuc: Imprimerie de L. Prud'homme, in-8o.
—. 1887. *Contes populaires de la Basse Bretagne*. Paris: Maisonneuve et Leclerc.
Lyon-Caen, Judith. 2008. "Un magistère social: Eugène Sue et le pouvoir de représenter." *Le Mouvement social*, Jul-Sept, 3.224, 75-88.
Lyons, Martin.1983., "Oral culture and rural community in nineteenth-century France: the *Veillée d'hiver*." *Australian Journal of French Studies*, 23.1, 102-114.
Maupassant, Guy de.1884. *Le Lit 29, Le Gil Blas*, 8 July.
—. 1885. *Toine*. Paris: Havard (dated 1886).
—. 2008. *Chroniques*, edited by Henri Mitterand. Paris: Livre de poche.
Merimée, Prosper. 1830. *La Partie de Trictrac*, *Revue de Paris*, 13 June, 15, 158-175.
—. 1846. *Carmen*. Paris: Michel Lévy Frères.
Minogue, Valerie, and Pollard, Patrick. 2008. *Visages de la Provence. Zola, Cézanne, Giono, Etudes du colloque d'Aix 19-21 oct. 2007*. London: Emile Zola Society.
Mistral, Frédéric. 1867. *Calendau, pouèmo nouvèu / Frederi Mistral; traduction française en regard*. Avignon: Roumanille.
Nerval, Gérard de. 1989-1993. *Oeuvres complètes*, edited by Jean Guillaume and Claude Pichois. Paris: Gallimard-Pléiade, 3 vols.
Nettement, Alfred 1845-6. *Etudes critiques sur le feuilleton-roman*. Paris: Lagny Frères. Ière et 2ème série, 2 vols.
Nisard, Marie-Charles-Edouard. 1854. *Histoire des livres populaires ou de la littérature du colportage depuis le XVe siècle jusqu'à l'établissement de la Commission d'examen des livres du colportage, 30 novembre 1852*. Paris: E. Dentu. 2 vols.
Pichois, Claude. 1979. *Littérature française*. Paris: Artaud, 3 vols.

Ponton, Rémy. 1991. "Sur la constitution de la catégorie du 'populaire' après 1848. A propos de quelques contemporains d'Alphonse Daudet," *Politix*, 2.4, 65-72.

Propp, Vladimir. 1973. *Morphologie du conte*, suivi de *Les transformations du conte merveilleux* et de Eleazar Mélétinski, *L'Etude structural et typologique du conte*, translated by Marguerite Derrida, Tzvetan Todorov & Claude Kahn. Paris: Seuil.

Rey, Alain, and Rey-Debove, Josette. 2005. *Le Nouveau Petit Robert. Dictionnaire alphabétique et analogique de la langue française*. Paris: Dictionnaires Le Robert.

Sand, George,1837. *Mauprat*, Paris: Félix Bonnaire.

—. 1858. *Légendes rustiques*, dessins de Maurice Sand. Paris: Morel.

—. 1873. *Le Château de Pictordu. Contes d'une grand-mère*. Paris: Michel Lévy.

—. 1876. *Le Chêne parlant. Contes d'une grand-mère.* Paris: Calmann-Lévy.

Strauss, Jonathan. 2002. "Political Force and the Grounds of Identity from Rousseau to Flaubert." *Modern Language Notes*, October, 117.4, 808-35.

Williams, Heather. 2007. *Postcolonial Brittany: Literature between Languages*. Oxford: Peter Lang.

Zola, Emile.. 1864. *Contes a Ninon,* Paris: Librairie Internationale, Hetzel et Lacroix.

—. 1874. Nouvelle édition, Paris: Charpentier.

# CHAPTER NINE

# EMPLOTTING THE FAIR: POPULAR FICTION AND THE WORLD'S COLUMBIAN EXPOSITION OF CHICAGO, 1893

BRENDA HOLLWEG

**1.** In 1893, Chicago was host to the World's Columbian Exposition – the greatest Fair the world had ever seen, as John Joseph Flinn claimed in his *Official Guide to the World's Columbian Exposition* (5). For the USA, the year 1893 "was a time of immense and lasting change. The precarious economic boom of the previous years tripped into a deep depression. Unemployment, strikes, business collapse, and political realignment changed America profoundly." (Gilbert 1991, 1) The nation, if it was to continue to thrive economically and ideologically and further expand internationally, needed a symbolic figure or space, which could encapsulate *in nuce* the multiplicity of interests and desires held and voiced by its contemporaries. The Chicago Columbian Exposition represented such an emblematic space: a testing ground for the representation, contestation and subversion of cultural norms, values and practices.[1]

The Fair commemorated the discovery of the Americas four hundred years earlier and celebrated the achievement and growth of the United States at the end of the 19th century. With its two sections – the grandiose White City with its Beaux-Arts palaces of national and international exhibits, and the Midway Plaisance, an exotic mile-long entertainment strip where the Ferris Wheel, Buffalo Bill's Wild West Show and the native

[1] I think here particularly of Michel Foucault's figure of the *heterotopia*, "a kind of effectively enacted utopia in which the real sites, all other real sites that can be found within the culture, are simultaneously represented, contested and inverted" (1986, 24).

villages of the *Völkerschauen*[2] were located – the Columbian Exposition was both a(n) (open-air) museum and a strange miniature version of the future metropolis. While the Fair propagated an urban concept of homogeneity, architectural symmetry, picturesque gardens and broad promenades, it also confronted its contemporaries with new, occasionally challenging, forms of urban life, commercialisation and ethnic diversity. Due to its far-reaching cultural significance the Fair was also responsible for a degree of publication activity that has no equal in any world's fair, either before or after 1893. The Exposition inspired, as one historian wrote, a "literary response big enough to have provided an exhibit in itself" (Smith 1984, 141).

From May through to October 1893, the Fair attracted more than 21 million visitors. Among them were also hundreds of journalists, writers and essayists who had been commissioned by their newspapers and publishing houses to enlighten their audiences on particular aspects of the Fair such as, for instance, the presentation of regional products, the collections of European art and technological innovation, the national parades and commemorative celebrations. Some writers and journalists had left their nearby hometowns in Illinois, Iowa or Wisconsin to be part of the event; others had come from the East Coast or undertaken transatlantic journeys from Europe where world expositions and international exhibitions of industrial goods had a 40-year long tradition. Quite a few, particularly women in their twenties, were amateurs in the writing profession, but they thought the Fair an opportunity to explore their writing skills, test their abilities to travel on their own and become more independent and self-reliant American citizens. For many, this Fair marked the divide between an outdated Victorian and an emerging Modern Age.

In their *Annotated Bibliography: World's Columbian Exposition, Chicago 1893* (1992) G.L. Dybward and Joy V. Bliss give a concise overview of the more than 2,500 titles published in conjunction with the Fair. These publications cover a wide range of different genres, including illustrated travel guides, cooking books, poems, picture books, theatre plays and satirical magazines but also romances, detective stories, utopian tales, travelogues, children's stories and many literary essays. It is these latter forms of storytelling that are of significance to my argument here. They

---

[2] The native villages on the Midway exhibited human representatives of various South American and African peoples – among them, for instance, the Dahomeys, a West African tribe who exemplified for many Americans what journalist Marian Shaw in her *World's Fair Notes* called a "primitive race": "people […] who, in the mad race of nations for power and pelf, seem to have been left far behind and, compared to the nations of today, are like untutored children." (1893, 56)

certainly continue a tradition of writing on Chicago that can be traced back to the immediate aftermath of the Great Fire in 1871.[3] The event, in which large parts of Chicago burned down and several hundred people were killed, constituted one of the major disasters in 19th-century US-American urban history. The fact that, only 22 years later, the city was again host to a World's Fair symbolised the stamina, enterprising spirit and inventiveness of its inhabitants. Following on from this earlier tradition, the Chicago Fair – like the Great Fire before it – quickly inscribed itself in the cultural imagination of the young nation. As products of a broad democratisation process and an expanding literary market, the Exposition texts supplied their readership amongst a growing urban and white middle-class with the necessary and latest news about the Fair. As dime novels or 10-cent magazines, as contributions to daily newspapers, weekly journals or monthly magazines such as *Chicago Tribune*, *Harper's Bazar*, *The Cosmopolitan*, *The Nation*, *The Century Magazine* or *Frank Leslie's Popular Monthly* they also offered inexpensive, accessible and portable reading material that could be consumed while commuting to and from work. In permanent dialogue with the official creed and messages of the Fair, these texts, perhaps most importantly, provided the open and basically plotless Exposition text with stories: proper beginnings, middles and endings. Their authors teased out the narrative potential that was encapsulated in the Fair's spatial arrangement and structure, its collections, classification systems and cultural events, and thereby actively participated in an on-going process of nation building and of re-inscribing and rewriting cultural identities. Despite the fact that these products of popular culture captured a significant moment in US-American history and reached a mass readership in the 1890s, today, they have almost slipped into obscurity.[4]

**2.** Similar to a museum, a World's Fair is a topographical, semiotic text; its three-dimensional elements can be called *semiophores* as they impart a network of metaphorical and metonymical relationships that can be read and, consequently, understood by its visitors (Pomian 1988, 50).

---

[3] A whole discourse on this subject matter is created in newspapers, journals and books on Chicago at the time. See, among many, *The Little Corporal* (1865-75), which published a special issue on the Great Fire in the immediate aftermath of the event. This and other issues of the magazine included editor's comments, literary essays, fictionalised first-hand accounts and children's picture stories about the incidents of the Great Fire. Subscribers were encouraged to contribute their own stories. Accessed 15 May 2012. http://www.merrycoz.org/MAGS4.HTM#relics.

[4] For an extensive study on this literature and its significance for the formation of cultural identity, see Hollweg 2001.

Like the theatre and on account of its more spectacular elements, an exposition also forms a synaesthetic text that potentially activates all human senses and makes use of a variety of visual, acoustic, olfactory and haptic codes (Pfister 1988, 24-25). As such, it constitutes a multi-faceted symbolic space, the identity of which is not monolithic and static but unstable and dynamic. Theorizing the Columbian Exposition as such a space allows me to trace the vital function specific literary forms had as meaning-making and discourse-generating components in a larger, cultural system of communication, which enabled society's members to communicate with and about themselves, and which attached sense and importance to their actions (Lüsebrink 1993, 89-90).

Kim Atkins has stressed the mediating function of emplotment, its explanatory role. "It configures," she writes, "events, agents and objects and renders those individual elements meaningful as part of a larger whole in which each takes place in a network that constitutes the narrative's response to why, how, who, where, when etc" (2003, n.p.). The World's Fair literature, equally important as the Exposition itself as an instrument of (inter)national instruction and enlightenment, education and edification, provided its readers with stories of both affirmative and resistant or counterpuntal readings. Although these stories often circulate around the same limited number of exhibits and events and are often situated in the same notorious Exposition places, it is the way they are being plotted that either turns the Exposition experience into a museum visit, an urban spectacle, a walk through/to the past or to a possible future and accounts for a story's specific educational or moral function. Typically, in the Exposition literature genre-specific plots (of love, romance, mystery etc) are called upon to increase the story's drama, the thrill of the reading experience and make up for its potentially uncomfortable moral and ideological lessons.

A nation or culture is not only an economic, social or discursive system but is also produced through emotions: feelings of love, anxiety, a sense of duty or desire for security. As a practice of communication emotions are important for plot development and storytelling: they draw attention to certain cultural phenomena, to concerns about social inclusion, cohesion or exclusion. The emotional intensity that characterises the Exposition visit in many literary texts is a signifier of a culture's both more euphoric and more anxious-ridden moments; it is certainly shown to transform the journey to Chicago and its Fair into something unique and memorable. In most plots emotions are "part of an on-going discourse production of subjects and power relations" (Harding 2009, 268).

**3.** Plotting-out routes through the Fair is probably one of the most distinct elements of Exposition literature. It is already noticeable in non-fiction text forms such as catalogues, travel guides and some journalistic articles, which are usually less known for their dynamic plots. But even here we encounter what could be taken as the simplest form of plotting, in the archaic sense of the word plot as a bounded area of ground, a pacing of measurements, giving directions for laying out a path on the ground, a dynamic act of interpretive ordering (Brooks 1984, 10-36). It is mostly through the selection and order of exhibits, their author's suggestions to look at a particular exhibit, follow a particular route or take part in a specific event, that we gain a sense of the text's "integrating dynamism that draws a unified story from a variety of incidents" (Ricoeur 1985, 8). Paratextually related to the Fair, these publications aimed to lead and guide the reader's impressions in advance, creating an imaginary Exposition-scape in which the disorienting experience of an actual visit could be placed and understood.

Equally important was their role of promoting and propagating the official creed of the Exposition, to present and develop what could be called its dominant ideology or preferred reading. This story consists of basically two competing narratives; each following a different logic. One narrative turns the Exposition into "a universal congress, which is no respecter of geographical boundary, race, color, party or sex" (Flinn, *Official Guide*, 7); the breakdown of distinctions between high-brow and popular culture, art and commerce, entertainment and learning, the foreign and the familiar is celebrated.[5] In the other, progress is plot. America is hailed as the new technological utopia, in which technological progress is synonymous with national progress and a vastly improved democratic community.[6] On a national level, the myth of *e pluribus unum*, of unity in diversity, is evoked, while – on a more international level – the image of the USA as *primus inter pares,* as a cosmopolitan nation to which all other nations are "bound […] by invisible but indissoluble ties," is propagated (Flinn, *Official Guide*, 7).

Repeatedly, these two narratives are re-affirmed, reworked and/or contested in the corpus of Exposition literature. It is not so much their degree of fictionalisation that matters here as the routes different

[5] See, for instance, Shaw's *World's Fair Notes*, 36 and 38.

[6] See Senator John J. Ingalls's *Lessons of the Fair* and John Brisben Walker's *A World's Fair Introductory: The Great College of Democracy* (both 1893), which celebrate peaceful and continuous democratic change based on technological innovation. This is a story that has shaped US-American history over the decades; for more recent examples, see Achter 2003, 308.

characters take through the Exposition and the ways subjects are emplotted to engage with the worlds on exhibition. One popular literary form of Exposition travel is the educational journey around the world, which, for the most part, is perceived as enlightening and entertaining. For Samantha Allen, Marietta Holley's female protagonist in her novel *Samantha at the World's Fair* (1893), the world on display is a cornucopia, a diverse yet unified collection of multiple objects and impressions, moods and materials, people(s) and regions. Over 700 pages, we are taken to the showcases of the White City, guided through the city maze and spectacle of the foreign peoples on Cairo Street (the reconstructed Egyptian bazaar on the Midway Plaisance), presented with a fake-historical site of a Spanish cloister and learn, among many more sites, about the three life-size ship models of Christopher Columbus.

Holley's accounts refer to an older travel custom, the Grand Tour, which flourished in Europe from the late 17th until the middle of the 19th century. It served as an educational rite of passage for members of the affluent classes, particularly wealthy young men. Here, in its Americanised version, the journey is undertaken by a middle-aged woman from the Midwest. The sites and exhibits Samantha feels drawn to become incentives for her to initiate a philosophical dialogue, touch upon political issues virulent at the time or voice her reformist ideas. As a devout Methodist, she repeatedly denounces the reprehensible consequences of alcohol abuse or informs her readers about the role women ought to have in modern society. Holley's voluminous novel is representative of a series of publications, which introduced their contemporary readers episodically to the plethora of new things, sites and experiences modern times had to offer.[7] Like Jules Verne's novel (and later stage adaptation of) *Around the World in Eighty Days* (1873), which pioneered the science fiction genre, Samantha's several days long journey around the fabricated worlds on display in Chicago proves to be mind-expanding, not only for her but also for her readers who are alternately positioned to observe these worlds through the eyes of a tourist, collector, adventurer, gallery visitor or amateur ethnologist.

The ritual of the museum or gallery visit often finds its narrative counterpart in a plot situated outside the Exposition halls proper. Subjects can be observed to climb towers, observation platforms or vantage points

---

[7] Other examples are Charles McClellan Steven's *The Adventures of Uncle Jeremiah and Family at the Fair*, Tudor Jenks's story for young folks, "The World's Fair Palaces", and his book for children, *A Century World's Fair Book for Boys and Girls*, the newspaper column "Captain Jack at the Fair" (all 1893) or H.C. Bunner's article "Making of the White City" (1892).

to enjoy bird's-eye views or panoramic vistas of the Exposition grounds and near-by metropolis. Following Michel Foucault's analysis on subtle power strategies in *Surveiller et Punir* (1975), I argue here for the important social and psychological functions such meticulous rituals can have; if practised often enough, they provide the individual with the illusion of security and orientation in an inherently transitive and unstable present. Reading about it had similar functions. Metropolitan life at the time was characterised by poverty, misery, corruption and scandal. Chicago, in particular, was notorious for its short but brutal labour history, marked by violent strikes, such as the Haymarket Riot in 1886, an influx of immigrants from Europe and, increasingly, farmers from the Midwest. (Gilbert 1991, 52) Emplotting the Fair as a space under/of control presents a useful, even pleasurable, literary strategy to counterbalance prevalent insecurities in times of rapid change and an emerging plurality of new phenomena and value systems.

Both activities, Holley's armchair travels to distant lands and the climbing of observation towers, however, are shown to lose their thrill. As Charles McClellan Steven's educational novel *The Adventures of Uncle Jeremiah and Family at the Fair* (1893) reveals, they can become tiresome or even exhausting reading exercises. The *objets d'art* of European Impressionism are not made for Uncle Jeremiah's gatepost at his Midwest farm and the technical wonders of Machinery Hall exceed his bucolic imagination. At some point Steven's elderly protagonist simply shuts his eyes and refuses to take in any more lessons the Fair has to offer. His spirits only re-awaken when he incidentally runs into like-minded folks from Kansas or Dakota outside the exhibition halls proper. In scenes of greeting and recognition humour is used in an ambivalent way, both to criticize America's lack of culture, particularly of its agrarian population, and to make fun of European cultural sophistication. Similarly, writer Julian Hawthorne in *Humors of the Fair* (1893) invents a series of subplots in which his bold, independent and patriotic Yankee-narrator makes a fool of any official authority, particularly of Exposition guides and wardens.

The desire to plot out different routes through the Exposition maze is also noticeable in a series of non-fiction essays, Teresa Dean's "Dispatches", which were later published as a collection entitled *White City Chips* (1895). As a journalist Dean visited the Fair repeatedly over the summer. In her essays, she practices a structurally open approach towards the Exposition. Repeatedly, she is seen to leave the well-trodden paths of the grounds and follow her own mental map through the Fair. She jumps over fences, walks along muddy roads and consciously ignores no-trespassing signs. While passing the exhibition halls of the White City or the villages and cafés on the Midway, she randomly selects objects, people and stories for their anecdotal, rather than strictly educational, character. Generally uninspired by the Fair's official programme she turns to the sightseers themselves who, "in their sense of the freedom of being part of the Midway, are more of a sight than the wildest Arab". (301) Many times she calls herself a "story hunter" or a "cosmopolitan vagabond". It is not the historical events, the big parades or the bombastic shows of the different American states that make up her stories, but the memorable and memorized chips, the little incidents that "just happen" on the fringe of the official Exposition spectacle.

**4.** The Chicago Columbian Exposition is also rewritten as dynamic and adventurous urbanity. The popular imagination is obsessed with a space that owes its existence foremost to the invention of specific theatrical spectacles of light, water and music. To be able to control light and avoid the dangers of fire was particularly important for Chicago whose inner city had suffered badly from the Great Fire. The illuminated White City symbolised the rebirth of the Chicago Phoenix from the ashes and sealed the triumph of the city over the unpredictability and fervour of nature. Furthermore, most texts support the image of a society in perpetual motion. Reminiscent of Jules Verne's world travellers in his various novels, the invented visitors of the Exposition literature are seen to explore the worlds on exhibition through rides in the elevated trains and on the Ferris Wheel or take a boat trip on the Grand Basin (the White City's artificial lake). Geographical mobility is complemented by emotional exaltations and the desire to transcend the material world.

This is particularly apparent in some of the journalistic essays and Exposition romances, occasionally with religious connotations. Clara Louise Burnham's *Sweet Clover: A Romance of the White City* (1894), for instance, recounts the well-known story of misplaced love between two pairs of young women and men who will only find each other in the predetermined pairings after a *tour-de-force* of emotion management, when they have learned how to decode the social sign-system and the more intimate gestures of their prospective partners. The Exposition spectacle with its sublime vistas, illuminated palaces and dramatic displays of light and water mirrors the protagonists' own agitations, false hopes of love and disappointments. The story culminates in a dramatic sensation scene, an apocalyptical spectacle of fire that destroys several central monuments within the White City section, reminding Chicago readers and those from adjacent regions, if only for minutes, that their city with its clean, controlled and basically safe exposition space could as easily become a place of destruction and potential death again.

A slightly different take on the tragic incident is staged in detective novelist E. Murdoch Van Deventer's *Against Odds: A Detective Story of the World's Fair*. Here, a series of titillating subplots show characters to be drawn visually and physically to the place of the tragedy, helping injured spectators or managing, just in time, to escape the falling pieces of the burning tower. In other stories, the trust in the Exposition managers' control over matter is described as so great that the quite real fire that destroyed the Cold Storage Building on the Exposition grounds, shortly after the World's Fair was opened, is misinterpreted by characters as a thrilling part of the staged spectacle.

Perhaps even more indicative of the allure of the Fair as a new form of urbanity are the many encounters with other visitors. Burnham in *Sweet Clover* has her protagonist Mildred mingle with the crowd of tourists visiting the Exposition. Even occasional unintended collisions with other by-passers, for Mildred, become part of the exhilarating experience of collectivity. In his literary essay "A First Impression", (1893) the English writer, critic and activist Walter Besant takes himself as the subject of critical observation of city life. At first, he appears to be distanced from the crowd. Questioning the national/istic education programme offered inside the White City palaces, Besant stylizes himself as a *flâneur*, sitting outside the buildings: reading, meditating, contemplating or simply dozing. Later, he is seen to take a walk on Wooded Island, a small, irregular green island in the midst of the symmetrically arranged promenades, or stroll along Midway Plaisance where he watches the multicultural hotchpotch of the foreign peoples from afar. But even he is taken in by the fervour and communal spirit of the mass spectacle and eventually aligns himself with the common man or "the Average People," as he calls them. (536-7) Here, as elsewhere, the Exposition visit is emplotted as offering the sightseer a unique chance to taste modern, metropolitan life without experiencing its harshness or bitterness. In most literary essays, romances and educational novels on the Exposition the urban horror of the masses with its implications of dirt, noise, rudeness, vulgarity, aggression or potential risks of getting mugged can still be appreciated as part of a staged spectacle.

A very different social and urban experience is emplotted in most detective stories. Van Deventer's *Against Odds*, John Harvey Whitson's *Chicago Charlie: A Columbian Detective* or Weldon J. Cobb's *A World's Fair Mystery* stress the fact that the proximity of the midwestern metropolis to the Exposition constantly led to transgressions of some sort or other, usually connected with violence and crime. Their stories are filled with criminal deeds and criminal hunts, with plots of disguise and mistaken identity, with transitory figures and doubles that resist interpretation and, finally, control. Rarely is there a text in which (good or bad) characters do not operate under two or three different names and are not able to change their identities as they change their clothes. When the villains in Van Deventer's *Against Odds* resort to deceptive methods in order to mislead the innocent or inexperienced visitor or hide within the Midway mazes to evade the detective's penetrating gaze, the urban setting is no longer a place where communality is practiced and the individual adheres to a collective system of rules.

Multiple forms of masquerade and camouflage, however, also allow the characters to invent and constantly reinvent themselves according to specific collective images, desires and expectations. Fictive members of the Chicago elite work disguised as Columbian guards on the Exposition grounds; white, upper-class women dress in men's clothes, carry pistols in their handbags and assume the attitude of amateur detectives; or young rural farm girls dress up as fashionable city women. One of these transitory figures is also Billy Stubbs in Whitson's *Chicago Charlie*. Billy assumes roles according to the situation he is confronted with. He changes from an orphaned newspaper boy to the heir to a large fortune; he also works as an informant for the detective. While chasing the criminals he suddenly finds himself in Buffalo Bill's Wild West Show. After a number of complications he is forced to enter the arena on the back of a wild pony. Within seconds the former newsboy and informant becomes "a figure of fame and an object of visual consumption." (Brodhead 1993, 62) His adventures symbolise a new approach towards the city: it is imagined as a space where the city walker or spectator now enters the performance arena as participant, and in which distinctions between viewer and doer begin to blur.

**5.** In *Imagined Communities: Reflections on the Origin and Spread of Nationalism* (1983) Benedict Anderson has stressed the role printed literature and its dissemination plays in constituting the nation as coherent, limited and sovereign. In line with Anderson's observation, most texts on the Fair, at some point, engage in retrospective views of classical Greece or the Venetian Republic to portray the White City as an ideal city comparable to ancient Athens, Rome or Venice. For one character in William T. Stead's romance *From the Old World to the New* (1892) boomtown Chicago is "the newest millionaire city in the world" on whose edge "the trophies of the civilisation that has subdued the Continent" are now on display. Its White City of Palaces stands on the shores of Lake

Michigan "like modern Venice on the shores of the Adriatic of the West." (3) Stead's comparison is representative of a majority of Exposition texts; its message remains equivocal. The analogy may refer to the scenic beauty of Venice, but it may also rekindle the city's Renaissance spirit of expansion and its success in establishing an Empire.

Among the texts that engage in classicist representations of the Fair are also non-fiction essays published in newspapers and journals, most prominently John J. Ingalls's essay "Lessons of the Fair" (1893-4), Murat Halstead's account of her visit in "Electricity at the Fair", John Brisben Walker's "The World's College of Democracy" or Marian Shaw's *World's Fair Notes* (all 1893). Less plot-driven than the detective stories or novels, these essayistic representations of the Fair owe their key position as repositories of cultural memory to the highly reproductive capacity of their *meme*: these are powerful myths, images and gestures that have mutated and matured over time reproducing themselves in an ongoing process of social change (Witoszek 1997, 246). In these essays, the use of old and new myths in tandem often breeds a collage of interrelated myths. The myth of the Phoenix or Judeo-Christian myths of creation are, for instance, combined with the myth of American exceptionalism, Columbus' discovery of the New World and his success story as a national hero, or the myth of the West and the frontier. The tenor of these texts is usually euphoric, following the official Exposition credo and re-affirming progress as plot. On account of the many mythological allusions the industrial products – machines, optical instruments and technological exhibits – achieve the status of sacred icons, just as the Beaux-Arts palaces of the White City resemble the sacred temples of ancient Greece.

Less common, but equally significant as both products and producers of cultural memory and mythical recollection, are literary emplotments of the Fair that actively engage in a counter-memory. Typically, these texts call attention to the presence of lives commonly neglected or silenced by the official celebrations. In *Amie Leslie at the Fair* (1893), Lilly Buck turns to "genuinely" American myths and mythical figures. Instead of "familiar old Ceres" or "inexhaustible Bacchus, sacred bovines and impious feasters," the author suggests Americans should admire "great pansy-eyed Texas steers, feather-crested Indians, a sundance, a Rocky mountain hero" (17-8) on the walls of Agricultural Hall. In Elbridge S. Brooks' book for children *The True Story of Christopher Columbus, called the Great Admiral* (1892), the myth of Columbus as America's grand discoverer and national hero is debunked, focus shifting instead to the indigenous population.[8] Likewise, the anonymous narrator of the short story "A Place of Mystery" (1893) is less interested in the grand spectacle than driven by a desire to encounter the marginalised, displaced, excluded or repressed parts of the Exposition. One subplot has her/him look out for an obelisk dedicated to the discovery of the Americas and peace among the nations. We learn that the monument has been transformed into a memorial of the other: in the evening hours, it is a regular meeting point for Indians, Arabs and female tourists visiting the Fair grounds. By sharing this knowledge with her/his readers the narrator calls attention to a moment of cultural contestation: a moment less marked by competition and the idea of progress than by equality and mutual recognition, rarely found amongst the patriotism and nationalistic drumming of many of the Exposition texts.

**6.** The Exposition literature provided its readers with a variety of symbolic stories which did not fail to hint at the many possibilities the permissive society offered its cultural participants: the education for citizens from remote and rural areas, the emancipation of women or the deconstruction of social, political and cultural hierarchies through plots of masquerade and performance. The typical perils and discomforts of modern metropolitan life, such as mugging, confidence tricks, disorientation in the city maze or traffic accidents, are here remodelled into experiences of a challenging, yet controllable, spectacle. These texts do not yet expose their readership to the cruelties of an urban world depicted by writers such as Frank Norris or Theodore Dreiser, who were inspired by the drama of the city streets, harbours and quotidian scenes. But they engaged their readers in plots by which questions of social, national and cultural identities could be broached and commented upon. As a playful version of the real experience – a "plaything" (Hawthorne), a "laboratory" (Dean) or "workshop" (McClellan Stevens) – in which different forms of narrative allowed for the negotiation and formation of diverse subjectivities, literary representations of the Fair give evidence to a *heteroglossia* of different voices dialogically at play. In the talk of a Kansas farm girl, the vocabulary and *blasé* attitude of the European intellectual, distancing himself from the crowd, in the public dispute between a native Chicago business man and a die-hard New Yorker we also hear the sound of the

---

[8] "If the native American were of a reflective turn of mind, all this [the Columbian Exposition] might awaken unpleasant thoughts. [...] And yes *he* is the American. He is the only one among us who had ancestors to be discovered. He is the aboriginal; the first occupant and owner; the only one here with an hereditary right to the country we are celebrating." (Mitchell 1893, 186).

human voice, or rather many voices, speaking in a variety of accents, rhythms and registers.

The inclusion of humorous or mysterious plots in encounters with other people(s) allows for the humane and poetic dimensions of the Exposition visit to shine through. Bill Schwarz reminds us that it was Walter Benjamin's life-long endeavour to uncover such experiences: personal and memorable moments which lie "deep in the heart of a commodified, standardized culture" and offer "the potential for disequilibrium, for re-enchantment". (Schwarz 2004, 95) Although only written at the beginning of Benjamin's "age of technological reproduction", these texts attempt to bestow upon the Fair a certain aura of undiminished authenticity, singularity and uniqueness. Contrary to the commercial, stage-like quality of the exhibits and the temporary character of the event itself, which is often bemoaned in these texts, the literature appeals to the commemorative qualities of the Fair and reinvents it as a *mnemotope* (Aby Warburg). As their authors criticize the transitory nature of the event and the invented authenticity of the buildings and Exposition displays, they also reflect upon their text's own function – namely, to embed the Columbian Exposition in a larger socio-historical context and add to the many existing *topoi* that of the World's Fair itself.

Emplotments of the Fair, however, are not without their blank spots. The symbolic space created collectively in these texts is, for instance, strongly marked by class and ethnic affiliations. While the cityscape is celebrated as being democratic and diverse, in reality, it was often exclusive and disunited, neglecting ethnic minorities and less privileged social groups. Although, in the 1890s, Chicago was increasingly becoming a center of black political and intellectual life, although a few black musicians played on the grounds, although former slave, abolitionist and statesman Frederick Douglass delivered his dedication speech at the Haiti Pavilion and although Frances Ellen Watkins Harper, speaking before the Exposition's Women's Congress, demanded justice for middle-class black women, African Americans were largely discouraged or barred from taking part in the Fair (VandeCreek 2002; Schechter 2001; Reed 2000). Fictionalized accounts of African American characters and their families or friends visiting the Exposition hardly feature in the popular imagination of the North at the time – they certainly play no significant part in the text corpus under investigation here. It was up to reformist, political activist and travelling lecturer Ida B. Wells who in 1894 published her by now renowned *The Reason Why the Colored American Is Not in the World's Columbian Exposition* to make the public aware of the institutionalized racism and systematic exclusion of black Americans from the Fair.

Underrepresented are also stories of working-class people and farmers who could not enter the grounds because they had neither savings nor spare time to embark upon the Exposition journey, let alone to pay the entrance fees for the exotic sights of the Midway Plaisance. Only very occasionally, issues of class and social inequality become the subject of more extensive plotting. Frances Hodgson Burnett's *Two Little Pilgrims' Progress: A Story of the City Beautiful* (1897) is such an exception, proposing a social critique representative of children's fiction written at the same time but not in relation to the Fair. Burnett's story circulates around two poor orphans who save up some money to travel to the Chicago Fair; but they must first overcome a series of obstacles and physical and financial restraints until they eventually get to realize their dream. From a closer analysis of Burnett's story but also other Exposition texts one can gain some notion of how the use of stock characters or genre-specific patterns and traditions can shape the content of national histories and memory culture.

Various texts also seem to reveal the crisis in communication characteristic of literary products towards the end of the nineteenth century. In his essay A First Impression, we hear Walter Besant lament the lack of "picturesque words" to describe his impressions of the Fair. "There is […] not a phrase left for me to invent," (530) he writes. Trust in human observation and the representational power of language seems to be eroded. When words fail their authors or do not feel adequate any longer to capture the complexities of a rapidly changing present, the invention of multiple plots rather than description, critical comment or analysis become both a pleasurable, compensatory literary strategy and a cultural necessity.

## Works cited

Paul J. Achter. 2004. "TV, Technology, and McCarthyism: Crafting the Democratic Renaissance in an Age of Fear". *Quarterly Journal of Speech* 90, 3: 307-326.

Anonymous. 1893. "A Place of Mystery". *Chicago Tribune* (10 September): 34.

Atkins, Kim. 2003. Paul Ricoeur (1913-2005). *Internet Encyclopedia of Philosophy: A Peer-Reviewed Academic Resource*. Accessed 15 May 2012. http://www.iep.utm.edu/ricoeur/.

Besant, Walter. 1893. "A First Impression". *Cosmopolitan Magazine* 15 (May-October): 528-539.

Brodhead, Richard. 1993. *Cultures of Letters: Scenes of Reading and Writing in Nineteenth-Century America.* Chicago: The University of Chicago Press.

Brooks, Elbridge S. 1892. *The True Story of Christopher Columbus, Called the Great Admiral*. Boston: D. Lothrop.

Brooks, Peter. 1984. *Reading for the Plot: Design and Intention in Narrative*. New York: Knopf Press.

Buck, Lilly West Brown (alias Amie Leslie). 1893. *Amie Leslie at the Fair*. Chicago: W. B. Conkey.

Burnham, Clara Louise. 1894. *Sweet Clover: A Romance of the White City*. Boston/New York: Houghton, Mifflin.

Cobb, Weldon J. 1892. *A World's Fair Mystery.* Chicago: Melbourne Publishing.

Crawford, Jack. 1893. "Captain Jack at the Fair". *Chicago Tribune* (10 September): 34.

Dean, Teresa. 1895. *White City Chips.* Chicago: Warren Publishing.

Dybward, G.L. and Joy V. Bliss. 1992. *Annotated Bibliography: World's Columbian Exposition, Chicago 1893*. Albuquerque, NM: The Book Stops Here.

Flinn, John Joseph. 1893. *Official Guide to the World's Columbian Exposition*. Chicago: The Columbian Guide.

Foucault, Michel. 1986. "Of Other Spaces". *Diacritics* (Spring): 22-27.

Gilbert, James. 1991. *Perfect Cities: Chicago's Utopias of 1893*. Chicago/London: University of Chicago Press.

Halstead, Murat. 1893. "Electricity at the Fair". *Cosmopolitan* Magazine (May-October): 577-83.

Harding, Jennifer. 2009. "Emotional Subjects: Language and Power in Refugee Narratives". In *Emotions: A Cultural Studies Reader*, ed. Jennifer Harding and E. Deirdre Pribram. London/New York: Routledge, 267-79.

Hawthorne, Julian. 1893. *Humors of the Fair*. Chicago: E. A. Weeks.

Holley, Marietta. 1893. *Samantha at the World's Fair*. New York: Funk & Wagnalls.

Hollweg, Brenda. 2001. *Ausgestellte Welt: Formationsprozesse kultureller Identität in the Texten zur Chicago World's Columbian Exposition (1893)*. Heidelberg: Winter.

Ingalls, John J. 1893-94. "Lessons of the Fair". *Cosmopolitan Magazine* (November-April): 141-9.

Jenks, Tudor. 1893. *The Century World's Fair Book for Boys and Girls: Being the Adventures of Harry and Philip with their Tutor, Mr.*

*Douglass, at the World's Columbian Exposition*. New York: The Century Co.

—. 1892-1893. "The World's Fair Palaces". *St. Nicholas: An Illustrated Magazine for Young Folks* 20, 2: 519-28.

Lüsebrink, Hans-Jürgen 1993. "Romanische Landeskunde zwischen Literaturwissenschaft und Mentalitätsgeschichte". In *Kulturbegriff und Methode: Der Stille Paradigmenwechsel in den Geisteswissenschaften*, ed. Klaus Peter Hansen. Tübingen: Gunter Narr.

Lynch, Lawrence L. (real name E. Murdoch Van Deventer). 1894. *Against Odds: A Detective Story of the World's Fair*. London: Ward, Lock & Bowden. Repr. in Donald K. Hartman, ed. 1992. *Fairground Fiction: Detective Stories of the World's Columbian Exposition*. Kenmore, NY: Motif Press, 1-254.

Mitchell, J. A. 1893. "Types and People at the Fair". *Scribner's Magazine* (July-December): 186-93.

Pfister, Manfred. 1988 [1977]. *Das Drama: Theorie und Analyse*. Muenchen: Wilhelm Fink.

Pomian, Krzysztof. 1988 [1986]. *Der Ursprung des Museums: Vom Sammeln*. Berlin: Klaus Wagenbach.

Reed, Christopher. 2000. *All the World is Here! The Black Presence at White City*. Bloomington: Indiana University Press.

Schechter, Patricia A. 2001. *Ida B. Wells-Barnett and American Reform, 1880-1930*. Chapel Hill: University of North Carolina Press.

Schwarz, Bill. 2004. Media Times/Historical Times. *Screen* 45, 2 (Summer): 93-105.

Shaw, Marian. 1992. *World's Fair Notes: A Woman Journalist Views Chicago's 1893 Columbian Exposition*. St. Paul, MN: Pogo Press. Originally published 1893 as a series of articles in *The Argus*, a small newspaper from Fargo, North Dakota.

Sims, A.K. (real name John Harvey Whitson). 1893. *Chicago Charlie: A Columbian Detective*. New York: Beadle & Adams. Repr. in Donald K. Hartman, ed. 1992. *Fairground Fiction: Detective Stories of the World's Columbian Exposition*. Kenmore, NY: Motif Press, 257-435.

Smith, Carl S. 1984. *Chicago and the American Literary Imagination, 1880-1920*. Chicago University Press.

Stead, William T. *From the Old World to the New: Or, A Christmas Story of the World"s Fair*, 1893 [Published as the Christmas issue of the *Review of Reviews* for 1892]. London/New York/Melbourne: Editorial Offices.

Stevens, Charles McClellan. 1893. *The Adventures of Uncle Jeremiah and Family at the Great Fair; their Observations and Triumphs*. Chicago: Laird & Lee.

VandeCreek, Drew. 2002. Race and Ethnicity. *Illinois During the Gilded Age*. Accessed 15 May 2012. http://dig.lib.niu.edu/gildedage/race.html.

Walker, John Brisben. 1893. "A World's Fair Introductory: The World's College of Democracy". *Cosmopolitan Magazine* (May-October): 517-27.

Witoszek, Nina. 1997. "Tradition: Erfunden oder Erinnert? Postmoderne Theorie und die Tartuer Semiotik". In *Vom Ende der Humboldt-Kosmen: Konturen von Kulturwissenschaft*, ed. Bernd Henningsen and Stephan Michael Schröder. Baden-Baden: Nomos Verlagsgesellschaft.

# CHAPTER TEN

# PICARESQUE PLOTS AND IMPROPER HEROINES: POPULAR HISTORICAL SAGAS IN $20^{TH}$ CENTURY FRANCE

DIANA HOLMES

Historical novels have been one of the major popular genres of the past century. Novels set in well known, dramatic and tumultuous periods of national history provide a readymade narrative framework for the adventures of fictional (or fictionalised) protagonists, bringing alive the documented reality of the past through vividly imagined personal experience, and lending to the private story the lustre of historical significance. The mimetic illusion is intensified by the knowledge that the underlying events of plot actually happened. Historical fiction has been particularly popular with a female audience, indeed "one of the major forms of women's reading and writing in the second half of the twentieth century" (Light 1989, 57). Not only does the genre enable the re-imagining of traditionally androcentric histories from a woman's perspective, what Alison Light calls "giving femininity, which normally has a walk-on part in the official history of our times, the lead role in the national drama" (Light 1989, 60), but it also offers a space in which to fantasize female experience outside the framework of contemporary norms and expectations.

Three of the most popular works of fiction in France since the Second World War belong to the category of the historical novel, each of them featuring a spirited, enterprising, beautiful heroine, through whose eyes and adventures an iconic period of French history is re-imagined. The "literary" novelist and historian Jacques Laurent turned to popular fiction in 1947, publishing *Caroline Chérie* under the pseudonym of Cécil Saint-Laurent: set at the time of the 1789 Revolution, it became the topselling French novel for the entire decade of the 1940s. Serge and Anne Golon's *Angélique*, set in the reign of Louis XIV, was published in 1956; widely translated, it sold in millions both in and beyond France. Régine Deforges's *La Bicyclette bleue*, the story of Léa Delmas and her adventures in the Occupied France of the Second World War, was published in 1983 and became the bestselling French novel of the decade. In terms of both plot and characterisation, Laurent, Golon and Deforges all acknowledge the influence of what is certainly one of the most popular novels of all time: Margaret Mitchell's 1936 story of the American Civil War, *Gone with the Wind* – a pre-war bestseller in France which topped the lists again in the late 1940s after the novel re-appeared in serialised form in *France-Soir*.[1]

Popular genres are often characterised by seriality, sequels and adaptation to other media: in commercial terms, this maximises the profit to be made, and in terms of reader satisfaction, it caters for the desire to repeat yet diversify pleasurable experience. The success of each of these novels led to the production of sequels, turning their stories into sagas. *Caroline chérie* was followed by two further volumes (*Le Fils de Caroline Chérie* in 1950; *Un Caprice de Caroline Chérie* in 1951); *Angélique*, to date, by thirteen (with her 88-year-old author apparently still writing); *La Bicyclette bleue* was the first of ten volumes. Each was also adapted very successfully for the screen. The film of *Caroline Chérie,* directed by Richard Pottier and starring Martine Carol, came out in 1951, and two sequel films (1952 and 1954) were also box office hits. *Angélique* was adapted into a series of five films between 1964 and 1967, all directed by Bernard Borderie and starring Michèle Mercier: successful at the time, they continued to be shown regularly on television for decades. *La Bicyclette bleue* became a TV mini-series in 2000, with Laetitia Casta as Léa, and continues to sell well as a box set.

Precisely because these are popular texts, in which suspenseful, immersive storytelling takes precedence over any overt concern with style or serious themes, they have attracted little critical attention. Yet they represent significant elements of twentieth- century French literature in the broad and inclusive sense, for each played a major part in the popular construction of a period of French history, and each added an iconic female figure to the repertoire of popular fictional heroines. Moreover, the structural similarities between these three bestsellers reveal much about the types of plotting that produce and reproduce reading pleasure, and about the specific appeal of the historical novel.

[1] Régine Deforges's *Bicyclette bleue* was so closely modelled on *Gone with the Wind* that she was sued by Mitchell's heirs for plagiarism.

## Narrative pleasures

Narrative tension, to use Raphaël Baroni's term (Baroni 2007), with its twin elements of suspense (what is going to happen?) and curiosity (how can these events be explained?), is central to the desire to keep turning the pages in any form of popular fiction. In the most classic of popular genres – the romance, the crime mystery – one central question drives that tension, and must be answered by the dénouement: will the lovers get together, and how? who committed the crime, and why? However, the narrative structure of these three novels is very different, the tension owing little to any drive towards an ending. Rather, their structure is picaresque: it is episodic, unified by a focus on the exploits, travels and amorous adventures of a single character, whose survival and well-being are at stake in each episode, as in the narrative as a whole. Narrative tension depends on the reader's concern for the hero: she (in this instance) will be at once the reader's stand-in in the text, the subjectivity through which much of the fictional world will be experienced, and the principal focus of narrative interest.

The characterisation of these saga heroines offers the reader a compelling and informative perspective on history. Like Margaret Mitchell's Scarlett O'Hara, Caroline, Angélique and Léa all come from families privileged by class, wealth or both, and grow up in relative security and comfort in a rural environment. It is the family's lack or loss of fortune, causally determined to some degree by real political events, that precipitates each heroine out of a predictably feminine story of protected girlhood followed by marriage, and into history. Youth, provincial origins, and the sheltered upbringing accorded to respectable girls mean that each heroine provides an initially ingenuous vision of national events: the 1789 Revolution (*Caroline*), the last years of the Regency and accession of Louis XIV to the throne (*Angélique*), the outbreak of World War 2 and Occupation (*Bicyclette Bleue)* are each seen through the eyes of a political *ingénue* whose gradual discovery of the public world makes her an effective intra-diegetic stand-in for readers unlikely to possess detailed knowledge of the period's history. An engaged, curious perspective on a partially familiar and dramatically conflicted period of French history is certainly one source of the novels' appeal. A very young Caroline witnesses the mob's attack on Versailles from a hiding-place within the palace, while Angélique is a naïve observer of plots against the throne before becoming closely involved in the life of Louis XIV's court. Positioned with the heroine through internal focalisation, the reader learns alongside her.

If one pleasure lies in the focalising of history from within, another lies in readerly identification with the attractive qualities that each heroine displays: energy, resourcefulness, courage, a voracious appetite for life. Given the female narrative perspective, and the stories' sustained emphasis on love and relationships, it seems safe to assume that women constitute the primary target readership for these novels, and that one element of the novels' appeal lay in their dramatisation of a tension, still unresolved for twentieth-century readers, between normative models of femininity and the will to pleasure and self-affirmation embodied by these heroines. Each novel represents the powerful pressure on girls to conform to a prescribed script of girlhood as preparation for a suitable marriage, followed by an adult life centred on domesticity and motherhood - a representation achieved in part, and in each case, through the secondary character of a more conventionally feminine sister who acts as foil to the central protagonist. Each heroine displays as a child an innate force of character that already resists this model, and then finds herself, thanks to the dramas of history, in a world that offers her the freedom to deploy her energies on a public stage. Alone and at mortal risk in revolutionary Paris, for example, Caroline feels more elation than fear: "Ainsi pour la première fois de sa vie, elle était libre" (Laurent 1947, 152). The heroines may deplore the historical upheavals that disrupt their lives and those of their contemporaries, and the violence that accompanies them, but they take full advantage of exceptional circumstances to escape the classic plot of a woman's life.

The picaresque novel traditionally features a hero who is also a rogue or rascal, such as Henry Fielding's Tom Jones or indeed Margaret Mitchell's ruthlessly egotistical Scarlett O'Hara. With such heroes the reader entertains an enjoyably ambivalent relationship that mingles identification with moral disapproval, the identification being all the more pleasurable for its transgression of moral and social laws to which, in everyday life, the reader may well subscribe and conform. This is certainly the process at work here: like Scarlett, Caroline, Léa and Angélique are morally flawed heroines, their appealing vitality shading into a ruthless will to survive, their joie-de-vivre into an uncompromising pursuit of their own pleasure. In the extreme circumstances provided by history, each heroine proves herself capable of killing, Caroline in particular repeatedly ensuring her own survival by deliberately sacrificing the lives of others. [2]

[2] In several episodes Caroline pragmatically sacrifices others to save her own skin, including Madame de Coigny who has sheltered Caroline in the past, but who – with only a fleeting moment of regret – she condemns to the guillotine by taking her place in a planned escape from the Conciergerie, the prison in which both have

They pursue the men they desire with a cheerful indifference to any existing commitments, their own or those of the potential lover: Caroline's inclination to seduce any handsome man she meets is only heightened by the knowledge that he is committed to another woman,[3] whilst in her pursuit of Laurent, Léa repeatedly endangers the happiness of his wife Camille, and this despite the fact that Camille is also a devoted friend to Léa herself.

Though each heroine undergoes a degree of "éducation sentimentale" whereby she learns to extend self-love to concern for others, the picaresque structure and avoidance of full *dénouement* (for sequels are planned) means that her conversion to virtue must always remain incomplete. It is a common feature of popular women's fiction to depict the improper, to imagine alternatives to normative models of female identity and behaviour: thus even the mildest forms of romantic fiction need a female rival or anti-heroine who acts out, for the reader's enjoyment, a refusal of female selflessness, and is then punished for it. The difference here is that the heroine herself, motivated and to some extent justified by exceptional historical circumstance, herself performs the transgressive role, and does so with impunity. In many senses far from feminist – individual self-interest trumps female solidarity throughout these stories, and extreme erotic beauty or "to-be-looked-at-ness"[4] is central to each heroines' characterisation[5] - these sagas nonetheless propose a radical alternative to the romantic, monogamous, selfless ideal of femininity that still underpinned most popular culture in the post-war

been incarcerated by the revolutionary government (Laurent 1947, 346-56). Angélique (Golon 1956b, 133) kills the evil Grand-Coesre with a knife blow to the heart. Léa calmly and accurately shoots a man who threatens her escape during exodus before the invading German army (Deforges 1983, 178).

[3] Caroline listens jealously to the handsome Louvet's story of his passionate, faithful love for his mistress, and reflects that 'il serait bien drôle, grâce à un léger manège de coquetterie, de lui prouver que cette passion ne peut résister au voisinage d'une autre femme', a thought that she rapidly translates into action (Laurent 1947, 244).

[4] Laura Mulvey's useful term for women's cinematic status as object of the male gaze (Mulvey 1989).

[5] This is the case to such a hyperbolic extent that it is hard not to detect a note of humour interlaced with the pleasures of vicarious narcissism. 'Par le diable', the Prince de Condé tells the adolescent Angélique early in the first novel, 'lorsque vous serez femme je prévois que des hommes se pendront pour vous avoir rencontrée' (Golon 1956a, 108), and in *La Bicyclette bleue* 'l'ascendant de Léa sur les hommes était total. Pas un qui ne lui résistât' (Deforges 1983, 15).

period, and remained active, if contested, when Deforges published *La Bicyclette bleue.*

## Eroticism and romance

The heroine sagas thus reference but also differ from the popular genre of romance. The basic, familiar narrative pattern of romance is that of girl meets boy, mutual desire and affinity is established, often after a period of its denial by one or both lovers, obstacles are overcome, and union is achieved or, in the case of the unhappy romance, proves unachievable (Holmes 2006). The romance indulges, knowingly, the ideal of the one true love, magically encountered and thereafter determining, completing, enriching the rest of life. This script is entirely present in these historical sagas, but it is modified in significant ways.

The sixteen-year-old Caroline moves to Paris with her family in 1789, as the novel opens: they are impoverished members of the minor nobility, and in Paris to try to improve the family fortunes. Caroline meets and falls for the handsome, seductive Gaston de Sallanches on page 31 of a near 900-page novel. At the end of Part I, she accepts a suitable marriage to the loving but far less seductive lawyer, Georges, whose role as a leader of the moderate, Girondist faction of the Revolutionary leadership then determines Caroline's necessary flight from Paris, urgent travels around France pursued by the Jacobin army, her arrest and imprisonment, escape to England, and eventual return to public life in Paris once Georges is reinstated in the early days of the Directorate. Throughout these colourful travels, Gaston (who has joined the Revolutionary army) remains the ultimate object of Caroline's desire, and reappears periodically for passionate trysts, fathering (unbeknown to himself) her son, and awaited, as the novel closes on a note of suspense, by a Caroline now returned to the family château:

> "Madame! Madame! C'est un cavalier. Il ne m'a pas dit son nom. C'est vous qu'il demande."
>
> (Caroline descends the stairs)
>
> Encore une marche, et elle saurait… (Laurent 147, 877)

Angélique, also the teenage daughter of impoverished minor nobility, is obliged to accept marriage to a rich, physically disfigured nobleman she has never met, Joffrey de Peyrac. In an erotic scenario familiar from many popular romances, the wedding is followed by a period of celibate cohabitation, for as a highly cultured *homme galant* of his era, a proponent of the art of love, Joffrey refuses to force himself on his young wife and undertakes instead a slow process of seduction. The deferred *nuit de noces* is a revelation to Angélique, "en quelques instants une nouvelle Angélique venait de naître, épanouie, libérée." (Golon 1956a, 226) and thereafter Joffrey remains, for the rest of the multi-volume saga, the love of her life. He too fathers her children, and when he disappears from the plot, burnt at the stake ostensibly for sorcery, though in reality for displeasing the King, doubt as to the truth of his death is kept alive in a number of ways. Joffrey remains Angélique's ultimate goal.[6]

Léa, in a plot closely calqued on *Gone with the Wind*, believes herself to be in love with Laurent d'Argilat (just as Scarlett covets AshleyWilkes), but soon meets her Rhett Butler, François Tavernier, again the dispenser of extreme sexual pleasure and a sense of emotional plenitude ("C'était donc ça l'amour, cet émerveillement de chaque parcelle de chair, ce miracle qui faisait tout oublier, même la guerre?" [Deforges 1983, 188]), and the narrative instigator of Léa's adventures as a Resistance liaison agent. François's role as Resistance leader means that he too is largely absent from the plot, but he reappears episodically for moments or nights of passion.

The same pattern is observed in each of the sagas. The heroes are all forms of that familiar figure, the alpha-male hero, whose most illustrious models in English literature are Mr Darcy and Edward Rochester, but who also bestrides the pages of international, including French, popular romance from Delly to Harlequin. He is sexually skilled (Caroline is always delighted to refind "cette extase que seules la présence et la tactique de Gaston lui avaient jamais donnée" [Laurent 1947, 679]) his mastery of the public world is signified not only by his role as a political and/or military leader, but also by his eloquence, irony and irreverence, and beneath his self-control and total competence lies the soft centre of his absolute love for the heroine. The underlying goal of the heroine's adventures is to find him again and to keep him. So far – so romance.

However – and it is a very large "however" – the hero's repeated and lengthy disappearances are an absolute narrative necessity, for they enable the heroine to engage in those solitary adventures that make up the bulk of each novel and constitute its picaresque structure. Despite the underpinning of a romantic commitment to the one true love, each heroine merrily engages in a whole series of what we might call, following

---

[6] Angélique re-finds her long-lost husband in volume 6, *Angélique et son amour* (*Angélique in Love*).

Beauvoir, *contingent* amorous affairs.[7] These episodes arise from a variety of motives, that range from irresistible if entirely carnal desire, to the use of sex as a pragmatic bargaining counter, and unlike the popular romance that tends to make female erotic pleasure inseparable from emotional commitment, these novels propose no moral disapproval of their heroines' promiscuity.

One example from each novel will illustrate their vision of sex as an activity with a variety of meanings and values, hence their divergence from the monogamous ideology of romance. Caroline, under the imminent threat of being guillotined herself, attempts to seduce Boimussy, a fellow aristocrat whom she believes to be rich, in the hope of extracting enough money to bribe her jailors. He turns out to be penniless himself and destined for the scaffold the next morning – but despite her disappointment, Caroline shares his bed for his last night of life, in a gesture motivated by a mixture of physical attraction and comradely sympathy. The narrator's tone is entirely uncensorious: morally, this is one of Caroline's finer moments (Laurent 1947, 396-99). Angélique makes a bargain with the blustering, corpulent commander of the women's prison to which she has been confined: a night with him in exchange for a period of freedom sufficient to allow her to rescue her infant son. It is out of an honourable commitment to keeping her side of the contract that once her son is safe Angélique duly returns to the prison: she dreads the experience, for the "Ogre" as the prisoners call him repulses her, but she goes through with it with a degree of good will that turns unwanted sexual congress into a human exchange that is perfectly tolerable.

> Cependant, ce n'était pas aussi terrible qu'elle se l'était imaginé. L'Ogre n'était pas méchant. Il agissait un peu en homme qui ignore son poids et sa force, mais, nonobstant cet inconvénient qui la laissait à demi écrasée, elle dut s'avouer qu'elle n'avait pas été loin d'éprouver quelque volupté à être la proie de ce colosse plein de force et d'entrain. Après, elle se sentit d'une légèreté de pierre ponce. (Golon 1956b, 147).

Léa, still convinced that she is in love with Laurent, meets up with her childhood companion Mathias when he is released from a German prisoner-of-war camp:

---

[7] In her memoirs, Beauvoir recounts how, early in their relationship, Sartre proposed and she agreed that alongside the "amour nécessaire" that united the couple, each should accept the other's right to "amours contingentes", for to do otherwise would mean to renounce at a very early age all the "séduisante diversité" of erotic and emotional encounters with others (Beauvoir 1960, 26).

> Léa ne bougeait plus, attentive soudain à l'écho que réveillaient dans sa chair les caresses brutales de Mathias. Elle se disait qu'elle ne devait pas, que c'était Laurent qu'elle aimait, qu'elle était folle et imprudente mais toute résistance était d'avance vaincue chez elle tant son désir d'un corps contre le sien, d'un sexe dans son ventre était fort. (Deforges 1983, 277).

In Léa's case then, the sexual exchange is motivated by a physical desire informed by memory and friendship, but again certainly not by romantic love. Sexuality in these novels is an essential component of romance, but the episodic plot structure, so opposed to the teleological drive of the popular romance, make love and commitment far from essential to satisfactory sex. It is Caroline who articulates her philosophy of love most clearly: "Parce qu'on aime un homme, les autres hommes ne restent pas moins plaisants, et du moment qu'il s'agit d'un caprice d'un soir, ou d'un devoir, le bien-aimé n'y perd rien" (Laurent 1947, 279), but the other two heroines would certainly agree. The many sexual encounters form an important element of the plot's rhythm, which is strongly erotic because it repeatedly charts the cycle of desire, its – generally deferred - satisfaction, and a brief ensuing calm before the next encounter.[8] These novels propose, or correspond to, a pervasive feminine fantasy of romantic commitment and durable, reciprocal love, underlying but not competing with a different ideal of female agency, freedom, and adventure which is simultaneously political/historical and erotic. The double narrative structure –the unconcluded love story underpinning a picaresque eroticism – is a striking element of similarity between the three bestsellers.

## History and Story

The most obvious point of resemblance between the three texts, however, is quite simply the fact that they are all historical novels. The pleasure of reading fiction is often described through metaphors of travel or displacement, as for example, in Marie-Laure Ryan's description of "getting lost in a book" as "the imaginative transportation of the reader's virtual body onto the scene of events" (Ryan 2001, 133). Immersion in story allows us to exit our own temporally and spatially contingent lives;

---

[8] Peter Brooks describes the ambitious heroes of the nineteenth-century novel as versions of the *picaro*, in terms that could equally apply to these twentieth-century heroines: "(they) may regularly be conceived as 'desiring machines' whose presence in the text creates and sustains narrative movement through the forward march of desire, projecting the self onto the world through scenarios of desire imagined and then acted upon." (Brooks 1984, 39-40).

the specific and lasting popularity of the historical novel can be attributed to its capacity to offer us time-travel, as well as a readymade set of dramatic determinants of plot. It is the cataclysmic nature of historical events that disrupts normal social relations and at once obliges and permits the heroine to leave behind a normal female destiny and set off on her epic journey. This journey involves - for the readers' pleasure and instruction – extreme mobility, both spatial and social, so that we traverse, with Caroline, Angélique and Léa, different regions of France, other countries, and a wide spectrum of experience from poverty and deprivation to luxurious living. The novels are all thoroughly researched and informative on both historical events and the texture of the everyday at another period, from food and clothing to fashion and entertainment.

At the same time, the choice of iconic historical moments heightens the narrative tension, for what is at stake in the survival of our heroine is also, in each case, the well-being of the nation. The lives of Caroline and Angélique will only cease to be at risk when stability and order return to France, for their stories are closely entwined with those of, respectively, the violent conflicts of post-revolutionary France, and the embattled regime of Louis XIV, externally threatened and internally torn between despotism and enlightenment. Léa's salvation depends on the triumph of the Resistance. Just as the reader's knowledge of the rules of genre promises the heroine's survival, so external knowledge of these iconic periods of history guarantees that France will emerge from crisis, but the interdependence of fictional plot and historical narrative amplifies the tension of reading. The heroine's fate is tightly interwoven with that of France itself.

Narrative also works to satisfy, provisionally, the human desire for the transformation of mere chronicity into meaningfully patterned time, or to turn succession, in Ricoeur's formulation, into configuration (Ricoeur 1991, 22). The sense of teleology – of each element of plot converging towards and gaining its significance from a coherent *dénouement* – is, as we have seen, relatively weak in these episodic and deliberately unconcluded plots, but history provides some of that sense of purposeful time, and of a promised conclusion conferring meaning on the whole. Whatever the twists and turns of the heroine's story, we know that it is leading towards the end of the Terror and Napoleon's accession to power, or to the lengthy and in some senses glorious reign of Louis XIV, to the defeat of Nazism and of its French collaborators. Published and massively read in the 1940s, 50s and 80s, respectively, each of these novels belongs to a different moment in a half-century characterized, in France as elsewhere in the West, by rapid, substantial and highly contested change in definitions of gender, and indeed of nation. Despite their striking similarities of narrative structure and technique, differences between the novels also situate them within particular decades. Jacques Laurent, a right-wing author who was briefly imprisoned post-war for collaboration, uses Caroline's self-absorbed contempt for politics to portray Revolutionary France cynically, as a country divided between equally self-interested factions. Caroline's contradictions help to explain her appeal for a 1940s readership: the ruthless determination and *débrouillardise* that ensure her survival surely resonated with readers recently emerged from the dark years of Occupation, whilst her furious dismissal of "ces passions politiques qui ruinaient le plaisir de vivre" (279) may well have tapped an undercurrent of anti-political sentiment, so soon after the violent internal conflicts of the Liberation period. In terms of gender roles, Caroline (perhaps unsurprisingly, as the creation of a right-wing male author) is also the least emancipated of the three: her disdain for politics is equally an aspect of her narcissism, for political passions tend to deflect male attention away from herself towards "des idées qui n'avaient pas de corps, pas de couleurs, qui ne vivaient que dans les livres et les discours" (263), and despite her energetic flouting of the rules of decorum, Caroline is happy to be the adored "other" of the male subject, a form of socially endorsed *mauvaise foi* in women that Beauvoir would brilliantly dissect the year after Caroline's invention.[9] In post-war France women had only just emerged from the extreme gender-conservatism of the Vichy years and had scarcely won the vote.

The success of the first *Angélique* dates from the late 1950s, when France was experiencing at once the loss of Empire and of any leading role on the world stage, and a dramatically rapid process of economic expansion and modernization. The reign of Louis XIV offered nostalgic appeal, as a high moment of the nation's political and cultural glory, and possibly too some analogy with the newly entrepreneurial, leisured and fashion-conscious mentality of the consumer age. Angélique as heroine can even be seen as the "new woman" emerging from the 1950s mix of improved opportunities for female education and employment, and promotion of motherhood and family – the model of femininity promoted by (for example) *Elle* magazine: she is educated, astutely enterprising (she re-makes her fortune and that of her children after Joffrey's death by setting up a successful restaurant, then gaining the royal patent for the

[9] In *Le Deuxième Sexe* (1949), Beauvoir shows how women's economic and social dependence on the "first" sex can produce a false sense of identity that depends on male perception: "la femme vassale [...] s'entête dans l'impossible poursuite de l'être à travers le narcissisme, l'amour..." (Beauvoir 1976, II, 597).

manufacture of chocolate), socially and sexually assertive - and at the same time an utterly devoted and competent wife (for the brief duration of her marriage) and mother.

*La Bicyclette bleue* was part of a wave of renewed French interest in the Occupation, triggered in part by the 1981 showing on French TV of Marcel Ophüls' revealing 1969 documentary on the collaboration, *Le Chagrin et la pitié*, long kept off the small screen by government censorship. Léa's cheerful assumption of her own right to pleasure might also chime with the values of what is generally seen as a strongly materialist decade, but above all her increasingly active and at times quasi-military role in the Resistance speaks to an era marked by second wave feminism's contestation of gender boundaries. Léa's story makes the fewest concessions to marriage and maternity as essential components of ideal femininity, and the development of the heroine's motivation from a personal will to freedom to a passionate defence of liberty and equality as collective values also translates Deforges' post-MLF (*Mouvement pour la libération des femmes*) feminism into narrative form.[10]

## Conclusion

Historical novels are inevitably shaped to some extent by the historical moment of their composition. More telling, though, than their historically located differences are the similarities of plot structure that connect these hugely popular fictions. In each, an initially naïve, high-spirited and adventurous heroine acts as both primary agent and focaliser of a colorful sequence of events that intertwine the fictional and the historic, immersing the reader in a compellingly plotted fictional world rendered the more mimetically plausible by its anchorage in documented history. The heroine's spatial and social mobility, determined in each case by political upheavals, lends itself to the exploration of different facets of the period – for example the Versailles court and Paris underworld, revolutionary Paris and the life of émigré aristocrats in London, the sinister luxury of collaborationist milieux in occupied Paris, and cold and hunger in the Maquis. The generic imperative to diversify the heroines' adventures, together with the saga's need to constantly defer full closure, produces a picaresque structure matched by the picaresque nature of the heroine, who

[10] As a publisher Deforges specialised in women's erotic writing, re-editing for example the work of the fin-se-siècle lesbian poet Renée Vivien, and herself authoring several erotic novels before launching into popular fiction with *La Bicyclette bleue*. She has always declared herself a feminist.

transgresses the norms of virtuous behavior in a way that invites a pleasurably ambivalent mode of identification. Caroline, Angélique and Léa perform all the major feminine roles: they each know what it is to be a loving daughter, a devoted wife, above all, in each case, a fiercely fond mother. But the open-ended plots mean that they never remain fixed in any of these roles: their adventures resume, connoting a restless desire that cannot be simply assuaged by romance or motherhood. Romantic historical novels are not widely seen as a radical or challenging genre of women's fiction. The heroine sagas, however, suggest otherwise: the narrative pleasures they offer include not only a retelling of history through a woman's eyes, but also a reworking of plot, both the plot of romance, and the traditional plot of a woman's life.

## Works cited


Baroni, Raphaël. 2007. *La Tension narrative.* Paris: Seuil.

Beauvoir, Simone. 1976. (1949). *Le Deuxième Sexe.* Paris: Gallimard, Livre de poche.

—. 1960. *La Force de l'Age*. Paris: Gallimard, Livre de poche.

Brooks, Peter. 1984. *Reading for the Plot. Design and Intention in Narrative.* Cambridge MA and London: Harvard University Press.

Deforges, Régine. 1983. *La Bicyclette bleue.* Paris: Fayard.

Golon, Serge et Anne. 1956a. *Angélique Marquise des Anges*. Paris: France Loisirs.

—. 1956b. *Marquise des Anges Le Chemin de Versailles.* Paris: France Loisirs.

Holmes, Diana. 2006. *Romance and Readership in Twentieth-Century France: Love Stories*. Oxford: Oxford University Press.

Light, Alison. 1989. "'Young Bess': Historical Novels and Growing up". *Feminist Review* No. 33 (Autumn), 57-71.

Mulvey, Laura. 1989 (1975): "Visual Pleasure and Narrative Cinema", in *Visual and other Pleasures*. Bloomington: Indiana University Press, 14-26.

Ricoeur, Paul. 1991. "Life in Quest of Narrative", in D. Wood, ed. *On Paul Ricoeur: Narrative and Interpretation.* London: Routledge, 20-33.

Ryan, M.-L. 2001. *Narrative as Virtual Reality. Immersion and Interactivity in Literature and Electronic Media.* Baltimore & London: The Johns Hopkins University Press.

Saint-Laurent, Cécil. 1947. *Caroline Chérie.* Paris: Éditions Jean Froissart.

# CHAPTER ELEVEN

# TELLING TALES ABOUT WORLD WAR TWO IN PHILIPPE GRIMBERT'S *UN SECRET*[1]

SUSAN BAINBRIGGE

Carlos Ruiz Zafón recently commented that making a distinction between high and popular cultures is tantamount to "cultural fraud", arguing that there is no "good literature", only good writing.[2] The text examined here has enjoyed popular widespread appeal as well as winning literary prizes, topping bestseller lists and achieving further recognition through a film adaptation by Claude Miller in 2007.[3] The plot-driven narrative (based on the narrator's personal "enquête") certainly engages "plaisir", but is not formulaic, and not to be dismissed by the Barthesian framework (whereby the "readerly" text engenders a lesser pleasure whereas the "writerly" text produces a superior kind of bliss ["jouissance"]) (Barthes 1973). What distinguishes the work as "good writing"? Why is telling the story important? This essay explores such questions in a text that is concerned with World War Two, that grapples with Holocaust testimony, public and private histories and stories, family secrets and childhood memory (or absence of it). So, whilst the subject matter opens up ethical, philosophical and political questions, the work can also be viewed in terms of its storytelling function. Pleasures are gleaned from the text through the creation of suspense, drama, and its resolution in the conclusion. Popular texts are known for their success in satisfying the reader by fulfilling various narrative desires, for example, in the pleasure of happy endings, or by offering a sense of "reconciliation" between the self and the world through the plot structure. Here, the

[1] I am grateful to the Carnegie Trust for a grant which enabled me to research this piece of work.

[2] See also Migozzi (2005) who affirms the "porosité des frontières entre littérature consacrée et littérature de grande consommation", 220.

[3] *Un secret*, first published in 2004 by Grasset. References here are to the Poche edition (2007), abbreviated in the text to *S*.

"sharing" of the secret between narrator, his entourage, and the reader plays an important symbolic role, and taps into a broader historical context. *Un secret* is part of a considerable œuvre of French writings, which deals with the subject of the Second World War by exploring both personal and collective trauma (many, although not all, autobiographical or at least autofictional). We could cite, for example, Georges Perec's *W ou le souvenir d"enfance* (1975), Sylvie Germain's *Magnus* (2005), Chantal Chawaf's *Le Manteau noir* (1998), Joseph Joffo's *Un Sac de Billes* (1973), and even Simone de Beauvoir's *Le Sang des autres* (1945).[4]

I will examine the credentials for considering *Un secret* as a popular text, before going on to some of the ethical dilemmas posed precisely by storytelling about the Second World War and Holocaust. Then the analysis will focus on how the story is told, the creation of suspense in the telling, and the way in which this impacts on the narrator, and, via identification with the narrator's point of view, on the reader. The story pivots around the Second World War, bringing this period of history into view via the intimate portrayal of one particular family. Their personal traumas are described in a way that situates them within a bigger socio-historical picture: the collective trauma of a whole generation is effectively encapsulated. My working definition of "trauma" is from Kai Erikson:

> By individual trauma I mean a blow to the psyche that breaks through one's defenses so suddenly and with such brutal force that one cannot react to it effectively… By collective trauma, on the other hand, I mean a blow to the basic tissues of social life that damages the bonds attaching people together and impairs the prevailing sense of community. (Erikson 1976, 153-54, in Alexander 2004, 4)

In *Un secret* the story itself focuses on the wartime and post-war childhood experiences of its male narrator and his family. We learn how as a young boy he felt out of place, and ill-at-ease physically. We discover that he invented an imaginary brother. He had fantasised about the existence of this brother: "un petit garçon qui se rêvait une famille idéale" (*S* 35). However, over the course of the story, the narrator uncovers a family secret, via the confidences of family friend Louise, revealing that one aspect of his fantasy does in fact have a basis in reality: that before his birth, and his parents' relationship, and prior to the outbreak of the Second

[4] For a comprehensive list of texts on the Second World War, see the database at the University of Leeds ("Narratives of the Second World War and the Occupation in France since 1939: Cultural Production and National Identity").

World War, his father had had a first wife and son ("Simon"), who were sent to Auschwitz, perishing there in the gas chambers.[5]

In terms of structure, the narrative consists of five short chapters followed by an epilogue. In the first chapter, we are introduced to the narrator and presented with the broad context in which the story takes place: where he lives, and who the central people are in his life. The second chapter presents the boy's imaginary construction of his "famille idéale": how his parents met, and the circumstances of his own birth. In the third and fourth chapters, we are given a new version of these events, informed by his conversations with Louise. This subsequent version, the "seconde histoire", reshapes the original narrative, and the narrator comments on their shared narrative project. In the fifth chapter the narrator considers his later teens and student days and juxtaposes these memories with the processing of discoveries which so dramatically shook his life at the age of fifteen. The epilogue follows up the story with a now older narrator who is himself a parent looking back over his past.

In terms of plot development, the discovery of a soft toy dog in the attic, which the young narrator (uncannily) calls "Sim", is the catalyst for the story of the narrator's discoveries. After sensing his parents' discomfort about the soft toy, he starts to delve further, gradually unearthing secrets from the family's past. This autobiographical novel, which is set in France, moves between past and present, between the depiction of the young boy and the older narrator's commentary, to tell us how the latter deals with the secrets and "unsayable" things that he confronts.

## *Un secret*: a popular text?

*Un secret* attracted a broad popular readership when first published. The Livre de Poche edition has sold over 900 000 copies.[6] It won the prestigious *Prix Goncourt des Lycéens* in 2004 and the *Elle Prix des Lectrices* in 2005. These two prizes contributed to a high volume of sales. The book and film adaptation have been used regularly in schools in France, evidenced by the numerous websites to be found which are devoted to the presentation of pedagogical materials and study aids.[7] The child as central protagonist contributes to the book's appeal: in such

---

[5] See *S*, p. 167.

[6] See http://www.info-culture.com/public/manifestation/51523 [accessed 23 February 2010].

[7] See http://www.bibliopoche.com/edition/Un-secret--Dossier-pedagogique/340493.html [accessed 4 May 2011].

contexts, children symbolise a certain vulnerability and innocence, and readily capture the reader's sympathies. The book's accessibility is also due in part to its presentation. Grimbert, who is a practising psychoanalyst, avoids writing a text filled with jargon. It is possible to identify psychoanalytical ideas and strands – he makes reference in interviews to Lacanian concepts (such as the "passe"), for example – but acknowledgement of such terms is not necessary for an understanding of the text.[8] *Un secret* forms part of an ever-increasing corpus of books that engage with the legacy of the Second World War and bears testimony to our ongoing fascination with this period of history.

Grimbert brings the trauma of the Holocaust to more recent generations, and presents a point of entry into a shared collective past. He thus opens up potential for discussion between older and younger generations. The author has specifically commented on the appeal of the work to adolescents in an interview on the film adaptation:

> Le thème du secret – au-delà du secret lié à l"Histoire, propre au livre –, les bouleverse et trouve des résonances dans leur propre vécu. Car le trauma se transmet de génération en génération, avec souvent des répercussions physiques (Ktourza 2007).

Grimbert's words echo the popularly held belief that trauma passes down from generation to generation (transgenerational trauma), as explored in Holocaust survivor testimony, or indeed more generally in explorations of memories of trauma and their impact on individuals and large groups.[9] In this respect, Nigel Hunt confirms in his study on memory, war and trauma, that it is important to "show how memory works in the social and collective sense, and how memories are transmitted and changed through generations" (Hunt 2010, 204-5).

## Telling the Story: the challenges of the "unspeakable"

Numerous writers (Primo Levi and others, for example) have asked whether it is actually possible to write about events of unspeakable horror, pondering the nature of the testimonial function of the survivor text, and

---

[8] "Si ce livre apporte un témoignage, c'est bien celui d"un travail sur moi-même déjà accompli. S'il fallait la rapprocher d'une expérience analytique – ce n'était pas le projet à l'origine – ce serait plutôt de l'ordre de la 'passe' au sens lacanien" (Cupa 2005).

[9] See, for example, the differing views of van Alphen (2006: 488), and Hirsch (2008).

the difficulties that this engenders. Others question whether a language exists to speak of trauma, or to evoke the trauma of loss – the "unsayables" or "unspeakables".[10] The acts of retelling, and reading, if they engender pleasure, also carry ethical risks. Professor Sean Hand, in a Warwick University website course description, identifies some of the problems posed by study of representations of the Holocaust. He asks whether any account would "run the risk of normalising the events, by introducing narrative construction and even aesthetic pleasure? On the other hand, if such a story was not told, would our culture not just rest on oblivion?" He asks whether "words such as "story" and "culture" [can] be even uttered in this context?"[11] We could also consider to what extent the motives behind the need to bear witness (the "besoin de témoigner", identified by Grimbert in an interview[12]), require examination. Factual documents might well be less controversial than an account containing, as here, a love story, and the depiction of eroticised, rather than, or as well as, victimised, bodies. Such texts may have narratives which engender pleasure in the reading and whose conclusions can offer satisfying resolutions. I will suggest that Grimbert's text offers a cathartic pleasure, experienced by virtue of the plot structure, and that its denouement offers the reader the vicarious experiences of redress and reconciliation (via their own "working through" the text).

## Telling the Story: the pleasures of the text

*Un secret* contains different types of narrative. There is romance (between the narrator's parents) and tragedy (the recounting of the narrator's discovery of the deaths of his father's first wife, Hannah (presented as a quasi-suicidal act) and their son Simon at the hands of the Nazis. There is suspense and drama, as the narrator's journey of discovery unfolds and his fantasised past is replaced by more concrete facts. There is

---

[10] There is an extensive bibliography on this subject, which includes, for example, Adorno (2003), Augé (1998), Ferenczi and Boltanski (2002), Hoffman (2004), Laub and Felman (1992), Caruth (1996), LaCapra (2001), Leys (2000), Rothberg (2009), Suleiman (2006), Todorov (2004), and Young (1988).

[11] See http://www2.warwick.ac.uk/fac/arts/ughandbook/french/ [website accessed 7 March 2010].

[12] "J'ai le sentiment, confirmé par l'écoute de mes lecteurs et par la lecture de leur courrier, que mon livre a souvent produit un effet du même ordre: un chemin accompli, dont j'ai éprouvé le besoin de témoigner, chemin qui s'offre à d'autres et leur ouvre la perspective d'une transformation. Un avant, un après: dans ce sens mon 'Secret' pourrait aussi se définir comme un acte" (Cupa 2005).

history, the story providing information about places and people (for example, in the attention to detail in the use of historical, geographical, cultural and architectural markers in key "scenes").[13] However, Grimbert has insisted that the book is not a historical novel: if it is an interweaving of stories and history, the emphasis is firmly on the uncovering of a secret (the existence of the narrator's father's first wife and a half-brother both of whom perished in Auschwitz):

> *Un secret* n'est effectivement pas un livre historique, même si l'histoire est présente de façon indirecte. J'avais surtout envie qu'on entende quelque chose sur la trajectoire d'un secret, ce qui est au fond le véritable sujet de ce livre. (Brunet 2006, 51)

This focus on the exploration of the "secret" does not nullify, however, other ways of viewing the text, precisely in terms of its straddling of history and (personal) story. Despite Grimbert's disavowals, his text is still positioned within a particular historical context, specifically the period of the Occupation in France, for a long time taboo, but now subject to intense, ongoing scrutiny. Henry Rousso's book titles, referring to the "syndrome de Vichy" and the "passé qui ne passe pas", encapsulate this tension between past and present (Rousso 1990; Conan and Rousso 1994). There is the ethical imperative "to tell" that makes storytelling a vital part of the "devoir de mémoire". Conan and Rousso's work outlines the danger that, in focusing on the past, we lose sight of the urgent demands of the present (Conan and Rousso 1994, 286).[14] Nonetheless Hirsch, in her writings on the Holocaust, refers to Raoul Hilberg's stress on the importance of storytelling "as a skill historians need to learn if they are to be able to tell the difficult history of the destruction of the Jews" (Hirsch 2008, 105).

Grimbert's double narrative, both personal *and* historical, engages us at different levels: if we are held in suspense about the outcome of his particular story, we are nonetheless familiar with the broader historical backdrop: we know what is coming. Structurally, there is a bifocal aspect to the text. Despite the author's emphasis on the book as an exploration of a particular "secret" (rather than as a "livre historique"), we are presented with a story that recounts the period of the Second World War, juxtaposed with the narrator's reflections on this narrative from the "present" time of writing. The dramatic present tense is particularly effective in creating

[13] The narrator refers to place names, newspapers, hotels, cemeteries etc.

[14] Robin (2003) also raises related questions about memory and commemoration (see pp. 341, 361-62, 375 in particular).

and sustaining tension in the story. All these features of the narrative contribute to its success in terms of the storytelling function. It is via the personal elements that the story takes hold – the reader empathising with the male narrator as he uncovers and confronts his past, charting his own evolution from frail, sickly child to writer and analyst. The personal and the public are of course not discreet spheres, but inevitably intertwined. The story is structured around certain key revelatory moments. Suspense is created via the revelation of secrets, in which the narrator's family friend Louise plays a central role. Both a personal journey and incursion into history, the narrative culminates in the narrator's satisfactory forging of a sense of identity via writing (where writing is understood to be an existential "act"). Since Louise is perceived to have played a key role in the construction of this identity, and in the revelation of secrets, it is to this central figure that the analysis now turns.

Louise is the catalyst; she is the messenger, and the "healer" in the story, the prime "fil conducteur". Her treatment room is next door to the narrator's parents' shop, and early in the story she is introduced as a constant in the narrator's life, with whom he and his family have considerable daily contact ("Louise faisait partie de notre famille, je l'avais toujours connue", *S* 28). She is both metaphorically and literally a healer, since she provides nursing care and "soins à domicile" from her small clinic (the narrator himself is the recipient of vitamin injections and the like during his childhood).

The narrator describes their meetings in terms of an ongoing dialogue ("Nous n'avions jamais interrompu nos conversations" [*S* 161]). She influences his choice of studies and career as a psychoanalyst: "[…] Louise, qui savait si bien écouter, m'avait ouvert les portes, elle m'avait permis de dissiper les ombres, m'avait restitué mon histoire" (*S* 169). The narrator emphasises his identification with Louise early on in the story. Her physical imperfections – a club foot – mirror his own perceived shortcomings ("Je la sentais proche de moi, sans doute en raison de sa difformité: elle devait sa démarche cahotante à un pied-bot dissimulé dans une chaussure orthopédique" [*S* 29]). Her childhood experiences chime with his own ("Louise racontait l'enfance d'une petite fille boiteuse, moquée, vivant dans l'ombre de ses camarades plus agiles. Je m'y reconnaissais" [*S* 32]). Described differently from his parents, her rheumatic joints and sagging skin contrast with their strong athletic bodies, which are frequently commented upon.[15] Ironically, she is the "survivante"

[15] Note the narrator's avowed fascination with bodies, which reflects the predominance of the body as a theme in the book as a whole. See *S* 26, 30.

par excellence, outliving his parents. Another crucial difference is that she, unlike his parents, claims to hide no secrets: "Elle se prétendait sans secrets" (*S* 31). The narrator's meetings with Louise in her "cabinet" resemble those between a therapist and her patient (this aspect of the relationship takes on greater significance as the story develops).[16]

Via Louise, the family secrets come to life. Suspense builds when Louise broaches taboo subjects, or when the narrator intervenes to comment. For example, when she comes to the facts about his half-brother, the narrator writes: "Louise venait *enfin* de prononcer le nom de Simon" (*S* 76, my emphasis). Life under the Occupation is described in a personalising of the history that the narrator has learned from his school books. Louise's narrative is described as a series of chapters ("de nouveaux chapitres", *S* 77), some of which are painful to recount, so that the narrator must urge her on (*S* 127).[17] He finds out that the brother of his fantasies had, in fact, existed: "Le frère que je m'étais inventé, celui qui avait rompu ma solitude, ce grand frère fantôme avait donc existé" (*S* 76). He learns of his parents' escape from Paris during the Occupation to a village in the Indre département. He discovers the tragic circumstances in which his step-brother and his father's first wife died, a version of which his parents preferred not to believe (that Hannah had given herself and her son up to the authorities in a suicidal gesture, fearing that her husband was developing a relationship with Tania, the narrator's mother). Louise is the lynchpin in helping the narrator to "find the plot".

The story that unfolds is both tragic and romantic. In her role as storyteller, we learn that Louise falls prey to silences, to "mutisme" (*S* 126). She is sometimes overcome by emotion and cannot continue: "Après m"avoir décrit ces lieux interdits, ces panneaux infamants, ces étoiles brodées des quatre lettres qui me désignaient aujourd'hui, Louise voulait me dire encore une chose, la plus douloureuse, mais sa voix s'est étranglée" (*S* 76). Meetings have to be interrupted, and the story resumed. This depiction of Louise's encounters with the narrator is interspersed with his analysis of what he is being told, and his reactions to his personal "enquête". Temporal shifts remind us of the way in which the story is being told, with flashbacks and flashforwards operating in tandem. For example, he interjects: "Louise me dira […]" (*S* 137); "je vais naître dans

---

[16] The narrator writes: "Alors je pouvais me laisser aller à lui raconter mes rêves" (*S* 32). He also comments that his parents would confide in her too.

[17] See also his reference to events in terms of a book: "[…] Louise tournait pour moi les pages d'un livre que je n'avais encore jamais feuilleté" (*S* 98), and "les pages tournent de plus en plus rapidement" with reference to Paris under the Occupation (*S* 102).

ce quartier […]" (*S* 153). With each revelation comes a change in the narrator's sense of self ("Je n'étais plus le même […]", *S* 77), just as his understanding of his loved ones changes in the light of his conversations with Louise. Her story enables the narrator to construct his own account, and this is why it is crucial to an understanding of the storytelling function of the book as a whole: "Grâce aux révélations de Louise j'avais bâti ce récit" (*S* 146). This story within a story, referred to in the text as "une seconde histoire" (*S* 85), counters the fantasy past that the narrator created for himself in the early part of the text. Thus the two narratives – the narrator's fantasised past and Louise's version of events (a further "phantasy" on the narrator's part? the figure of a beneficent good mother and ideal interlocutor?) – can be compared.

The telling of the story becomes bound up with the narrator's construction of his identity via the construction of a narrative. The latter encompasses the imagined story of his conception, the discovery of the existence of his half-brother, and incorporates comments on his education and the charting of the direction of his future life. Likened to a therapeutic process, the writing of the narrative opens up an exploration of the disparate strands of the past. It is a grieving process, movingly told. As the narrator becomes mentally more robust, he describes how he improves physically too. By the end, he presents himself as an adult, with a more secure sense of self and with a purpose in life (as an analyst, a writer, and a father). He negotiates a less fraught and confused relationship with his parents, especially his father.[18] The story takes on a more upbeat, redemptive quality that is typical of many popular novels. Where his imperfections (his "maigreur" [*S* 15], "pâleur maladive" [*S* 20], and "anatomie défaillante" [*S* 21])[19] had been highlighted in contrast with his parents' taut, athletic bodies ("Mes parents, mes bien-aimés, dont chaque muscle avait été poli, comme ces statues qui me troublaient dans les galeries du Louvre" [*S* 20]), he now comments that a certain role reversal has taken place. His father's frailty informs the narrator's perception of a change in the dynamic of their relationship. In fact, the death of their dog occasions a particularly poignant moment of reflection and reconciliation in which the narrator broaches the traumatic family experiences that have hitherto remained taboo:

---

[18] For example, regarding his father's ambivalence about his Jewish identity.

[19] He also comments: "je haïssais mon corps et mon admiration pour le leur ne connaissait plus de limites"; "l'éclatante santé de mes parents contrastait encore davantage avec mon aspect souffreteux" (*S* 25).

> Je l'ai serré dans mes bras, ce que de ma vie je n'avais encore jamais fait. Son corps m'a paru frêle, celui d'un homme âgé que je dominais maintenant d'une tête. Me sentant étrangement fort je n'ai pas versé une larme, la mort de notre chien avait été l'occasion d'un nouveau retournement: je venais de délivrer mon père de son secret (*S* 173).[20]

The book's concluding message seems to be that the narrator has surmounted the physical and psychological challenges of his childhood, and reached a greater understanding of self and significant others.

The writing of the story itself takes on physical aspects too: it is compared both to the construction of a monument and the healing of a wound. Words related to "restitution" and "construction" are used, emphasising the focus on the narrator's psychological scaffolding as he pieces together different experiences from his past and thus re-examines his own changing sense of self. It is a process which the narrator links to grief and mourning, writing that "Dans ses pages reposerait la blessure dont je n'avais jamais pu faire le deuil" (*S* 180). Of course, it is important here to make the distinction between narrator and author, between actual and fictional dramatisation of self.[21] The construction of a *récit*, deemed to have released the narrator from the dead weight of grief, is a well-known strategy for processing traumatic events. According to Stéphanie Orace, language inscribes loss: "la perte, pour l'écrivain, s'expérimente aussi dans la langue. L'écriture répète le deuil en inscrivant la disparition en son cœur même: écrire le vide, l'accepter, le dépasser peut-être" (Orace 2005, 392). These are the stories we tell ourselves, and by exploring loss through narrative, we make better sense of its meaning for us.

At the end of the story, in the "epilogue", we find out how the idea for the book came about: the narrator, now a father, recounts a visit to a nearby property inhabited by a member of the Laval family in which he and his daughter find a dog cemetery. They see the loving care lavished on the memory of the animals, when members of that same family had participated in sending so many people to their deaths (*S* 180). The very fact that the story features an epilogue in which the narrator now has a daughter indicates that, in addition to the writing of the story, the narrator has reached a new stage in his life – in therapeutic terms (from a Freudian

---

[20] At the end of the story, when the narrator observes his own ageing hands, he registers a further identification: "Elles [ses mains] m'ont fait penser à celles de mon père, telles que je les avais connues dans ses dernières années. Je lui ressemblais enfin" (*S* 182).

[21] On this subject the author is purported to have told readers that Louise is the only wholly fictional character in the book.

perspective), he has been able to reinvest in the future after a period of mourning lost "objects" and is now investing in new "objects".[22]

The memories have become story, a vital story, in which the presence of a caring and listening "Other" (Louise) is key. Grimbert has affirmed the need to tell stories in order to understand the world around us: "On ne peut connaître son histoire qu'à travers une fiction. Le mémoire elle-même étant toujours une fiction" (Brunet 2006: 57). As Scott McCracken comments: "Despite the fact that it is often thought of as a passive and purely recreational activity, reading popular texts is part of the process of change. Popular fiction can supply us with the narratives we need to resituate our*selves* in relation to the world" (McCracken 1998, 16-17).[23]

To conclude, this volume of essays provides ample evidence to support the argument that stories are important. Diana Holmes highlights elsewhere the function of literature in helping us to make sense of the world, citing Todorov"s essay *La Littérature en péril*, in which he reasserts a "therapeutic, moral and social function" to literature, a focus frequently dismissed in contemporary French literary and cultural critiques (Holmes 2010, 85). Stories about the Holocaust present their own particular challenges. There is a wealth of commentary on testimonials and their purpose, but such comments do not necessarily fit with analyses of the pleasures of the text. According to David Grossman, author of *See Under: Love*, such literature enables us to engage with the other, to feel empathy, and to make us more accountable for our actions:

> At its best, literature can bring us together with the fate of others, distant and foreign. It can create within us, at times, a sense of wonder at having managed, by the skin of our teeth, to escape those strangers' fates, or make us feel sad for not being truly close to them. For not being able to reach out and touch them. I am not saying that this feeling immediately motivates us to any form of action, but certainly, without it, no act of empathy or commitment or responsibility can be possible (Grossman 2007, 6).

---

[22] Séverine Bourdieu (2005: 396) refers to Freud's analysis of mourning: "chacun des souvenirs, des espoirs par lesquels la libido était liée à l'objet est mis sur le métier, surinvesti et le détachement de la libido est progressivement accompli sur lui".

[23] In addition to this relational aspect, see also Baroni (2007, 26), who stresses the importance of telling stories from anthropological and psychological points of view: "[…] ces productions culturelles sont en mesure de produire une tension plus ou moins éphémère, qui passe pour un plaisir 'gratuit' mais dont on aurait tort de minimiser la portée anthropologique et la valeur psychologique".

In *Un secret*, I would argue that the reader is involved in the way Grossman suggests: in addition to the prospect of offering an aesthetically pleasing story, with a satisfying resolution, the narrative takes us through drama and suspense, through romance, fantasy (phantasy?) and horror. Diana Holmes, in an article on Nancy Huston, wrote of Huston's commitment to the "historical, the particular, the empathetic" (Holmes 2010, 92). Grimbert's commitment could be described in similar terms; he focuses on the experiences of embodied selves in his/stories to which the reader can relate, offering the possibility of broader vicarious identification with this period via the story of a young boy. Catharsis and immersion in historical legacy intersect. The textual scars of the Holocaust form a crucial part of the narrative, intrinsic to the plot. Theorists, critics, writers, and survivors, such as Primo Levi, writing about treatment of the Second World War, remind us of the dangers of losing sight of key political and historical contexts in theorisations of trauma. We are reminded of the power of the story itself to return us to those contexts, by our own affective and intellectual engagement with the book, and by our own processing of that transformation of memories into narrative.

The book concludes with the narrator's dedication of his text to his half-brother, Simon: "Ce livre serait sa tombe" (*S* 185). In the preceding paragraph, mention is made of a book of photographs devoted to the memory of all the children who were deported during the Holocaust and died. The book concludes, then, on both personal and collective fronts, for Simon and for all the children who perished. The therapeutic function of literature would seem to be here. *Un secret* is a cathartic text through the telling of a compelling story, which engages the reader in both cerebral and visceral ways. If the narrator's paralysis when faced with the subject of "Laval" as an oral exam question for the baccalauréat formed an important strand of the story that could not be told, the text we have here seeks to fill that gap, to avenge his own, and others' "mutisme" (*S* 166), to make the seemingly unsayable, sayable. The text also makes this "unsayable" accessible to a wide audience.

## Works cited

Adorno, Theodor W. 2003. *Can One Live After Auschwitz?: A Philosophical Reader*. Stanford: Stanford University Press.

Augé, Marc. 1998. *Les Formes de l'oubli.* Paris: Payot.

Alexander, Jeffrey C. et al. 2004. *Cultural Trauma and Collective Identity.* California: University of California Press.

Bacqué, M.-F., and M. Hanus. 2000. *Le Deuil.* Paris: PUF.

Baroni, Raphaël. 2007. *La Tension narrative: suspense, curiosité et surprise*. Paris: Seuil.
Barthes, Roland. 1973. *Le Plaisir du texte*. Paris: Seuil.
Beauvoir, Simone de. 1945. *Le Sang des autres*. Paris: Gallimard.
Bourdieu, Séverine. 2005. "Le passé en pièces détachées", in *Deuil et littérature*. Études réunies par Pierre Glaudes et Dominique Rabaté (Modernités, 21), 393-412. Bordeaux: Presses Universitaires de Bordeaux.
Brunet, Olivier. 2006. *Un secret,* dossier d'accompagnement. Paris: Livre de poche.
Caruth, Cathy. 1996. *Unclaimed Experience: Trauma, Narrative and History*. Baltimore; London: Johns Hopkins University Press.
Chawaf, Chantal. 1998. *Le Manteau noir.* Paris: Flammarion.
Conan, Éric, and Henry Rousso, 1994. *Vichy: Un Passé qui ne passe pas.* Paris: Fayard, 1994.
Cupa, Dominique. 2005. "Interview de Philippe Grimbert". *Champ psychosomatique*. 1, 37: 13-16.
Erikson, Kai. 1976. *Everything in its Path*. NY: Simon and Schuster.
Ferenczi, Thomas, and C. Boltanski (eds). 2002. *Devoirs de mémoire et droit à l''oubli*. Bruxelles: Complexe.
Germain, Sylvie. 2005. *Magnus*. Paris: Albin Michel.
Grimbert, Philippe. 2006 [2004]. *Un secret*. Paris: Livre de poche.
Grossman, David. 2007. "Confronting the beast", *The Guardian*, 15 September 2007, pp. 4-6.
—. 2001. *See Under: Love*. London: Vintage.
Hirsch, Marianne. 2008. "The Generation of Postmemory", *Poetics Today*, 29, 1: 103-28.
Hoffman, Eva. 2004. *After Such Knowledge: Memory, History and the Legacy of the Holocaust*. New York: Public Affairs.
Holmes, Diana. 2010. "To write is a transitive verb: Nancy Huston and the ethics of the novel", *Contemporary French and Francophone Studies*, 14, 1: 85–92.
Hunt, Nigel, C. 2010. *Memory, War and Trauma*. Cambridge: Cambridge University Press.
Joffo, Joseph. 2002 [1973]. *Un Sac de Billes*. Paris: Hachette.
LaCapra, Dominic. 2001. *Writing History, Writing Trauma*. Baltimore; London: Johns Hopkins University Press.
Laub, Dori, and Shoshana Felman. 1992. *Testimony: Crises of Witnessing in Literature, Psychoanalysis and History*. NY; London: Routledge.
Leys, Ruth. 2000. *Trauma: A Genealogy*. Chicago; London: University of Chicago Press.

McCracken, Scott. 1998. *Pulp: Reading Popular Fiction*. Manchester: MUP.

Migozzi, Jacques. 2005. *Boulevards du populaire*. Limoges: PULIM.

Orace, Stéphanie. 2005. "L'expression muette du deuil", in *Deuil et littérature*. Études réunies par Pierre Glaudes et Dominique Rabaté (Modernités, 21), 375-92. Bordeaux: Presses Universitaires de Bordeaux.

Perec, Georges. 1975. *W ou le souvenir d'enfance*. Paris: Denoël.

Robin, Régine. 2003. *La Mémoire saturée*. Paris: Stock.

Rothberg, Michael. 2009. *Multidirectional Memory: Remembering the Holocaust in the Age of Decolonisation*. Stanford: Stanford University Press.

Rousso, Henry. 1990. *Le Syndrome de Vichy: de 1944 à nos jours*. Paris: Seuil.

Suleiman, Susan Rubin. 2006. *Crises of Memory and the Second World War*. Harvard: Harvard University Press.

Todorov, Tzvetan. 2004. *Les Abus de la mémoire*. Paris: Arléa.

van Alphen, Ernst. 2006. "Second-Generation Testimony, Transmission of Trauma, and Postmemory", *Poetics Today*, 27, 2: 473-88.

Young, James E. 1988. *Writing and Rewriting the Holocaust*. Indiana: Indiana University Press.

## Online resources

"Interview with Sandra Ktourza", 3 October 2007, "Pédagogie et culture". http://www.vousnousils.fr/page.php?P=data/ca_vous_parle/pedagogie_et_culture/&key=itm_20071003112440_philippe_grimbert_le_film_un_sec.txt [accessed 26 January 2010].

http://www2.warwick.ac.uk/fac/arts/ughandbook/french/ [accessed 7 March 2010].

http://www.info-culture.com/public/manifestation/51523 [accessed 23 February 2010].

# PART III:

# BENDING GENRES

# Chapter Twelve

# Le Plaisir du polar et ses paradoxes

Natacha Levet

Le mot "polar", en français, renvoie à différents types de productions romanesques, et il est nécessaire, avant toute chose, d'en préciser le sens et de déterminer quel sera le genre support de cette étude, afin d'éviter tout malentendu. Ce terme, selon une première acception, désigne l'ensemble du roman policier saisi en tant que fiction romanesque mettant en scène le récit d'une transgression criminelle; il recouvre dans ce cas aussi bien le récit d'énigme que le *thriller* ou le roman noir. Selon une seconde acception, il désigne une variété spécifique de romans policiers, on parle alors de polar ou de "roman noir", et dans ce cas il se distingue du récit d'énigme ou du *thriller*. C'est cette seconde acception qui sera retenue ici: polar et roman noir seront donc employés comme des synonymes. En tant que fiction policière, le genre met bien sûr en scène, dans la majorité des cas, une transgression criminelle, mais il a aussi ces traits spécifiques, dont certains sont liés entre eux: une certaine variabilité structurelle, une forme de regard voire d'engagement social ou politique, un parti-pris d'écriture réaliste et le recours au registre tragique. Ces différents traits sont du moins repérables dans le roman noir français de la fin du 20ème siècle à nos jours.

Pourquoi évoquer le plaisir de l'intrigue dans le polar? Parce que le polar français, à l'instar de l'ensemble du genre policier, n'a cessé de le revendiquer comme un trait générique fondamental, le fondement du plaisir du texte, et ce constat n'est pas sans poser question: d'abord parce qu'on a coutume de dire que le polar est aujourd'hui un genre en grande partie reconnu et légitime: or, au regard des valeurs littéraires dominantes affichées dans la seconde moitié du 20ème siècle, le plaisir de l'intrigue ne pouvait que contribuer à dévaloriser le genre. Nous verrons comment les auteurs s'accommodent de cela. Ensuite parce que l'on peut être perplexe devant le goût des lecteurs pour des textes sombres, tragiques, flirtant avec les marges et la morbidité. Qu'est-ce qui provoque le plaisir du lecteur dans ces fictions? De quel type est le plaisir du noir? Cernons donc les spécificités du plaisir de l'intrigue, aussi bien dans leurs enjeux que dans leurs apparents paradoxes et ambiguïtés.

## 1. Le plaisir de l'intrigue et ses enjeux symboliques

De fait, comme l'ont établi Erik Neveu et Annie Collovald, le plaisir de l'intrigue est au premier plan pour les lecteurs de romans policiers. Sans surprise, on constate que les lecteurs du genre policier, et donc du roman noir, aiment à se laisser prendre par le plaisir de l'intrigue. Erik Neveu et Annie Collovald écrivent ainsi:

> L'un des bonheurs de lire un policier c'est d'être embarqué dans une histoire, et même une intrigue. Par-delà la diversité des sous-genres, il existerait une unité des lectures policières autour d'un contrat de lecture qui promet au lecteur de lui raconter une histoire avec un début, des rebonds, une issue. La narration est, presque au sens propre, un véhicule. Elle embarque le lecteur, le saisit, oblige – si du moins le livre est réussi – à ne plus lâcher le volume. (Neveu et Collovald 2004, 171)

Ce discours est largement repris par les auteurs et les éditeurs de polar. Les auteurs insistent sur leur caractère de "raconteurs d'histoires". Ainsi, Patrick Raynal, auteur de polar et directeur de la Série Noire durant les années 90, écrit dans un numéro des *Temps modernes*:

> Le combat qu'a mené alors le roman noir, mais aussi, avec lui, toute la littérature vraiment romanesque, et tout ce que, par exclusion, on a appelé « paralittérature », c'était en fait de dire: « Attention, nous sommes des romanciers, nous voulons simplement raconter des histoires. » (…) Les éditeurs, le public, les journalistes, la critique s'intéressent enfin de nouveau aux raconteurs d'histoires. (Raynal 1997, 91-92)

"Raconteur d'histoires"… L'expression est reprise par Jean-Hugues Oppel, qui confesse qu'une question le taraude tout au long de l'écriture d'un roman: "le lecteur va-t-il marcher dans ma combine ? (…) Mon métier de raconteur d'histoires est de vous manipuler rien qu'avec des mots". Tonino Benacquista dit encore: "Je suis un 'fictionneur'. Mon but est d'inventer des histoires". Chez certains, on trouve une assimilation du plaisir de l'intrigue pour le lecteur et pour l'écrivain, comme si l'auteur était, au fil de l'écriture, son propre lecteur. Fred Vargas écrit: "J'aime bien me raconter des histoires (…) Pour chacun de mes romans, je connais le meurtrier à l'avance, mais j'ignore ses motivations, et je ne connais pas toute l'histoire". Pour Claude Amoz enfin, le premier moteur de l'écriture est l'envie de "raconter des histoires", et elle ajoute : "je ne fais jamais de plan: si je sais la fin de l'histoire, je n'ai plus aucun désir de la raconter". Ecrire, c'est raconter une histoire et *se* raconter une histoire. Amoz précise d'ailleurs ce qu'elle entend par raconter une histoire:

> Avec le polar, je suis dans un espace de liberté. J'ai le plaisir de lire ou d'écrire un récit auquel je crois, avec des rebondissements qui me font battre le cœur, rire ou pleurer, des personnages auxquels je m'identifie ou que je déteste, bref, je me prends naïvement au jeu, en tant que lectrice, et, en tant qu'auteur, j'espère y prendre mon éventuel lecteur…
> (www.romanpolicier.com, site consulté le 18/08/2005)

Or, cette revendication s'accompagne d'une opposition de valeurs. Bien sûr, il s'agit là du point de vue des auteurs du polar, qui ne correspond pas nécessairement à une vue juste du champ littéraire, mais qui permet à ces acteurs de se positionner. Le roman noir revendique ce que la littérature blanche, légitime, a refusé dans la seconde moitié du 20ème siècle: l'intrigue, l'identification, l'adhésion émotionnelle, le romanesque, la naïveté (cf. Amoz). Cette opposition est très perceptible dans les propos de lecteurs que rapportent Neveu et Collovald. On retrouve là, en partie, l'opposition des valeurs telle que l'avait évoquée Jean-Louis Dufays dans un article (Dufays 2000), opposition que l'on pourrait compléter.

| Valeurs fonctionnelles classiques et dominées | | Valeurs littéraires modernes et dominantes |
|---|---|---|
| correction linguistique | vs | transgression linguistique |
| richesse du contenu | vs | beauté, richesse de la forme |
| réalité ou vraisemblance | vs | fictionalité |
| moralité, bonté | vs | transgression éthique |
| unité, clarté | vs | polysémie, complexité |
| conformité | vs | subversion, nouveauté |
| émotion | vs | impassibilité |

Il est évident que certaines de ces oppositions sont revendiquées par les auteurs français des années 1990 et 2000: l'exigence de réalisme renvoie à la valeur "réalité, vraisemblance", tout comme l'émotion s'oppose souvent, dans l'esprit des auteurs, à l'impassibilité qu'aurait cultivée le roman français depuis les années 50.[1] Cependant, dans leurs propos, les auteurs de roman noir font apparaître d'autres polarités, qui apparaissent ici en italiques:

| Valeurs fonctionnelles classiques et dominées | | Valeurs littéraires modernes et dominantes |
|---|---|---|
| correction linguistique | vs | transgression linguistique |
| richesse du contenu | vs | beauté, richesse de la forme |
| réalité ou vraisemblance | vs | fictionalité |
| moralité, bonté | vs | transgression éthique |
| unité, clarté | vs | polysémie, complexité |
| conformité | vs | subversion, nouveauté |
| émotion | vs | impassibilité |
| *"écriture d'une aventure"* | *vs* | *"aventure d'une écriture"* |
| *narration romanesque* | *vs* | *formalisme* |
| *raconteurs d'histoires* | *vs* | *écrivains* |

Les auteurs de polar opposent le plaisir de la narration romanesque au formalisme littéraire, et ce faisant, ils endossent des valeurs dominées, les revendiquent même. Le Nouveau Roman est particulièrement désigné comme le mouvement littéraire marquant une rupture avec le récit, imposant la mise en abyme (d'où la reprise des expressions de Jean Ricardou dans le tableau); au final, le roman de la seconde moitié du 20ème siècle est jugé stérile, ennuyeux, nombriliste ou tout simplement intimidant, comme en témoignent ces propos d'auteurs. Claude Amoz dit ainsi en 2005: "Quand j'ai commencé à écrire, on était en plein règne du 'nouveau roman', un mouvement qui a apporté beaucoup, mais qui, pour moi, avait quelque chose de stérilisant, dans la mesure où il dénonçait le caractère artificiel du personnage romanesque, de l'intrigue, des dialogues... ".

[1] Il n'est pas certain en revanche que les auteurs de polar revendiquent la correction linguistique: au contraire, depuis les pères fondateurs que sont Jean Amila, Léo Malet et les auteurs de la Série Noire dans les années 50 et 60, le roman noir français cultive une forme de transgression linguistique par le maniement de l'argot. Les enjeux sont certes bien différents du polar américain, qui participe à la fondation d'une langue américaine en se distinguant de la "correction" de l'anglais britannique (cf. Tadié 2006), mais ils sont tout aussi fondateurs du genre.

Didier Daeninckx écrit (propos extrait des archives du site *Mauvais Genres*):

> La lecture du roman contemporain français, du Nouveau Roman, de Tel Quel, était totalement décourageante. (…) Je me suis dit que c'était dans cet espace de la Série Noire qu'il était possible de contourner l'interdiction du roman qui planait comme une loi depuis les Surréalistes jusqu'à Tel Quel.

En quelque sorte, l'opposition entre roman noir et littérature blanche est une opposition entre "raconteurs d'histoires" et "écrivains". Si Tonino Benacquista se définit comme un "fictionneur", dont le "but est d'inventer des histoires" (propos recueillis par *L'Express*, 03/01/2002), il ajoute: "J'aimerais bien me qualifier d'écrivain, mais cela suppose une recherche sur la langue, une invention stylistique". Se poser contre, c'est fonder sa propre identité, sa spécificité.

## 2. Suspense ou curiosité: les ambivalences de la mise en intrigue du roman noir

Mais qu'en est-il des romans noirs eux-mêmes? Sont-ils des mécaniques textuelles à happer le lecteur, à l'embarquer, comme le disaient Collovald et Neveu? Le roman noir rejette-t-il du même coup la complexité narrative et fictionnelle, le travail sur la forme? Peut-on le distinguer clairement sur ce plan du récit d'énigme? La réalité des textes – et aussi des lectures – est complexe. Dans la citation de Collovald et Neveu apparaissait l'idée d'une histoire avec "un début, des rebonds, une issue", donc d'un récit linéaire et régi par le suspense. L'idée que le roman noir serait gouverné par la seule stratégie du suspense est fréquente, énoncée par exemple par Todorov dans sa "Typologie du roman policier", qui oppose sur ce point le roman noir au récit d'énigme. C'est pourquoi, selon lui, il s'agit d'un récit prospectif: "La prospection se substitue à la rétrospection. Il n'y a plus d'histoire à deviner; et il n'y a pas de mystère, comme dans le roman à énigme". Le roman noir relèverait donc du seul suspense: "On va ici de la cause à l'effet: on nous montre d'abord les données initiales (…) et notre intérêt est soutenu par l'attente de ce qui va arriver, c'est-à-dire des effets". (Todorov 1971, 14).

Le lecteur fait un pronostic, c'est-à-dire qu'il anticipe le développement futur de la fable; les rapprochements avec le roman d'aventures sont d'ailleurs assez fréquents. Voici la définition de la mise en intrigue par le suspense selon Baroni:

> Il y a création d'un effet de suspense quand, face à une situation narrative incertaine (disjonction de probabilité importante) dont l'interprète désire impatiemment connaître l'issue, il y a retardement stratégique de la réponse par une forme quelconque de réticence textuelle (fin de chapitre ou d'épisode, péripétie, ralentissement de l'action, relation chronologique ne comprenant pas de résumé synthétique dans la phase d'exposition, etc.). Une question typique du suspense: "Que va-t-il arriver?" (Baroni 2007, 99)

Cette modalité de mise en intrigue s'opposerait à celle de la curiosité, pour laquelle Baroni prend d'ailleurs l'exemple du récit d'énigme:

> Il y a création d'un effet de curiosité quand on constate que la représentation de l'action est incomplète. Quand l'incomplétude du texte s'accompagne de l'attente que le texte fournira une réponse après un certain délai, la curiosité produit l'une des modalités de la tension narrative. Dans ce cas, il y a également une forme quelconque de retardement stratégique de la réponse qui oriente l'interprétation vers un dénouement à venir. Une question typique de la curiosité: "Qui l'a fait?" (le fameux "whodunit?" du roman policier) (Baroni 2007, 99-100)

Qu'en est-il dans les textes eux-mêmes? Il suffit de mener quelques analyses structurelles et narratologiques pour voir que les choses sont plus complexes. Les analyses chiffrées qui vont suivre sont fondées sur un corpus de 138 romans noirs français des années 1990-2000.[2] Un meurtre est l'élément déclencheur, ou plutôt le nœud de l'intrigue, présent à l'ouverture du récit, dans 56,5% des romans, de manière comparable au récit d'énigme; et la tension narrative est fondée sur la résolution d'une affaire criminelle dans 67,4% des œuvres. Dans ce dernier cas, la résolution de l'affaire a pour enjeu la mise à jour de l'identité du criminel dans 75,5% des œuvres (cela pouvait s'ajouter à d'autres enjeux résolutifs). Le récit est structuré autour d'une enquête dans 55,1% des œuvres. On remarque que les romans ne proposant aucune enquête ne représentent que 11,6% des romans, et que ceux qui sont organisés autour de l'organisation d'actes criminels, cas emblématique du roman noir selon Todorov, ne représentent que 14,5% des romans. En revanche, au niveau de la narration, le corpus se caractérise majoritairement par la prospection et la linéarité évoquées par Todorov puisque cela concerne 65% des romans. Reste que dans 35% des romans, ce n'est pas le cas, et ce n'est pas une proportion négligeable. C'est trop en tout cas pour que l'on puisse faire de la structure prospective et linéaire une caractéristique générique.

---

[2] Ce corpus est celui d'un travail de thèse de littérature française soutenu en 2006: Levet, Natacha, "Le genre, entre pratique textuelle et pratique sociale: le cas du roman noir français (1990-2000)", Université de Limoges.

Dans 35% des cas, il y a distorsion de l'ordre d'exposition des événements, ou une diminution de leur clarté.

Tous ces indicateurs montrent que le roman noir repose aussi bien sur la curiosité que sur le suspense, contrairement à ce que disent les critiques qui y voient un type d'intrigue configuré par le seul suspense et une logique d'action et de conflit. On a donc tort d'opposer roman noir et récit d'énigme sur le plan de la tension narrative.

De fait, l'effet de curiosité est mobilisé dans le roman noir, parce qu'il repose dans de nombreux cas sur une enquête, sur la découverte du coupable, comme dans le récit d'énigme. Mais l'effet de curiosité est également mobilisé d'une autre manière. Le texte peut en effet dissimuler des éléments cruciaux d'une autre nature, comme par exemple l'identité de la victime. Le roman *Dans la tourbe*, de Claude Amoz, leurre son lecteur (et ses personnages) de bout en bout, puisque la tension narrative est fondée sur la recherche angoissée du corps d'une victime de meurtre, victime dont on comprendra à la fin qu'elle n'a jamais existé: il y a ici jeu avec les codes du genre. De même, certains débuts de récits engendrent de nombreuses questions, un nœud et une tension liés à l'impossibilité de comprendre pourquoi les événements se produisent, ou ce qui se passe. Ainsi, l'incipit du roman de Gilles Del Pappas, *Massilia Dreams*, nous montre l'agonie d'une femme assassinée:

> Elles n'étaient pas mal, là, dans la gangue de terre glaise. Bien sûr, elles ne brillaient pas de mille feux, elles savaient bien qu'un jour ou l'autre, elles resplendiraient à nouveau dans les yeux des femmes jalouses. Elles se reposaient dans ce berceau, un peu comme au jour de leur naissance, du temps où, pas encore taillées par des mains expertes, elles dormaient, d'un sommeil sans ombre.
>
> De son ventre le sang gicle, elle pense à la malédiction de ces maudits cailloux. C'était leur faute. Oh! Elle était bien persuadée que c'était du possible. Pas superstitieuse, non… Ça pouvait arriver. Les missions qu'on lui confiait étaient parfois dangereuses, mais là… Elle n'en voulait pas à son assassin. Bien sûr il était déçu. Elle n'aurait jamais pensé que… Et surtout, elle n'aurait jamais dû toucher ces merveilles. Non, jamais. Elle gémit. La blessure lui fait horriblement mal. Elle sait qu'elle va mourir. Avant, il y a très longtemps, elle avait fait des études de médecine. Elle était douée. Pourquoi n'avait-elle pas poursuivi? Oui pourquoi? Elle s'était souvent posé la question, en vain. Peut-être à cause de ce viol incestueux subi lors de son enfance. Ce désir paternel, le ruptus…
>
> Ses pensées dérivent. Mourir! Bizarrement ça ne l'affecte plus. Elle a bien vécu, ne regrette rien. Elle n'aurait pas dû toucher ces pierres maléfiques… (Del Pappas 2000, 7)

À la page suivante, le récit embraye sur une narration homodiégétique, un chauffeur de taxi marseillais raconte son quotidien: la rupture est totale. Rien ne permet de comprendre ce qui se passe à la première page. Cela suffit à nouer l'intrigue, le lecteur peut échafauder des hypothèses et formuler des questions: Qui est-elle? Qui l'a tuée? Pourquoi? Que sont ces pierres? Quel lien avec le chauffeur de taxi? Les deux actions surviennent-elles au même moment?

C'est un exemple: nombreux sont les romans noirs qui s'ouvrent sur des faits totalement ou partiellement incompréhensibles, ou qui commencent par ce qui, dans une narration linéaire, constituerait un élément du dénouement.

Ainsi, le plaisir de l'intrigue tient à la fois à la stratégie du suspense et de la curiosité dans le roman noir, sans qu'il soit possible d'opposer par ce critère roman noir et récit d'énigme. C'est aussi une manière de jouer avec les codes du genre, d'endosser certaines valeurs littéraires dominantes comme la subversion (*vs* la conformité), la complexité (*vs* la clarté)…

## 3. Le plaisir de l'intrigue dans le polar: un plaisir paradoxal?

Il est un autre aspect qui pose question dans le plaisir de l'intrigue: que le polar tienne en haleine un lecteur captivé par le suspense ou saisi par la curiosité, cela ne fait aucun doute. La majorité des romans offre une résorption de la tension narrative: la quasi-totalité des œuvres dénoue la tension et répond aux questions du lecteur (92%). Cependant, le polar offre une spécificité par rapport aux autres types de récits policiers: le lecteur peut avoir tous les éléments de compréhension sans que cela représente pour les personnages une issue positive car la restauration de l'ordre initial, jugée typique du récit d'énigme, n'est pas fréquente dans le roman noir. En effet, la fin peut être qualifiée de négative dans 68,1% des cas; une fin négative signifie la mort des personnages ou de leurs proches, des pertes irrémédiables pour les personnages, l'absence de sanction des coupables, le triomphe des valeurs négatives (corruption, injustice, etc.). Le roman noir est sombre, propose des destins marqués par la mort, la perte, le désastre; il dénoue la tension narrative de manière funeste, sans offrir de consolation évidente pour le lecteur. La fréquence de ces dénouements négatifs fait que le lecteur, lorsqu'il ouvre un roman noir, sait à quoi s'attendre: il en est parfois informé par le titre, par les premières pages, mais plus globalement, cette anticipation d'un dénouement funeste relève des compétences architextuelles du lecteur.

Globalement, le roman noir correspond au "suspense paradoxal" défini par Raphaël Baroni:

> Ce cas semble attester le maintien d'une certaine tension quand s'opposent dans notre conscience ce que nous pensons (ou savons) devoir survenir et ce que nous souhaiterions voir advenir. Ce désir d'une issue alternative nous pousserait ainsi à produire des anticipations improbables qui entreraient en tension avec celles fondées sur la probabilité. L'anticipation de la "catastrophe" crée alors une émotion dénuée d'incertitude: il ne s'agit plus de crainte ou d'espoir, mais d'un affect enraciné dans une passivité encore plus fondamentale que l'imprévisibilité du futur, dans l'anticipation d'un malheur inexorable, modalité thymique fataliste que l'on peut malgré tout rattacher encore au phénomène global du suspense. Nous retrouvons ici la dualité des émotions tragiques évoquées par Aristote: d'un côté la crainte – que nous assimilons au suspense classique fondé sur l'incertitude du devenir –, et de l'autre la pitié qui, bien que dépourvue d'incertitude, se fonde sur une contradiction entre le vouloir et le savoir de l'interprète (Baroni 2007, 288).

Ce cas de figure s'applique au roman noir en tant que récit déterminé génériquement. La fin de la définition est particulièrement intéressante parce qu'elle réintroduit le plaisir tragique, fondamental dans le plaisir de l'intrigue du roman noir.

Suspense paradoxal, mais aussi plaisir paradoxal, parce que l'attente d'un dénouement négatif semble entraver le suspense, mais aussi parce que cela pourrait mettre à mal la fonction consolatoire de ce type de fiction. En effet, outre les éléments structurels mentionnés, qui annoncent au lecteur une intrigue qui se dénoue dans la mort et le désastre, un examen des thèmes fréquemment exploités par le roman noir révèle que c'est un type de récit qui exploite souvent les milieux et les personnages à la marge, le meurtre et la violence. Ainsi, 84,1% des romans examinés mettent en scène directement des actes violents. Le roman noir français des années 1990-2000 est fidèle à sa mauvaise réputation. Il en va ainsi de *Versus*, roman d'Antoine Chainas paru en 2008 en Série Noire, salué par les critiques et lecteurs de polars comme un ouvrage remarquable, en tout cas remarqué. Son personnage principal, le major Nazutti, est un anti-héros auquel il serait étonnant de s'identifier: c'est en effet un personnage en perdition, mais surtout une boule de haine raciste, homophobe, entre autres. Il mène une croisade d'une violence inouie contre les criminels, et rien dans sa trajectoire ne s'apparente à la rédemption ou à la sublimation. Le roman est d'une violence et d'une morbidité presque insoutenables, explorant ce qu'il y a de plus sombre dans l'âme humaine, sans qu'aucune lueur d'espoir soit permise. Comme il se doit, le dénouement est tragique.

Nazutti meurt et a contaminé de sa violence et de sa haine le jeune Andreotti qui lui est adjoint pendant cette enquête.

En voici un extrait, qui donne une idée de la tonalité de l'ensemble, l'hôpital étant en quelque sorte une métaphore du roman noir ou de sa vision du monde:

> Le major entra dans l'hôpital au pas de charge. Il le connaissait par cœur. Tous ceux qui survivaient aux faits divers de la mégapole atterrissaient ici. Pour un temps du moins.
> Il y avait les viols, les plaies par balles, les blessures par arme blanche, les coups de tête, les passages à la batte de base-ball.
> Il y avait les tentatives de suicide, veines fendues et médocs plein la tronche. Les coups de fusil, les morsures animales et humaines, accidentelles et volontaires.
> Il y avait la stupidité absolue des imprudents.
> Il y avait de la médiocrité, de la crasse et des larmes.
> Des accidents de la route, des fractures ouvertes, des côtes broyées, des traumatismes crâniens et des hémorragies internes.
> Il y avait du blanc, du rouge, du jaune, du bleu et du violet: toutes les couleurs du sang sous la peau.
> Il y avait de la salive, des sécrétions vaginales, du pus, de la pisse et des restes d'os pulvérisés. De la vermine dans les plaies.
> Il y avait des pleurs, de l'abattement, de la confusion et de la colère.
> Il y avait la mort, partout, en filigrane.
> Mais de salut point.
> Ce n'était pas un endroit où l'on soignait les gens.
> Ce n'était pas un endroit où l'on s'occuperait de toi, où tu pouvais te dire que tu serais considéré comme un être humain.
> C'était une usine. Un lieu de passage d'où, si tu ne mourrais pas, on te rejetait au plus vite, là-bas, dans le grand bordel du monde extérieur, celui-là même qui t'avait amené ici.
> Pour libérer des lits.
> Du temps et de l'espace. (Chainas 2008, 300-301)

Tragique, le roman noir n'épargne rien au lecteur, et est même l'expression d'un tragique radicalisé.[3] Pourquoi s'infliger de telles

[3] Il expose des souffrances infligées à l'homme non par des valeurs positives (condition du tragique selon Max Scheler) mais par les forces mêmes qui devraient le protéger. Il exprime un pessimisme radical, face à un monde que nulle valeur positive ne vient organiser. Certains romans vont réintroduire un espoir d'action ou en tout cas d'humanité face à une telle déréliction, ou même réintroduire dans leur univers romanesque du réenchantement (cf. Vargas et Pennac), mais le registre tragique reste un trait fondamental du genre, et le plaisir tragique est à l'œuvre dans la lecture du polar.

lectures? Précisément parce que le roman noir réactive le plaisir tragique, fait de crainte et de pitié, crainte face à ce qui va advenir, pitié née de la tension entre ce que nous savons devoir advenir et ce que nous aimerions qu'il advienne (cf. Baroni). Le plaisir tragique est également lié à la catharsis : le roman noir offre une vision sombre de ce monde qui est le nôtre sans être tout à fait notre vie. Il offre ainsi ce mélange entre la proximité de l'expérience et la distance nécessaire. Cette dimension apparaît dans l'enquête sociologique de Neveu et Collovald, qui parlent de "lectures exutoires" à propos du roman noir, lequel proposerait une "évasion dans la réalité". Les lecteurs trouvent dans leurs lectures des émotions fortes et une vision du monde qui fait écho à leur propre expérience ou leur ressenti, comme cette lectrice:

> C'est un peu, comment dire, l'exutoire des temps modernes, le roman policier. C'est-à-dire qu'il y a à la fois des romans, certains auteurs que j'ai pu citer, très, très durs, au sens où c'est noir, c'est sombre comme littérature. J'aime les lire, il y a sûrement une part, comme une référence à un monde dans lequel on vit qui n'est pas toujours très, très simple quoi. (Collovald et Neveu 2004, 165)

Dans le cas de *Versus*, d'Antoine Chainas, on constate chez les lecteurs cette volonté de trouver un univers romanesque proposant à la fois la noirceur du monde avec une dimension réaliste exacerbée et une force émotionnelle propre à empoigner le lecteur. Les commentaires laissés sur les sites de vente en ligne ou sur certains blogs ayant chroniqué le roman sont éloquents. Qu'ils aient aimé ou non, tous soulignent la noirceur sans concession de l'intrigue, le mélange de fascination et de répulsion que le lecteur éprouve face au personnage principal, Nazutti. Certains évoquent ce qui assure malgré tout le plaisir de la lecture : pour quelques-uns, c'est précisément le caractère éprouvant qui est mis en avant. Roman "qui déménage et qui secoue", *Versus* est apprécié parce qu'il "vient nous chercher, nous déranger et ne nous laisse pas de répit", assure un lecteur. Ainsi, la force émotionnelle du récit est un de ses atouts: le plaisir peut naître d'émotions fortes et a priori négatives. D'autres lecteurs ont réussi à adhérer à cet univers et à s'attacher aux personnages, qu'il s'agisse de l'adjoint Andreotti, "binôme auquel on peut se rattacher, heureusement", ou Nazutti lui-même, car "Chainas parvient à le rendre attachant en s'attardant également sur ses failles", "à lui apporter une touche d'humanité". Surtout, Antoine Chainas propose un "Epilogue" qui assure, en dépit de cette noirceur, une forme de consolation: on y apprend ce que deviennent les différents protagonistes. Parmi eux, Rose, la mère de la fillette enlevée au début du roman, parvient à refaire sa vie en se remariant et en adoptant trois enfants:

> Ce fut dur. Ce fut incroyablement long. Ce fut difficile. Il y eut des éclats de rire, quelques fulgurances et un peu de calme.
> Ils vécurent. (Chainas 2008, 531)

Si Nazutti meurt, Andreotti, quoique sérieusement atteint par sa collaboration criminogène avec son supérieur, parvient à renouer le contact avec Nathalie, ce qui lui ouvre la voie de la rédemption:

> Ils en étaient là. Sur le quai de gare.
> Délicatement.
> Tendrement.
> Elle était tout ce qui lui restait.
> Elle était tout ce qui lui restait… (Chainas 2008, 537)

Ainsi que le dit un lecteur, cet épilogue permet au roman d'être noir sans être désespéré: sans doute est-ce la condition pour adhérer à une fiction qui se distingue par son extrême violence et sa dureté sans concession.

Complexe, le plaisir de l'intrigue dans le roman noir l'est assurément, tout comme il est difficile d'enfermer le genre dans des codes structurels fermes: faite de suspense et de curiosité, la tension narrative va générer des postures de lecture variées. En revanche, il est un dénominateur commun aux œuvres qui s'y rattachent: le plaisir tragique. Le roman noir offre, comme le disent Neveu et Collovald, une fiction qui ne console pas mais qui rassure et réassure l'individu dans sa vision de l'homme et peut même lui donner des explications sur les dysfonctionnements du monde. Le lecteur de noir n'est donc pas un lecteur masochiste, sadique, ou qui se complairait dans des lectures sordides, mais un lecteur qui trouve un écho de sa propre vision dans une fiction "si loin, si proche".

## Références


Baroni, Raphaël. 2007. *La Tension narrative. Suspense, curiosité et surprise*. Paris: Seuil.

Chainas, Antoine. 2008. *Versus*. Paris: Gallimard.

Collovald, Annie, Neveu, Erik. 2004. *Lire le noir. Enquête sur les lecteurs de récits policiers*. Paris: Bibliothèque Publique d'Information/Centre Pompidou.

Del Pappas, Gilles. 2000. *Massilia Dreams*. Paris: Librio.

Dufays, Jean-Louis. "Lire, c'est aussi évaluer. Autopsie des modes de jugement à l'œuvre dans diverses situations de lecture", *Revue de didactologie des langues-cultures* 119 (2000): 277-90.

Levet, Natacha. "Le genre, entre pratique textuelle et pratique sociale : le cas du roman noir français (1990-2000)." Thèse, Université de Limoges, 2006.

Raynal, Patrick. "Le roman noir est l'avenir de la fiction", *Les Temps modernes* 595 (1997): 88-99.

Tadié, Benoît. 2006. *Le Polar américain, la modernité et le mal.* Paris: PUF.

Tadié, Jean-Yves. 1996. *Le Roman d'aventures*. Paris: PUF.

Todorov, Tzvetan. 1971. *Poétique de la prose*. Paris: Seuil.

# CHAPTER THIRTEEN

# TRANS-BOND-EXPRESS, OU LES PLAISIRS MOBILES (1953-1965)

LOÏC ARTIAGA

James Bond entre dans le champ des études littéraires dans les années 1960, avec l'essor de la narratologie structuraliste. D'une certaine façon, le succès planétaire de la *fabula* bondienne est simultanément livré au monde avec des clés d'interprétation (Artiaga 2007). L'étude d'Umberto Eco intitulée *Le strutture narrative in Fleming*, parue à Milan en 1965, traduite et rééditée à plusieurs reprises jusqu'au début des années 2000, reste en Europe la plus citée, mais aussi celle qui a réussi à déborder le seul champ de la critique.[1] Pour Umberto Eco, les romans de Fleming fonctionnent comme une machine, reposant sur la base "d'unités très simples, régies par de rigoureuses règles combinatoires". Le récit est d'abord construit sur une série de couples d'oppositions fixes (Bond-M, Devoir-Sacrifice, etc.), dont l'issue est fixée par avance, comme à la mourre chinoise (pierre-feuille-ciseaux): M. bat Bond, Bond bat le Méchant, le Méchant bat la Femme, le Monde Libre bat l'Union soviétique, etc. L'intrigue se présente au lecteur comme un jeu produisant invariablement une suite en neuf coups: M confie une mission à Bond, Le Méchant apparaît à Bond, Bond inflige un premier échec au Méchant, La Femme se présente à Bond, Bond souffle la Femme, Le Méchant capture Bond, Le Méchant torture Bond, Bond bat le Méchant, Bond convalescent s'entretient avec la Femme, qu'il perdra par la suite. Cette approche a été critiquée dans les années 1980, par Teresa de Lauretis, puis par Tony Bennett et Janet Woollacott. Ils font du lecteur/joueur d'Umberto Eco, uniquement décrit dans sa relation de coopération avec les invariants du texte, un ressort commode utilisé par le

[1] Traduite en anglais puis en français pour la revue *Communication* dans les deux années suivantes, cette étude est notamment reprise et augmentée en 1978 dans le recueil *Il Superuomo di massa* (publié en France en 1993) et publiée à nouveau dans *The James Bond Phenomenon: A Critical Reader* (Lindner 2003).

sémioticien pour donner chair à sa théorie. Umberto Eco ôterait à son lecteur toute caractéristique liée au temps, à l'âge, au genre et à la culture et ne le déterminerait finalement que par rapport au texte (Baroni 2004).[2]

Ces limites sont moins à considérer comme des angles morts remettant fondamentalement en question le travail d'Umberto Eco sur Bond – lui-même indique en 1978 que "les vérifications définitives devront être faites dans le cadre non du livre mais de la société qui le lit" (Eco 1993 [1978], 163-207) – que comme les symptômes d'un contexte intellectuel. Le sémioticien fait de la combinatoire narrative qu'il décrit chez Fleming "l'origine du succès de la saga 007". C'est parce que la machinerie narrative fonctionne que les masses adhèrent aux livres, qui mettent en mouvement "un réseau d'associations élémentaires" et appellent "à une dynamique originelle et profonde" (Eco 1966). Préoccupé même pour s'en détacher de la légitimité de son objet d'étude, pris dans un champ qui garde malgré tout le texte imprimé - voire le volume, comme principal support de l'analyse - Umberto Eco en néglige la transmédialité. Prisonnier par son époque, il ne distingue pas l'originalité de l'économie des plaisirs qui se déploie dans la *fabula* bondienne. Le lecteur/spectacteur des premiers temps de la société industrielle de consommation n'est pas uniquement lecteur jouissant parce que "plongé dans un jeu dont il connaît les pièces et les règles" (Eco 1966); son immersion dans la fiction dépend des conditions historiques et des transformations que connaît alors l'industrie du divertissement. Ressaisir Bond et ses lecteurs dans ce contexte des années 1950-1960 permet de s'interroger sur les plaisirs esthétiques des masses dans le second vingtième siècle mais aussi de comprendre comment cette notion de plaisir a été abordée et questionnée par des intellectuels qui ont été les premiers à se frotter à ces fictions populaires. Des livres aux films, que nous considérerons ici ensemble, comme "des textes de Bond",[3] du point de vue de l'auteur à celui de ses critiques, le plaisir suscité par ces œuvres semble se déplacer. Situé par Ian

---

[2] Raphaël Baroni souligne les limites de la représentation de la séquence narrative réduite à la forme aseptisée "d'une opposition structurale ou du devenir d'une action" et notamment quand ce type de constructions produit une échelle des effets esthétiques dépréciant ceux typiques des productions populaires, comme le suspense.

[3] Cette notion plurielle englobant un ensemble d'œuvres en constante augmentation et en permanente mutation est expliquée par Bennett et Woollacott (1987, 46-53). Elle permet d'éviter de faire des romans de Ian Fleming "un point statique de référence" (traduit par nous) à partir duquel seraient vues et analysées les autres productions mettant en scène le personnage, considérées comme des adaptations plus ou moins fidèles de l'œuvre originale.

Fleming "quelque-part entre le plexus et le haut de la cuisse" pour un lectorat masculin, il devient ainsi un plaisir intellectuel chez Eco pour une frange étroite de lecteurs.

Une cartographie de ces mouvements s'impose. Il s'agit ici d'en expliquer les significations et de comprendre ce qu'ils disent de l'évolution des plaisirs en régime médiatique. Ceux-ci ne sont pas uniquement répétition du même, fruit de la machine "à produire de la redondance" que décrit Umberto Eco. Ils peuvent être marqués par un goût pour l'écart, la différence, la distance, à l'intérieur d'un même réseau d'œuvres et témoigner d'un appétit pour l'exploration d'un monde social en pleine mutation.

## Jouissances esthétiques d'une œuvre transmédiale

La question de la transmédialité et de ses origines historiques travaille/traverse le champ des études sur la culture médiatique. Si les chercheurs étasuniens, comme Henry Jenkins, situent volontiers les prémices de la convergence au sein de l'industrie du *pulp* américain de l'entre-deux-guerres, les recherches européennes montrent la mise en place de processus identiques dès le XIXe siècle (Kalifa 2001). On sait avec Marc Lits que "ce qui caractérise la culture médiatique, c'est à la fois l'émergence massive de l'image, du visuel, et la mobilité des récits dans des logiques de migrations transsémiotiques. L'hybridité, y compris des supports, est constitutive de ces productions" (Lits 2009, 118-123). On pourrait ajouter que la transnationalité devient la règle dès la Belle Epoque, comme le montrent les incessants passages de frontières des figures archétypales de bandits, de génies criminels ou de justiciers chez les éditeurs populaires européens (Popular Roots of European Culture 2010).

Les "textes de Bond" sont donc dans les années 1950-1960 les héritiers d'une culture médiatique déjà séculaire. Mais, au moment où les fans étasuniens de Tolkien s'arrachent les versions pirates d'une œuvre en passe de devenir *culte*, ces récits amorcent une rupture. Alors que les œuvres subissaient des "incarnations" successives (feuilleton *puis* volume *puis* théâtre, *puis* cinéma, par exemple), les "textes de Bond" apparaissent de manière quasi-simultanée: premier volume en 1953, première adaptation pour la télévision en 1954, investissement des colonnes du *Daily Express* en 1957 sous forme de bande dessinée. Deux ans plus tard, le *New York Times* annonce que Fleming travaille à l'écriture d'un scénario pour le cinéma. La *fabula* bondienne ne s'incarne pas en une oeuvre *princeps*, marquée à jamais par le sceau d'un auteur et régénérée dans le temps par la capacité d'étoilement de supports inédits. Elle propose un réseau d'œuvres, renforcé par une foultitude d'objets derives, codés et signifiants, marqué par des transactions incessantes. Ces ramifications se font plus denses au mitan des années 1960, après les trois premiers films portant sur grand écran 007, mais aussi à travers la duplication de la figure de Bond, reprise dans des imitations nombreuses[4]. L'intermédialité, qui sert la construction d'un réseau d'œuvres, assouvit l'attente de "lecteurs avides de mondes fictionnels les plus complets et autonomes possibles", d'œuvres sans fin productrices de renvois référentiels multiformes (Besson 2006). Rappeler ces faits permet de se placer dans la perspective de la majorité des lecteurs découvrant les livres signés par Fleming *après* avoir vu les films de Terence Young et de Guy Hamilton. En Angleterre, Pan Books vend en 1960 323,000 exemplaires des romans de Fleming. Cinq ans et quatre films plus tard, le nombre est multiplié par vingt, et atteint les 6,782,000. L'essentiel de la circulation de la figure de James Bond repose dès les années 1960 sur une culture dominée par l'image – le cinéma, l'affiche, les publicités, la bande dessinée. Le lecteur d'Umberto Eco, pris dans les seuls rets des versions imprimées des "textes de Bond", n'existe déjà plus dans la société occidentale des *sixties*.

## Retour à Fleming

Si l'on considère les œuvres de Ian Fleming dans un contexte marqué au mitan du XXe siècle par la transmédialité, on ne peut réduire le plaisir qu'elles suscitent à celui d'une plongée sous contrôle dans une intrigue au dénouement prévisible. L'auteur déploie lui-même une toute autre argumentation pour parler de son œuvre. Identifiant Bond à sa propre *catharsis*, il explique la création du personnage comme un moyen commode pour oublier l'ennui du mariage et combler la perte d'une sorte de plaisirs. En 1960, dans une conversation avec Georges Simenon sur le *thriller business*, Fleming explique ses livres en usant d'une rhétorique du plaisir et du divertissement:

> I write about what pleases and stimulates me. I greatly enjoy knowing that other people, quite intelligent people, find my books amusing and entertaining. But I'm not really surprised, because they entertain and amuse me, too (Lane 1966).

---

[4] On peut penser à *The Ipcress File* en 1965, à la série des *Flint* amorcée en 1966, ou en Allemagne aux *Rolf Torring* (les aventures d'un agent secret en Asie), aux *Kommissar X* (sept films entre 1965 et 1971).

La société capitaliste défendue par 007 est représentée comme un possible de plaisirs, qui se manifestent dans la profusion dans les romans et à l'écran d'objets de consommation. Leur exposition dans les "textes de Bond" participent pleinement au dispositif décrit en 1966 par Guy Debord de l'ostentation de marchandises "montrées et abstraitement disponibles" (Debord 1966, 3-11). Chez Fleming, les loisirs ne comblent pas des temps morts dans le récit, ils sont, en soi, une aventure chargée de sens. Le lecteur est donc appelé à s'identifier à des personnages qui prennent du plaisir et le formulent.

Prompts à distinguer les parentés de l'auteur avec les romanciers du XIXe siècle, les commentateurs de Fleming ont laissé de côté le fait que Fleming inscrit dans la diégèse bondienne des références nombreuses à la culture médiatique, liant ainsi consciemment son œuvre aux productions de masse de son temps. Dès *Casino Royale* (1953), les personnages principaux sont campés à travers leurs ressemblances avec des musiciens ou des acteurs. Felix Leiter, l'agent étasunien, ressemble à Frank Sinatra et James Bond à Hoagy Carmichael. Le roman *Live and Let Die* (1954) plonge aussi le lecteur dans un fourmillement référentiel, associé aux rebondissements de l'intrigue: si Leiter a la vie sauve lorsqu'il est fait prisonnier par les hommes de mains de M. Big, c'est parce qu'il partage avec eux le goût pour les *jazz band.*[5] Ian Fleming n'enferme pas ses lecteurs dans un jeu intertextuel circonscrit à l'espace de la littérature. Il assume le caractère transmédiatique de ses récits. Après 1962 il déclare même que dans son imaginaire, James Bond a désormais les traits de l'acteur Sean Connery (Denning 2003). Rémanence du film *Dr. No*, la silhouette d'Ursula Andress apparait en 1963 aux lecteurs de *On Her Majesty's Secret Service.*

## Les plaisirs pop des *sixties*

La pochette de la compilation *Music to Read James Bond by* (1965) ramasse en une seule image ce processus de coalescence, proposé au lecteur/spectateur/auditeur des œuvres liées à Bond. Figurant une jeune

[5] "When no instructions came from The Big Man they got bored and I got to arguing the finer points of Jazz with Blabbermouth, the man with the fancy six-shooter. We got on to Duke Ellington and agreed that we liked our band-leaders to be percussion men, not wind. We agreed the piano or the drums held the band together better than any other solo instrument — Jelly-roll Morton, for instance. A propos the Duke, I told him the crack about the clarinet – 'an ill woodwind that nobody blows good'. That made him laugh fit to bust. Suddenly we were friends" (Fleming, 1973, 90-91).

femme couverte d'une pellicule d'or feuilletant *You Only Live Twice*, elle invite ainsi à croiser les univers esthétiques et musicaux des films avec ceux des livres. C'est une esthétique et un rapport pop à la culture qui planent sur les "textes de Bond". Les films de Terence Young et de Guy Hamilton sont en eux-mêmes des objets pop, répondant parfaitement aux qualificatifs énoncés en 1957 par le peintre Richard Hamilton pour définir le Pop Art : populaire, transitoire, consommable, bon marché, fabriqué en série, jeune, spirituel, sexy, astucieux, glamour et lucratif. "Que proposent les premiers Bond en effet, sinon la sérialité, les couleurs vives, l'esthétique populaire de la bande dessinée [...], les plaisirs narratifs de la littérature feuilletonesque, l'érotisme *cheap* de *Playboy*", écrit Olivier Maillart. Les films du milieu des années 1960 empruntent au Pop Art les à-plats de couleur, avec pour chaque œuvre des teintes dominantes – or pour *Goldfinger*, bleus et rouges pour *Thunderball*, "qui saturent le plan pour en atténuer la profondeur, le travailler comme un espace plat, ironiquement faux, dessiné" (Maillart 2007). Certaines images rappellent l'évident recyclage pop à l'œuvre, comme celle du corps recouvert d'or de Jill Masterson (*Goldfinger*, 1964), si proche des anthropométries d'Yves Klein (1960).

Cette dimension pop éminemment visuelle rejoint les livres dans leur usage de la "technique du regard". Dans la version augmentée de son article de 1965 parue dans *Il Superuomo di massa* (1978), Umberto Eco associe les longues descriptions de l'auteur à une "technique du regard sans but", qui nourrit "des passages pleins de virtuosité, feignant une technique du regard [...] que non seulement le mécanisme narratif du récit ne requiert pas mais qu'il rejette". Cette "technique du regard" toute "photographique" n'a pas pour Eco de fonction narrative, elle repose sur le redondant, elle fait naître la jouissance par le repos plus que par l'excitation. Insistant sur ce qu'il nomme le *déjà-vu*[6], Umberto Eco néglige ici l'importance du *vu*, la conversion forcée du lecteur en spectateur/voyeur. Comme le prouve Michael Denning, cette position du

---

[6] Eco, dans "Les structures narratives," explique ainsi le recours littéraire au *déjà-vu* : "Il est en effet surprenant de constater la minutie acharnée et oiseuse de ses interminables descriptions d'objets, de paysage ou de gestes en apparence non essentielles à l'aventure [...]. Fleming [...] décrit une partie de canasta, une voiture de série, le tableau de bord d'un avion, le wagon d'un train, la carte d'un restaurant, le paquet de cigarettes d'une marque trouvable dans n'importe quel bureau de tabac. Il liquide en quelques lignes un assaut donné à Fort Knox parce qu'il sait qu'aucun de ses lecteurs n'aura jamais l'occasion de dévaliser Fort Knox [...]. Fleming s'attache à nous restituer le *déjà-vu* [...] puisque c'est sur le *déjà-vu* que fonctionnent nos capacités d'identification".

lecteur en “regardeur” se révèle en particulier dans la façon dont Ian Fleming choisit de montrer la sexualité (Denning 2003).

Sans faire des “textes de Bond” des manifestes cachés pour le Pop Art, on peut aussi interpréter ce *déjà-vu* dans les perspectives que Andy Warhol dessinent pour le monde de l’art, où l’œuvre parce qu’elle est objet de consommation devient “toujours multiple même si identique” (Fongond et Lesourd 2009). Avec le Pop Art, loin d’y être une représentation fidèle du monde, l’image se trouve toujours volontairement filtrée par sa mécanique de production, de reproduction et de circulation. Au diapason des fondements esthétiques de ce mouvement, les “textes de Bond” montrent des œuvres périssables, que l’on peut détourner, reproduire, mélanger ou ignorer. Dans *The Man with a Golden Gun* (1965), James Bond, que le lecteur a auparavant vu tirer un livre de sa valise, l’ouvrir et ne pas le lire, brutalise un groupe de musiciens, sautant sur scène, imposant un changement d’intensité et de rythme de la musique, dégrafant au passage le décolleté de la danseuse. Au cinéma, Bond règle de manière définitive leur compte aux symboles de la culture classique. Les bibliothèques et les œuvres d’art sont soit placés du côté des opposants comme éléments de décor, soit volés, détruits, voire saccagés. Le salon du Dr No héberge un portrait du duc de Wellington par Goya, effectivement volé en 1961. *Thunderball* s’ouvre sur la destruction d’une salle de château remplie de pièces rares, dans une séquence dont le montage rapide rappelle le découpage des planches de bande dessinée.

## Bond ou le fantasme de la mobilité

La culture est donc inscrite, chez Ian Fleming et dans les films des années 1960, dans une économie du déplacement – d’un lieu à l’autre (Goya chez *Dr No*), d’un support à un autre (du livre au film et vice-versa), d’une strate de la hiérarchie culturelle à un autre (de la bibliothèque de M au feuilletage discret de *Playboy* dans lequel sont publiés par tranches les histoires de Fleming). En réponse, le plaisir s’inscrit aussi, dans les récits bondiens, dans la mobilité. Si, comme l’écrit Eco, la narration reste arc-boutée sur des structures fixes (autant chez Fleming que dans les films de Terence Young et de Guy Hamilton), le personnage immuable de 007 traverse un monde en changement. Il est d’abord un héros mobile, voyageur maîtrisant les codes et les moyens du déplacement dans l’espace. Il est aussi un héros qui voyage à l’intérieur du feuilleté du monde social et des différents plaisirs de classe.

Le récit, chez Fleming, est souvent réduit par ses commentateurs savants à l’accomplissement de plaisirs facilement identifiables. Anthony

Burgess résume ce qu'il retient de Bond à une simple énumération: la voiture de sport, le bon dosage pour une vodka martini, un dîner et un bridge chez *Blade's*, les noms de marques de parfum, la séduisante chevelure désordonnée d'une belle fille (Burgess 1988). L'étude sérielle révèle cependant une cartographie des plaisirs plus complexe, variant dans ses formes, ses significations et le genre.

**Tableau n° 1 : Plaisirs, formes et personnages dans *Casino Royale* (1953)**[7]

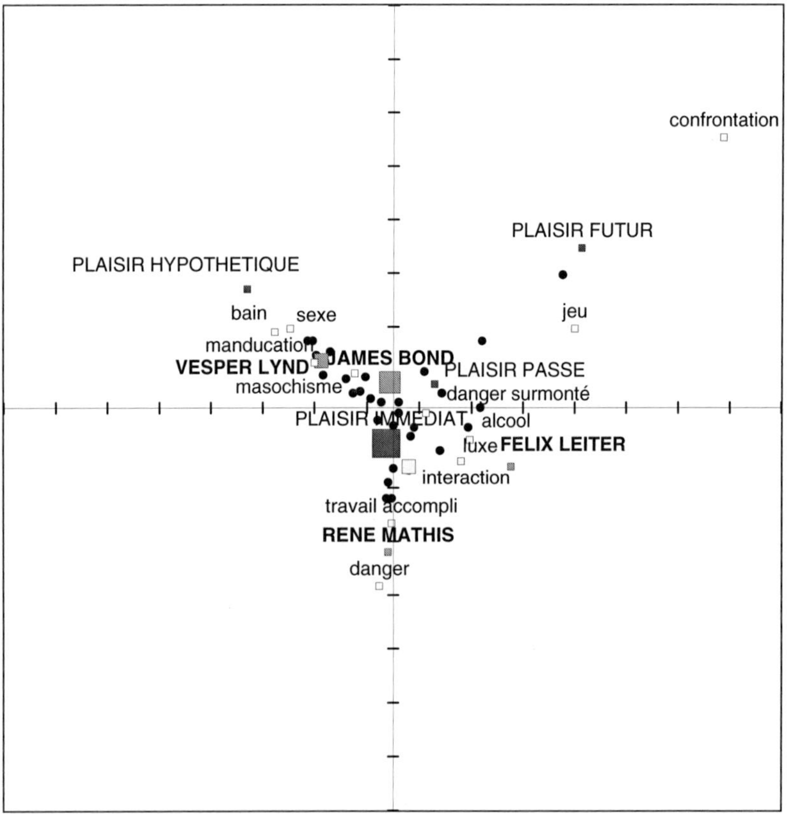


[7] La carte montre les positions de 20 modalités et les coordonnées de 42 observations. 9,09 % de la variance est expliquée par les deux axes représentés.

Le tableau n°1 figure une analyse factorielle de correspondances (AFC), fondée sur les occurrences dans le roman *Casino Royale* (1953) des notions de plaisir, associées à des personnages, des thématiques et un rapport au temps. L'AFC montre deux "axes" hédonistiques. Le premier rassemble des formes de camaraderies masculines, solides parce qu'elles se fondent à la fois sur la rémanence de plaisirs passés et qu'elles restent actives dans le temps présent. Le second est propre au couple d'amants, entre jouissance du présent et plaisirs hypothétiques. James Bond a en commun avec les agents René Mathis et Felix Leiter l'immédiateté du goût de l'interaction sociale, du travail accompli et du danger surmonté. Avec Vesper Lynd, il partage les joies de la nourriture, les plaisirs du bain et ceux du sexe. Le schéma souligne la position centrale qu'occupe Bond dans ce dispositif. Le personnage assure les transactions et la synthèse entre des univers hédonistiques différents. Comme l'a montré Matthieu Letouneux, l'omniprésence de l'argent chez Fleming fait naître un "exotisme de classe sans lutte des classes" (Letourneux 2007). L'auteur convertit l'or en arme (*Goldfinger*, *The Man with a Golden Gun*) et place toujours l'argent au cœur de ses intrigues. Dans *Casino Royale*, Bond ne fait rien moins que de tuer Le Chiffre en le ruinant. Mais le rappel permanent de plaisirs simples – prendre un bon petit déjeuner, avec du café, des œufs et du bacon, ce que le personnage de 007 accomplit de manière quasi-compulsive dans *Live and Let Die* (1954) permet de mesurer l'écart entre ces plaisirs et ceux qu'offrent des loisirs en passe de se démocratiser, comme jouer au golf ou fréquenter un casino.

Ce thème de la mobilité fait écho, dans les années 1950-1960, aux changements profonds que connaissent les classes populaires anglaises. Comme le notent Michael Young en 1958 puis Ferdynand Zweig en 1961, celles-ci s'inscrivent alors dans un mouvement de rapprochement avec les valeurs et le mode de vie de la bourgeoisie. Ces changements atténuent la conflictualité entre l'idéologie des classes populaires et *l'éthos* dominant de la société anglaise. Comme le suggère Christophe Lindner, la figure de Bond, surtout lorsqu'elle est incarnée par Sean Connery, est à rapprocher de celles des "nouveaux aristocrates" décrits dans les années 1960 par Christopher Booker qui, à l'instar de Mick Jagger ou de David Bailey, mêlent un *background* de la classe ouvrière avec des attitudes bourgeoises. Dans les romans comme à l'écran, le personnage incarne à merveille, dans l'économie de ses plaisirs, le processus d'acclimatation à marche forcée des classes populaires aux changements culturels et sociaux de l'après-guerre, tel que l'explique Richard Hoggart en 1957:

> Dans les situations de changement, les individus tendent à réagir en se référant alternativement à plusieurs systèmes de valeurs [ ...] Les formes

> modernes du libéralisme s'appuient sur une réinterprétation constante des traditions (Hoggart 1991 [1957], 223).

Les "textes de Bond" offrent la traduction narrative de cet accompagnement des classes populaires vers les usages, les représentations et les loisirs de la bourgeoisie. Ian Fleming joue en permanence avec des effets de mise à distance et de rapprochement, d'invraisemblance et d'effets de réel. Le lecteur est à la fois confronté au retour du *même*, à la redondance, comme l'écrit Umberto Eco. Mais dans le même temps, parce qu'il est aussi un *spectateur*, il goûte aux variations d'un réseau d'œuvres dans ses écarts et ses changements. Le livre de Fleming qu'il découvre dans la plupart des cas *après* le film qui l'a adapté ne présente pas un récit strictement identique au second. Les "textes de Bond" accoutument leurs lecteurs/spectateurs à une société qui change, en usant d'un ressort propre à la culture pop – la variation sur un même motif ou un même thème. Prises dans leurs répétitions, les structures narratives chez Fleming, comme la signature sonore du personnage à l'écran reprise à l'infini, ont finalement plus en commun avec les sérigraphies qu'Andy Warhol entame en 1962 qu'avec Novalis ou Goethe, "bonnes lectures d'un gentilhomme aisé" qu'Umberto Eco prête à l'auteur (Eco 1993).

## Epilogue. Les transgressions du chercheur pop

La question du mouvement et de la répétition dans les "textes de Bond" apparaît en creux dans les critiques faites aux films à la fin des années 1970. Les médias occidentaux leur reprochent alors une trop grande fidélité à la formule originelle. Lorsque le lien avec les mouvements culturels qui traversent les sociétés occidentales disparaît et qu'il ne reste plus des films que la structure narrative reproduite à l'identique, l'intérêt s'émousse. Janet Maslin l'exprime dans les pages du *New York Times* en 1977 à propos de *The Spy Who Loved Me*:

> James Bond [...] hardly ever comes to grips with his most insidious adversary, the James Bond formula...a Bond film is interesting only insofar as it quietly subverts the series' old tricks (Maslin 1977).

Meilleur agent de la société de consommation, 007 semble alors atteindre sa propre date de péremption: "fifteen years ago, at the time of *Dr No* this sort of thing was a great deal more effective than it is today", poursuit Janet Maslin. En réalité, le plaisir bondien se déplace à nouveau, la diffusion des films devenant, comme Tony Bennett et Janet Woollacott l'indiquent, un moment ritualisé dans l'Angleterre fin de siècle (Bennett et Woollacott 1986, 13-33).

Interroger la notion de plaisir à travers les "textes de Bond" montre combien l'univers créé par Ian Fleming a pu jouer avec les aspirations et les frustrations des populations occidentales dans les années 1950 et 1960. Comme Violette Morin le mentionne en 1965, le "phénomène Bond" est alors aussi le premier de la culture de masse à requérir l'analyse d'intellectuels. C'est aussi dans cette perspective de la construction d'un discours savant sur les débuts de la société de consommation industrielle que l'étude d'Umberto Eco doit être appréhendée. Le sémioticien donne lui-même en 1964 sa version de la reconfiguration du champ intellectuel face à l'irruption de nouvelles formes de consommations culturelles. Le clivage s'opère entre "apocalyptiques" se plaignant du déclin de l'autorité savante et "intégrés" prenant en compte les mutations techniques visibles dans le champ de la culture (Eco 1964).

Lisons différemment l'introduction de *Il Superuomo di massa* et l'étude des structures narratives chez Fleming. N'en faisons pas uniquement des analyses à partir desquelles il s'agit de se situer, mais considérons-les comme des documents historiques. Apparaît ainsi un plaisir passé jusque-là inaperçu. Etalant ses *comics* pour illustrer son propos lors d'un congrès organisé par le Centre international des études humanistes et l'Institut des études philosophiques de Rome, Umberto Eco est mu au début des années 1960 par une douce "intention provocatrice" et subversive (Eco 1993). Son plaisir repose alors sur une transgression qu'il reconnaît volontiers trente ans plus tard: travailler avec des cadres rigoureux sur une fiction populaire. Soit une parfaite posture pop, ironique, décalée et distanciée, qu'il ajuste avec habileté au monde universitaire. Reprise avec des variations de langue ou de présentation mais toujours identique dans sa structure initiale, son étude répond ainsi parfaitement à ce qui définit, depuis la fin des années 1950, un objet pop.

## Références


Artiaga, Loïc. 2007. "James Bond: mode(s) d'emploi (1965 – années 1990)", in *James Bond (2)007. Anatomie d'un mythe populaire*, in Boully, Chenille and Hache-Bissette (eds), 18-28.

Baroni, Raphaël. 2004, "La valeur littéraire du suspense," *A Contrario*, 2: 29-43.

Bennett, Tony et Woollacott, Janet. 1987. *Bond and Beyond. The Political Career of a Popular Hero.* London: Macmillan.

Besson, Anne. 2006. “Le cycle dans la science-fiction anglo-saxonne des années 80-90,” in Bozzeto and Menegaldo (eds), 137-160.
Booker, Christopher. 1969. *The Neophiliacs: A Study in the Revolution in English Life in the 1950s and the1960s*. London: Collins.
Boully, Fabien, Chenille, Vincent, and Hache-Bissette, Françoise (eds). 2007. *James Bond (2)007. Anatomie d'un mythe populaire*. Paris: Belin.
Bozzeto, Roger et Menegaldo, Gilles (eds). 2006. *Colloque de Cerisy. Les Nouvelles Formes de la Science-fiction*. Paris: Bragelonne.
Burgess, Anthony. 1988. “Introduction,” in *Ian Fleming's James Bond Novels*. London: Coronet.
Debord, Guy. 1966. “Le déclin et la chute de l'économie spectaculaire-marchande.” *Internationale Situationniste* 10: 3-11.
Denning, Michael. 2003. “Licensed to look: James Bond and the heroism of consumption,” in Lindner (ed), 2003, 56-75.
Eco, Umberto. 1964. *Apocalittici e integrati: comunicazioni di massa e teorie della cultura di massa.* Milan: Bompiani.
—. 1966. “James Bond: une combinatoire narrative,” *Communications* 8: 77-93.
—. 1993 [1978]. *De Superman au surhomme.* Paris: Grasset.
Fleming, Ian. 1973. *A James Bond Omnibus*. London: Jonathan Cape.
—. 1963. “How to Write a Thriller.” *Books and Bookmen*, May 1963.
Fongond, Marie and Lesourd, Serge. 2009. “Warhol, une esthétique ‘consumatoire’ ou l'art comme modernité,” *Cliniques méditerranéennes* 80: 165-176.
Hoggart, Richard. 1991 [1957]. *La Culture du pauvre*. Paris: Éditions de Minuit.
Jenkins, Henry. 2006. *Convergence Culture: Where Old and New Media Collide*. New York: New York University Press.
Kalifa, Dominique. 2001. *La Culture de masse en France*, 1860-1930. Paris: La Découverte.
Lane, Sheldon. 1966. *For Bond Lovers Only.* London: Panther Books, 81-97.
Lauretis, Teresa de. 1984. *Alice Doesn't: Feminism, Semiotics, Cinema.* London: Macmillan.
Lindner, Christopher (ed). 2003. *The James Bond Phenomenon: A Critical Reader*. Manchester: Manchester University Press.
Lits, Marc. 2009. “Populaire, idéologie, argumentation : un trio infernal,” *A Contrario* 2, Migozzi, Jacques, and Artiaga, Loïc (eds), 118-123.

Letourneux, Matthieu. 2007. "'Le Monde ne suffit pas'. Les univers en tension des romans de Ian Fleming," in Boully, Chenille and Hache-Bissette (eds), 29-37.

Maillart, Oliver. 2007. "Une beauté de circonstance. James Bond, le cinéma d'action et l'esthétique pop," in Boully, Chenille and Hache-Bissette (eds), 209-218.

Maslin, Janet. 1977. "'Spy Who Loved' a Bit Long on Bond," *New York Times*, 28 July 1977.

Young, Michael. 1958. *The Rise of the Meritocracy.* Harmondsworth: Penguin.

Zweig, Ferdynand. 1961. *The Worker in an Affluent Society: Family Life and Industry.* Londres: Heinemann.

Section "Détectives et enquêteurs" du Musée Virtuel "Popular Roots of European Culture," (2010), http://www.popular-roots.eu/, vérifié le 3 mai 2012.

# CHAPTER FOURTEEN

# COURIR APRES LES INTRIGUES… DYNAMIQUE NARRATIVE ET PLAISIR DU RECIT DANS LES FASCICULES POUR LA JEUNESSE DES ANNEES 1900-1930

MATTHIEU LETOURNEUX

L'une des formes importantes et méconnues de la production populaire est celle des récits en fascicules pour la jeunesse diffusés massivement du début du XXe siècle à la veille de la Seconde Guerre mondiale. Citons les quelque 26 séries d'aventures de petits héros d'Arnould Galopin publiées pour la plupart chez Albin Michel, parmi lesquelles *Le Petit Chasseur de la pampa* (1925-1926), *Le Petit Chasseur de panthères* (1928-1931), les *Aventures d'un petit buffalo* (1930), *Les Aventures d'un apprenti parisien* (1928), celles d'un *écolier parisien* (1931-33), en tout, plus d'un millier de fascicules dans 26 séries d'aventures aux héros interchangeables[1]; les séries scoutes de Jean de La Hire, comme *L'As des boy-scouts* (1925), *Les Trois boy-scouts* (1913-1921 et 1935), *Les Grandes Aventures d'un boy scout* (1926) et autre *Roi des scouts* (1931)[2]. Pensons encore aux récits de René-Marcel de Nizerolles, José Moselli, Roger Salardenne et quelques autres[3]. Ces formes de récits en épisodes ont connu un très grand succès dans la première moitié du XXe siècle: Annie Renonciat donne le chiffre

---

[1] On peut trouver la liste complète de ces séries à l'adresse suivante: http://www.roman-daventures.com/auteurs/france/galopin/galopin-biblio.htm (consulté le 11 mars 2012).

[2] Sur ces séries, voir Letourneux 2006.

[3] René Marcel de Nizerolles (Marcel Priollet), *Les Voyages aériens d'un petit parisien à travers le monde* (1933-1935), *Les Aventuriers du ciel* (1935-1937), *Les Robinsons de l'île volante* (1937-1938), Roger Salardenne, *Jack le petit sans famille* (1937), *Les Aventures d'un petit parachutiste* (1938); pour connaître la litanie des fascicules de José Moselli, on consultera Touchant 2001.

de 100 000 exemplaires par fascicule en moyenne pour Arnould Galopin (Renonciat 2004). Les chiffres de Jean de La Hire étaient probablement moins importants: 25 000 exemplaires environ pour *Scouts service secrets*, la dernière collection lancée chez Tallandier[4], beaucoup plus sans doute pour les collections antérieures – on a pu avancer un chiffre avoisinant les 100 000 exemplaires pour les premières collections de chez Ferenczi, comme *Les Trois Boy scouts*.

Pressés par la nécessité de produire un fascicule par semaine, ces auteurs n'avaient guère le temps de fignoler des intrigues, et livraient les premières parties de leurs romans bien avant de les avoir achevés. Tous enchaînaient les romans, sans pause, souvent chez le même éditeur. Cette façon de procéder se traduisait par des récits dans lesquels l'intrigue se défaisait en une rhapsodie épisodique. C'est nous inviter tout à la fois à interroger la notion même de *plot*, d'intrigue, et celle du plaisir, dans ces récits qui, *a priori*, sont *sans* intrigue délimitée.

Face à ces productions sérielles, la question de la "bonne intrigue" se pose en termes assez différents de ceux qui prévalent habituellement: le plaisir du lecteur n'est pas fondamentalement provoqué par la surprise qu'il éprouverait à découvrir l'intrigue ou les trouvailles narratives de l'auteur, puisque ces récits, produits à la chaîne, ne peuvent guère être qualifiés d'originaux. Mais cela ne veut pas dire pour autant qu'il faille leur faire un sort en réduisant le plaisir qu'ils procurent au simple mécanisme de ratiocination, satisfaction du même éternellement répété. Par-delà le charme de la répétition, les mécanismes de variation caractéristiques de la sérialité offrent, même dans ces œuvres produites à la chaîne, des formes et des modes de lecture et d'écriture spécifiques, hors de toute stratégie de distinction. L'intrigue peut être banale au plus haut point, la façon dont elle sera configurée dans sa relation au support ou au genre pourra en redéfinir profondément le sens.

La logique de la livraison engage en effet une façon de concevoir son intrigue: quand Arnould Galopin ou Jean de La Hire se lancent dans l'un ou l'autre de leurs romans en plus de cent livraisons à peine le précédent achevé, ils ne peuvent guère connaître le détail de leur récit. Ils ont peut-être une idée de son architecture, ils peuvent avoir en tête ses premiers épisodes, mais les épisodes suivants sont repoussées dans les limbes. Aussi doivent-ils penser une intrigue très largement ouverte, ce qu'ils thématisent généralement à travers un voyage improvisé, à l'aventure. Si les héros s'engagent dans une course frénétique et erratique à l'instar de

[4] Ce sont du moins les chiffres qui prévalent pour les publications de cet éditeur dans les années 1930.

*Freddy la bougeotte*, héros qui porte bien son nom[5], c'est que les auteurs ne savent pas eux-mêmes où ils vont.

La deuxième contrainte tient à la périodicité des œuvres et à leur présentation. Les éditeurs publient un numéro de la série par semaine, et le support joue sur l'ambiguïté entre l'unité du fascicule et celle du roman: chaque fascicule porte une couverture et un titre propres et la présentation peut laisser croire au lecteur qu'il existe une relative indépendance entre les livraisons. C'est le cas par exemple des séries scoutes de Jean de La Hire, dont les publicités annoncent un récit complet. Suivant les cas, auteurs et éditeurs choisissent de mettre l'accent sur l'unité de la superstructure, présentant la série comme une œuvre unique découpée en livraisons, ou sur celle du fascicule, faisant de la série une collection de récits d'aventures.[6]

Ces effets significatifs de variation affectent en retour la structure même des œuvres, conduisant d'une logique de feuilleton à une logique de série. Mais on peut repérer dans tous ces ouvrages une même tension, dans le mode de publication, entre l'unité de la livraison et celle de l'œuvre. De fait, même quand le découpage des livraisons ne coïncide pas exactement avec l'unité épisodique, par exemple chez Arnould Galopin, la logique du fascicule impose à l'auteur un rythme événementiel qui reste très largement déterminé par les dimensions de la publication. Plus largement, on distingue une tendance des œuvres à adopter une régularité rythmique des épisodes qui s'explique sans doute en grande partie par l'incidence du support, débitant le récit en livraisons hebdomadaires. Il s'agit clairement ici de thématiser, dans la structure narrative de l'œuvre, cette double saisie contradictoire du support, entre collection de récits et roman en livraisons.

On le voit, les contraintes liées aux supports affectent l'intrigue elle-même, dont la structure reproduit la tension entre hétérogénéité des fascicules et unité de l'œuvre. Il existe une unité narrative de l'épisode qui

---

[5] [Delubac] *Les Aventures de Freddy La Bougeotte*, Mulhouse, S.E.P.E.L., 1946, 20 fascicules.

[6] Le support affecte ces découpages: le format du journal rattache davantage la structure à la logique de la livraison, coupant parfois le récit au milieu d'un chapitre. A l'inverse, le format en volume, même modeste au point d'être proche de la brochure, suppose une unité narrative. Mais les variations d'une série à l'autre semblent témoigner que la structure du récit n'est pas commandée par les seules contraintes du support, mais qu'elle repose sur une décision commune de l'éditeur et de l'auteur, définie dès l'origine, sans doute contractuellement, pour faire coïncider ou non épisodes et support: ainsi Tallandier choisit-il de recourir presque systématiquement à un tel principe de coïncidence, Albin Michel presque jamais, Ferenczi le fait après la Première Guerre mondiale et Offenstadt tente les deux techniques.

le rend en partie indépendant de la structure d'ensemble. Cette logique de contiguïté explique que l'intrigue prenne presque toujours la forme d'un voyage: dans sa gestion d'un espace saisi en une série d'étapes, le voyage permet de concrétiser dans la trame continue d'un trajet-intrigue la logique discontinue des épisodes juxtaposés. La superstructure du récit privilégie en outre une forme ouverte. La séquence conduisant de la crise à sa résolution, matière du récit, n'est unifiée que par une intrigue prétexte: défi extraordinaire, voyage autour du monde, poursuite sans fin, etc. De telles trames ne sont contraintes qu'à leurs seuils (crise et résolution), et n'impliquent pas d'inscription dans un chronotope déterminé, pas de chronologie événementielle, elles se contentent d'indiquer l'unité du récit, mais comme simple horizon du texte. Si le *plot*, comme superstructure, offre la garantie qu'il s'agit bien d'un seul roman (comme unité de sens), le plaisir que procure ce livre réside essentiellement dans les *subplots* (comme unités secondes assurant l'essentiel de la tension narrative).

Il faut dire que si l'auteur insiste sur la péripétie, c'est qu'il ne sait probablement pas lui-même exactement quelle extension il va donner au récit. En effet, les contrats supposaient de pouvoir rallonger et raccourcir l'œuvre en fonction de son succès. Il faut dire aussi que l'intrigue d'ensemble tend à se perdre, au fil des milliers de pages que distille l'auteur durant des mois et parfois des années – et qu'il serait difficile de maintenir la tension narrative sans le relais des péripéties. Il faut dire enfin que l'auteur cherche à séduire également les lecteurs irréguliers, en leur offrant des héros récurrents dont les aventures peuvent se lire d'une façon presque indépendante.

Thématisée à travers le voyage et ses étapes, la logique du support à diffusion hebdomadaire peut décomposer le récit en unités secondaires, déterminant des intrigues fondées sur chacun des espaces traversés: une aventure en Amérique, une autre dans le Grand Nord, une troisième en mer, etc. On voit comment la relation entre le récit-cadre et les récits secondaires peut être lue en termes architextuels. La première unité détermine un genre de récit, le roman d'aventures géographiques, et un sous-genre, le roman de voyage encyclopédique. Elle en définit aussi les protagonistes (les scouts, le chasseur, le "petit explorateur", l'aviateur, le reporter, le détective, etc.), lesquels sont des types engageant des scénarios intertextuels (voyages patriotiques, chasses extraordinaires, courses technologiques, poursuites autour du globe, etc.). Dans tous les cas, la logique est celle d'un cadrage, très largement dominé par une perspective générique. Mais ce cadrage générique est littéralement *mis en intrigue*, au sens où le récit matérialise la relation de l'architexte aux intertextes à travers cette intrigue organisée en un récit cadre décomposé en récits secondaires. De fait, les épisodes peuvent être lus comme autant de variantes au sein de l'intrigue-cadre à valeur architextuelle: à chaque région traversée, son lot d'aventures attendues, avec leur propre cohérence narrative, mais sans déranger les contraintes et la structure d'ensemble. L'architexte "roman d'aventures géographiques", cadre du roman, sera ainsi décliné, d'un fascicule à l'autre, en sous-ensembles plus identifiés: récits maritimes, westerns, chasses au trésor ou robinsonnades se succéderont d'un numéro à l'autre. Dans les œuvres qui jouent le plus clairement sur l'unité entre la forme de l'intrigue et celle du support, comme les récits scouts de Jean de La Hire, cela se traduit souvent par l'évocation d'une région distincte par fascicule, déterminant une unité de cadre et d'intrigue et souvent de nouveaux protagonistes: chaque pays impose ses propres scénarios intertextuels et son unité narrative. Dans ce cas, la logique est près de basculer du côté de la série à héros récurrent.

On voit comment la logique narrative contradictoire permet la lecture discontinue que supposent les fascicules: l'auteur peut ajouter des épisodes ou en soustraire, le lecteur peut éventuellement manquer un ou deux fascicules, la saisie de l'intrigue n'en sera guère affectée. Les résumés figurant généralement au début de chaque fascicule, chez Jean de La Hire, R.-M. de Nizerolles ou José Moselli, disent cette tendance au ressassement, puisque d'un numéro à l'autre, le texte en reste dans ses grandes lignes le même, preuve que les épisodes ajoutés ne font guère progresser l'intrigue.

Au niveau des intrigues secondaires déterminées par les limites du fascicule, l'auteur ou l'éditeur obéissent à une logique contradictoire: ils proposent au lecteur une unité narrative identifiable, susceptible de lui procurer un plaisir complet, qui l'invitera, la semaine suivante, à acheter un nouveau numéro. Mais ils produisent *a contrario* un effet d'inachèvement, proposant une forme, même limitée, de *suspens*: les rivaux des scouts de Jean de La Hire ont pris de l'avance dans la course autour du monde tandis que ceux-ci aidaient l'armée française attaquée par les bédouins dans le désert; le petit aventurier de Galopin a pu fuir les Indiens, mais il lui faut à présent retrouver son redoutable ennemi; et le héros de Nizerolles n'échappe à un péril dans les airs que pour en pressentir immédiatement un nouveau. Chez Moselli (par exemple dans *Les Mystères de la mer de corail*, 1925), cet effet de suspens est mis en scène dans l'espace du fascicule, à travers une ultime page proposant les premiers paragraphes du prochain volume, et introduisant la crise qui servira d'unité au récit d'ensemble.

Tous les auteurs ne conçoivent pas de la même façon cette relation du support au *suspens*: là où un Jean de La Hire propose des fascicules à l'intrigue bien délimitée, chez Nizerolles et Galopin au contraire, la plupart des fascicules s'achèvent sur une sorte de *cliffhanger* qui n'est pas sans annoncer la logique des séries télévisées modernes. On pourrait penser qu'il y a une contradiction entre ce qui vient d'être dit et le fait que le découpage de certains romans (ceux de Galopin par exemple) soit en partie arbitraire, s'achevant souvent au milieu d'un chapitre à la façon des livraisons du XIXe siècle. Mais ici encore, c'est négliger combien l'auteur pense la tension narrative en fonction de son support: les fascicules très brefs de Galopin (16 pages) le contraignent à inscrire son récit dans une tension constante, une logique de l'acmé permanent. On peut trouver toutes les vingt ou trente lignes un de ces effets de *suspens* sur lequel pourrait s'arrêter le fascicule. Autrement dit, il n'est pas certain que le choix du découpage des fascicules soit opéré par l'auteur, mais la logique tensive est telle que l'éditeur pouvait aisément trouver de quoi couper le texte à n'importe quel moment tout en produisant un tel effet d'attente.[7] Ici encore, le support détermine une logique narrative, et imprime à l'intrigue son rythme. Narrativement, cela suppose de multiplier vertigineusement les péripéties, de supprimer presque entièrement les passages descriptifs ou l'idée même de pause dans le récit, en maintenant une pression constante. Cela implique encore de mettre en scène cette tension dans un style recourant à des effets de parataxe suspensive: exclamatives, phrases et paragraphes brefs inscrivent dans la page cette volonté de toujours mettre en scène l'attente du lecteur.

La tension entre totalité romanesque et unité épisodique produit un plaisir lui-même en tension. D'un côté, la cohérence de l'épisode répond à la volonté de complétude qu'ouvre toute crise narrative, en offrant des récits brefs aux structures bien repérables; de l'autre, la logique ouverte de la série conjure le caractère frustrant du récit clos en promettant d'en renouveler le charme par un effet de relance des aventures des protagonistes. Le plaisir du récit ouvert installe une tension avec le désir d'une clôture du texte qui en déterminera le sens global, quand bien même cette clôture, dans sa forme ultime (celle de l'ensemble de l'œuvre comme roman) devrait être constamment repoussée.

Cette logique contradictoire possède une explication historique. Nées au début du XXe siècle, au moment où la collection se substitue aux livraisons comme support populaire privilégié (Hogg-Grandjean 1996), les séries de fascicules font transition, et tentent de combiner la trame ouverte du système déclinant des romans en livraisons et la clôture narrative en

---

[7] Chez José Moselli, l'effet de *suspens* et d'unité narrative est en grande partie une production éditoriale, puisque les œuvres étaient à l'origine conçues pour être publiées en feuilletons dans *L'Intrépide*.

une trame resserrée du roman sériel issu d'une collection. Cela explique l'ambiguïté de la présentation des volumes, entre numéros d'une collection et livraisons d'un roman, comme s'il s'agissait de concilier l'ancienne forme et la nouvelle. Le choix du genre et les scénarios intertextuels privilégiés thématisent cette tentative pour inventer une forme transitoire entre deux logiques différentes d'intrigues liées à deux supports successifs. Le récit de tour du monde illustrait dans sa forme ouverte les contraintes du feuilleton. Il disparaîtra très largement des collections d'aventures de chez Fayard, Ferenczi et Tallandier, supports moins adaptés, avec leur nombre de pages limité, aux intrigues paratactiques et ramifiées. Il survivra cependant dans les fascicules, au prix néanmoins d'un ajustement à l'évolution du canon narratif, puisque les auteurs mettent en scène dans l'intrigue l'oscillation entre la logique du fascicule et celle du roman publié en collection – c'est-à-dire entre la prolifération événementielle et l'unité narrative.

Mais ce recours aux stéréotypes du récit de tour du monde a d'autres conséquences. On sait que leur vogue est née de la tendance de la littérature populaire à adopter, au XIXe siècle, une perspective panoramique – et en ce sens, Jules Verne est un descendant de Balzac et des physionomistes (Thérenty 2007). Traverser tous les continents, en peindre les peuples, la faune et la flore, c'est affecter au roman une forme et une fonction encyclopédique; c'est prétendre aussi faire de l'œuvre un alter-ego du monde. C'est un effet similaire que produisent les romans de Jean de La Hire, Arnould Galopin ou Raoul de Nizerolles qui définissent, au fil des pages, un univers de fiction cohérent, avec sa poignée de protagonistes récurrents. Mais si ce monde ressemble fort au nôtre, il détermine également ses règles propres, indépendamment du référent extralinguistique. C'est d'autant plus vrai que les héros des fascicules se ressemblent tous, du "petit buffalo" au "petit chasseur de la pampa" chez Arnould Galopin, de "l'as des boy-scouts" au "roi des scouts" chez Jean de La Hire. On le voit, par-delà la clôture des séries, ce sont bien, en un sens, toujours les *mêmes* aventures du *même* personnage, dans le *même* univers de fiction qui sont racontées. Jean de La Hire ne propose-t-il pas à quelques années d'écart deux séries des *Trois boy-scouts* avec des personnages différents qui vivent à peu de choses près la même aventure (au niveau de l'intrigue cadre), mais déclinée en une série de mésaventures originales? Effets de continuité d'un fascicule à l'autre et effets de continuité d'une œuvre à l'autre tendent à produire une sorte de confusion généralisée qui témoigne de ce que c'est toujours un peu le même récit, la même intrigue ouverte qui se prolongent pour les lecteurs, parce que la clôture du récit importe moins (tant qu'elle reste promise à l'horizon du récit) que son interminable prolongement.[8] Quand un roman de Galopin ou de Jean de La Hire s'achève, les auteurs en commencent aussitôt un autre, avec des personnages identiques au nom différent, ce qui permet de prolonger virtuellement à l'infini le plaisir du récit: *Julot, tueur de tigres* cède la place, la semaine suivante, à *Toto explorateur*, et les *Grandes aventures d'un boy scout* font immédiatement suite à *L'As des boy-scouts*, créant une sorte de continuité des aventures et des univers de fiction.

L'impression d'unité diégétique est encore accrue par le fait que les intrigues se déroulent dans des univers de fiction similaires. Ce monde est réduit dans les faits à un très petit nombre de *topoï*, et se cantonne à des zones de délimitations architextuelles servant de réservoir de thèmes et de scénarios intertextuels: l'Amérique (ses Peaux-Rouges, ses *outlaws*, son attaque du train), l'Afrique noire (ses bêtes féroces, ses cannibales), l'Inde (sa chasse au tigre, son voyage à dos d'éléphant), etc.

Par-delà la limite des séries, par-delà même l'hétérogénéité des auteurs, il existe une cohérence entre les univers de fiction, dans la mesure où le monde auquel ils renvoient est déterminé par une double logique référentielle: la première désigne les régions géographiques réelles; mais la seconde, plus essentielle à la structuration des imaginaires, renvoie clairement à des espaces dont les caractéristiques sont déterminées de façon intertextuelle. Jean-Marie Seillan a ainsi pu montrer combien l'Afrique du roman d'aventures était réduite à un tout petit nombre de *topoï* inlassablement convoqués par les auteurs (Seillan 2006). On pourrait faire, après Paul Bleton (Bleton 2002), les mêmes remarques pour l'Amérique à l'imaginaire directement repris des fascicules de chez Eichler et des premiers *westerns*, et décliner ainsi ces effets de vraisemblance architextuelle pour toutes les régions du globe (Letourneux 2010). Ainsi les intertextes des œuvres de genre viennent se substituer, dans les récits, à la réalité que les espaces sont sensés désigner. Contrairement aux textes des générations précédentes, il n'y a plus de passages didactiques, parce que l'œuvre à renoncé à parler du monde pour ne plus évoquer que d'autres récits. On en voudrait pour preuve l'extraordinaire faculté de Jean de La Hire, de reprendre *in extenso* des chapitres entiers de romans écrits par ses prédécesseurs dans l'un ou l'autre de ses fascicules, en se contentant de modifier le nom des

---

[8] D'ailleurs, en un sens, c'est bien *la même* série qui est proposée par-delà les titres différents, puisque les éditeurs (Albin Michel, Offenstadt, Ferenczi) invitent à les associer à travers la présentation matérielle des volumes ou l'absence de discontinuité entre les publications: les couvertures et les mises en pages sont standardisées, et une nouvelle série débute, à peine la précédente achevée, avec une présentation similaire.

protagonistes, produisant de la sorte des séries entières de fascicules par simple collage de textes. Il ne fait rien d'autre, dans ce cas, que de pousser à l'extrême la tendance, qu'on retrouve chez Galopin ou Nizerolles, à reformuler platement (mais en prenant cette fois la peine de les réécrire), des épisodes de romans d'aventures. De la citation plate au plagiat, la distance n'est pas toujours très grande.

Dès lors qu'elle s'inscrit dans une perspective intertextuelle et architextuelle plutôt que référentielle, la logique encyclopédique des œuvres n'a plus vocation à offrir une vision panoramique de la réalité géographique, mais à décliner les scénarios intertextuels du genre associés aux espaces traversés par les héros. De l'encyclopédie didactique du récit de tour du monde au XIXe siècle, on glisse vers une encyclopédie du roman d'aventures. Il s'agit moins de se singulariser en se démarquant, que d'offrir une vision synoptique du genre, qui passe par une nécessaire schématisation. Si les auteurs proposent des intrigues rudimentaires et stéréotypées, ce n'est pas nécessairement parce qu'ils sont incapables d'être originaux, mais c'est parce que le pacte de lecture défini par le support et sa reformulation générique et narrative supposent une simplification extrême, comme condition de possibilité de l'encyclopédisme de l'œuvre. La conséquence en est la grande prédictibilité du récit: les épisodes se suivent, attendus, et l'on pourrait presque deviner, à l'arrivée des protagonistes dans une région, quelles aventures ils vont rencontrer: on l'a dit, rares sont les épisodes en Amérique sans Indiens, ou l'absence de chasse au tigre en Inde. Or, dès lors qu'elle est remotivée dans le pacte de lecture, cette prédictibilité, loin de susciter l'ennui est, selon nous, à la source du plaisir du lecteur et de la tension narrative.

En se contentant de reprendre des scénarios attendus pour chaque cadre-type du roman d'aventures, l'auteur crée un effet d'anticipation qui n'a pas le temps, pour le lecteur, de se transformer en ennui, parce que le rythme et l'enchaînement des épisodes ne le permettent pas. Au contraire, une tension narrative est produite par l'invitation, pour le lecteur, à anticiper constamment sur la suite du récit, à partir de ses compétences de lecteur sériel. Cette invitation est d'autant plus forte que tout, de l'évidence des événements au paratexte, sollicite en permanence ce mécanisme d'anticipation. Ainsi en est-il des couvertures: l'importance de ces images grossièrement colorées dans l'orientation de la lecture est d'autant plus grande qu'elles illustrent des textes brefs, et qu'elles en disent par avance le scénario, le décomposant parfois, à la façon d'un récit en images, en une série de scènes intermédiaires. On voit combien cette tendance à concevoir l'intrigue à travers des séries de *scripts* que le lecteur peut anticiper tend ici à modeler la lecture avant même que celle-ci ne débute – dès le titre, dès la couverture. Loin de jouer avec les attentes du lecteur (en les trompant ou en les dévoyant), le récit actualise la plupart des scripts que ce dernier, en bon amateur du genre, est en droit d'attendre. Le plaisir du lecteur tient certes au fait qu'il voit ses attentes confirmées, mais il repose aussi, en amont, sur cette dynamique de lecture anticipatrice que sollicite le texte.

Dans ces conditions, la tentation est forte, pour définir le plaisir du récit, d'en revenir au principe du ressassement régressif. Mais pour qu'il y ait tension dramatique, il faut que le plaisir du même s'affronte avec celui de la variation. Cette tension passe ici encore par la dynamique du récit, qui ne cherche pas tant à varier par rapport au modèle qu'à varier *au sein du modèle*: les intrigues sont certes stéréotypées, et n'innovent guère par rapport aux intertextes qui les nourrissent, mais le lecteur qui achète la série des aventures peut lire, au fil des numéros, un vaste éventail de récits: il découvrira tour à tour une robinsonnade, un naufrage, un combat contre des bandits, un périple dans les pôles, bref tous les sous-genres du roman d'aventures. La fuite en avant du récit est aussi déclinaison inlassable des possibles narratifs du genre, qui tient au caractère encyclopédique de ces œuvres. Certes, le lecteur n'est pas vraiment surpris par ce qu'il lit au fil des pages, en revanche, il est comblé par la profusion des aventures et des variations infinies qu'elles offrent dans une trame narrative continue et virtuellement sans fin. Ici, la variation vaut pour déictique d'une infinité d'autres récits possibles.

On comprend mieux alors pourquoi cette forme encyclopédique s'accommode d'une logique aussi stéréotypée. Le stéréotype accompagne la dynamique de variation et le plaisir qu'en tire le lecteur. Ce dernier avance, saute d'un fascicule à l'autre, et s'oublie au fil du récit, ayant le sentiment d'embrasser dans le texte le genre dans sa totalité, suivant un plaisir qui repose sur un principe de *collection*. L'intrigue vise à mettre en scène un tel plaisir totalisant à travers un voyage du personnage *dans le monde* qui vaut pour métaphore du trajet du lecteur *dans le genre*. Dès lors, on voit combien la tension narrative que produit l'attente chez le lecteur d'événements qu'il pressent mais dont il ignore les modalités de déroulement se double d'une attente des nouvelles variations produites, et d'un plaisir à découvrir un récit dont il connaît les rouages mais dont il découvre l'infinie variété.

"To find the plot", "trouver le récit", c'est aussi en suivre les ramifications et les virtualités dans une sorte de logorrhée narrative: c'est dans ce cas poursuivre un récit qui se présente moins comme une œuvre individualisée que comme une mécanique visant à parcourir toutes les travées du genre dans une dynamique narrative virtuellement sans fin. En recrachant du stéréotype au kilomètre, les auteurs de fascicules plongent à la source du conte. Il ne s'agit pas là de la forme sophistiquée du conte mettant en scène la voix originale du conteur et son habileté à narrer autrement ou à réarticuler de façon originale le déjà là, le déjà connu. Il s'agit de cette ivresse devant les infinies virtualités et l'arbitraire du conte. Le conteur devient ainsi une machine à générer du récit à l'infini – et à révéler de la même façon que les récits sont eux-mêmes potentiellement infinis. On assiste, à la façon des *1001 nuits*, à un récit sans fin véritable, sinon promise et toujours repoussée jusqu'au moment où le lecteur lui-même se lassera, comme Shâhriar face à Shéhérazade.

C'est précisément cette dynamique du récit que ressaisit l'intrigue, avec ses courses sans fin dans lesquelles il s'agit pour le héros d'avaler les kilomètres comme le lecteur avale les fascicules, sans jamais faire de pauses. Et l'on pourrait trouver un témoignage de cette logique d'un récit emporté par la dynamique de la narration dans l'importance des titres de fascicules à sémantisme vide, qui renvoient simplement à une pure promesse de tension: *Une affaire délicate*, *Difficultés imprévues*, *L'immense tragédie*, *Nouveaux dangers*, *Nouvelles complications*... De tels titres disent bien que l'essentiel est de relancer la machine, de maintenir la pression, mais que le contenu importe peu, parce que le pacte de lecture sériel le prédétermine très largement et que, quelle que soit l'intrigue, le lecteur sait d'avance qu'il aura droit à l'une ou l'autre des aventures conventionnelles du genre.

Le caractère encyclopédique du récit lui permet de fonctionner comme une machine combinatoire produisant de l'événement à la chaîne en puisant dans le répertoire du genre. La vraisemblance est certes fondée sur une logique architextuelle, mais elle s'intéresse moins à la cohérence du récit, à son architecture, qu'à sa dynamique. Si le lecteur accepte de jouer le jeu de la fiction, ce n'est pas tant parce que l'intrigue est bien conçue, ni parce qu'elle est originale, ni même parce qu'elle est bien contée, que parce qu'elle va de l'avant et qu'elle offre de la sorte une profusion, un trop plein de récits. Dans cette dynamique, le traitement du stéréotype, saisi par son côté le plus rudimentaire, participe de la vraisemblance, puisqu'il conditionne l'efficacité d'un récit et le plaisir que le lecteur en tire.

On dit souvent que pour que la séduction du récit sériel opère, il faut que les auteurs soient capables de donner un nouveau visage aux éléments sériels. Certes, ce nouveau visage peut prendre la forme d'intrigues originales, de variantes astucieuses, d'autres façons de conter ou de proposer une lecture renouvelée de vieux stéréotypes, mais ce que montrent les exemples que nous avons choisis, c'est que la capacité à investir des supports et à en ressaisir les spécificités en termes d'intrigue et de dynamique narrative peut aussi permettre de réarticuler le connu, le déjà là, pour lui offrir un nouveau visage. Dans nos exemples, les récits de tour du monde que narrent les auteurs permettent de mettre en intrigue la dynamique du fascicule, ce support combinant la logique de la livraison et celle de la collection, et d'en saisir les virtualités en termes de relation au récit et au genre, en terme également d'un plaisir particulier du pur vertige de la collection que l'on ressentirait face à la profusion même d'un conte emporté dans sa course sans fin à travers le monde et les intrigues, exploration inépuisable des conventions du roman d'aventures.

## Références


Bleton, Paul. 2002. *Western, France*, Amiens: Encrage.

Hogg-Grandjean, Sophie. 1996. *L'Evolution de la Librairie Arthème Fayard (1857-1936)*, thèse de l'université de Versailles-Saint-Quentin-en-Yvelines, sous la dir. de J.-Y. Mollier.

Letourneux, Matthieu. 2006. "*L'As des boys scouts* de Jean de La Hire ou le tour du genre en 52 fascicules", *Mélanges en l'honneur d'Isabelle Nières-Chevrel.* Sous la direction de Cécile Boulaire. Rennes: Presses de l'Université de Rennes.

Letourneux, Matthieu. 2010. *Le Roman d'aventures, 1870-1930.* Limoges: Pulim,

Rennonciat, Annie. 2004. 'Production du 'populaire' dans l'édition pour la jeunesse', in Migozzi, Jacques and Le Guern, Philippe (eds). *Production(s) du populaire.* Limoges: PULIM.

Seillan, Jean-Marie. 2006. *Aux sources du roman colonial.* Paris: Kathala.

Thérenty, Marie-Eve. 2007. 'Avant-propos', *Romantisme*, 136, 'L'œuvre-monde', 2002-7.

Touchant, Jean-Louis. 2001. *L'Apothéose du roman d'aventures.* Amiens: Encrage.

# CHAPTER FIFTEEN

# INEVITABLE PLOTS IN THE SYMBOLIST NOVEL? GEORGES RODENBACH'S *BRUGES-LA-MORTE*

RICHARD HIBBITT

The existence of the Symbolist novel has exercised critics intermittently for over a century. At one extreme we find the view that it is a contradiction in terms, based on the argument that Symbolism's interest in suggestiveness and polyvalence found its natural manifestation in the poem, painting, prose poem or play, rather than in the unavoidably linear and expository structure of the novel.[1] At the other, we find the view that the experimental novels of the late nineteenth century by Barrès, Dujardin, Gourmont, Gide, Schwob and others paved the way for the great Modernist novels – for Joyce, Faulkner, Proust and Woolf – and thereafter for the experiments of the *nouveau roman* and all subsequent variations on the autotelicity of fiction.[2] My aim here is not to reiterate the tenets of this debate or to support one particular camp – both arguments have their validity – but to explore the role played by plot in the Symbolist novel and to examine the relationships between Symbolism, plot and popularity, taking Georges Rodenbach's 1892 novel *Bruges-la-morte* as a case study.[3]

---

[1] See Poulliart 1974 and Mourier-Casile 1982 for a consideration of these difficulties. See also Swift 1973 for a nuanced and succinct consideration of the debate.

[2] The standard text here is Wilson 1961. An even broader definition is proposed by Friedman (Friedman 1991).

[3] The most comprehensive recent study of the Symbolist novel is Michelet Jacquod 2008. Michelet Jacquod surveys the preceding debate and offers a new definition of the novel as a text of 'extreme consciousness'. The second part of her book focuses on works by Dujardin, Gide, Gourmont and Schwob; the first part provides a thorough discussion of the problematics of the debate and discusses a number of other authors and examples. See also Uitti 1961 and Wiesław Malinowski 2003.

This exploration will lead to a consideration of the extent to which reader response to the Symbolist novel inevitably involves the identification and processing of a plot, however unconventional the text may be in terms of causality and chronology. Beyond this, the essay considers the extent to which reading a novel entails an inevitable teleological operation which enables the reader to find an interpretative key to the text, irrespective of the writer's intention. In other words, can we read a narrative without reconstituting some kind of plot?

Symbolism was not an organized movement or school, despite the 1886 article in *Le Figaro Littéraire* by Jean Moréas, entitled "Un manifeste littéraire" and subtitled "Le symbolisme", which is known in English as the Symbolist manifesto (Moréas 1973). It should be seen rather as an artistic current based around the potential of the word and the image, a current which is epitomized by the semantic plenitude of Mallarmé's poetry, the paintings of Moreau and Redon, and the theatre of Maeterlinck and Villiers de l'Isle-Adam. Indeed, it is perhaps within Mallarmé's own theoretical writings that we find the best account of the need for language to reinvent itself and to explore the fullness of its possibilities.[4] Although his manifesto is predominantly concerned with poetry, in the penultimate paragraph Moréas writes that "la conception du roman symbolique est polymorphe", suggesting (without giving any examples) that the Symbolist novel will be characterized by its protean qualities and its emancipation from the restrictions of Naturalism. But other critics argued that the novel would remain outside: in 1886 Alfred Vallette suggested that Symbolism would remain in the domain of poetry; similarly, in 1891 Ferdinand Brunetière minimized the contribution of Symbolism in "Le roman à venir", his essay on the future of the novel.[5] However, various writers themselves were experimenting with the possibilities of renewing the novel in line with the developments seen in poetry and of liberating it from both Naturalist and Decadent constraints. André Gide's early *récits* of the 1890s, such as *Les Cahiers et les Poésies d'André Walter* and *Paludes*, constitute one example of this experimentation; after completing the first work, Gide declared himself to be a Symbolist, remarking in a letter to Valéry dated 26 January 1891 that he hoped to achieve for the novel what Mallarmé had achieved for poetry and Maeterlinck for the play: "Donc Mallarmé pour la poésie, Maeterlinck pour le drame – et, quoique auprès d'eux deux je me sente bien un peu

---

[4] Among the many short pieces on poetics that Mallarmé wrote, see *Crise de vers* (1886-92-96) (Mallarmé 2003), and the 1891 interview he gave to Jules Huret, in *Enquête sur l'èvolution littéraire* (Mallarmé 1982).

[5] See Vallette 1886 and Brunetière 1891.

gringalet, j'ajoute Moi pour le roman" (Gide 2009, 52). Although Gide's explicit adherence to Symbolism gradually disappeared, it should be understood here as part of his ongoing desire to renew the form of narrative prose; indeed, his wish to write a new kind of novel was partly responsible for his long-standing reluctance to use the term "roman" to refer to his works. But the possibility of a Symbolist novel remained a niche interest, which is evident from the fact that it is rarely mentioned in the interviews with contemporary writers collected in Jules Huret's 1891 survey *Enquête sur l'évolution littéraire* (Huret 1982). Nor is it considered in Pierre Bourdieu's analysis of the *fin-de-siècle* literary field in *Les Règles de l'Art*, which uses Huret's survey as one of its source texts: although Bourdieu acknowledges the innovative novels of the period by writers including Gide, Maurice Barrès, Édouard Estaunié, Camille Mauclair and Paul Margueritte, he simply concludes that they can be read "comme des poèmes en prose" (Bourdieu 1992, 172), considering Symbolism to be the domain of poetry.

In *Le Roman symboliste: un art de l'extrême conscience*, Valérie Michelet Jacquod (2008) argues that the Symbolist novel is not simply an attempt to invest prose with the qualities of poetry, but also an attempt to explore notions of musicality, dream and the unconscious. Michelet Jacquod posits it as both referential and auto-referential, therefore a paradox, but very much an existing paradox, and one which contributes to the renewal of the genre of the novel as a whole. Her discussions of novels by writers including Gide, Édouard Dujardin, Rémy de Gourmont and Marcel Schwob focus on aspects such as the condensation of action, the frequent focus on the (fragmented) consciousness of one character, and the early usage of the interior monologue. As far as plot is concerned, she describes how the Symbolist novelists wanted to combine certain elements of their nineteenth-century heritage with the suppression of conventional narrative:

> En effet, pour les auteurs, le roman du symbolisme est appelé à devenir le creuset où doivent se fondre la psychologie héritée de Stendhal, la vision exaltée de Balzac, le rythme cadencé de la prose de Flaubert et l'impressionnisme des Goncourt, tout cela s'articulant autour d'une intrigue presque absente, drame intériorisé de la pensée ou mouvement imperceptible de la foule [...]. (Michelet Jacquod 2008, 34)

The reference here to "une intrigue presque absente" raises an immediate question: to what extent can a plot be *almost* absent? Of course it can be reduced or minimized, and conventional causality can be replaced by atmosphere, tonality, *leitmotifs* or the recreated non-sequiturs of interior monologue; as Michelet Jacquod puts it above, the interiorized drama of thought processes or the imperceptible movement of the crowd. The standard elements of the *romanesque*, or novelistic, can even be replaced by tableaux, seemingly as interchangeable as the prose poems collected in Baudelaire's *Le Spleen de Paris*, which he compares to pieces of a snake (Baudelaire 1962, 6), or to the pieces that make up Rimbaud's *Illuminations*. However, the integrality and linearity of prose narratives (as opposed to collections of prose poems) suggests that the virtual absence of the plot is perhaps rather a question of the absence of an explicit plot; the plot itself may be implicit, or latent, but it is always present.

Michelet Jacquod does not develop her reference to the virtual absence of the plot, but she makes the interesting proposition that the Symbolist novel occupies a distinct place with regard to the adventure novel, the realist novel and the poem. Using the narrative theory of Gérard Genette, she argues that metalepsis is the distinguishing feature of Symbolist narrative:

> La composition de l'œuvre symboliste, organisée par la métalepse, possède une autre caractéristique qui la distingue à la fois de la structure du roman d'aventure – linéaire et contingente – , de celle du roman réaliste – linéaire et métonymique – mais encore de la forme du poème, pourtant dévoilante et circulaire, qualités vers lesquelles tend le récit symboliste. (Michelet Jacquod 2008, 139)

Her hypothesis is that the pervasive metalepsis in the Symbolist novel is evident in the texts' awareness of their own literariness: here metalepsis is understood as the collapsed division between narration and narrated, or simply as "frame-breaking", with possible connotations of metafiction. This is based partly on Genette's analysis of metalepsis in *Figures III*, where he refers to the transgressive intrusion by an extradiegetic narrator (or author) into the diegesis (Genette 1972, 243-45); it also draws on his later work in *Métalepse*, where he expands the notion that metalepsis is a particular type of metonymy, which can substitute cause for effect (and vice versa) (Genette 2004, 13-14). In this respect metalepsis also displays its original rhetorical function, where one trope is substituted for another which may appear to have nothing to do with it. Here we can see another link with Symbolism, in the sense that one meaning can trigger off another seemingly unrelated one, be it the non-sequitur or flight of fancy. Moreover, both the narratological and the rhetorical definitions of metalepsis can be evident if the narrative mode is broken by such a metonymic shift. For Michelet Jacquod, the Symbolist novel therefore gravitates toward the circular and revealing quality of the poem but crucially differs from it, in the same way that it differs from the linear and contingent adventure novel and the linear and metonymic realist novel. I agree with her distinction with one reservation: the word "linear" should be added to the definition of the Symbolist novel, which might be described as quintessentially linear, metaleptic and poetic. The remainder of this essay will examine this theory by considering the example of Georges Rodenbach's *Bruges-la-morte.*

Published in 1892, *Bruges-la-morte* is a short novel which contains thirty-five photographs of the city of Bruges, from which human figures are almost entirely absent. The genesis of the text raises interesting questions regarding popularity, commercial dictates and reception. Rodenbach initially wrote a short prose piece – *une nouvelle* or *un récit* – that was serialized in thirteen short chapters in *Le Figaro* between 4 and 14 February. When a possible book publication was mooted, the publisher (Ernest Flammarion) wanted to enlarge the text so that it could be marketed as a *roman*. This was achieved by the addition of two new chapters and the photographs, which are placed at intervals throughout the text. It is however not an illustrated text: the images are simply juxtaposed with the text and do not systematically correlate to specific parts of it, thereby providing a hybrid text, or two concurrent texts.[6] Rodenbach then wrote a well-known retrospective "Avertissement" to the book, a preface where he emphasizes the role played by the city of Bruges as a character that exerts an influence on the narrative, which justifies the subsequent addition of the images. Ironically, a work which is frequently cited as both the first *récit-photo* and the quintessential Symbolist novel owes its *avant-garde* quality to commercial criteria rather than to the author's initial artistic aims. With further irony, the addition of the photographs to bulk out the text meant that it was not as successful as hoped because of the

[6] See the Gallimard edition of *Bruges-la-morte* edited by Jean-Pierre Bertrand and Daniel Grojnowski for a reproduction of the original edition (Rodenbach 1998). The Labor edition edited by Christian Berg (Rodenbach 1986) contains extensive supplementary material and a copy of the original frontispiece by Fernand Khnopff, but does not contain the original photographs. Some of the later Flammarion editions miss the point completely by combining the photographs with conventional pen-and-ink illustrations of the characters, such as the 1919 "nouvelle edition", which contains "similigravures d'après les dessins de H. Delavelle". For an English version, see the Dedalus translation by Mike Mitchell (Rodenbach 2005), with an introduction by Alan Hollinghurst. This edition replaces the original photographs with new ones of the city taken by Will Stone, who also provides a translation of Rodenbach's 1888 essay "Agonies des Villes" ("The Death Throes of Towns").

prohibitive cost of each book, which meant that only 14,000 copies were sold after four years, to Flammarion's apparent disappointment. Although Philip Mosley refers to it as "the most successful publication of 1892" (Mosley 1996, 20), this success was due more to its aesthetic interest than to its sales figures. The popularity of *Bruges-la-morte* can therefore be seen in a number of different ways. It started out as a *feuilleton* in *Le Figaro*, ending each day with the words "la suite à demain" beloved of television cliffhangers today, and was intended to help sell daily newspapers in the popular late-nineteenth-century fashion associated with Zola, Maupassant and a host of other writers.[7] It became less popular in the commercial sense as a book, yet now owes a different kind of popularity as part of the *fin-de-siècle* canon to the same combination of text and image that hindered its initial commercial success. One might argue that the transformation of the text enabled it to enjoy both its initial and subsequent popularity; if Flammarion had not suggested adding the photographs after its initial serialization, it may well have been relegated to the status of many other short stories and novels of the period, which are now semi-forgotten and out of print.

It is a trope of critical literature on the period to refer to *Bruges-la-morte* as a Symbolist novel. Jean-Pierre Bertrand and Daniel Grojnowski consider it both "comme un "récit-photo" et comme un roman symboliste, l'un des plus représentatifs, sans aucun doute" (Bertrand and Grojnowski 1998, 10). Michelet Jacquod similarly describes it as the "roman symboliste modèle", referring to it as an example of the "roman-poème" and suggesting that it can be seen as a successful synthesis of the novel and the prose poem (Michelet Jacquod 2008, 43 and 20).[8] This emphasis on the poetic qualities of the text can be partly attributed to Mallarmé's letter to Rodenbach of 28 June 1892, in which he praises the prose as a poem: "j'apprécie en ce livre le poème, infini par soi et littérairement un de ceux en prose les plus fièrement prolongés" (Mallarmé, cited in Rodenbach 1998, 292). These poetic qualities are evident in the use of repetition and evocation, the employment of *leitmotifs*, the blank pages which separate text and image, and in the cadences of the prose itself, exemplified by the incorporation of alexandrines such as "l'ombre des hautes tours allongée sur le texte" (Rodenbach 1998, 50). Most critical

---

[7] For an account of the genesis of *Bruges-la-morte*, see the Introduction by Bertrand and Grojnowski (Rodenbach 1998), especially pp. 10-15. For an account in English, see Mosley 1996. For an interesting discussion of the use of photography, see Edwards 2000.

[8] On this subject see also Gorceix 1985, and Malinowski 2003 which devotes an entire section to it.

interest in *Bruges-la-morte* has focused on the idea of the *roman-poème*, the innovative use of images, the attempt to posit the city as a determining force akin to a character, and the creation of a Symbolist urban landscape which mirrors and affects the protagonist's "états d'âme".[9] In their presentation of the text, Bertrand and Grojnowksi argue that one distinguishing feature of the Symbolist novel is its desire to break determinist narrative causality:

> Si le roman symboliste se définit par la raréfaction des procédures romanesques, il se distingue plus encore des productions concurrentes par le rapport au déterminisme qu'il tente de briser. C'est dans le traitement de la causalité narrative, en effet, que se mesure sa différence avec le roman naturaliste ou le roman psychologique. (Bertrand and Grojnowski 1998, 41)

In *Bruges-la-morte* this attempt to subvert standard causality is evident in the role that the city plays in creating a non-rational, non-human influence; in other words, the city is transformed from realist backdrop into a symbol with both rich semantic potential and connotations of the fantastic, developing the prosopopoeia suggested in the "Tableaux Parisiens" section of Baudelaire's *Les Fleurs du Mal*. Yet these undoubted Symbolist qualities should not conceal the fact that the narrative of the novel is constructed around a surprisingly conventional plot: linear, causal, chronological, teleological and, crucially, *vraisemblable*, in the sense of realistic or plausible. The conventionality of the plot, which is ideally suited to serialization, has been largely ignored, although a few critics have considered it in passing. In his introduction to the recent English translation of the novel, Alan Hollinghurst writes of the "[t]he elaboration of mere atmosphere into a principle of action" (Hollinghurst 2005, 12). Yet he is aware that this aim to conflate atmosphere and action – or stasis and motion – leads in practice to a combination of evocation and narration, identifying the "inherent paradox of the Symbolist novel: how is the inwardness, the fatalistic paralysis of Symbolist art to be wedded to the demands of narrative?" (Hollinghurst 2005, 12). This idea has been developed in greater detail by Philip Mosley, who writes of how "the sustained integration of its poetic language into the narrative structure of the text allow[s] for a heightened, at times almost ethereal, dimension to coexist with the forward thrust of the plot" (Mosley 1996, 23). Mosley also notes how "[t]he plot of *Bruges-la-morte* builds steadily to a crime of

[9] The Gallimard edition of *Bruges-la-morte* (Rodenbach 2008) contains a detailed bibliography, as does *Georges Rodenbach: Critical Essays*, the collection of essays edited by Philip Mosley (1996).

passion" (1996, 26), and is clearly aware that both the determinist and psychological elements of *Bruges-la-morte* sit uneasily with what he rightly refers to as the "so-called" and "problematic" Symbolist novel (1996, 20 and 24-25). Bertrand and Grojnowski are similarly aware of the apparent contradictions between Symbolist theory and Rodenbach's practice, acknowledging that he was able to combine his experimental objectives with conventional traits such as "le maintien d'une intrigue, des personnages et d'un chronotope" (Bertrand and Grojnowski 1998, 34). In the section of their presentation entitled "Un roman hybride", they point out how this dual nature of the text enabled it to appeal both to Mallarmé and to the readers of *Le Figaro*, emphasizing the "pluralité des codes de lecture" which also enable this experimental text to be read as a crime story and as a *conte fantastique* (Bertrand and Grojnowski 1998, 35).[10] However, I would argue that their discussion of the novel's plot does not go far enough: they refer to Rodenbach's aim to compress it ("resserrer"), but the episodic plot of *Bruges-la-morte* is not particularly compressed (Bertrand and Grojnowski 1998, 37). Similarly, they argue that the coherence of the plot resides in its interior system of references rather than its mimetic relationship to the exterior world (Bertrand and Grojnowski 1998, 37), whereas in my view the plot makes perfect sense according to both an auto-referential / Symbolist reading and a mimetic / Realist one. To illustrate this hypothesis, two alternative summaries of the text's plot are provided below:

1) Symbolist reading:

> A rich widower moves to Bruges because the city constitutes the ideal place to mourn his deceased wife. Five years later he sees his wife resurrected in the form of a dancer. When he betrays both the city and his dead wife with this dancer, the city and/or his wife's ghost takes its revenge by compelling him to kill the dancer in order to keep their pact.

This Symbolist reading attributes the causality of the narrative wholly to the interior structure of the text itself: to the influence of the city represented verbally and visually by its religious sites, its canals, the sound of its bells, and the ambiguous dancer who may be the ghost of his wife or the city itself made incarnate. However, it is also possible to summarize the plot of *Bruges-la-morte* without any recourse to Symbolist polyvalence and indeterminacy, in what we might call a Realist reading:

2) Realist reading:

---

[10] On the evolution of a hybrid form of prose poem and story, see Raitt 1981, 156.

> A rich widower moves to Bruges because he believes that the city constitutes the ideal place to mourn his deceased wife. Five years later he begins an affair with a dancer who reminds him of his wife. When the dancer tries to touch his dead wife's hair, which he has kept as a type of relic, he loses his temper and strangles her with it.

In this reading the Symbolist function of the city can be completely omitted and the causality of the text can be understood in purely plausible terms, similar to the cause of the initial murder and eventual double suicide in Zola's *Thérèse Raquin*, for example. Perhaps surprisingly, given its reputation, *Bruges-la-morte* is even more plausible than Oscar Wilde's *The Picture of Dorian Gray*, where the fantastic transformation between Dorian and his portrait cannot be rationally explained. The same argument even applies to Balzac's *La Peau de Chagrin*, one of the source texts for *Dorian Gray*, where the plot similarly rests on an element of the fantastic breaking the pact of verisimilitude (the magical properties of the ass's skin as a variation on the legend of Faust). In this respect I would dispute Hollinghurst's claim that "the conventions of realistic fiction are almost completely abandoned" (2005, 17): although he rightly notes that the proliferation of exterior descriptions is drastically reduced, in terms of plot the conventions of the realist novel are faithfully observed.

The co-existence of these two readings of *Bruges-la-morte* suggests that it is fallacious to argue that the Symbolist novel is by definition not determinist and that plot in the Symbolist novel is virtually absent. Instead, we need perhaps to talk of co-existent determinisms and plots and propose a third, hybrid reading of *Bruges-la-morte* which develops the above readings, among others:

3) Hybrid reading(s)

a) It is a poetic work of prose: the prose aspires to the literariness of poetry with regard to the use of rhythm, repetition, symbol and motif.
b) It is an exploration of the power of the symbol, i.e. a Mallarméan exploration of the suggestive potential of the word, which also supports Moréas's view of the symbol as adumbrated in the Symbolist manifesto.
c) It is a Naturalist novel: the actions of the principal character are determined by his social position and by the environment where he lives (to this can be added the plausibility, rationality and recognizable socio-economic contexts characteristic of Realism).
d) It is a long *conte fantastique*, which combines the plausible and the oneiric to produce an uncanny effect.

e) It is an allegorical *récit édifiant* (cautionary or moral tale) which warns the reader of the danger of confusing art with life, reinforcing its affinity with *The Picture of Dorian Gray*.

This attempt to outline various possible readings of *Bruges-la-morte* aims to show that its polyvalence – and therefore its successive forms of popularity – can be attributed as much to its conventional plot as to its Symbolist credentials. If we think of it in terms of Barthes's distinction between the *texte lisible* and the *texte scriptible* (readerly and writerly text), it can be interpreted as both a readerly *texte de plaisir* which proceeds chronologically to a plausible dénouement and a writerly *texte de jouissance* where the potential meanings of the text exist in the spaces between the words and images. Although one might think that the Symbolist novel would exemplify the "texte scriptible", where the reader becomes co-author, in this reading, *Bruges-la-morte* should also be seen as a "texte lisible" which can be read in different ways, but crucially incorporates these readings into its teleological linearity. In this respect it suggests an interesting affinity with Valéry's much-quoted remark that the novel could no longer begin with a sentence such as "La marquise sortit à cinq heures".[11] The second sentence of *Bruges-la-morte* can be read as a variation on this example: "Hugues Viane se disposa à sortir, comme il en avait l'habitude quotidienne à la fin des après-midi" (Rodenbach 1998, 51-52). The elements identified by Valéry – name or social position, time, denotation of a completed action by the use of a preterite – are all present in this sentence, which initiates a narrative sequence that leads to Hugues's meeting with Jane Scott and culminates in her murder. Although it may come as a surprise that a work championed as *avant garde* can be viewed in such conventional terms, this causal and chronological reading co-exists with its Symbolist qualities. The narrative proceeds towards its *telos* in a way that prefigures two works of similar length, Thomas Mann's *Death in Venice* and Gabriel Garcia Márquez's *Chronicle of a Death Foretold*; although the title *Bruges-la-morte* denotes the dead city, the worshipped dead wife and Jane herself, it is the literal death which constitutes the end of the plot and the text.

This reading of *Bruges-la-morte* as a variation on a conventional popular thriller also invokes the role of the reader. In the "Avertissement", Rodenbach argues that those who will read the text will also undergo the influence of "la Ville", which is capitalized as a proper name. This is

[11] For a discussion of this remark, see *inter alios* Nathalie Sarraute, 'L'ère du soupçon' (Sarraute 1956, 70). Frank Kermode also refers to it in his discussion of Camus's *La Peste* in *The Sense of an Ending* (Kermode 1966, 22).

undoubtedly true, since those who have read the book will surely attest to the influence of the city in word and image on the narrative. Indeed, as many critics have pointed out, the photographs are not crucial to this representation of the city – the idea of the city as a symbol and an agency was already in the first serialized version - but they certainly enhance and develop its effect. However, despite Rodenbach's claims and Bertrand and Grojnowski's emphasis on the Symbolist novel's attempt to break narrative causality, surely here one form of causality is simply replaced by another one. As readers, we can doubtlessly acknowledge the success of Rodenbach's retrospective explanation of his artistic attentions. We can agree that the images of the city could be in any sequence, that the bells are diurnal like the movement of the sun as opposed to chronological like the yearly calendar. We can acknowledge the Symbolist metalepsis in both its narratological and rhetorical senses, constituted here as the breaking of the frame by the unconventional metonymy of the city as the vengeful ghost of the protagonist's dead wife. We can acknowledge certain elements of indeterminacy in the text. Yet at the same time, our attempts to understand the text still depend on the need to reconstitute a plot – and, rather than subverting this, *Bruges-la-morte* actually provides us with an alternative plot, as outlined above.

*Bruges-la-morte* can therefore be seen as *sui generis* in its particular hybridity. Although it can of course still be seen as a Symbolist novel, it seems difficult to sustain the view that it might be the quintessential Symbolist novel because of this conventional plot. In fact any attempt to posit a characteristic Symbolist novel seems destined to fail, as Michelet Jacquod shrewdly points out in the introduction to her study. The importance of plot to other novels from the period would entail a wider study, but a few initial thoughts can be mentioned here. For example, Edouard Dujardin's 1887 novel *Les Lauriers sont coupés*, renowned as a pioneering example of interior monologue and as a formative influence on James Joyce's *Ulysses*, traces one evening in the life of its narrator, Daniel Prince, and his relationship with an actress, Léa d'Arsay (Dujardin 2001). The plot could be summarized to varying lengths, but any summary would reflect on the chronological and causal nature of the narrated events and thoughts as the narrator prepares for his next meeting with Léa. Despite the use of the first-person narrative and the employment of the present tense, the study of an individual consciousness can still be interpreted in terms of a plot. This suggests an affinity with Frank Kermode's argument in *The Sense of an Ending* concerning Sartre's *La Nausée*, where he invokes Aristotle to argue against the success of Sartre's attempt to replicate the contingency of existence in the form of the novel:

> No novel can avoid being in some sense what Aristotle calls "a completed action". This being so, all novels imitate a world of potentiality, even if this implies a philosophy disclaimed by their authors. They have a fixation on the eidetic imagery of beginning, middle, and end, potency and cause.
>
> Novels, then, have beginnings, ends, and potentiality, even if the world has not. (Kermode 1966, 138)

In one sense here Kermode is of course stating the obvious, but the validity of his point resides in reminding us of the novel's unavoidable linearity. In terms of finding the plot, can we justifiably argue that all forms of reading involve finding a plot, or transforming a *szuhet* into a *fabula*? The immediate counter-argument here is that the examples discussed above – *Bruges-la-morte, Les Lauriers sont coupés, La Nausée* – are characterized by a chronology lacking in other, more experimental novels, such as Alain Robbe-Grillet's *La Jalousie* or his screenplay for Alain Resnais's *L'Année dernière à Marienbad*. But even *La Jalousie* and *L'Année dernière à Marienbad* need to be processed by the reader/viewer in a way which entails treating them as a completed action with some form of progression: repetition, circularity and non-sequitur do not alter the essential linear unity of novel or film. The critical cliché which states that "nothing happens beautifully (or otherwise)" can never be entirely supported. As Kermode writes, "the making of a novel is partly the achievement of readers as well as writers, and readers would constantly attempt to supply the very connections that the writer's programme suppresses" (Kermode 1966, 139). Even in the most experimental texts, can a modicum of plot always be found?[12]

As far as the Symbolist novel is concerned, the co-existence of Symbolist qualities and conventional narrative ensures that the reader reads the text on a number of different levels: in the case of *Bruges-la-morte* not only does the reader find the Symbolist/Realist plots, but the novel encodes these two readings. This does not however make the Symbolist novel a contradiction in terms; rather, it shows that Symbolism in the novel necessitates the co-existence of aesthetic intentions and generic conventions. Both the initial and subsequent popularity of *Bruges-la-morte* can be attributed to this successful hybridity, which enables the text to be read as both Gothic thriller and disquisition on the power of the

[12] I am aware of course that there are large lacunae in my knowledge of the novel that might contradict this argument – James Joyce's *Finnegan's Wake* is often cited as the *nec plus ultra* as far as plot is concerned – but I am too cowardly to follow Pierre Bayard's advice here (apart from citing his own book).

symbol. The power of the symbols in *Bruges-la-morte* recall Oscar Wilde's aphorisms in the preface to *The Picture of Dorian Gray*: "All art is at once surface and symbol. / Those who go beneath the surface do so at their peril. / Those who read the symbol do so at their peril" (Wilde 1985, 22). There is another similarity between the novels with regard to their geneses and their popularity: both were initially serialized and in both cases the publishers asked for additions to be made to the published novel version; in Wilde's case the six added chapters shift the balance from the disquisition on aesthetics and morality towards a plot-driven, late Victorian Gothic thriller, which would have greater appeal to a mass audience.

The popularity of the text also suggests an interesting response to Pierre Bourdieu's argument in the essay "The Field of Cultural Production, or: The Economic World Reversed" (Bourdieu 1983).[13] Bourdieu chooses the example of late nineteenth-century French literary production to illustrate his thesis that the symbolic capital of art or literature is in inverse proportion to the economic capital or its market value, arguing that this is "the period in which the literary field attained its maximum autonomy" (Bourdieu 1983, 328). However, there is no place for the Symbolist novel in his diagrammatic representation of the period: the novel is outside the "artistic field" of poetry that appeals to either an "intellectual audience" or "no audience" (Bourdieu 1983, 329). Bourdieu posits a hierarchical relationship where the "psychological novel" and "society novel" have more symbolic capital than, in descending order, the "Naturalist novel (Zola)", the "novel of manners", the "popular novel (serial)" and the "rural novel" (Bourdieu 1983, 329). According to this schematic reading which separates the disinterested autonomy of Symbolist poetry from the box office appeal of novels or plays produced for mass audiences, the Symbolist novel would appear to be a mutually exclusive phenomenon. Bourdieu also makes an interesting distinction between "the principle of legitimacy" that resides solely in the recognition by one's peers rather than by a wider audience, in other words "art for artists", and the 'principle of legitimacy which its advocates call "popular", i.e. the consecration bestowed by the choice of ordinary consumers, the "mass audience"'

---

[13] This is an English translation of a presentation Bourdieu wrote in 1982 and gave at a conference in Bad Homburg, Germany in 1983. The French version, first published in 1991 as "Le champ littéraire", is a slightly revised version of the original text. See Pierre Bourdieu, "Le champ littéraire", *Actes de la recherche en sciences sociales*, 89 (1991), 3-46. The ideas in this essay are developed in the first part of *Les Règles de l'Art* (Bourdieu 1992).

(Bourdieu 1983, 331-32). In his reading, the nineteenth-century novel by definition combined both symbolic and economic capital:

> The novel, occupying a central position in both dimensions of the literary space, is the most dispersed genre in terms of its forms of consecration. It was broadly perceived as typical of the new mercantile literature, linked to the newspaper and journalism by serialization and the impact they gave to it, and above all because, unlike the theatre, it reached a "popular audience"; […]. (Bourdieu 1983, 332)

*Bruges-la-morte* is both a popular serialized *nouvelle* that became a novel and an attempt to emulate the artistic autonomy of Symbolist poetry, which might seem to indicate a flaw in Bourdieu's model. However, I would suggest that the Symbolist novel could simply be added to his scheme as another example of the novel's ability to appeal to both "intellectual" and "mass" audiences. Later in the essay Bourdieu refers to "the reconversion of one kind of specific capital into another (e.g. the case of the Symbolist poets who moved into the psychological novel)" (Bourdieu 1983, 346, n. 25). To my mind, this process can not only be seen as a sequential development but also a simultaneous form of literary production: the Symbolist novelists who combined the symbolic capital of poetry with the economic capital of the *feuilleton* and the novel. In this respect, Georges Rodenbach's *Bruges-la-morte* is both a plot-driven traditional novel and an experimental Symbolist text which owes it enduring popularity to the possession of both kinds of capital.

## Works Cited


Baudelaire, Charles. 1962. *Le Spleen de Paris*. Paris: Garnier.

Bertrand, Jean-Pierre and Grojnowski, Daniel. 1998. Introduction to Georges Rodenbach, *Bruges-la-morte*. Paris: Garnier-Flammarion, 7-44.

Bourdieu, Pierre. 1983. "The Field of Cultural Production, or: The Economic World Reversed", trans. Richard Nice, *Poetics*, 12, 311-56.

—. 1992. *Les Règles de l'Art: Genèse et Structure du Champ littéraire*. Paris: Seuil.

Brunetière, Ferdinand. 1891. "Le roman à venir". *Revue des deux mondes*, no. 105, 685-99.

Dujardin, Édouard. 2001. *Les Lauriers sont coupés*, ed. Jean-Pierre Bertrand. Paris: Gallimard.

Edwards, Paul. 2000. "The Photograph in Georges Rodenbach's *Bruges-la-morte* (1892)". *Journal of European Studies*, 30, 71-89.

Friedman, Melvin J. 1991. "The Symbolist Novel: Huysmans to Malraux". In *Modernism: A Guide to European Literature 1890- 1930*, edited by Malcolm Bradbury and James McFarlane, 2nd edn. London: Penguin, 453-66.

Genette, Gérard. 1972. *Figures III*. Paris: Seuil.

—. 2004. *Métalepse*. Paris: Seuil.

Gide, André. 2009. *André Gide, Paul Valéry: Correspondance 1890-1942*, ed. Peter Fawcett. Paris: Gallimard.

Gorceix, Paul. 1985. "*Bruges-la-morte*, un roman symboliste". *L'Information littéraire*, 37.5, 205-10.

Hollinghurst, Alan. 2005. "Introduction", in *Bruges-la-morte*, trans. into English by Mike Mitchell. Sawtry, Cambs: Dedalus, 11-19.

Huret, Jules, 1982. *Enquête sur l'évolution littéraire*, ed. Daniel Grojnowski. Paris: Thot.

Kermode, Frank. 1966. *The Sense of an Ending: Studies in the Theory of Fiction*. Oxford: Oxford University Press.

Malinowski, Wiesław. 2003. *Le Roman du symbolisme.* Poznan: Wydawnictwo Naukowe UAM.

Mallarmé, Stéphane. 1982. Interview with Jules Huret, in *Enquête sur l'évolution littéraire*, ed. Daniel Grojnowski. Paris: Thot, 73-80.

—. 2003. "Crise de vers", in *Œuvres complètes*, ed. Bertrand Marchal, Vol. II. Paris: Gallimard; Bibliothèque de la Pléiade, 204-13.

Michelet Jacquod, Valérie. 2008. *Le Roman symboliste: un art de l'extrême conscience.* Geneva: Droz.

Moréas, Jean, 1973. "Un Manifeste littéraire", *Le Figaro littéraire*, 18 September 1886, reprinted in *Les Premières armes du Symbolisme*, ed. Michael Pakenham. Exeter: University of Exeter Press.

Mosley, Philip. 1996. "The Soul's Interior Spectacle: Rodenbach and *Bruges-la-morte*", in *Georges Rodenbach: Critical Essays*, ed. Philip Mosley. Madison, NJ: Fairleigh Dickinson Press, 17-40.

Mourier-Casile, Pascaline. 1982. "Figures et formes de la clôture dans le récit symboliste". *Romanica Wratislaviensia*, 18 (1982), 75-92.

Poulliart, Raymond. 1974. "Problèmes du roman symboliste", *Revue de l'Université de Bruxelles*, 3-4, 334-56.

Raitt, A.W. 1986. *The Life of Villiers de l'Isle-Adam.* Oxford: Clarendon Press.

Rodenbach, Georges. 1986. *Bruges-la-morte*, ed. Christian Berg. Brussels: Labor.

—. 1998. *Bruges-la-morte*, ed. Jean-Pierre Bertrand and Daniel Grojnowski. Paris: Gallimard.

—. 2005. *Bruges-la-morte*, trans. into English by Mike Mitchell. Sawtry, Cambs: Dedalus.

Sarraute, Nathalie. 1956. *L'Ère du soupçon: Essais sur le roman*. Paris: Gallimard.

Swift, Bernard C. 1973. "The Hypothesis of the French Symbolist Novel". *Modern Language Review*, 68, 776-87.

Uitti, Karl D. 1961. *The Concept of Self in the Symbolist Novel.* The Hague: Mouton & Co.

Vallette, Alfred. 1886. "Les Symbolistes", *Le Scapin*, 16 October, 81.

Wilde, Oscar. 1985. *The Picture of Dorian Gray*, ed. Peter Ackroyd. London: Penguin.

Wilson, Edmund. 1961. *Axel's Castle: A Study in the Imaginative Literature of 1870-1930*. London: Fontana.

# CHAPTER SIXTEEN

# FINDING THE PLOT IN FRENCH *CHANSON*: ÉDITH PIAF AND THE NARRATIVE SONG

DAVID LOOSELEY

This chapter offers some reflections on the familiar view that, unlike Anglo-American popular music, French *chanson* is a narrative form. I want in particular to look at how *chanson* sets about telling a story: what the distinctive conditions of the song form are for narrative. I shall do so by turning to the classic *chanson* star most closely (though not altogether accurately) identified with this narrative tradition: Édith Piaf.

## *Chanson* and Popular Music Studies

Schematically, twentieth- and twenty-first-century popular songs may be divided into two capacious categories: those capturing a fleeting moment of emotion in the present, and those telling a story, usually set in the past. Of course, the first category might also include narratives in a broad sense; but the second is distinguished by an explicit plot. And whereas, in the first, the narrative is conducted through music as much as if not more than words, in the second, music is generally thought of as secondary to words, an embellishment of the story rather than its medium. Anglophone popular music studies has tended to be somewhat more preoccupied with the first category, particularly in the context of pop and rock. French writing on *la chanson française*, on the other hand, has conventionally placed *chanson* in the second category, as a narrative or literary form whose cultural legitimacy rests not on sales but on its ability to blur the boundaries between "high" and "low" culture, "literature" and mere "fiction". Yves Salgues's introduction (Saka 1994, 8) to a collection of Piaf's lyrics is a case in point: "Populaire certes, mais littéraire à l'image de celui des plus grands (Trenet, Gainsbourg, Montand, Ferré, Brassens, Aznavour, Souchon…), le répertoire d'Édith Piaf [. . .] fait partie de notre patrimoine national". Despite the influence of international pop and rock since 1960, which led French popular song along multiple other routes, this representation of *la chanson française* as literary by nature remains intact and is regularly renewed in the form of sightings of a revived, supposedly indigenous narrative tradition, as in the following example: "Les années 2000 ont ramené la tradition narrative disparue: c'est une autre grande vague, celle de la nouvelle *chanson* française portée par Bénabar, Delorme, Renan Luce" (Davet 2009, 2).

Certainly, Simon Frith (1998, 169-71) maintains that "all songs are implied narratives. They have a central character, the singer; a character with an attitude, in a situation, talking to somebody (if only to herself). [. . .] to sing a song is to tell a story, and to tell a story is to be a storyteller." Yet he too sees *chanson*, and Piaf's work especially, as a case apart: a more directly narrative genre, "as much a verbal as a musical form" (Frith 1998, 170). But, although what he has to say about *chanson* and Piaf is pertinent and suggestive, it is also relatively brief. Indeed, popular music studies generally has had little to say about *chanson*. This is because, in addition to being objectively anglocentric, it has tended to decentre the lyric, arguing as Frith does that popular lyrics are "sound acts" and cannot be seen in isolation from melody, arrangement, performance, and so on. This is a perfectly viable position generally speaking, but it does not help make sense of the special status of lyrics in French *chanson*, acknowledged by Frith. Surely this special status calls for a specific mode of analysis? Piaf serves as a *cas de figure* for addressing this question.

## Piaf and auteurism

A story needs an author. But the question of who the author is in Piaf's work requires some unpicking. Her career and the myths surrounding it are too well known to need more than a brief summary here. Born in 1915, she began as a street singer in the early 1930s before being discovered by night-club owner Louis Leplée, then rediscovered by Raymond Asso after Leplée was murdered. Her first recordings are from 1936 on Polydor. By 1940, she was a major star, at least in France. Although the songs recorded before then are less well known today, they are more interesting from the point of view of this volume, because it is here that storytelling is most prominent.

The roots of this narrative tradition in *chanson* lie in folk song (Looseley 2003). But in the late-nineteenth century, with the dawning of mass culture, performing rights and professionalisation, folk narratives were steadily adapted to urban settings in the form of the *chanson réaliste*. This genre was initially identified with the social realism of Aristide Bruant (1851-1925) and Montéhus (Gaston Brunschwig, 1872-1952) in the last decades of the nineteenth century. But it was revived and renewed in the early twentieth by female performers such as Berthe Sylva (1885-1941), Fréhel (1891-1951) and Damia (1892-1978). *Chanteuses réalistes* often began their careers recycling the songs of Bruant or Montéhus, but they soon transformed the masculine rhetoric of social populism into narratives of female suffering and dependency in the form of weepy melodramas about unrequited love among the urban poor. Already, in the first decades of the twentieth century, their appeal lay in nostalgia for a disappearing lowlife exoticism. Piaf is a late exponent of the style but, by the 1930s, in a rapidly modernising Paris, the realist narrative had become even more anachronistic and stylised, intertextually related to the similarly nostalgic cinema of Carné, Duvivier, Clair and the actor Jean Gabin (several *chanteuses réalistes* in fact appeared in such films) (Vincendeau 1987). In Piaf's hands, however, the seam was re-worked and re-imagined, before being watered down and eventually abandoned in her later work.

She did not achieve this, or the stardom that came with it, alone. Rather, "la môme Piaf", the stage name she initially took when still only nineteen, was from the outset a collective creation, a composite artefact. Up to a point, she was her own invention: not only by virtue of her talent and the bodily properties of her voice, its "grain" to use Barthes's term, but because from the outset she evolved narratives about herself, building her future myth. Her early companion Simone Berteaut (1970) recounts how, even before she was famous, Piaf would identify instantaneously with certain songs performed by others, seeing them as being in some prophetic sense about her, telling her personal story. "La Légion, c'est à moi, à personne d'autre!", she insisted, on first hearing "Mon légionnaire" (Asso-Monnot 1936), originally sung by Marie Dubas (Berteaut 1969, 129).

Piaf was also the product of the two Pygmalions who helped launch her career. Leplée heard her singing in the street and began to train her to sing in his club, and it was he who selected her stage name. More importantly, Asso, who seems to have had a subtle understanding of the idiom of mass-cultural stardom, took this construction work much further, developing her stage performance and attire (the iconic little black dress, adapted from other *chanteuses réalistes*) and her off-stage demeanour. Crucially, he also wrote her an entire repertoire. I shall pay particular attention to Asso's work, even though other lyricists of the 1930s made significant contributions to the Piaf persona, in particular Robert Malleron, author of the seminal *L'Étranger* (1934), and Roméo Carlès, the first to write a lyric especially for her, entitled "Simple comme bonjour" (music by Louiguy, 1936). A third set of creators were her composers, most notably Marguerite Monnot, who wrote the melody to *L'Étranger* and regularly put Asso's lyrics to music, though she remained Piaf's chief composer, and friend, long after Piaf broke with Asso around 1940. According to Simone Berteaut (1970, 119), Monnot was in fact as important to Piaf's career as Asso: "C'est elle qui lui a appris ce qu'était une chanson, qui lui a fait comprendre que la musique n'était pas qu'un air, que, suivant la façon dont on l'interprétait, il pouvait dire autant de choses que les paroles—avec autant de nuances."

What we arguably see, then, in the Piaf-Asso-Monnot collaboration is a *chanson d'auteur* aesthetic in the making, one which reveals the collective nature of auteurism in song as much as in cinema. The *chanson d'auteur* would eventually be identified with the *auteur-compositeur-interprète* trope (ACI), in which the respective roles of Asso, Monnot and Piaf were subsumed into a Brassens or a Ferré. Piaf herself is not primarily thought of as an ACI (although she did write a lot of her own material from around 1940). But the "realist" stories devised for her were dramatised narratives of Piaf's own narratives. The singer could therefore be identified with the song in a constructed notion of "authenticity" (Vincendeau 1987; Looseley 2003). And even though this authenticity was in one sense a commodity manufactured by the male-dominated music business, Piaf's appropriation of that commodity manufacture through her astonishing vocal and expressive abilities transcended and transformed it far beyond the standard image of the manipulated star. In this sense, we can speak of *la môme Piaf* as a composite auteur, prefiguring the expressive possibilities of the *chanson* later realised by postwar ACIs.

## Storytelling in the *Chanson*

Asso's songs, reflecting Piaf's early life experiences (and indeed his own as a former legionnaire) are skilfully plotted. Telling a story in three minutes, the length imposed by the 78 rpm record, was no easy task. Asso's solution was, as with the three unities in classical theatre, to make a virtue of constraint. Of all Piaf's lyricists, he is the most gifted at plotting a spare, intense narrative akin to a synopsis for a film, play or short story. Event, characterisation and psychology are pared down to the barest essentials. Indeed, reading his lyrics on the page, one is reminded by their formal simplicity and moral content of La Fontaine's fables, or of Camus's literary maxim "dire moins". The need for economy, the impossibility of building sophisticated characterisation or psychology in three minutes are turned to advantage in the creation of mysterious, unfathomable strangers, fragmented events, and bleak, inconclusive outcomes.

There are three basic modes of narrative address in these early songs: the straightforward third-person narrative in the past (for example "Ding Din Dong", Asso-Dreyfus, 1936); the first-person narrative in the past, in either the singular ("Mon amant de la Coloniale", Asso-Juel, 1936) or the plural ("Browning", Asso-Villard, 1938); and the third-person narrative in the present, usually an historic present ("Le Fanion de la légion", Asso-Monnot 1936). There are, though, numerous variants and permutations of these three modes, including from time to time a first-person narrative in which the "je" is explicitly framed as a narrator. This is the case in "J'entends la sirène" (Asso-Monnot, 1936: Saka 1994, 33-4), where the female narrative voice begins with a present tense as she remembers a past encounter, then slips into the past historic and imperfect tenses once the internal narrative or flashback begins. In some cases, a narrative may become self-referential, as the narrators explicitly draw attention to their role as storytellers; though this happens somewhat more in the lyrics of others than in Asso's songs: for example Carlès's "Simple comme bonjour" and "La Petite Boutique" (Carlès-Hodeige, 1936) (see Saka 1994, 34-6 and 45-6 respectively).[1]

As regards characterisation, Asso's songs are mostly love stories peopled by the poor and downtrodden. His characters are conventionally gendered, reflecting the patriarchal vision of the times and more specifically of the torch song.[2] Women are rejected lovers, seasoned street girls with a heart, or innocents forced to turn to the sins of the flesh; one way or another, they are the helpless victims of desire and emotion. Like Zola's characters, they are also determined and essentialised by their socio-urban status, as in "Elle fréquentait la rue Pigalle" (Asso-Maitrier, 1939: Saka 1994, 81-2), where a street girl, smelling of "cheap vice" and "black with sin", is fleetingly lifted out of her milieu and moment by a lover who finds her beautiful. At her request, he whisks her away to Montparnasse, only to have the scales fall abruptly from his eyes. Once

---

[1] One exception in Asso's own work is "On danse sur ma *chanson*" (Asso-Poll, 1940: Saka 1994: 85-6), which concerns the writing of a song, possibly this one. But significantly, in this case the usual narrative element is less prominent.

[2] For further discussion of gender in the torch song, see Moore 2000 and, in a specifically French context, Vincendeau 1987. For an even more graphic instance of the assumed fatalism of gender roles in Asso's songs, including male violence and female submission to it, see "C'est toi le plus fort" (music by J. Cloërec, 1936: Saka 1994: 51-3).

she is outside her "natural" topography, he sees her for what she is and promptly sends her back to Pigalle, whose physical mark is indelible. Men, on the other hand, are freer, more mobile geographically, socially and emotionally; or they are tied yet empowered by their gendered thirst for adventure or by elemental forces like the sea or the desert: colonial soldiers (zouaves, legionnaires), sailors, underworld villains, mysterious strangers passing through and therefore unreliable, though some reveal a more vulnerable side which only enhances the irresistible attraction they exert.

Another feature of the Asso-Piaf repertoire is that one can detect the plot conventions and resources of popular narrative, taken from folk-tales, film or fiction: the pathetic fallacy, love at first sight, the irresistible lure of sex; and most of all, melodrama. These early songs are three-minute soap-operas, characterised by extreme emotions and searing conflict, painted with bold rather than subtle strokes. At the same time, what distinguishes them from soaps is the need for economy: in a three-minute plot, there is no room for the self-indulgent, set-piece tirade. There are also significant elements of crime fiction and *film noir* in Piaf's early repertoire generally, and in Asso's work particularly: "Browning", "Le Contrebandier" (Asso-Villard 1936 and 1938), "Paris-Méditerranée", "Le Chacal" (Asso-Seider 1938). In most cases, however ("Browning" is a rare exception), the *noir* element is inseparable from the "realist" romance. Starting out as powerful sexual encounters in which the woman is happy to be swept away, the love affairs of Piaf's cast of unfortunates and marginals almost always go wrong, though again it is occasionally the man who ends up getting hurt ("Ding Din Dong", "Le Petit Monsieur triste", Asso-Monnot 1939). But whether the man is victim or villain, Asso's songs, despite being written for a female performer, are male-centred in so far as the lyrics give him *le beau rôle*. Ultimately, however, the tragic flaw in all such encounters is neither the man's nor the woman's. The real culprits are simple twists of fate that symbolise social and sexual determinism.

Of course, what this synoptic analysis of the narrative lyric omits are in fact the song form's major resources: musicality and performance: that is, the creative inputs of the singer and composer. There is in Piaf's renditions of Asso's songs a musical narrative which complements and sometimes contradicts the narrative of words: melody, arrangement, instrumentation, staging, lighting, recording, the microphone, and above all voice. We talk metaphorically of a narrative "voice" in fiction, but in song, that "voice" is quite literal, embodied and signifying. And in Piaf's particular case, the voice self-consciously *performs* narration. In recordings of "Mon Amant de la Coloniale" and "Le Fanion de la Légion" (Asso-Monnot, 1936), for example, she half-speaks her lines, using the amazed, totally engaged, dramatising delivery that an adult employs when telling a story to a child. The musical arrangement here has a similarly narrative function, as in "Le Fanion de la Légion", where a Hollywoodised, stereotypically sinister "Arab" drum and pipe motif contrasts with stirring bugle calls.[3] In this performance of storytelling and the assumption of a childlike audience, there is in fact an implied conception of the popular. But to show in more detail how this works, I shall analyse just one song.

**Paris-Méditerranée** (1936)
1. C'est une aventure bizarre,
Comme le train quittait la gare
L'homme a bondi dans le couloir
Et le front contre la portiere
Il regardait fuir la lumière
De Paris mourant dans le soir.
[Refrain :]
Un train dans la nuit vous emporte
Derrière soi des amours mortes
Mais l'on voudrait aimer encore
La banlieue triste qui s'ennuie
Défilait morne sous la pluie...
Il regardait toujours dehors

2. Le train roulait dans la nuit sombre,
L'homme déjà n'était qu'une ombre,
Et d'être seule j'avais froid
S'il a parlé qu'a-t-il pu dire ?...
Je ne revois que son sourire
Quand il vint s'asseoir près de moi.
[Refrain :]
Un train dans la nuit vous emporte
Derrière soi des amours mortes
Et dans le cœur un vague ennui

---

[3] There are at least two recorded versions of this song, only one of which features the drum and pipe musical setting. This appears on a vinyl compilation, *Édith Piaf: Ses plus belles chansons. A Commemorative Album*, Contour 1969, no. 6870505. The alternative version, recorded in January 1937 and probably more common on compilations today, can be heard on the CD *Éternelle: les plus grandes chansons d'Édith Piaf*, EMI Music France, 2003, no. LC0542, CD no.1. On this and other representations of the Legion in popular culture, see Cooper 2006.

Alors sa main a pris la mienne
Et j'avais peur que le jour vienne
J'étais si bien tout contre lui.

3. Lorsque je me suis éveillée
Dans une gare ensoleillée
L'inconnu sautait sur le quai.
Alors des hommes l'entourèrent
Et tête basse ils l'emmenèrent
Tandis que le train repartait
[Refrain :]
J'ai regardé par la portiere
Comme en un geste de prière
L'homme vers moi tendait les mains
Le soleil redoublait ma peine
Et faisait miroiter des chaînes
C'était peut-être un assassin
Coda :
Il y a des gens bizarres
Dans les trains et dans les gares…

*Paris Méditerranée*
Words & Music by Raymond Asso & Rene Cloërec


This song is a first-person narrative in the past, the female narrator being a character in the drama that unfolds. Although in this instance Piaf sings rather than using the semi-spoken delivery I have just alluded to, the song is explicitly framed as a tale being told from the very first line: "C'est une aventure bizarre". But it is a tale which, even for Asso, has a singularly spare plot. A man leaps on a train just as it is leaving Paris heading south. The narrator watches him as night falls; she feels cold and alone. Looking back at the incident now, she is unsure who made the first move, the one that led him to sit beside her, or even what was said. But he takes her hand and they spend the night together on the train, though a

[4] I reproduce exactly the punctuation as it appears in the sheet-music supplied by the publisher. The version in Saka (1994: 74-5) has different punctuation. In Piaf's 1938 recorded version, 'L'homme' in the third line of the first verse is replaced with 'Il'.

cinematic fade discreetly excludes us from how the night passed. She wakes up to sunshine in time to see her new companion jump off at a station, where he is immediately arrested and led away in handcuffs. Perhaps he was a murderer, she muses as the train pulls out, though like her we never find out whether he was, nor indeed anything else about him. And the narration finishes with a coda containing a disconcertingly banal, apparently unemotional and uninformative narratorial observation: "Il y a des gens bizarres/Dans les trains et dans les gares". So how exactly are meanings made and performed in this curiously flat narrative?

First, I suggest, the very banality of this coda from the narrator is not to be taken at face value but serves as abbreviated characterisation, indicating her emotional vacancy, not unlike Meursault's "Aujourd'hui, maman est morte. Ou peut-être hier, je ne sais pas" in *L'Étranger* (1957, 9). The song form also provides additional layers of signification. Three key features help achieve this: the relationship between lyrical content and musical setting, the refrain, and the voice.

The narrative framing of the lyric is underscored by a classically cinematic "soundtrack" of train music straight out of Hitchcock and Hollywood, made up of the thundering wheels and urgent whistles of a steam engine, interlaced with the rising and descending minor cadences of a string section, suggestive of at once adventure and pathos. As so often in early cinema, the train connotes the sadness of departures, being carried away helplessly down life's track. This is confirmed by pathetic visual imagery: "la banlieue triste", "morne sous la pluie", and the city "dying" as night descends. The two characters remain anonymous and unknown, at least to the listener. He is clearly on the run, the fact of his leaning his head on the carriage door giving a visual sign that he is desperate and needy, qualities which in Piaf's universe always have sex-appeal. The first refrain then allows us, without effort, to sense that the narrator too is needy, with a past freighted with heartbreak and yearning. Here, the verse/refrain alternation in the standard popular-song format is set to work to particularly good effect. Any refrain tends to impede the simple linear progression of a sung narrative, its recurrence providing a musicality which in Piaf is also a fatalism, a poetic sign of tragic destiny, though it can also surreptitiously advance the narrative by taking on a slightly different meaning after each verse, or when the refrain's set lyrical pattern is changed slightly, as here. Whereas the train music mercilessly drives the narrative forward in time and space, the refrain acts as punctuation, pausing the story's linearity and hinting at emotional baggage: "Un train dans la nuit vous emporte/Derrière soi des amours mortes/Mais l'on voudrait aimer encore". The sequential use of "vous", "soi" and "on" distances and universalises the narrator's personal experience, while the inbuilt melodic recurrence of the refrain underscores the atemporality of this reflection.

Piaf's contralto contributes further layers of meaning here. In the verses, her vocal is essentially narrative, full of the thrill of travel, adventure and storytelling and adding colour to the *noir* narrative. Then in the first two lines of the refrain, her voice soars and becomes more emotionally involved, before assuming a softer, affectively ambivalent texture in the third line when the irrepressible desire to love again is evoked. This texture remains for the next three lines, underscored by a melancholy string accompaniment coupled with a softer chugging of the train, which slows as it passes through the dismal suburban landscape. Meanwhile, the man looks wistfully out of the window—the wistfulness communicated not by words but again by Piaf's voice. Then the melody and vocal delivery of the second verse pick up speed again, jolting us back to the feverish forward rhythm of the train until the second refrain repeats the vocal modulations of the first, with the softer, slower third line returning even though the line itself is different this time— "Et dans le coeur un vague ennui"—suggesting a deeper, unknowable, spiritual malaise.

There are, then, two distinct time zones in the song: real, narrative time and complex emotional time, though these are unobtrusively communicated through the formal verse/refrain alternation. But, significantly in this context, the refrain's distinctive melody and vocalisation are repeated for a third and last time, though in this case emptied of the hinted-at emotional content of the first two refrains and refilled with pure narrative, as she looks out of the window to see the man's cuffed hands gesture pleadingly towards her. Since there is now nothing to hope for from this "brief encounter", no emotional possibilities left, only story remains, as the tale, like the train, follows the tracks to a geographically unspecified but predictably barren destination. The banal narratorial remark in the coda, about the odd people you meet on train journeys, now assumes its full, powerful meaning, with the help of the frail, sorrowful quality of the vocal at this point. Its very banality is the narrator's way of denying disappointment and arming herself for the return to solitude that awaits her down the track. This was, after all, nothing to get excited about, nothing more than a curious *fait divers*, underscored by a final, bathetic toot from the train.

What we have, then, in this song is the semiotic coupling of words and music, narrative time and emotional time, illusion and reality. It is a miniature *film noir*. And the *noir* trope of the wanted man is ideal for the purpose, as it has, built into it, the classic theme of all Piaf's early work: a love that can never be. Piaf-Asso songs offer cheap admission to a fictional cinematic short.

There is, however, as I have tried to show, much more psychological complexity in the recorded performance than the lyric on the page suggests. In particular, the gendering of the protagonists is more complex. Asso's lyric does indeed place action, adventure and danger on the side of the dashing male criminal, while the female character becomes a passive observer of her troubled emotional life. And yet *le beau rôle* is still ultimately hers. For the narrator in this *film noir* is both actor and director: it is she who teases out the meaning of the melodrama as it unfolds, who has the freedom to produce a final shot in which only she and her emotional landscape are left on screen before the fade. While this is not quite metafiction (or *metachanson*[5]), it moves in that direction.

## After Asso

In 1940, Piaf broke with Asso personally and professionally. From that point on, the sense of there being a unified, narrative repertoire in her work disappears. On the one hand, she started writing her own lyrics, not many of which are very good. On the other, her regular lyricists for the next few years, Henri Contet and Michel Emer,[6] produced material that was both more varied in content and more variable in quality. But most of all, whereas the Piaf-Asso-Monnot team was creatively inventing a persona through repertoire, by the time Contet and Emer came on the scene, that persona was already established, so they were working intertextually and writing to a known formula, or at best refining it, good though many of their lyrics were. A case in point is Emer's "De l'autre côté de la rue" (1943; Saka 1994, 108-10), a complaint by a poor girl about the rich girl on the other side of the street who has had all the breaks she has not. One recognises only too well the remnants of the *chanson réaliste* but, significantly, the song is now made more commercial by a happy ending. Piaf too attempts to work the exhausted realist seam in her own compositions, such as "J'ai qu'à l'regarder" (1943, music by Siniavine; Saka 1994, 112-13), where the narrator, again irresistibly drawn to a good-looking man with a winning smile and hoping this time it will be the real thing, slips into the lyrical clichés of happiness: spring, running

---

[5] See Harrison 2005.

[6] Emer somewhat less until 1945, since he was Jewish and had to flee south, with Piaf's help.

through meadows, and even a "tra la la". It is as if a conscious effort is being made to build a more commercial, less sleazy, less class-based repertoire, with a larger palette of moods, scenarios and compositional techniques, where love as suffering is balanced with both love as joy and music as celebration. A statement made to the press in 1943 confirms this: Piaf now claimed to dislike the *chanson réaliste*, preferring "flowers, simple love stories, health, joie de vivre and Paris" (quoted in Vincendeau 1987, 123). It was only when Piaf started using a wider range of lyricists (though still including Emer and Contet) and a wider range of subjects that the quality became more consistent, although her work after Asso was never again to be so consistently narrative.

Another critical factor in this change of repertoire was that, at the end of the war Piaf went to New York where, after a difficult start, she won over American audiences and became an international star. As a result, her most iconic numbers, "La Vie en rose" (1946), "Hymne à l'amour" (1949), and of course "Non, je ne regrette rien" (1960), float in the mid-Atlantic idiom of the torch song, moving into that first category of song I identified at the start of this chapter. In this respect, Piaf comes to resemble other female international singing stars in the torch song tradition: Judy Garland, Barbara Streisand, Shirley Bassey, and so on. So there is inevitably an extent to which some of the specificity of French *chanson*, its national locatedness, is lost, although it is debatable whether this should be a subject of lament. Essentially, her career may be read as symbolising the shift in the notion of the popular from a French working-class particularism to a universalism in which a "popular" song is one appreciated by a sociologically diverse and increasingly international audience. Her early work in fact embodies a narrative, quasi-folk conception of the authentic popular, redolent of the Popular Front; and, musically as much as politically, this conception was finished after the Occupation.[7]

Even so, I suggest that in her later songs narrative is not so much abandoned as relocated. Even in the songs where the element of plot disappears, or is only very thin as is often the case, there is a narrative of arrangement, performance and voice. And an additional layer of narrative meaning now appears, irrespective of the quality of the lyric, provided by Piaf's own, now iconic identity, as autobiography intrudes ever more into the perceived meanings of her songs, once again prefiguring the more

[7] I borrow here from my chapter 'Authenticity and appropriation in French popular music: a discursive history' in D. Holmes and D. L. Looseley (eds). *Imagining the Popular in Contemporary French Culture.* Manchester University Press, forthcoming 2012.

personal work of the *auteur-compositeur-interprète*. Arguably, then, by moving away from the national specificity of the lyric-centred *chanson*, her later work becomes better suited to the kind of holistic analysis characteristic of anglophone popular music studies, where the lyric becomes just one of a panoply of resources that make a popular song popular and meaningful. In her hands, French *chanson* changes meaning.

## Works Cited

Berteaut, Simone. 1969. *Piaf*. Paris: Robert Laffont.

Camus, Albert. 1957 [1938]. *L'Étranger*. Paris: Gallimard (Folio).

Cooper, Nicola J. 2006. "The French Foreign Legion: Forging Transnational Identities and Meanings". *French Cultural Studies* 17 (3) (October): 269-84.

Davet, Stéphane. 2009. "La Chanson française résiste à toutes les modes". *Culture Communication: le magazine du Ministère de la culture et de la communication*, 171 (June): 1-2.

Harrison, Kim T. 2005. The Self-Conscious *Chanson*: Creative Responses to the Art versus Commerce Debate. PhD thesis, University of Leeds.

Looseley, David L. 2003. *Popular Music in Contemporary France: Authenticity, Politics, Debate*. Oxford and New York: Berg.

Moore, John. 2000. "'The Hieroglyphics of Love': The Torch Singers and Interpretation", in R. Middleton (ed.) (2000). *Reading Pop: Approaches to Textual Analysis in Popular Music*. Oxford: Oxford University Press: 262-96.

Saka Pierre (ed.). 1994. *Édith Piaf: L'Hymne à l'amour* (préface de Yves Salgues). Paris: Librairie Générale Française.

Vincendeau, Ginette. 1987. "The *Mise-en-scène* of Suffering: French *chanteuses réalistes*". *New Formations* 3 (Winter): 107-28.

# CHAPTER SEVENTEEN

# REWRITING THE PLOT: DANIÈLE SALLENAVE'S REWORKED FICTION

IMOGEN LONG

"Je quitte l'avant-garde pour le plaisir de lire"
—Danièle Sallenave, 1980 (Garcin 1980)

Born in 1940 in the French provincial town of Angers, Danièle Sallenave is an academic, writer and intellectual with many novels, short stories, essays and articles to her name.[1] Her early texts were well received critically but reached a limited audience because of the experimental nature of their literary form and it was not until her more conventional novel *Les Portes de Gubbio* was awarded the *Prix Renaudot* in 1980 that she came to the attention of a wider reading public. In recognition of her successful writing career and wider public interventions, Sallenave was elected to the *Académie Française* in 2011. As a public intellectual, she is known for her involvement in key debates particularly on issues relating to the Republic and universalism; her vocal opposition to the political parity legislation in the 1990s on the grounds that it contravened the founding principles of equality underpinning the Republic is an illustrative example of her *engagement*.

Sallenave first made her entry into the literary world through the avant-garde review *Digraphe*[2], co-founded with Jean Ristat in 1973, which published theoretical and literary pieces by writers and thinkers such as Louis Althusser, Roland Barthes and Jacques Derrida amongst others. Her connections with the experimental, revolutionary set also extended to

[1] Sallenave has written over twenty works in addition to translating various Italian works by Paolo Pasolini, Luigi Pirandello and Italo Calvino into French.
[2] The first editorial board was composed of Luce Irigaray, Jean Ristat, Jean-Joseph Goux, Jean-Claude Lebensztein and Danièle Sallenave.

collaborations with the *Tel Quel* group on occasion[3] but ultimately she felt that the evolution of her own writing practice left her little choice but to withdraw from active involvement with such journals: "Apres m'être rapprochée du groupe de *Tel Quel* autour de Philippe Sollers, j'ai compris, il y a quelque temps, qu'il y avait un décalage entre la théorie que je défendais et la pratique que j'affichais."[4] Over time she has become more involved in the public arena, making high profile and controversial interventions, as with her vehemently anti-Israeli stance of 2002.[5] Sallenave's increasingly political position, reflected in the changes in her writing styles, abandons the purely abstract in favour of commitment, as Bruno Thibault affirms : "A l'instar de Milan Kundera, Sallenave engage l'écrivain à sortir de son laboratoire et à aborder les questions qui touchent l'homme du commun" (Thibault 1997, 77). She has always combined purely "literary" concerns, and thus work aimed at a specialised audience, with the wider concerns of a public intellectual who seeks to be read or heard by a public extending well beyond the elite.

In the course of her trajectory as a writer, Sallenave has experimented with literary genres and modes of writing, reconfiguring various themes in alternative forms and it is this rewriting of the plot and the implications of the move from the literary, the writable to the popular, the readable – in Barthesian terms from *le scriptible* to *le lisible*[6] – which will form the central focus of study here. In particular, this chapter will examine her 1986 *La Vie fantôme*, in which she returned to an earlier novel published as *Le Voyage d'Amsterdam ou les règles de la conversation* (1977), rewriting it in a more accessible and "popular" style. Elements of this novel, a love story, again reappeared in her 2002 novel *D'Amour*, illustrating the ongoing significance of this story for her (Sallenave 2003, 94). Further, all these texts have their roots in an unpublished manuscript now kept in the Sallenave archives. The unpublished source manuscript entitled *Histoire d'amour en cent phrases* comprises around a hundred fragments reminiscent of the maxims of La Rochefoucauld. The later works can be traced from this manuscript and the same essential narrative

---

[3] For more on the history of *Tel Quel* see Ffrench 1995.

[4] Garcin, Jérôme, "Je quitte l'avant-garde pour le plaisir de lire," 30.

[5] Her political engagement has seen her at the centre of controversy via the *Le Monde* case and her article on the Israel-Palestine question, "Israel-Palestine: Le Cancer," *Le Monde*, June 4, 2002, written together with Edgar Morin and Sami Nair.

[6] Terms used in Barthes's *Le Plaisir du texte*. Barthes argues that, although more challenging, a greater sensation of "jouissance" is to be had from writerly texts which demand much more of the reader.

strand remains discernible in all the published texts. In *La Vie fantôme*, the story already told in *Le Voyage d'Amsterdam* is expanded and given a more traditional, less experimental retelling, resulting in considerable commercial success but also in a negative response from critics who decried this move from avant-garde to "railway station" novel.[7]

Critics viewed *Le Voyage d'Amsterdam ou les règles de la conversation* as an avant-garde novel and therefore inaccessible or difficult to read and Sallenave's early texts undoubtedly do reveal the influence of practitioners of the *nouveau roman* such as Alain Robbe-Grillet and Nathalie Sarraute. Dubbed one of the "*nouveau roman's* prodigal children" (Garcin 1976), she recognises her debt to the exponents of this genre: "J'adore les descriptions. J'adore en lire et j'adore en faire. C'est ce que j'aime dans le nouveau roman [...] y'a deux choses que j'aime dans le nouveau roman: les dialogues chez quelqu'un comme Sarraute, par exemple, et les descriptions chez Claude Simon. Ce sont mes deux grands attachements nouveau roman" (Sallenave 1992).

Irrespective of the literary style she employs, Sallenave returns to the subject of women's roles and status throughout her writing, forming constant themes across the reworked texts. The question of women's place within the boundaries of marriage and love is addressed from different vantage points. Although Sallenave is an avowed critic of *écriture féminine*, which she associated with essentialism, *Le Voyage d'Amsterdam* does share certain stylistic traits with the *écriture féminine* genre. The lack of punctuation, the fragmented prose and elliptical syntax clearly locate the novel in the *nouveau roman* experimental writing field while in *La Vie fantôme*, a more traditional novel in tone and approach, the narrative is clearly outlined: Pierre, a married teacher has a four-year affair with the young and single librarian Laure. Laure experiences conflicting feelings about marriage and adulterous affairs. By accepting the situation she is forced to live a "phantom life" (a hollow simulacrum of meaningful existence) and it is this liminal position that Sallenave intends to explore, not only in *Le Voyage d'Amsterdam* but in its subsequent reincarnation as *La Vie fantôme,* as she observes:

> Il me semble pourtant que la logique voudrait qu'à partir du moment où l'on se marie, on respecte la règle du jeu. A travers Pierre et Laure, je montre la polygamie institutionnelle qu'est devenu l'adultère dans nos sociétés. Je ne juge pas, j'expose une impasse de l'adultère: une vie qui n'en est pas une, qui n'a aucun prise sur le temps. J'ai eu envie d'écrire un

---

[7] An apt translation for railway station novel would be "airport novel" with its depreciative connotations in English of light, "pot-boiler" holiday literature.

> roman sur la suite continue et banale des jours et la méditation du narrateur sur cette médiocrité. J'ai écrit plusieurs versions du livre, séparées par de longues périodes et à chaque fois dans l'emportement. C'est Delacroix dans son journal qui parle de la vitesse d'exécution nécessaire pour donner du mouvement à une toile. (Sallenave 1986, 33).

So by rewriting *Le Voyage d'Amsterdam* as *La Vie fantôme* in this way, by transforming an avant-garde text into an accessible one, Sallenave makes a return to the story and storytelling. Peter Barry, drawing on Russian formalism, offers a general distinction between story and plot when he writes:

> The story is the actual sequence of events as they happen, whereas the plot is those events as they are edited, ordered and packaged, and presented in what we recognise as narrative. This is a crucial distinction; "the story", being the events as they happen, *has* to begin at the beginning, of course, and then move chronologically, with nothing left out. The "plot" on the other hand, may well begin somewhere in the middle of a chain of events, and may then backtrack, providing us with a "flashback" which fills us in on things that happened earlier. The plot may well have elements which flash forward, hinting at events which will happen later. So the "plot" is a version of the story which should not be taken literally. (Barry 2009 [1995], 223).

In the light of Barry's distinction, *Le Voyage d'Amsterdam* can be seen to demand considerable decoding by the reader to reveal the story that underlies the plot. In a way, the reader has to construct the text for themselves as the story of *Le Voyage d'Amsterdam* is hazy, no chain of events is clearly perceptible and a sequential chronology is not a discernable element of the novel's structure. Instead, Sallenave presents the reader with fragments of events and plot elements to be reassembled and reordered. In keeping with the spirit of many post-structuralist works, multiple interpretations exist concurrently in *Le Voyage d'Amsterdam* and remain open to navigation by the reader. There are however some clues that may be interpreted as narrative anchors in space and time, for example the characters appear to bear witness to the events of May 1968 thus contextualising the fiction in relation to real historical events. Yet the intersection between actual historical events and the universe of the characters is less evocative of social reality than it is a means to suggest the problems of reality within the fictional context. When alluding to May 1968, Sallenave, interestingly, focuses on the aftermath of the protests, rather than their zenith, and on their impact at a personal level in terms of sex and desire, rather than broader political or social change: "A l'automne, il y avait encore des grèves, et au matin, des tas de journaux salis, piétinés dans les caniveaux avec la boue; des arrêts imprévus du métro et des autobus, de sorte qu'ils se manquaient souvent, obligés de descendre à une station inconnue, loin de leurs rendez-vous habituels, ce qui exaspérait leur dési." (VA, 17). Even when the reader succeeds in identifying some temporal markers, it is only to find that the characters' preoccupations lie firmly within themselves and their own world rather than in any connection with external developments.

In the same way that the 1961 film *L'Année dernière à Marienbad,* based on a script by Robbe-Grillet, puzzles the viewer with its disjunctive snapshots of memory from which the viewer must assemble some kind of meaning, so the act of remembrance is foregrounded in *Le Voyage d'Amsterdam,* which is largely composed of overlapping, repeated recollections that are not necessarily connected. Indeed, the text is interlaced with almost identical recurring dialogue and the novel's chronological structure is fragmented with flashbacks interspersed with narrative: "Elle tourne le dos à la fenêtre, le rideau retombe sur la vitre froide; toutes lumières éteintes, couchée, dans le noir, elle écoute le bruit de la pluie, et se souvient" (VA, 58). The dislocated nature of the text challenges the reader's conception of exactly how memory is constructed and reconstituted. The first section of *Le Voyage d'Amsterdam* owes much to the style of *Histoire d'amour en cent phrases,* the unpublished fragmentary text, in that it makes similar use of short paragraphs and aphoristic sentences. The unpublished manuscript of the first version of *Le Voyage d'Amsterdam*, now in the Sallenave archive in Angers university library, is revealing, for it shows that a distinct narratorial voice "je" was at times part of the original work, but was then dropped in the published version. For example sentence number ninety-eight states: "il n'y a aucune photo d'eux, à cette époque, je veux dire d'eux ensemble, mais des quantités de photographies séparées, qu'on peut associer à son gré; cette solitude, cette exclusion ont quelque chose d'absolument nécessaire et qui frappe".[8] Although the punctuation is conventional in this early version of *Le Voyage d'Amsterdam*, later segments are written without the usual functions and closures of punctuation. There are no full stops or capital letters and the semi-colon replaces the full stop. Despite the strong autobiographical elements in *Le Voyage d'Amsterdam* which will be reworked in *La Vie fantôme*, the narrative reveals a depersonalised story. Anonymity is achieved in part through the use of pronouns: the characters are largely referred to as "il/elle" (he/she) maintaining a sense

[8] Manuscript in dossier *Le Voyage d'Amsterdam ou les règles de la conversation* R 813 003-7.

of detachment; the absence of names reinforces the sense of generic experiences. Rather than highly individualised characters, Sallenave's principal protagonists could be anybody or everybody. In the later *La Vie fantôme*, however, Pierre and Laure are described and narrated in great detail, complete with their innermost thoughts and feelings, in a much less knowingly "literary" style. The narrative tropes Sallenave employs in this later incarnation to convey the mundane and the commonplace, coupled with the extremely well worn plotline of an affair, are redolent of those used in popular novels.[9]

The importance of the body is in evidence in *Le Voyage d'Amsterdam*, a point very much in keeping with the feminist concerns of the second wave women's movement to speak and write openly about the body from women's perspective. The descriptions of sex are notable for their frankness and there are many examples to be found, particularly in the opening section of the novel:

> Ils revenaient souvent à une figure simple: elle, à cheval sur lui, les jambes repliées sous ses fesses, tandis qu'il la tient aux hanches, le sexe brandi, mais ne la pénétrant pas; elle la tient la verge dans sa main fermée, comme un garçon qui se branle; lui, de son côté voit son propre sexe tendu vers les seins de la femme; ils revenaient souvent à cette figure simple (VA, 30).

The style here avoids the clichéd metaphorical vocabulary usually associated with such scenes in the novels of the romance genre. Corporeality is highlighted and its subsequent implications for the relationship between body and soul, self and Other follow from this frank emphasis. Sallenave, like others associated with the feminism of the 1970s, asserts the right to speak openly of the female body and female desire.[10] By contrast, the portrayal of sex is much more euphemistic in the reworked *La Vie fantôme* from which candid references to the body are erased. It is as though the emphasis on corporeality in *Le Voyage d'Amsterdam* has been sanitised, following the waning of the women"s movement; instead we witness a return to the type of discourse frequently found in conventional popular women's romance fiction, as can be seen in

---

[9] See Gelder 2004 for an interesting discussion of the difficulties of defining 'popular' fiction.

[10] By point of contrast, Sallenave's *La Vie fantôme* sees sex depicted much more euphemistically. For example Pierre and Laure's last physical encounter is described thus, "A peine sur le lit, il avait été en elle, le visage enfoncé dans le cou qu'il mordait. Elle avait gémi, et bientôt, elle était en larmes et pour la première fois Pierre aussi, et ils laissèrent couler sur leur visage cette eau tiède qui les lavait de tout", *La Vie fantôme*, 289.

the following sexual encounter between Pierre and Laure: "Ils avaient gagné la chambre, on ne sait comment, sans y voir, sans se lâcher. Ils se révélèrent un peu plus tard, honteux, heureux, épuisés, et ils prirent une douche ensemble, les yeux fermés dans la mousse parfumée du savon" (VF, 45).

Somewhat predictably, given its experimental nature, *Le Voyage d'Amsterdam* did not prove to be a popular text with the reading public, unlike the reworked version of the story as *La Vie fantôme*, which was very successful with readers and provided the inspiration for a Quebecois film of the same name.[11] Arguably, the very popularity of *La Vie fantôme* had an impact on its critical reception. Critics used to Sallenave's abstruse and ludic texts replete with symbols and poetic language found this a surprising departure. When evoking this unforeseen development, Josyane Savigneau spoke of a transition from laboratory literature to railway station novel (Savigneau 1984: 14). Laboratory literature could be perceived as a reference to the interest of many *nouveau-romanciers* in the physical sciences and the scientific backgrounds of writers such as Robbe-Grillet, whose experimental fiction has been likened to scientific experiments. The critical reaction to *La Vie fantôme* calls to mind the mixed responses to Marguerite Duras's 1984 novel *L'Amant* (Duras 1984) which similarly was seen as an unprecedented departure from her characteristic oeuvre, hitherto notable for its experimental and innovative nature. Like Sallenave, Duras had reworked the themes of childhood she had previously explored in texts such as *Un Barrage contre le pacifique* for the later, more widely acclaimed work.[12]

Commentators like Savigneau criticized *La Vie fantôme* on the grounds that its representation of middle-class characters displaying a languid indifference to life amounted only to an uninspired portrayal of bourgeois mediocrity. Similarly, Jacqueline Forni critiques *La Vie fantôme* for its plotline which she terms banal: "C'est une histoire à deux sous, « banale à pleurer » comme le chantait Piaf: il n'y a même pas de mélo dans ce roman d'amour de Français moyens dans une petite ville de province" (Forni 1986, 9). In the earlier *Le Voyage d'Amsterdam*, the characters appear to embrace platitudes and make a virtue out of the commonplace:

---

[11] *La Vie fantôme*, a 1992 film by Jacques Leduc, adapted for the cinema by Yvon Revard and Jacques Leduc. A copy of the film and related documents including publicity items are kept in the archives in Angers.

[12] Elizabeth Fallaize explores the question as to "why, in the mid-1980s did a 70-year old woman with a reputation for difficult, avant-garde texts, read by left-wing intellectuals top the French best-seller lists and become an international star?" in Fallaize 1986.

"Ils usaient avec prédilection de formes toutes faites, de phrases banales, de clichés vulgaires, pour dire leur désir ou leur satisfaction; ils se défendaient de rien inventer" (VA, 28). In both texts Sallenave sanctions reference to the everyday yet, interestingly, this decision is more heavily censured by critics when explored in the more readable *La Vie fantôme*. Just as in *Le Voyage d'Amsterdam*, Sallenave confirms that depicting everyday life remains one of her prime concerns, and indeed this became a central focus of *La Vie fantôme*:

> J'aime beaucoup regarder les gens […] L'écrivain doit être objectif et passionné. Car l'objectivité n'est pas la froideur et la passion n'est pas forcement subjective. J'ai passé des années à vivre en province, j'observais les gens et j'avais peur de ne pas pouvoir échapper à cette atmosphère. Je suis à la fois fascinée et effrayée par l'existence ordinaire. J'ai eu envie de raconter cette tentative de vraie vie qui devient Vie fantôme.[13]

In *La Vie fantôme* Sallenave wishes to convey this oppressive atmosphere of ordinary life in the French provinces, and the "tyranny of meaning" from which there is no escape. For her, the everyday life of the provinces is a stifling state of mind:

> Quand nous étions des adolescents, dans le milieu des années cinquante, nous ne pensions pas que « la province » fut seulement une catégorie de la géographie ou de l'histoire de la France, mais que c'était un état: une pesanteur, un destin, une séduction peut-être, une douceur même, et aussi une menace, toujours: celle de ne jamais réussir complètement à s'éveiller. (Sallenave 1986a, 56).

Rooted firmly in the mundanity of lived experience, the storyteller is thus an observer whose tales are based on what is seen firsthand; it is this role of "reality observer" that Sallenave herself adopts in her fiction. The narrator's role consists of preserving and collating facets of everyday life and presenting them for the reader to disentangle. When speaking about the reworked *La Vie fantôme*, Sallenave rejected the notion that the role of narrator should be that of analyst, arguing rather that the narrator merely lays out an arrangement of happenings: "moi, je donne à voir. Et la psychologie se déduira toute seule des situations. Je recueille des morceaux, les expériences, les gestes et j'unifie tous ces fragments. C'est cela le rôle du narrateur: unifier l'épars". (Sallenave 1986b, 46-7). By gathering up and reassembling these "scattered elements", Sallenave

[13] Interview with Jean-Henri Fabre in "Regard d'entomologie," unsourced article in *les archives littéraires Danièle Sallenave*, Angers *Coupures de presse* dossier R 813 020-2.

constructs disparate entities into a plot which she invites her readers to interpret; they can immerse themselves in the fictional universe of the author by suspending disbelief. Her narratives are neither pure invention nor dramatised fact and indeed such divisions remain blurred. Thus, via her stories, she allows a form of dialogue between author and reader which challenges the reader to do more than simply disarm him or herself before the author's text. For her the importance of writing is central, it is everywhere, it is a way of life and she brings to the reader issues of metaphysical examination of being, intersubjectivity, interdependence and loneliness through her texts, worked and reworked:

> L'écriture, pour moi, est absolument nécessaire. Ce n'est pas son utilité, sa fonctionnalité qui est importante, c'est sa présence, partout, à tous moments qu'il s'agisse de cinéma, de théâtre ou de photographie. C'est une réponse à tout ce qui se présente, quelque chose d'absolument continu, une question d'état d'existence, de manière de vivre (Le Bihan 1986).

In both versions of her text Sallenave deals with the everyday, transforming the ordinary into writing and in so doing offers a response to lived experience which forms a vital part of the writer's mission; the writer invites the reader to recognise their own agency in interpreting and shaping experience, providing the reassurance in Sartre's words "that we are essential in relationship to the world" (Sartre 1988, 49). In *La Vie fantôme* this fascination with the everyday is recounted more fully and integrated into the diegesis, marking a shift from the elliptical, oblique narration of everyday acts so prevalent in *Le Voyage d'Amsterdam.* In this way, the everyday is treated differently in the more popular text as the more abstract emphasis on human agency takes second place to a theme of the monotony of the everyday and its stultifying effects. For example, everyday objects and gestures are central to Sallenave's narration of Laure's ennui at waiting for Pierre to leave his wife and commit himself fully to their relationship, and to Pierre's dissatisfaction with married life, his career as a literature teacher and his lot generally. Pierre's sense of malaise is captured, for example, in the following passage:

> Ainsi le mois d'août s'avança. Deux semaines passèrent et Pierre ne s'était pas encore mis au travail. Un matin, debout devant les rayonnages, il se mit à bâiller. Il était dix heures, il avait faim. Il s'assit dans la cuisine sur un tabouret de formica et resta un moment devant le frigidaire ouvert, dans l'odeur des légumes et du poisson, un bout de comté à la main. Il se vit soudain dans la porte vitrée [...] Est-ce que ce travail-là lui convenait? [...] Au fond, il ne savait ni qui il était, ne ce qui lui aurait convenu. (VA, 81)

In *La Vie fantôme* therefore, details of the domestic milieux which resist decoding in *Le Voyage d'Amsterdam* are fleshed out fully, revealing in the process the extent to which the monotony of the central characters' daily routines stultify their own existence and impinge on their relationships with each other.

In this way, *La Vie fantôme* is a useful tool as it may serve to unlock precisely these ambiguous elements of *Le Voyage d'Amsterdam*. Much of what happens in *La Vie fantôme* can be transposed onto the outline extant in *Le Voyage d'Amsterdam*: the narrative mode of the novels and the texts are very different but viewed together they form a whole. Bruno Thibault goes further by asserting "il s'agit d'une ré-écriture du *Voyage d'Amsterdam*, mais sur le mode réaliste" (Thibault 1991, 91), from which we may deduce that he means a classic, conventional non-experimental writing style cast in a "popular" mould. On a structural level, the two texts are composed in a binary format: both books are constructed in discrete halves and Sallenave's notes make clear that she selected the dual format to act as a mirroring device. Her annotations state: "construire le livre en deux parties – miroir/inversion." [14] The bipartite structures suggest two separate phases of the characters' lives and also echo the division that exists in the "vie du couple" and the schism between "I" as subject and the other, between "je" and "autre". Examination of the opening sections of each novel in particular allows a close comparison of Sallenave's shifting writing styles. For instance, while *Le Voyage d'Amsterdam* has no clearly identifiable narrator the explicit presence of an unnamed, omniscient intradiegetic narrator in *La Vie fantôme* indicates the development of Sallenave's style in the later text. A comparison between the two descriptions of the female characters' solitude, for example, is revealing. In *Le Voyage d'Amsterdam* the writing is elliptical and gnomic, recalling the work's aphoristic origins, *Histoire de l'amour en cent phrases*. In common with the *nouveau roman*, the emphasis here is on description rather than any understanding of the characters' motivations or of interpretation of the plot. Leaving the reader a challenging task of piecing together the plot in this "writerly" text, Sallenave's writing style here is sparse and minimal with experimental pagination and punctuation:

> couchée, dans la nuit, elle écoute; elle, solitaire en ce soir obscur traversée de brumes, en ce soir abrité au cœur de la ville par le repliement protecteur

[14] Manuscript in Cahier 1. F1.46 in dossier *La Vie fantôme* R 813 007-1.

> de ses murs, leur appareil fragile de briques et de parpaings légers, la toile, le papier peint, les rideaux et les fenêtres aux vitres froides ... (VA, 5) [15]

A similar scene in *La Vie fantôme* reprises the central theme of the solitude of the "other woman" and her existential angst but is here much more conventionally narrated. Unlike the first text, here the characters are ascribed names and clearly delineated identities. Laure is left alone after Pierre leaves to resume his routine with his wife and family; since her isolation has been explained, Laure's plight is much easier to decipher:

> Laure va et vient, passe d'une pièce dans l'autre, revient s'étendre un moment dans les draps chauds et froissés, puis elle se relève, remplit la baignoire et reste immobile dans l'eau chaude, les yeux fermés, tandis que la vapeur monte autour d'elle, poisse ses cheveux, ternit les carreaux de céramique vernie. Le sommeil la gagne. Il est huit heures, la nuit est tombée (VF, 12).

Nonetheless, despite the perception that *La Vie fantôme* was in some ways simply a more "popular" version of a literary text, both versions eschew the happy ending associated with "popular" fictions. The traditional pleasure of a satisfying resolution of the story is conspicuous by its absence since, as in the earlier text, Pierre relinquishes his lover at the end of the narrative: "Il [Pierre] n'éprouvait pas le besoin de donner de ses nouvelles [...] Il est vrai qu'aujourd'hui ils étaient peut-être définitivement séparés" (VF, 281). Sallenave's later text therefore is not a simple move towards populism and the formulaic; her straightforwardly popular telling of the earlier tale contains the same elegiac themes of mourning engendered by a failed relationship and the search for women's identity. Even if the way in which the plot is presented evolves over the course of its rewriting, the story remains the same in essence.

By taking the decision to forsake *avant garde* and experimental writing to express herself in a popular vernacular, using more established narrative forms, Sallenave, in keeping with postmodern tenets, refuses to privilege elite and difficult forms of writing. In such a context, she rejects the hierarchies of good and bad fictions and moves consciously from ambiguity to clarity, from mimesis and showing to diegesis and telling. The tale is an effective way to transmit a message, as Walter Benjamin noted when he lamented the fact that "the art of storytelling is coming to an end" (Benjamin 2002, 146) and with it the ability to exchange experiences. His assertion that storytelling belongs to the real world, the

[15] Layout as in the original.

living world,[16] helps us to understand Sallenave's choice to return to the realist mode. As she herself contends, storytelling brings life to a given society and breathes life into it: "raconter fait exister une société. Raconter est le tissu même de la vie" (Sallenave 1992). Via her multiple rewritings, she finds or comes to the plot through her repetition and, as Benjamin affirms, "storytelling is always the art of repeating stories".

As Peter Brooks argues in his *Psychoanalysis and Storytelling* (Brooks 1994, 20-46), stories are one possible way of giving expression to desire; in much the same way as analysands unburden themselves to reveal repressed or subconscious desire, so the author, through the relating of the story, may articulate fundamental desires, thus making the realist mode an interesting choice for Sallenave's story of an ultimately unsatisfactory adulterous love affair. Sex, desire and the workings of the subconscious therefore find expression in the revisiting of previous incarnations of the text: by enhancing, embellishing, embroidering upon, or, at times, even erasing altogether, what went before the author produces a body of interconnected work intrinsically bound up with her own personal trajectory. Sallenave's *La Vie fantôme* deploys certain recognised tropes of popular romance fiction, but not simply for their own sake.[17] Rather, her unsentimental tale of the impossibility of reconciling desire and personal freedom looks to a post-1968 feminist context where the relationship between sex and women's identity is often presented as unfulfilling and difficult to negotiate.

Sallenave takes this same story and rewrites it in different forms, defending her decision against negative critical opinion which regarded conventional plotting and characterisation as necessarily inferior and "populist". Similarly, defying the view that the domestic everyday is a fundamentally trivial theme embraced in the main by women writers in light, lesser literature, she instead insists on the importance of engaging with the everyday in her writing. It can then be seen that a fundamental plot of love, desire, adultery and separation is present in each text, together with the thematic of the everyday as both deadening routine and as raw material for creation; by translating these into a more familiar and hence "readable" form, with its pleasures of a compelling story, she does not dilute the literary quality of her work. In fact, even if it goes against the grain of dominant critical opinion, the reworking of the texts represents, for her, a kind of progress: the emphasis on the surface of the text, the

[16] "Experience has fallen in value [...] Experience which is passed on from mouth to mouth is the source from which all storytellers have drawn" (Benjamin 2002, 144). For more on this point see Brooks 1994, 82.

[17] See Holmes 2006.

opacity of words themselves, in the earlier more experimental version serves only to lessen the emotional charge of the plot which is central to her project as a woman writer; thus to categorise her move away from experimentalism, *le scriptible*, towards narrative realism, *le lisible*, as "populist" is reductive and ultimately belies the complexity of the relationship between her writings.[18]

## Works Cited

Barry, Peter. 2009 (1995). *Beginning Theory*. Manchester: Manchester University Press.

Barthes, Roland. 1975. *Le Plaisir du texte*. Paris: Seuil.

Benjamin, Walter. 2002. "The Storyteller". In *Walter Benjamin Selected Writings Volume 3 1935-1938*, edited by Howard Eiland and Michael W. Jennings, 143-166. Cambridge, MA and London: Belnap Press of Harvard University.

Brooks, Peter. 1994. *Psychoanalysis and Storytelling*. Oxford: Blackwell.

Duras, Marguerite. 1984. *L'Amant.* Paris: Gallimard.

—. 2007 (1950). *Un Barrage contre le pacifique*. Paris: Gallimard.

Garcin, Jérôme. 1980. "Je quitte l'avant-garde pour le plaisir de lire". *Nouvelles littéraires*, November 20-27, 30.

Garcin, Thierry. 1976. "Les enfants prodigues du nouveau roman". *Quotidien de Paris*, 10 February.

Fallaize, Elizabeth. 1996. "The Story of her life: Marguerite Duras's *L'Amant* (1984)". In Colin Davis and Elizabeth Fallaize, *French Fiction in the Mitterrand Years*, Oxford: Oxford University Press, 18-37.

Ffrench, Patrick. 1995. *The Time of Theory: A History of Tel Quel.* Oxford: Clarendon Press.

Forni, Jacqueline. 1986. "Entre l'amour et les obligations sociales: *La Vie fantôme* de Danièle Sallenave". *La Quinzaine littéraire,* 470, 1-15 October, 9.

Gelder, Ken. 2004. "Popular Fiction: The Opposite of Literature". In *Popular Fiction: The Logics and Practices of a Literary Field*, London, New York: Routledge, 11-40.

Holmes, Diana. 2006. *Romance and Readership*. Oxford: Oxford University Press.

[18] I am very grateful to Margaret Atack and Diana Holmes for their comments and suggestions on this chapter.

Le Bihan, Odile. 1986. “L’homme partagé de Danièle Sallenave”. *Lire*, 21 September.
Sallenave, Danièle. 1977. *Le Voyage d'Amsterdam ou les Règles de la conversation*. Paris: Flammarion.
—. 1980. *Les Portes de Gubbio*. Paris: Hachette.
—. 1986. *La Vie fantôme*. Paris: POL.
—. 1986a. “Simone de Beauvoir: Mémoires. La Vie avec la pensée,” *Révolution*, 321, 25 April, 56.
—. 1986b. Interview with Michelle. Grazier. *Télérama*, 24 September, 46-7.
—. 1986c. “Sallenave: La Vie Bovary”. *Libération*, 25 September, 33.
—. 1992. Discussion with Bruno de Cessole, "Les livres de leur vie". *Bibliothèque publique d’information* (Code: Sallenave 31* Doc).
—. 2002. *D’Amour*. Paris: Gallimard.
Sartre, Jean-Paul. “Why Write?” In *What is Literature and other essays,* edited by Stephen Ungar, 48-69. Cambridge, MA: Harvard University Press.
Savigneau, Josyane. 1986. “La Vie perdue”. *Le Monde des livres*, 19 September, 14.
Thibault, Bruno. 1991. *Danièle Sallenave et le don des morts*. Paris: Gallimard.
—. 1997. “Danièle Sallenave et le thème de la vie séparée dans les nouvelles d’*Un printemps froid*”. *French Forum,* 22, 1, 75-91.

# Part IV:

# In a Spin: Storytelling in the Postmodern Era

# CHAPTER EIGHTEEN

# LES FANS ET LES HISTOIRES : CONSTRUCTION CONTEMPORAINE D'UN PARADIGME DU RÉCIT COMME LIEN

ANNE BESSON

Depuis le milieu des années 90, l'explosion de l'Internet haut débit a inauguré une nouvelle ère pour la consommation culturelle, et notamment le récit de fiction. Si la situation n'est pas la même pour les travaux anglophones, force est de constater que la théorisation critique française commence seulement à célébrer deux des acquis les plus visibles de cette donne inédite, dont les promotions furent contemporaines, parallèles et s'avèrent pourtant largement antinomiques: d'une part la construction d'une figure de récepteur "actif" et passionné (mise à l'honneur de ce qu'on appelle au choix *fan*, *nerd* ou *geek*[1]); d'autre part, avec le *storytelling*, la réhabilitation d'une toute-puissance de "l'histoire": elle vient se substituer au douteux "plaisir de la non-histoire" naguère théorisé par Umberto Eco au sujet de la lecture populaire (Fabbri-Bompiani-Senzagno, 1978: 158) mais en conserve cependant l'image peu nuancée d'une emprise, voire d'une manipulation, de ces mêmes consommateurs dont on annonce ailleurs le réveil critique.

Je commencerai donc par faire le point, dans une perspective métacritique, sur l'appréhension de ces deux phénomènes – montée en puissance de la figure du "fan" et prise en compte des pouvoirs du récit – qui se présentent pour moi, même si le lien entre eux n'est en général pas effectué, comme les deux faces d'une volonté d'analyse surplombante des

[1] Les trois termes présentent des nuances de sens (le *nerd* est plus exclusivement associé aux technologies informatiques, le *geek* chargé de connotations plus positives), mais se rencontrent le plus souvent employés en synonymie. Leurs apparitions dans la langue française ont été successives (*geek* n'a guère que quelques années), mais ils sont aujourd'hui employés en simultanéité. Pour une ébauche d'histoire et d'étymologie de ces termes, voir Faucher, 2010.

tendances culturelles contemporaines. D'un côté on s'intéresse à leur réception: que veulent, que font, que disent les consommateurs? De l'autre, on cherche à déterminer les objectifs des producteurs derrière ce qui est ainsi livré au public. Mais on aboutit, dans les deux cas, au même type de questionnement binaire, véritable serpent de mer pour qui s'intéresse aux cultures de grande diffusion: le public d'aujourd'hui est-il "empowéré"[2] ou toujours plus aliéné, esclave de passions qu'il a seulement désormais de multiples façons inédites d'alimenter? Et parallèlement, le pouvoir du récit est-il un outil au service de notre manipulation quotidienne par les discours dominants, ou bien est-il, de plus en plus, approprié par des consommateurs qui s'en saisissent et le détournent à leur propre profit?

Je présenterai ensuite mon point de vue sur ce débat qu'il ne s'agit aucunement de trancher: il me semble en effet que les tenants des deux positions extrêmes disent en partie la même chose. On peut alors estimer que cette part commune, celle du consensus sur la façon dont *on raconte et se raconte l'histoire*, est ce qui nous permet d'approcher au mieux une réalité contemporaine dont le propre, on doit le garder à l'esprit, est de nous échapper toujours par manque de distance et par effet de sidération. Or, ce que partagent ces discours antagonistes, c'est en tout premier lieu une même foi, parfois attaquée mais cependant centrale, dans les pouvoirs du symbolique, qui font ici un retour frappant. Ceux-ci se trouvent à nouveau pensés comme une capacité de configuration, de mise en ordre dans les différents sens du terme, que l'ordre en question soit celui du pouvoir en place ou la restauration d'une prise de chacun sur ce qui l'entoure. Toujours le récit de fiction se voit envisagé comme le nouveau lieu de construction possible d'une identité partagée, comme si l'humanité – ce qu'il nous est possible de partager en tant qu'êtres humains – avait trouvé refuge dans les histoires.

[2] Je choisis de "franciser" l'adjectif construit sur le bien connu "empowerment", "empowered". Une traduction existe, "encapacité" (sur "encapacitation"), mais elle apparaît pour l'heure moins parlante, et si possible encore plus laide!

Les *fan studies* n'existent pas encore véritablement en France,[3] en partie parce que les intellectuels de gauche qui auraient pu s'y consacrer sont demeurés marqués par la sociologie bourdieusienne, si pertinente qu'elle en a étouffé longtemps toute piste discordante. Or elle égale culture et capital, faisant de la possession des codes culturels dominants un instrument d'affirmation et surtout de maintien de la domination culturelle. La pensée de Bourdieu, largement diffusée, s'attache notamment à éclairer les stratégies et les leurres, l'arsenal trompeur qui vient garantir cette pérennité: ainsi, le fait de *mimer* un partage possible, de *faire croire*, fallacieusement, à une porosité des hautes et basses cultures, alors que la capacité à naviguer de la sorte entre plusieurs régimes d'adhésion serait en réalité l'apanage des seuls mieux dotés. A l'évidence pourtant, la démocratisation de l'accès à une culture multiforme impose désormais des ajustements à ce postulat (Lahire 2004), si bien que le temps semble aujourd'hui venu pour que se développent des travaux consacrés aux modalités de réception les plus récentes des récits de genre et des nouveaux médias par leur public passionné. Les premières thèses sont en cours ou juste soutenues sur cette réception et les types de socialisation qu'elle met en place (David Peyron en SIC, Vincent Berry en science du jeu[4]), les premiers articles paraissent qui émanent de très jeunes

---

[3] Pour citer les rares ouvrages disponibles: *Les Fans. Les dieux de nos nouvelles mythologies* de Vincent Rousselet-Blanc, J-C Lattès, 1994; *Fan Attitude* d'Eliane Girard et Brigitte Kernel, 2002 (recueil de témoignages de fans s'exprimant depuis 1996 dans la séquence "Fan Clubbing" de l'émission "Noctiluque", sur les ondes de France Inter) – ces deux exemples sont de bons échantillons de l'ancienne perception du fan, qui apparaît datée et caricaturale: les chanteurs populaires sont les seules idoles prises en compte, et le fan caractérisé par un fétichisme dans l'identification, souligné à grands traits. Du côté des travaux universitaires, on signalera les actes de colloque *Les Cultes médiatiques, Culture fan et œuvres cultes*, sous la direction de Philippe Le Guern, PUR coll. « Le sens social », 2002 : dans son introduction, Le Guern formule d'ailleurs le même constat d'un faible nombre de travaux français par opposition au cas anglo-saxon (p. 19-20). Fort intéressant, le recueil souffre toutefois du phénomène d'obsolescence rapide qui guette ce type de publication: il n'y est quasiment pas question d'Internet, le magnétoscope à cassettes vidéo est analysé comme une nouveauté…

[4] Sur les "guildes" de MMORPG, Vincent Berry a soutenu en novembre 2009 une thèse en sciences de l'éducation, sous la direction de Gilles Brougère (Paris 13, EXPERICE): "Les cadres de l'expérience virtuelle: jouer, vivre, apprendre dans un monde numérique. Analyse des pratiques ludiques, sociales et communautaires des joueurs de jeux de rôles en ligne massivement multijoueurs: Dark Age of Camelot et World of Warcraft." David Peyron prépare à l'heure où nous écrivons une thèse en sciences de l'information et de la communication, sur la "culture *geek*" et la

chercheurs, prenant la suite de pionniers comme Marc Lits ou les sociologues Philippe Le Guern ou Eric Maigret.[5]

Les représentations fictionnelles, l'évolution des "images" associées à la nébuleuse nerd/geek/fan/otaku, ont précédé, et imposé, cette prise en compte académique. Autour de deux grands pôles où se focalisent les représentations, eux-mêmes très différents puisqu'il s'agit d'une part de récits de science-fiction mettant en scène des techno-futurs proches (réflexions et fictions de William Gibson ou Neal Stephenson[6]), et d'autre part d'œuvres audio-visuelles "réalistes" humoristiques, nombreuses à avoir récemment mis au premier plan des personnages de ce type,[7] s'étend tout un réseau d'images en expansion rapide: des variations féminines sur ces mêmes figures de scientifiques de génie, plus ou moins gothiques mais toujours imbattables en informatique, apparaissent ainsi, en tant que membres d'une équipe, seconds rôles plébiscités par le public (Abby dans la série télévisée *NCIS*[8]), ou même en anti-héroïne de *best seller* dans le

convergence intermédiatique, sous la direction de Jean-Pierre Esquenazi (Lyon 3, HELICO).

[5] Marc Lits, Professeur de communication à l'Université catholique de Louvain (Belgique), est spécialiste des cultures populaires, télévision et "récits médiatiques". Philippe Le Guern, Maître de conférences à l'Université d'Angers, travaille sur les séries télévisées, les fans, et ces dernières années surtout sur les musiques populaires actuelles. Eric Maigret, Professeur de sociologie des médias à l'Université Paris 3-Sorbonne Nouvelle, s'attache à la sociologie de la réception et des publics; il est un des pionniers de l'introduction des *Cultural Studies* en France (voir Maigret, 2008).

[6] William Gibson, fameux prophète de l'ère des réseaux, aux héros dotés de connexions neurales, a notamment abordé le thème dans *Idoru* (1997), ainsi que dans l'article "Modern boys and mobile girls" (Gibson 2001). Neal Stephenson a également mis en vedette des personnages de joueurs, hackeurs, spécialistes en cryptologie, par exemple dans ses romans *Snow Crash* (1992) ou dans *Cryptonomicon* (1999). Il évoque justement l'évolution des perceptions à leur égard dans une conférence, "Science Fiction as a Literary Genre", donnée au Gresham College le 8 mai 2008 (Faucher 2010: 9).

[7] La plus fameuse, et hilarante, est la série américaine *The Big Bang Theory* (*sitcom* créée par Chuck Lorre et Bill Prady en 2007, 4 saisons diffusés sur CBS), précédée chronologiquement par la britannique *The IT Crowd* (*sitcom* créée par Graham Linehan, diffusée depuis le 3 février 2006 , soit 4 saisons, sur Channel 4). En France, les vignettes *NerdZ* (sur NoLife depuis 2007, 4 saisons) ou le film *Cyprien* (de David Charhon, 2008, avec Elie Seimoun dans le rôle-titre), surfent sur la tendance avec une tendance certaine à l'amateurisme assumé, dans le premier cas, à la caricature dans le second.

[8] Créée par Donald P. Bellisario et Don McGill, diffusée depuis le 23 septembre 2003, soit 7 saisons, sur CBS; avec Pauley Perrette dans le rôle d'Abby Sciuto.

cas de Lisbeth Salander, de la trilogie *Millenium*.[9] S'y ajoutent, hors fiction, d'innombrables manifestations de cette "mutation sociologique" que les médias s'attachent à enregistrer et/ou exploiter. Il en est de très confidentielles, comme le magazine culturel *Geek*[10] ou la chaîne de télévision "Nolife", mais d'autres aussi qui s'imposent dans notre quotidien commun, comme la fusion plus qu'amorcée entre les mondes *a priori* peu compatibles de la technophilie et de la mode: à côté de l'ouvrage encore assez spécialisé de Diana Eng, *Fashion Geek*, on ne compte plus les articles consacrées aux "geekettes", curieux néologisme associant féminisation et francisation qui fait actuellement recette dans les magazines de mode les plus diffusés (Pietrois-Chabassier 2010).

L'extension assez abusive de ce qui devient au fil des exemples une catégorie "socio-culturelle" en vogue (il suffit désormais d'aimer son IPhone et Facebook pour se retrouver au cœur de cette nouvelle cible) m'intéresse comme symptomatique d'une valorisation extrêmement rapide: il y a cinq ans encore, non seulement le mot *geek* n'existait pas dans le vocabulaire français, mais encore les rares travaux français sur les fans s'intéressaient, pour le dire vite, aux seuls fétichistes du PSG ou de Mylène Farmer. Or, si l'on se penche sur ce qui est mis en valeur pour justifier l'émergence de ce nouveau héros de notre temps, on rencontre, en vrac: l'enthousiasme passionné (puisqu'on est toujours envahi d'anglicismes, le fait d'être "dedicated to": une forme d'engagement, quoi qu'on en ait); l'importance de la démarche créative où on retrouve "l'activisme" sous la forme du consommateur actif, à son tour producteur des constellations de *fan films*, *fan fictions*, *fan arts*; l'érudition qui, même spécialisée, est analysable comme une stratégie herméneutique pionnière adaptée à la révolution de notre écosystème culturel (Faucher, 2010). En outre, ou plutôt, en conséquence, les champs de spécialisation traditionnels du *fan/nerd* (un mélange d'innovations technologiques, de genres de l'imaginaire, de "pulp" et "pop" culture) en sont venus à se confondre avec les goûts du plus grand nombre, devenu dès lors capable de comprendre, de mesurer l'étendue de ses connaissances sans toutefois l'égaler – elles sont désormais moins l'objet de l'habituelle ironie un peu

[9] Les romans de Stieg Larsson, parus en Suède en 2005, ont fait l'événement de la rentrée littéraire 2008 en France avec leur traduction chez Actes Sud. La hackeuse néo-punk est réapparue dans des versions audiovisuelles (série télévisée et films pour le cinéma) sous les traits de Noomi Rapace, puis dans le *remake* hollywoodien de David Fincher (2011), incarnée par Rooney Mara.

[10] Magazine bimestriel édité par Dinosaur, Cyborg and Fish Consulting (!), dont le premier numéro a paru en mai-juin 2009. Le numéro de juin-juillet 2010 est présenté comme "saison 2 épisode 3".

méprisante ("get a life!") et davantage d'une fascination parfois mêlée d'inquiétude (voici à quoi ressemblerait notre futur?).

Cette réhabilitation, relecture des asociaux *borderline* en consommateurs actifs et avertis, est en réalité l'aboutissement de réflexions qui existent aux Etats-Unis depuis les années 1980 au moins au sein des *cultural studies*, sous le nom de *fan studies*. Celles-ci tendent en général à adopter, par empathie ou même participation à leur objet, un caractère très enthousiaste et unilatéral – ainsi les travaux importants de Henry Jenkins, qui se qualifie lui-même de "aca/fan".[11] Il existe certes des voix plus discordantes, comme celle de John Tulloch, reprise par Richard Saint-Gelais, pour qui les fans, loin de détenir les clés d'un plaisir synonyme d'émancipation symbolique, demeureraient une "élite sans pouvoir" (Saint-Gelais 2011: 398) dont l'expertise ne trouve pas à se convertir en influence réelle. Mais de telles positions, prudentes ou lucides, ne semblent viser qu'à nuancer ce qui apparaît comme l'appréhension majoritaire aujourd'hui, à savoir une vision globalement positive des effets d'appropriation interactive permis par le développement d'Internet.

Le débat sur le degré d'aliénation des consommateurs semble donc tranché, en tout cas provisoirement. Il remonte pourtant aussi loin que les premier travaux critiques sur la réception, et se confond quasiment avec leur histoire. La ligne de fracture, *empowerment* vs. manipulation, structure le champ dès les années 40. Se mettent alors en place, autour des notions de persuasion et de gratification, les grands paradigmes inverses des écoles de Francfort d'une part, de Columbia et Chicago d'autre part. L'optimisme américain conçoit déjà des consommateurs responsables capables de choix éclairés tenant compte de leurs besoins spécifiques, quand la méfiance européenne construit une condamnation de la culture populaire, qui fournirait des gratifications trompeuses à la société massifiée et aliénée. Cette même opposition apparaît toujours centrale, dans les années 60 et 70, lors de la naissance et du développement des *cultural studies* à Birmingham.

Il me semble que le débat s'est en réalité plus déplacé que réglé: déplacé sur le terrain du *storytelling*, une fois que les travaux des *cultural studies* ont atteint une masse et une visibilité critiques, à l'évidence couplées à de fortes évolutions sociologiques. On n'a plus vraiment la possibilité, sauf à s'assumer comme penseur élitiste/réactionnaire, de prendre les gens pour des idiots, ni non plus de leur reprocher d'aller

---

[11] Le blog de Jenkins (http://www.henryjenkins.org/) est intitulé "Confessions of an Aca/Fan".

chercher leur plaisir fictionnel ici plutôt que là. Dès lors, le débat actuel autour du *storytelling*, qui se confond quasiment en France avec les textes qu'y consacre Christian Salmon (depuis 2007 seulement), peut apparaître comme le revers de la valorisation récente d'une certaine catégorie de public, spécialiste et active dans ses choix de consommation. J'y vois le souci, louable, que cette existence désormais reconnue de "récepteurs" avertis, du moins dans une certaine mesure et pour certains d'entre eux, n'amène pas à sous-estimer l'insidieuse entreprise de reconfiguration du monde par le récit dont nous serions menacés; et donc, comme la queue de comète d'une méfiance profondément ancrée chez les intellectuels français vis-à-vis de la manipulation idéologique venue d'Outre-Atlantique.

Je voudrais souligner, avant de revenir sur cette question de l'assujettissement des imaginaires, qu'il s'est tout de même produit un glissement majeur dans la représentation de l'aliénation par les histoires, parallèle bien entendu au nouveau respect dû à l'évasion fictionnelle: il y a eu réhabilitation du plaisir pris à la lecture, au visionnage, à l'écoute ou à la pratique, c'est-à-dire de la capacité à se passionner pour un cours d'événements (Baroni 2007) – dont on constate qu'ils ne sont plus, ces plaisirs, assimilés à une stase. On est passé du "plaisir de la non-histoire", "un plaisir où la distraction tient au refus du développement des événements, au fait de se soustraire à la tension passé-présent-futur pour se retirer vers un *instant*, aimé parce que récurrent" - je cite un des textes fondateurs d'Eco, toujours autant repris par les universitaires qui s'intéressent à la question (Fabbri-Bompiani-Senzagno, 1978: 158) - au plaisir (et éventuellement au danger) de *l'histoire*. Ça n'est pas rien: cela implique qu'on a constaté l'inadéquation partielle du paradigme d'Eco, qui faisait du texte populaire une compensation des modèles sociaux ayant pour rôle d'en équilibrer les effets: le roman-feuilleton, "triomphe de l'information", était ainsi la forme adaptée à une société stable et hyper-normée, et la " narrativité de la redondance" fournissait quant à elle la détente nécessaire pour faire face à "notre société industrielle contemporaine" et son "incessante charge informative avançant par à-coups brutaux, impliquant constamment des réajustements" (Ibid). Or il se trouve que, si ce dernier paramètre n'a cessé de se renforcer, cette évolution n'a en revanche pas été compensée par une redondance de plus en plus importante des fictions consommées. Au contraire, même en gardant à l'esprit qu'on reste dans le récit de genre et de grande diffusion, fondé sur le respect de codes récurrents, il s'est produit un retour manifeste à l'intrigue dans son suivi et ses rebondissements.

Qu'on pense aux formats télévisuels: les deux traditions standardisées de la série (non évolutive: *Starsky et Hutch*) et du feuilleton (dont les rebondissements constants imposaient un suivi contraignant) ont été détrônées par la systématisation d'une formule qualifiée de "série feuilleton" (Benassi 2000 and Winckler 2002). Celle-ci combine en effet les techniques d'écriture de l'épisode indépendant à "l'arc" du suivi narratif: elle se base bien sur un dispositif récurrent (à chaque épisode, un nouveau cas pathologique, une nouvelle enquête, un nouveau phénomène inexpliqué…), mais en déportant l'essentiel de l'intérêt narratif sur l'évolution des personnages et de leur interrelation. Les ensembles romanesques sur lesquels j'ai surtout travaillé (Besson 2004) ont effectué en quelques décennies un passage comparable et désormais complet de la série (où le temps intervolumique se suspend au profit d'une reprise éternelle des mêmes aventures et des mêmes combats) au cycle, qui au contraire intègre le passage du temps à la construction de son récit "à suivre", et se contraint à diverses stratégies de renouvellement. Deux exemples qui contredisent l'équivalence entre demande de répétition et réalité sociale heurtée et nous amènent à avancer qu'au contraire, nos pratiques culturelles *reflètent* nos vécus quotidiens autant ou plus qu'ils ne les compensent, leur rôle étant de les modéliser pour les rendre vivables – concevables, conceptualisables: soit le rôle attribué, par Ricœur, notamment, à la mise en intrigue (Ricœur 1984)!

Pour y revenir, le *storytelling* selon Salmon, constat d'un "nouvel ordre narratif" présenté sous l'angle de l'avertissement contre les manipulations idéologiques, s'avère à mon sens victime de cela même qu'il prétend dénoncer – à savoir de la façon dont les puissants essaient de raconter l'histoire, en l'interprétant en leur faveur, comme si la capacité d'influencer nos représentations n'était pas de leur part la moindre des choses… La réussite dans la manipulation des esprits, c'est en effet bien le but, totalement affiché, de techniques d'abord appliquées au management, au marketing publicitaire, à la communication politique. Autrement dit, si une chose est sûre c'est qu'il n'y a guère de machiavélisme là-dedans – au contraire, les promoteurs du *storytelling*, qui ont une nouvelle "formule" à proposer, présentent une nette tendance à se survendre: ils s'attribuent des pouvoirs qu'ils n'ont pas, et c'est s'y laisser prendre que de tant les prendre au sérieux.

Pourquoi ne pas y lire davantage comme une tentative de récupération, alors que tout a échoué et que la méfiance règne? Ces dirigeants qui s'avisent qu'autour de la machine à café les employés discutent, et en tirent une théorie sur "l'entreprise comme construction narrative", non seulement, bien entendu, cela ne veut pas dire grand-chose (les notions de récit, d'histoire, de narration, sont très diluées: le plus souvent, il s'agit de courtes anecdotes exemplaires), mais en outre, ils ne font guère que réinventer l'eau tiède, se raccrochant tant bien que mal à la pratique millénaire des fictions, et plutôt mal que bien. Les nouveaux gourous barbus du *storytelling* ont beau se réclamer de Propp ou de Barthes, le niveau de leurs productions n'en reste pas moins affligeant. Dans l'objectif qu'ils disent viser, l'exploitation de mythes ou, disons, de représentations collectives, ils s'avèrent, par exemple, totalement dépassés par les réussites des littératures de genre, comme nous allons le voir rapidement pour finir.

On ne peut que tomber d'accord avec le constat, point de départ de *Storytelling*, d'un "nouvel âge de la fiction". Seulement, et sans naïveté aucune, cela n'implique pas forcément que ses velléités manipulatrices soient dominantes. Pour citer après Salmon un éditorial du *New York Times*, "beaucoup de gens ont redécouvert le pouvoir qu'ont les histoires de constituer une réalité […] et commencent à réaliser que les histoires peuvent avoir des effets réels qui doivent être pris au sérieux" (Smith 2011). Le postulat, ici très explicite, est celui d'un *efficace* de la représentation symbolique: mais pourquoi toujours le faire contribuer à l'effroi paranoïaque, alors qu'ailleurs la même pensée "pessimiste de gauche", quand il s'agit des combats féministes par exemple, va souligner au contraire avec hauteur que les gains symboliques ne sont jamais que des cache-misères. Yves Citton, dans son récent *Mythocratie. Storytelling et imaginaire de gauche*, invite bien à pratiquer la scénarisation au service des valeurs d'émancipation, mais il s'inscrit encore dans la logique selon laquelle il faudrait détourner les moyens de l'ennemi. Je crois qu'il vaudrait la peine de formuler *aussi* le constat inverse, postulant que les moyens nous ont été donnés en partage, et font l'objet de constantes tentatives de récupération: c'est peut-être *parce que* les gens " s'échappent" que les emplois du *storytelling* essaient de les *retenir* en usant des outils même de leur évasion.

Pourquoi, comme le fait Citton, s'arrêter en chemin et prendre, comme exemple des pouvoirs de la "réinvention de soi", un musicien de jazz expérimental, Sun Ra, qui revendiquait son origine saturnienne, plutôt que les fans de *Star Trek* qui communiquent en klingon? Pourquoi un obscur collectif d'artistes italiens retravaillant les codes du récit du genre en rêvant de susciter des interventions "d'en bas",[12] et non directement des

[12] "...chaque livre sortant de Wu Ming s'inscrit dans une communauté et une transmédialité en devenir, puisqu'il 'est potentiellement entouré d'un nuage quantique d'hommages, de spin-off et de narrations «latérales»: des récits écrits par des lecteurs (fan fiction), des bandes dessinées, des dessins et des illustrations, des chansons, des sites web, et même des jeux en réseau ou sur table inspirés des livres, des jeux de rôle avec les personnages des livres et d'autres contributions

exemples de l'inventivité de ces derniers, qui suscitent de telles activités, les foisonnantes *fanfics* en premier lieu? Il semble bien que les intellectuels les plus engagés, quelle que soit leur bonne foi, achoppent toujours sur l'impossibilité de prendre en compte ce que font, ce que sont, déjà, ces cultures réellement "marginales" dans le sens où elles ne sont pas inscrites dans une perspective de légitimation, et qui cependant "font culture" d'une autre façon, en se dotant de hiérarchies et de spécialistes.

Le lien est direct, dans les visées du moins, entre les techniques du *storytelling* et les genres populaires de grande diffusion contemporains: à côté de l'insistance, dans les discours des *storytellers*, sur un art immémorial du récit (on pourrait aussi parler de "vieilles recettes"), on note parallèlement, en France, ce qui est quasiment une rengaine, la célébration d'un récent (plus ou moins récent, plus ou moins net aussi!) "retour au récit", "aux personnages"… qui viendrait rompre avec des travers que notre production en littérature générale hérite du Nouveau Roman. Bien sûr, l'histoire est un peu plus complexe et plus longue que cela, mais c'est en tout cas ainsi qu'on nous la raconte. Or, la manière dont on choisit de se raconter l'histoire constitue précisément ce que doit s'efforcer de déterminer et d'analyser notre réflexion: ce récit partagé d'aujourd'hui est celui d'un pays (d'un monde, à quelques nuances près) qui longtemps ne voulut plus raconter d'histoires, et dont la méfiance ces derniers temps s'érode, peut-être à ses dépens, au profit d'un désir d'histoires "sans fin", qui se présentent comme des "mythes", au syncrétisme caractérisé.

Relier, mettre en ordre, donner sens: autant de fonctions par nature collectives, qu'on attendait naguère du côté du religieux bien sûr, puis du politique ou du social, et qui sont aujourd'hui réinvesties par les récits fictionnels réappropriés. Activités des fans et pouvoirs du récit se rejoignent dans ce mythe contemporain qui n'est déjà plus à construire, qui constitue déjà une réalité de nos imaginaires. C'est ainsi que les nouveaux lecteurs donnés en modèle prennent leur plaisir spécifique à anticiper, à combler les blancs, à faire sens du détail, à investir des espaces d'intrigue potentielle, qu'ils produisent leurs propres récits dans les interstices du "canon" et les hypothèses participant aux quêtes herméneutiques orchestrées sur la Toile. Les tendances contemporaines, formelles et génériques, de la fiction de grande diffusion vont quant à elles dans le sens du développement des cycles à suivi chronologique au détriment de la

---

venues «d'en bas», à la nature ouverte et changeante de l'œuvre et au monde qui vit en elle'." Je souligne le "potentiellement" (Citton, *ibid.*, intermède « Du mythe interrompu à l'épopée en chantier », reproduit en ligne sur le site Fabula (page consultée le 04/07/10): http://www.fabula.org/atelier.Du_mythe_interrompu.)

série, on l'a dit, et sont en outre marqués par l'explosion d'un genre, la *fantasy*, caractérisé par son travail sur les archétypes et les fusions génériques. Ce genre du merveilleux contemporain, qui fonctionne comme le creuset où se refondent les codes hérités des différents récits de genre, exhibe en effet à la fois son rapport aux mythes, matière première à recycler, et sa nature paradoxale de réinvention du passé aujourd'hui (Besson 2007).

Qu'il s'agisse de volumes et épisodes, désormais systématiquement reliés, des médias en phase ultime de convergence, des époques décrites, librement revisitées en uchronies, ou encore des genres, aujourd'hui travaillés sous l'angle du mixage, contenus et supports de nos fictions se doivent d'être poreux, connectés, appropriables. Les évolutions observables, du côté des récepteurs comme des producteurs, eux-mêmes conçus comme de moins en moins distincts ou séparés, vont alors toujours dans le sens d'une mise en continuité généralisée du divers et du multiple. Elles participent ainsi d'un puissant imaginaire contemporain du lien, du réseau, par lequel ces "communautés" réunies dans des "univers" réinvestissent le sens d'une humanité partagée dans la faculté d'invention collective d'un nouveau monde des histoires.

## Références


Baroni, Raphaël. 2007. *La Tension narrative: suspense, curiosité et surprise*. Paris: Seuil.

Benassi, Stéphane. 2000. *Séries et feuilletons TV. Pour une typologie des genres fictionnels*. Liège: Editions du CEFAL.

Besson, Anne. 2004. *D'Asimov à Tolkien, cycles et séries dans la littérature de genre*, Paris: CNRS.

—. 2007. *La Fantasy*. Paris: Klincksieck.

Bourdieu, Pierre. 1979. *La Distinction: critique sociale du jugement*. Paris: Minuit.

—. 1992. *Les Règles de l'Art, genèse et structure du champ littéraire*. Paris: Seuil.

Citton, Yves. 2010. *Mythocratie. Storytelling et imaginaire de gauche*. Paris: Editions Amsterdam.

Eng, Diana. 2009. *Fashion Geek: Clothes Accessories Tech*. Cotati, CA: North Light Books.

Fabbri-Bompiani-Senzagno (eds), Bouzaher, Myriem (trans). 1978. *De Superman au Surhomme*. Paris: Grasset.

Faucher, Benoit. 2010. "La figure du 'geek' comme stratégie de lecture. Naviguer dans la 'pop culture' à l'ère du surplus culturel". *TRANS*. 9:

http://trans.univ-paris3.fr/spip.php?article397
Gibson, William. 2001. "Modern boys and mobile girls". *The Observer*: http://www.guardian.co.uk/books/2001/apr/01/
Girard, Éliane, and Kernel, Brigitte. 2002. *Fan Attitude*. Paris: Librio.
Glévarec, Hervé, Macé, Éric, and Maigret, Éric (eds). 2008. *Cultural Studies*. Paris: Armand Colin.
Jenkins, Henry. 1992. *Textual Poachers: Television fans and participatory culture*. New York/London: Routledge.
—. 2006. *Fans, Bloggers and Gamers: Exploring Participatory Culture*. New York/London: NYUP.
—. 2006. *Convergence Culture: Where Old and New Media Collide*. New York and London: NYUP.
Lahire, Bernard. 2004. *La Culture des individus, dissonances culturelles et distinction de soi*. Paris: La Découverte.
Pietrois-Chabassier, Thomas. 2010. "Ma nuit chez les geekettes", *Grazia*, February 2010.
Ricœur, Paul. 1984. *Temps et récit II: La configuration du temps dans le récit de fiction*. Paris: Seuil.
Rousselet-Blanc, Vincent. 1994. *Les Fans. Les dieux de nos nouvelles mythologies*. Paris: J-C Lattès.
Saint-Gelais, Richard. 2011. *Fictions transfuges. La transfictionnalité et ses enjeux*. Paris: Seuil.
Salmon, Christian. 2007. *Storytellling, la machine à fabriquer des histoires et à formater les esprits*. Paris: La Découverte.
—. 2009. *Storytellling, saison 1:chroniques du monde contemporain*. Paris: Les Prairies Ordinaires.
Smith, Lynn. 2001. "Not the same old story", *New York Times*, 11 November, 2001.
Winckler, Martin. 2002. *Les Miroirs de la vie, histoire des séries télévisées*. Paris: Le Passage.

# Chapter Nineteen

# Du cœur au prisme : mise en intrigue et réflexivité dans la science-fiction

Marc Atallah

Trop souvent mise à l'écart, voire carrément exclue, des recherches universitaires en raison, paraît-il, de son orientation "populaire", de sa "pauvreté" stylistique ou encore de ses "carences" esthétiques, la littérature de science-fiction souffre d'un manque crucial de légitimité académique qui, s'il était comblé, autoriserait pourtant à préciser les contours génériques, les innovations poétiques et les apports pragmatiques de quantité de récits pour l'instant encore étonnement indifférenciés, si ce n'est par leur inclination thématique (et encore). En effet, quiconque s'est un jour intéressé à approfondir ses connaissances sur ce genre littéraire, aura fait la surprenante expérience de constater le peu d'essais critiques publiés sur lui dans le monde francophone jusqu'à présent. Au demeurant, et même si nombre d'analyses étudient l'évolution des formes prises par les motifs traditionnels du genre au cours de la diachronie ou mettent au jour les plus ou moins subtiles interrogations métaphysiques qui peuvent être dégagées synchroniquement des textes, on ne dénombre que quelques ouvrages théoriques qui centrent expressément leur réflexion sur les richesses *littéraires* propres à la science-fiction[1]: la conjecture romanesque ,[2]

---

[1] Voir par exemple Angenot 2003,193-214, Langlet 2006 ou Saint-Gelais 1999.

[2] Originellement qualifiée de "rationnelle" par Pierre Versins (1972), la conjecture romanesque a été pour la première fois évoquée sous la plume du fondateur de la Maison d'Ailleurs (www.ailleurs.ch) pour caractériser l'élément commun irréductible qui sous-tend les récits utopiques, science-fictionnels et ceux narrant des voyages extraordinaires. Or, au cours de mon étude doctorale, je me suis attelé à l'étude minutieuse de ce concept – et c'est à la suite de cette dernière que j'ai été conduit, d'une part, à supprimer le prédicat "rationnelle" en raison de son appartenance analytique au substantif "conjecture" et, d'autre part, à regrouper les trois genres susmentionnés sous l'appellation "littératures conjecturales": à un

les mondes possibles alternatifs (au sens que ce concept prend chez les sémioticiens) et, surtout, l'élaboration, la configuration et le déroulement d'intrigues autant originales que troublantes. Cette observation sera rendue encore plus inquiétante si l'on se rappelle que la science-fiction est une des seules familles discursives, si ce n'est la seule, à focaliser ses investigations – n'est-ce pas d'ailleurs le fondement intime de ses récits? – sur la corrélation typiquement moderne qui s'est établie dès la seconde moitié du XIX^e^ siècle entre les technosciences, les sociétés et les individus. Parcourir les œuvres de science-fiction, c'est, à n'en point douter, découvrir des mises en intrigue axées sur des relations singulières entretenues par les subjectivités humaines avec les disciplines constitutives du champ technoscientifique et à leurs réalisations d'une part, et, d'autre part, c'est être incité à revenir, réflexivement, à l'origine – coïncidant avec notre monde empirique – de ce que Darko Suvin (1977) appelle le *cognitive estrangement*.[3] En ce sens, la science-fiction est bel et bien à la croisée des cultures (pour reprendre la dichotomie instituée à la fin des années 1950 par Charles Percy Snow (1959) ou, plutôt, elle est une réintégration, *par le biais de la diégèse*, des deux cultures: les technosciences ne sont plus considérées dans les seuls progrès technologiques qu'elles promettent, mais sont sommées d'entrer en résonance avec les impacts socio-anthropologiques plausibles de ces mêmes progrès.

Au vu de ce qui précède, il est alors justifié de s'interroger: les productions littéraires sont-elles nécessairement, et de tout temps, vouées à être superbement ignorées par la critique, dès l'instant où elles entrent en dialogue avec l'imaginaire provenant des sciences dites "de la nature" et celui des concrétisations technologiques que ces sciences autorisent à concevoir? Les limites de cette contribution m'empêchent de répondre de manière exhaustive à ce qui semble bien circonscrire un objet d'investigation passionnant pour une certaine sociologie de la lecture. Par contre, ces mêmes limites me permettent d'esquisser ce à quoi pourrait donner naissance une enquête narratologique fondée sur le matériau des études littéraires, c'est-à-dire le texte – en l'occurrence ici, science-fictionnel [4]: l'*exemplum* servira la poétique et le recours à la grammaire de

---

même processus logique doit correspondre une même identité générique (Atallah 2008).

[3] Le *cognitive estrangement* peut être aisément défini comme l'ensemble des connaissances que le lecteur doit convoquer pour rendre intelligible un monde décalé.

[4] En raison de l'amplitude du champ de la science-fiction, un critère restrictif devait être trouvé afin que mon enquête puisse rester pertinente. Puisque je cherche à interroger le rapport {imaginaire technoscientifique ; société ; individu}, et que

l'intrigue, la pragmatique. Or, travailler le texte en décortiquant les options diégétiques pour lesquelles il a opté, c'est aller à l'encontre d'un certain réductionnisme idéologique fréquemment opéré par les chercheurs: en préconisant l'exploitation de ses thématiques au détriment de ses ressources formelles, ceux-ci restreignent en effet la science-fiction critique à n'être qu'une littérature d'idées. Il m'a alors paru judicieux de montrer le caractère étriqué, voire même franchement erroné, d'une telle réduction qualitative. Mais quelle voie suivre pour prouver que les récits incriminés étaient bien plus que des "idées"? La voie qui s'est imposée consistait à élaborer, à partir d'un roman de science-fiction critique récent - *Le Dernier de son espèce* d'Andreas Eschbach (2006) - et de quelques réflexions théoriques sur la fiction – ici celles proposées par Jean-Paul Sartre, Paul Ricœur, Jean-Marie Schaeffer et Raphaël Baroni –, une grille de lecture spécifique. L'usage de cette grille, que j'ai appelée "matrice minimale d'intrigue", peut être conçue comme une procédure analytique révélant, non la distance esthétique séparant les récits science-fictionnels de ceux, "canoniques", valorisés par la critique littéraire contemporaine, mais l'appartenance des premiers à la classe des objets, dont les seconds peuvent néanmoins aussi ressortir, qui accordent à l'organisation narrative des fonctions littéraire et pragmatique capitales. C'est d'ailleurs pour cette raison que cette matrice a été dirigée sur l'étude des formes: je souhaitais montrer comment les formes propres à la science-fiction critique interagissaient avec celles, plus traditionnelles, des autres genres romanesques, afin de produire des effets, par exemple herméneutiques, inédits.

L'idée ayant servi d'assise liminaire à cet exposé rappelle que, parmi la pléthore des récits disponibles sur le marché, ceux qui, comme *Le Dernier de son espèce* de l'écrivain allemand, doivent être acceptés comme les plus stimulants autant intellectuellement qu'existentiellement, puisqu'ils mettent en intrigue de manière ingénieuse et inédite des conjectures romanesques – se manifestant linguistiquement par le biais de signes (mots

---

nous savons tous que la plausibilité d'un élément textuel conditionne l'herméneutique des textes, j'ai décidé de ne m'occuper que des récits basés autour de conjectures *vraisemblables*, c'est-à-dire pertinentes eu égard aux paradigmes technoscientifiques en vigueur à l'époque d'écriture. J'appellerai ce sous-genre de la science-fiction, "science-fiction critique", et j'ai montré ailleurs (Atallah 2008) que ses mises en intrigues possèdent deux propriétés principales: 1/ elles rappellent que les technosciences sont des dimensions de l'agir humain, vu qu'elles présentent des personnages en proie à de nouveaux savoirs ou de nouvelles technologies influençant leurs rapports aux autres et à eux-mêmes; 2/ elles offrent une image plausiblement distanciée de la sphère empirique.

ou syntagmes) nommés "novums" par Darko Suvin (1977, 12) ou "mots-fictions" par Marc Angenot (1978, 196) –, qui décalent intelligemment notre univers réel vers un de ses pendants fictionnels. C'est aux développements de ce constat que je dois alors me dédier à présent. Plus concrètement, je débuterai mon propos par l'éclaircissement de la structure logique du processus conjectural, "cœur" de l'intrigue science-fictionnelle, car pourvu de la propriété formelle d'unir rationnellement et tensivement deux temporalités distinctes (monde réel, monde fictionnel). Il faudra en fait montrer par quels procédés textuels cette conjecture, au-delà de son contenu sémantique, crée la possibilité d'une tension non seulement *narrative*, mais encore, suite aux effets thymiques de curiosité et de suspense décrits par Raphaël Baroni (2007)[5], *réflexive*. J'orienterai ensuite l'argumentaire vers les richesses qui peuvent surgir de ce processus conjectural: ce qui était initialement un "cœur" structurel deviendra alors un "prisme" épistémologique, celui d'une piste originale qu'il nous est loisible d'emprunter pour penser nos rapports subjectifs quotidiens aux technosciences ainsi qu'à leurs avancées pratiques. Autrement dit, la tension bidirectionnelle évoquée ci-dessus, conduira à dégager une construction diégétique particulière et les effets pragmatiques qui y sont associés: une structure insoupçonnée de mise en intrigue viendra se greffer à la structure narrative traditionnelle {nœud → dénouement} et ce, grâce aux modalités qui accompagnent la textualisation de la conjecture (notamment la perspective narrative):

{<u>nœud :</u> apparence d'un scénario stéréotypé → <u>dénouement :</u> situation-limite}

Il me faudra alors montrer qu'à la direction tensive de cette nouvelle structure narrative – elle suit l'ordre: d'abord le nœud, ensuite le dénouement – doit nécessairement correspondre, dans le cas d'une littérature conjecturale comme la science-fiction critique, une tension "à rebours", c'est-à-dire une structure réflexive:

{<u>dénouement:</u> situation-limite → conjecture → <u>réflexion:</u> monde réel}

---

[5] Rapidement, le *pronostic* est "l'anticipation incertaine d'un développement actionnel dont on connaît seulement les premises" et le *diagnostic*, "l'anticipation incertaine, à partir d'indices, de la compréhension d'une situation narrative décrite provisoirement de manière incomplete" (Baroni 2007, 110).

En cela, je rejoins – tout en prenant la liberté de l'augmenter par les résultats obtenus lors des enquêtes que j'ai menées sur les récits de science-fiction, entre autres critiques – le constat posé par Raphaël Baroni:

> [C]'est bien toujours dans une interaction entre ces deux niveaux – d'une part, la tensivité inhérente à l'action représentée et, d'autre part, son mode de textualisation – qu'il faut rechercher l'origine de la *tension narrative*, et non dans l'un ou l'autre de ces aspects du récit pris isolément (Baroni 2007, 152).

Un truisme lancera mon argumentaire: tout lecteur qui en est familier, sait que les récits de science-fiction critique sont narrativement informés par la conjecture romanesque, c'est-à-dire par l'extrapolation rationnelle d'un élément technoscientifique [6] (savoirs, technologies) déjà présent, au moins sur le mode du projet, dans le monde empirique. Le déploiement conceptuel de cet état de fait m'autorise à postuler que, grâce à la réflexivité consubstantielle à ce processus logique, ces narrations doivent être conçues comme des *miroirs distanciés* de ce même monde empirique: si les contours de notre avenir sont esquissés, c'est avant tout pour revenir à notre présent. En d'autres termes, si la science-fiction critique décale ses univers fictionnels, c'est pour évoquer, en creux, et penser, réflexivement, le monde duquel ces univers sont tous rationnellement inspirés - c'est-à-dire, excepté dans le cas particulier de l'uchronie, le nôtre - et c'est cette particularité de la tension narrative propre à la science-fiction critique que j'aimerais, *in fine*, exhiber. Or, bien que la conjecture mette à distance l'univers fictionnel en imaginant ce à quoi notre sphère pratique pourrait éventuellement conduire ou propose d'interroger la direction et les conséquences supposées prises par la recherche technoscientifique d'une époque donnée, elle donne surtout naissance à une intrigue, c'est-à-dire, dans la perspective aristotélicienne, à la représentation d'êtres agissants dans un contexte spécifique, ici conditionné par l'actualisation fictionnelle de la conjecture romanesque: la science-fiction critique est avant tout une *mimèsis* littéraire, la conjecture, une opération textuelle. C'est ainsi dans l'art que ces récits ont de raconter leur histoire, c'est-à-dire dans le savoir-faire d'un *storytelling* spécifique, que réside l'apport le plus fécond des textes du genre discursif que j'ai choisi d'étudier: ici, la beauté ne vient pas en premier lieu des innovations esthétiques, mais s'origine dans les

[6] À des fins de distinction taxinomique, je souhaiterais ajouter ici que la science-fiction (critique) regroupe l'ensemble des récits fondés autour d'une conjecture romanesque de coloration technoscientifique, contrairement à l'utopie ou à la dystopie qui, elles, se concentrent autour de conjectures essentiellement sociopolitiques.

rapports, toujours singuliers, établis par les auteurs, entre les conjectures romanesques, les mondes possibles qui en résultent et les configurations adoptées par la mise en intrigue. Afin de montrer, par l'analyse d'un exemple précis, comment les récits de science-fiction critique construisent leurs intrigues[7] avec, pour finalité, d'inciter le lecteur à prendre en charge subjectivement les réflexions inhérentes au mode de traitement de la conjecture, je vais tout de suite me pencher de manière approfondie sur le récit d'Andreas Eschbach, évoqué plus haut.

*Le Dernier de son espèce* raconte l'histoire de Duane William Fitzgerald, soldat américain qui, tout comme d'autres de ses collègues, a accepté au début des années 1980 de subir de nombreuses interventions chirurgicales, secrètement financées par le gouvernement des Etats-Unis, visant à le transformer en "soldat doté de capacités surhumaines" (Eschbach 2006, 156). Vu qu'il a secrètement espéré ressembler aux icônes du cinéma hollywoodien populaire depuis son adolescence, le gouvernement américain lui a permis de réaliser son rêve. Pourtant, suite à un nombre conséquent de dysfonctionnements internes de toutes sortes, Duane et cinq de ses camarades se voient retirés, en 1994, du projet auquel ils appartenaient: le projet "Steel Men".[8] Chacun est alors invité à vivre le reste de son existence paisiblement, à l'écart du monde, sans tenter de reprendre contact avec un de ses anciens compagnons d'infortune; disparaître, en somme. Suite à cette proscription et à un concours de circonstances, Duane s'est exilé dans le petit village portuaire de Dingle (Irlande), jusqu'à ce qu'il se rende compte qu'un inconnu, "écuma[nt] la ville en sonnant de porte en porte" (Eschbach 2006, 31), cherche à le retrouver. L'action narrative paraît lancée; elle décollera peu, voire pas du tout. C'est plutôt aux états d'âme désenchantés, parfois nauséeux, souvent désespérés du narrateur autodiégétique que nous aurons affaire au gré des

---

[7] J'ai dit, plus haut, que l'objectif de cet exposé était de constituer une "matrice minimale d'intrigue". Par là, je ne veux pas signifier que les récits doivent nécessairement articuler l'ensemble des traits qui seront évoqués lors de l'analyse, mais plutôt de montrer une tendance discursive préconisant certaines propriétés formelles et thématiques lorsqu'il s'agit de conduire le lecteur à interroger, par l'intermédiaire des personnages, les relations s'établissant entre technosciences, société et être humain.

[8] L'intertextualité avec l'homme d'acier, c'est-à-dire *Superman* ou *Terminator*, est claire: *Le Dernier de son espèce* instaure un dialogue implicite avec les grandes figures de la science-fiction. Cela a pour conséquence de réfléchir non seulement à la direction empruntée par notre réalité en vue de perfectionner l'espèce humaine, mais aussi aux textes (ou aux films) ayant alimenté cet espoir et offert quantité de scénarii stéréotypés.

(rares) péripéties, Duane prenant peu à peu conscience qu'il est à la fois le dernier cyborg survivant du fiasco Steel Men et le dernier témoin d'une expérience militaro-technologique gênante qui a mal tourné. Une seule chose lui semble alors impérative: trouver un sens, humain, à cette vie, fondamentalement inhumaine.

Quelques minimes vérifications contextuelles suffisent pour accepter le monde inventé par Eschbach comme structurellement [9] et thématiquement [10] analogue à celui dans lequel nous évoluons: les éléments textuels œuvrent donc de concert en faveur de l'établissement d'une familiarité, d'une proximité – typique du roman réaliste –, entre l'Irlande des premières années du XXI$^{e}$ siècle et l'univers fictionnel du romancier allemand. Un même sentiment se fait d'ailleurs jour quant aux technologies mentionnées et articulées au sein de la narration, puisque nous ne sommes pas le moins du monde surpris de constater qu'elles sont bien intégrées à notre quotidien ou, du moins, qu'elles commencent à y prospérer. Les yeux artificiels ou bioniques existent déjà, les batteries nucléaires et les pompes à sédatifs aussi. Il en va de même pour les technologies de la chirurgie micro-invasive, de la tomographie par émission de positrons, et de la robotique ou encore des chimères, évoquée à la fin du roman. On ne peut manquer de l'observer, toutes les conditions sont réunies par Eschbach pour que nous puissions percevoir l'univers représenté comme une variante quasi identique de notre sphère réelle et, partant, pour que nous soyons en mesure d'emprunter, réflexivement, le "pont référentiel" ainsi créé: monde possible proche du nôtre, thématiques connues, décalage cognitivo-critique limité à une conjecture (celle du "cyborg"), immersion fictionnelle "maximisant" l'identification du lecteur au personnage principal grâce au point de vue narratif adopté (autodiégétique)[11]. Or, malgré cette assise réaliste du récit, une particularité – et non des moindres – distingue le personnage principal du roman, du reste de l'espèce humaine: c'est un cyborg, c'est-à-dire "un être vivant pourvu d'implants technologiques qui renforcent au-delà de la normale les capacités de l'organisme, notamment ses facultés d'adaptation à un environnement

[9] Pour ne citer qu'un exemple prouvant cette similarité structurelle, pensons à la nature des inférences herméneutiques qu'il est nécessaire d'actualiser pour rendre le texte intelligible: elles sont identiques à celles qu'il faut former pour comprendre un roman réaliste.

[10] Une seule illustration concourant à l'effet de réalisme suffira ici. Dingle est bel et bien la ville principale de la péninsule irlandaise éponyme, située entre les bourgades de Tralee et Killarney, toutes deux aussi mentionnées.

[11] La définition des concepts d'"immersion" et d'"identification" peut être trouvée chez Jean-Marie Schaeffer (1999).

hostile" (Eschbach 2006, 66); et ces implants sont décrits quelques lignes plus loin:

> Des amplificateurs de force ont été implantés dans vos muscles. Des pans entiers de votre squelette – votre bras droit par exemple – ont été remplacés par des armatures en titane hautement concentré. Des capteurs électroniques vous permettent de percevoir les ultraviolets, les infrarouges, les rayons X et gamma, les virus, les armes chimiques, etc. (Eschbach 2006, 67)

En plus de celles évoquées ci-dessus, d'autres innovations technologiques envahissent la constitution de Duane: œil artificiel, pompe à sédatifs, batterie nucléaire, ordinateurs, appareils de navigation, unités de stockage, réservoirs, turbocœur, commandes bioneuroniques. C'est un homme-machine, ou une machine-homme, en somme. Évidemment, un tel amalgame, souvent fantasmé, n'existe pas et n'a jamais été réalisé, du moins jusqu'à aujourd'hui. En cela, Duane doit avant tout être perçu comme un "novum", c'est-à-dire l'incarnation diégétique d'une conjecture romanesque, qui, d'une part, met rationnellement à distance l'univers de la fiction et, d'autre part, représente le "cœur" intime de la narration. Ce sont bien les aventures de l'homme que nous suivons, mais tout ce qui lui arrive est conditionné par sa constitution hybride. Aidé par l'effet de réalisme instillé depuis le début du roman et suite à l'extension de sa propre encyclopédie paradigmatique (si besoin est)[12], cette conjecture est cependant facile à accepter comme *vraisemblable*: une lecture conjecturale et référentielle de l'œuvre peut alors être activée. Toutefois, comme indiqué plus haut, le récit de l'écrivain allemand n'est pas construit comme le sont la plupart de ceux qui prennent le cyborg comme motif principal. Rien d'exceptionnel ne se passe, l'action est réduite, par exemple à la question de savoir si Duane pourra manger à sa faim, ou fuir ses opposants. La problématique n'est donc pas, nous le découvrons petit à petit, celle du vaillant cyborg riche de ressources surhumaines – comme c'est le cas dans les romans ou les films racontant l'histoire d'un "homme de fer" – mais celle d'une subjectivité tellement "mécanisée" qu'elle se doit de rechercher en elle et autour d'elle, les traces d'humanité auxquelles elle pourrait s'accrocher pour exister avec dignité: la quête d'identité remplace les combats sensationnels. L'incipit du roman est révélateur de cette liberté prise vis-à-vis du scénario attendu – liberté dont il faudra

---

[12] Le cyborg est en effet une conjecture romanesque vraisemblable et j'en ai pour preuve les travaux de Kevin Warwick (2002), l'expansion de la biomécatronique, les recherches effectuées au département américain officiel de la DARPA, l'apparition imminente d'exosquelettes, etc.

encore mesurer la fonction – car le micro-suspense qui s'y fait jour, émergeant d'une situation qu'il est difficile de ne pas ressentir comme ironique, nous met déjà sur la piste de la spécificité narrative propre à la science-fiction critique [13]:

> *[1 : cadre]* Je m'éveillai ce samedi matin aveugle et hémiplégique.
>
> *[2 : SF + ?]* Je me suis souvent retrouvé aveugle, hémiplégique également, mais la concomitance de plus en plus fréquente des deux types de crises commence à m'inquiéter.
>
> *[3 : ?]* Allongé sur le flanc droit, le visage partiellement enfoui dans l'oreiller, je ne pouvais plus bouger que la tête, le bras gauche et quelques muscles qui, en l'occurrence, ne m'étaient d'aucune utilité.
>
> *[4 : ...]* Agacé, je fus tenté de somnoler encore un peu en espérant que le malaise s'estomperait de lui-même. Je savais pourtant que ce ne serait pas le cas. Qui plus est, ma vessie réclamait d'être soulagée.
>
> *[5 : !]* De la main gauche, je fis donc quelques moulinets arrière et, vainquant tant bien que mal oreiller et matelas, je réussis à empoigner le montant du lit.
>
> *[6 : ...]* Changer de position à la force d'un seul bras, de surcroît démis,
>
> *[7 : SF + !]* n'est pas une sinécure, surtout pour un colosse d'un quintal et demi aussi raide qu'un mannequin. Mais à cœur vaillant rien d'impossible.
> Je tirai de toutes mes forces.
>
> *[8 : !]* Frôlant la déchirure musculaire, je culbutai enfin et m'écrasai l'omoplate gauche contre le rebord. Malgré la douleur,

[13] Je me permets ici d'utiliser la signalétique proposée par Raphaël Baroni (2007, 139) : "... pour les macro-propositions relatives au nœud [...] pour celles associées au retard (péripéties ou autres) et pour les macro-propositions liées au dénouement." J'y ajoute le symbole [SF], pour les macro-propositions typiques des narrations science-fictionnelles et je développerai leur signification contextuelle lors de l'analyse.

j'étais désormais idéalement placé pour glisser ma main valide sous le sommier.

*[9 : ...]* Depuis des années, je garde là-dessous un gourdin de bois en prévision d'occasions comme celle-ci. Jusqu'alors, m'en asséner deux ou trois coups sur la calebasse ou sur un membre récalcitrant avait systématiquement payé.

*[10 : SF + !]* Mes rouages internes diffèrent peu de ceux d'un vieux distributeur de boissons : j'ai parfois besoin d'être un tantinet bousculé pour retrouver mes facultés.

*[11 : !]* Ce matin-là, cependant, rien n'y fit. Je cessai de me cogner dessus avant de m'infliger plus que de simples ecchymoses. J'étais toujours aveugle et paralysé.

*[12 : ...* et *SF]* [Puis, après avoir identifié le problème comme un problème d'alimentation générale, Duane, dont la nature de cyborg ne nous est maintenant plus inconnue, utilise un couteau pour réactiver l'interrupteur hors service]

[…] [13 : !] La paralysie se dissipa instantanément, je retrouvai le contrôle de mes membres et de mon œil droit. Mes muscles émirent une espèce de sifflement quand je me remis en mouvement. Quel bonheur de pouvoir court-circuiter la douleur et réguler l'afflux veineux! Je me redressai, trempé de sueur et de sang, et me dirigeai d'un pas chancelant vers la salle de bains. Main comprimée sur la blessure, je commençai avec délice par vider ma vessie. (Eschbach 2006, 7-13)

L'analyse séquentielle de ce passage m'intéresse grandement, car elle fait apparaître deux points essentiels pour la suite du propos: (a) l'importance de la conjecture pour la formulation de diagnostics et de pronostics autant réflexifs que narratifs; et (b) la résolution d'un nœud stéréotypé au cours d'un dénouement inattendu. Tout d'abord, on le constate lors de cet *incipit* débutant *in medias res* [macro-proposition 1], il y a formation rapide d'un double nœud à fonction cataphorique [macro-proposition 2 et 3]. Le premier nœud [macro-proposition 2] relève de la stratégie d'ébranlement habituellement préconisée par les auteurs de science-fiction – la distanciation cognitivo-critique opérant par un dépaysement radical amorcé en général dans les toutes premières lignes de l'œuvre –, puisque la proposition "Je me suis souvent retrouvé aveugle, hémiplégique également, mais la concomitance de plus en plus fréquente des deux types de crises commence à m'inquiéter", introduit une inintelligibilité par la présence de l'adverbe "souvent" et du syntagme "de plus en plus fréquente", associés à deux états physiologiques qui ne se vivent normalement pas de manière récurrente. Le lecteur, étonné, doit alors se référer à ses connaissances encyclopédiques (ou au paratexte [14]), afin de produire des inférences et donner du sens à ce qu'il lit. Il doit, en fait, inférer sur le mode du diagnostic pour saisir comment un homme peut être "souvent" aveugle et hémiplégique – il y a donc création de curiosité. Il faudra attendre les macro-propositions 7, 10 et surtout 12, pour que les inférences puissent prendre une coloration rationnelle et, partant, pour que la curiosité soit satisfaite, du moins en partie. Le lecteur a décrypté la conjecture et sait maintenant que Duane est un cyborg - les indices des macro-propositions 7 et 10, "un colosse d'un quintal et demi" ou "mes rouages internes", conduisent aux preuves explicites données par la macro-proposition 12 - mais l'effet thymique de la curiosité ne peut être dit entièrement épuisé, vu que le lecteur doit encore découvrir comment Duane est devenu un homme-machine et pourquoi il semble défectueux. Quant au second nœud [macro-proposition 3], il relève de la structure plus classique {nœud → dénouement}, car, à partir d'une incertitude (le héros va-t-il s'en tirer?), il plonge le lecteur dans l'attente et l'oblige à produire des inférences – mais sur le mode du pronostic cette fois-ci – pour imaginer, à partir des scénarii stéréotypés qu'il a mémorisés au cours de ses lectures antérieures, comment Duane va récupérer sa vue et sa motricité. Il y a donc, ici, création de suspense. Or, même si c'est la macro-proposition 13 qui met fin à ce dernier (après maints retards représentés par les macro-propositions 4, 6, 9 et 12, et les fausses résolutions des macro-propositions 5, 8 et 11), le lecteur est confronté à un dénouement un peu particulier. Il lui a en effet fallu, lors de son parcours de l'incipit, accepter la conjecture et rejeter ses schèmes diégétiques *a priori*, vu que ceux-ci postulent toujours la toute-puissance de l'homme-machine et, de ce fait, sont difficilement compatibles avec la situation d'un cyborg incapable de se lever de son lit sans explication extérieure. En ce sens, il est aisé de relever que si ces schèmes diégétiques *a priori* peuvent être court-circuités, c'est en raison de la nature même de la conjecture (un surhomme transformé en infra-homme). Celle-ci amorce une réflexion, existentielle, fondée sur le fait que la technoscience est avant tout une

---

[14] La quatrième de couverture, ou l'illustration de Manchu de l'édition utilisée, offrent déjà la clé de l'étrangeté science-fictionnelle: la puissance d'ébranlement de l'incipit est par conséquent fortement réduite.

dimension de l'agir humain perturbant, voire mettant en péril l'humanité des individus (et non une réflexion portant exclusivement sur le devenir actionnel d'un événement problématique: le handicap de Duane). La richesse réflexive de ce qui vient d'être mentionné est facilement perceptible dans le dénouement de la séquence étudiée. Celui-ci n'a en effet pas pour fonction d'affermir l'omnipotence de l'homme-machine (ce serait le cas dans les scénarii-clichés), mais, au contraire, de le montrer dans sa fragilité, dans son humanité, car, pour ne pas mourir, il doit choisir de risquer sa vie – dilemme qui s'incarne, diégétiquement, dans ce que Jean-Paul Sartre nomme une "situation-limite" [15] et dont la fonction est, par essence, de favoriser le questionnement du lecteur sur la condition humaine telle qu'elle est problématisée dans la situation décrite. Ici l'homme-machine ne restera humain qu'à condition d'être toujours en mesure d'exercer sa liberté:

> [Fin de la macro-proposition 12] Étape suivante: inciser. Ce genre de multilames est difficile à ouvrir, surtout quand on prétend dégager l'une des petites piques acérées et rarement usitées […] La main tremblant sous l'effort, je finis pourtant par réussir.
>
> L'euphorie s'évanouit dès que je me remémorai ce que je prévoyais de faire.
>
> [...] J'analysai une dernière fois la situation, en quête d'une alternative… et d'un ultime sursis. Évidemment, je n'en trouvai pas. Si ma folle entreprise était couronnée de succès, je pourrais m'estimer vernis. Dans le cas contraire, je n'aurais plus qu'à m'époumoner en priant pour que quelqu'un m'entende et se précipite à mon secours – hypothèse tristement illusoire. (Eschbach 2006, 12)

Cette brève analyse nous montre donc, d'une part, que l'incipit du roman d'Eschbach crée une tension narrative originale, ébauchée par une

[15] Ce concept, forgé en vue d'une nouvelle poétique dramaturgique, représente le choix existentiel que doit opérer un personnage, pris dans un monde et dans son parcours de vie, pour se découvrir liberté et se choisir dans son être. L'objectif visé par Sartre est essentiellement pragmatique: "éclaire[r] les principaux aspects de la condition humaine et […] faire participer le spectateur au libre choix que l'homme fait dans ces situations" (Sartre 1946, 57). Or, vu que ces situations "explore[nt] la condition [humaine] dans sa totalité et présente[nt] à l'homme contemporain un portrait de lui-même, ses problèmes, ses espoirs et ses luttes" (Sartre 1946, 61), il ne fait aucun doute qu'elles sont, pour Sartre, le vecteur idéal de toute prise en charge par le lecteur. Considérées comme les moments d'intensité où la subjectivité s'éprouve en tant que subjectivité, les situations-limites conduisent le spectateur à être ébranlé, à prendre conscience et à s'interroger sur les réalités problématiques de son temps.

dysphorie passionnante, qui, comme toute tension narrative, produit un effet thymique spécifique (le suspense) et conduit le lecteur, non à valider des hypothèses reposant sur des scénarii stéréotypés, mais à éprouver, par l'intermédiaire d'un narrateur autodiégétique, une situation-limite inattendue (dysphorie conclusive): le "cœur" de la science-fiction critique s'oriente ainsi vers une expérience existentielle. Cette situation-limite, autorisant le lecteur à accompagner le narrateur-personnage dans l'exercice de sa propre subjectivité, est, en fait, une des options de configurations textuelles les plus usitées dans les récits de science-fiction critique – à tel point qu'il me serait possible d'affirmer que la tension narrative au sein de ce genre littéraire, se dénoue toujours, micro-textuellement comme macro-textuellement, de cette manière:

$$\{\underline{\text{nœud :}}\ \text{apparence d'un scénario stéréotypé} \xrightarrow[\text{(suspense)}]{\text{(pronostic)}} \underline{\text{dénouement :}}\ \text{situation-limite}\}$$

D'autre part, l'analyse ponctuelle menée ci-dessus, associée aux résultats obtenus lors de l'analyse abstraite du processus conjectural (" pont référentiel", miroir décalé de la réalité), autorise à comprendre l'omniprésence du sentiment de curiosité dans la science-fiction critique, puisque ce sentiment, en premier lieu, pousse le lecteur à chercher l'origine thématique de la tension narrative (c'est-à-dire la conjecture technoscientifique) et, en second lieu, l'incite à revenir au monde à partir duquel cette conjecture a été formée: le sien. Un tel retour réflexif est peut-être une des stratégies textuelles les plus puissantes, surtout si elle est accordée avec une perspective narrative de type autodiégétique, pour conduire le lecteur à s'interroger, toujours sur le mode du diagnostic [16], sur les conséquences socio-anthropologiques des innovations ou des projets technoscientifiques. Ici, le "cœur" narratif représenté par la conjecture, se cristallise dans un "prisme" épistémologique, c'est-à-dire une multiplication des interrogations que le lecteur peut mener subjectivement sur les virtualités technoscientifiques:

---

[16] Il y a ici deux niveaux hiérarchisés de diagnostic: le premier s'identifie aux anticipations produites par le lecteur pour saisir l'origine thématique (la conjecture) de la situation-limite; le second, aux anticipations produites par ce même lecteur pour comprendre que le résultat du premier diagnostic est déjà une anticipation faite par un autre (le romancier) d'un état de fait antérieur (le monde réel). La conclusion est triviale: le premier diagnostic est la mise en abyme textuelle du second.

{dénouement : situation-limite $\xrightarrow[\text{(curiosité)}]{\text{(diagnostic)}}$ conjecture $\xrightarrow[\text{(réflexivité cognitivo-critique)}]{\text{(diagnostic)}}$ réflexion : monde réel}

Pour résumer, l'œuvre d'Eschbach, quoique limitée pour l'instant à son incipit, utilise diverses stratégies rhétoriques pour produire des effets thymiques (suspense, curiosité) et pour agencer la diégèse en vue d'instiller un questionnement critique: une double tension – narrative et réflexive – se fait alors jour. Or, il s'avère que l'ensemble du récit de l'écrivain allemand est construit sur le même *pattern* que celui adopté par l'incipit, puisque l'intrigue générale s'articule autour d'un nœud apparemment stéréotypé (on recherche Duane pour le mettre à mort) [17], qui se résoudra contre toutes attentes, dans un dénouement inédit. La situation-limite finale déjoue les pronostics élaborés et rend non-pertinent le scénario premier – Duane fuit pour survivre –, vu qu'il se donne la mort afin de devenir, finalement, humain. Au demeurant, on s'aperçoit que la double tension mise en lumière plus haut se retrouve ici aussi au centre de l'analyse: la tension narrative "standard" se résout après avoir créé un effet de suspense: on cherche Duane → il arrive tant bien que mal à se protéger *[...]* → il se tue pour sauver celle qu'il aime. Quant à la tension réflexive, elle se résout également lorsque l'effet de curiosité a reçu toutes les informations nécessaires pour ne plus pouvoir être alimenté: Duane est un cyborg dysfonctionnant → on apprend petit à petit ce qui lui est arrivé (rêves de toute-puissance, fiasco du projet "Steel Men", mort de ses compagnons, etc.) et on chemine avec lui dans sa quête existentielle → il a trouvé que pour recouvrer son humanité, il doit accomplir un acte purement altruiste, en l'occurrence, dans sa situation, se tuer par amour. Or, même si la tension narrative trouve dans la situation-limite finale du récit sa conclusion euphorique, la tension réflexive, elle, atteint son paroxysme. En effet, vécu par le lecteur en état d'immersion fictionnelle, ce dénouement, succédant à l'échec de l'évasion ultime tentée par Duane, propose au lecteur de revenir sur un mode critique à sa réalité, enrichi par le détour fictionnel:

> Quand Sénèque mourut, il eut ces mots: "C'est en homme accompli que je m'en vais". J'aimerais pouvoir m'exprimer ainsi. Je ne le peux pas. Pourtant, aujourd'hui, en prenant la ferme décision de vous [Bridget] protéger, j'étais habité pour la première fois d'un sentiment qui dépasse toutes les

[17] Un ancien soldat exilé à l'autre bout du monde et poursuivi pour être mis à mort, parce qu'il détient des secrets sur les recherches confidentielles menées par l'armée américaine: le scénario semble *a priori* peu original.

> peurs. Si dans ma vie je me suis trompé de route, je suis quand même arrivé là où elle m'est devenue précieuse. Je m'en vais à présent, et j'ose le dire: c'est en homme aimant que je m'en vais. Je pars le cœur plein d'amour, Bridget Keane. Où que vous alliez, je vous en prie, gardez-moi comme tel dans votre souvenir. Comme un homme qui était perdu et a été sauvé. Comme un homme que vous avez profondément touché, sans même jamais l'effleurer. (Eschbach 2006, 291-92)

Au seuil de sa mort, Duane découvre finalement un sens à sa vie et le lecteur, un sens à l'œuvre. En effet, ce dernier a suivi, tout au long du récit, "un homme qui était perdu" et qui s'est aliéné à lui-même, en accordant sa confiance aux rêves de grandeur qu'un système réifiant lui faisait miroiter. Puis, grâce à la situation-limite de la fin du roman, le lecteur, d'une part, éprouve l'intensité de sa subjectivité: il a compris, avec le narrateur [18], qu'il n'y avait "ni issue ni salut" (Eschbach 2006, 290) et il a fait le choix, toujours en la compagnie de ce dernier, de mourir – fictionnellement – en être humain. D'autre part, conjuguée à la vraisemblance de la conjecture romanesque, cette situation-limite aura probablement pour incidence de créer un malaise émotionnel. Ébranlé dans ses valeurs par l'agencement narratif et le décalage cognitif, le lecteur se voit conduit, en premier lieu, à se questionner sur ce qu'il aurait fait à la place de Duane et, en second lieu, à revenir, réflexivement, à l'origine de la distanciation – à son quotidien, donc. Pour le dire autrement, c'est parce que cette situation-limite anticipe sur des interrogations qui ne peuvent exister qu'à condition d'imaginer la technologie "cyborg" réalisée, que le lecteur est amené, grâce à la nature cognitivo-critique du décalage conjectural, à penser les technosciences et les technologies informant la sphère pratique: leurs projets, les directions qu'elles préconisent, les valeurs implicites sur lesquelles elles se fondent et les questions qu'elles passent, trop souvent peut-être, sous silence.

---

[18] Il est à noter que même si le narrateur-personnage est ici à la fois celui qui décrit la situation-limite dans laquelle il se trouve (rôle du narrateur) et celui qui la vit (rôle du personnage), les romans de science-fiction critique ne sont pas tous nécessairement construits autour d'une telle modalité narrative. Il s'avère que dans le cas extrême où le caractère de la fiction ne semblerait pas mettre à l'épreuve sa subjectivité (en ne réagissant pas à la situation-limite dans laquelle il se trouve, par exemple), le lecteur pourra quand même exercer la sienne: une situation-limite bien construite crée une tension réflexive qui pourra toujours être ressentie et prise en charge par le lecteur.

Il est temps de synthétiser le parcours suivi et d'étendre ce qui a été découvert à travers l'analyse de l'œuvre d'Andreas Eschbach, à la science-fiction critique – c'est-à-dire, il me faut le rappeler, l'ensemble des œuvres construites autour de conjectures plausibles relativement au paradigme technoscientifique en vigueur. Aux récits de science-fiction critique, et non à tous les récits de science-fiction, car si ces derniers inventent aussi un monde possible et racontent l'histoire de plusieurs individus dans ce même monde, seuls les premiers cristallisent dans une situation-limite, la description de l'univers fictionnel, les événements diégétiques et le parcours de vie des personnages. La plupart des récits de science-fiction critique regroupent en effet les éléments qui viennent d'être évoqués: une conjecture vraisemblable de nature technoscientifique, un monde possible aliénant [19], des narrateurs-personnages [20] nécessairement aliénés que l'on accompagne dans un parcours de vie rendu possible par la conjecture, et des situations-limites, également influencées par cette même conjecture, par le biais desquelles ces personnages pourront s'éprouver dans leur liberté. On peut au demeurant supposer que si la tension structurant le récit est orientée vers une situation-limite – indépendamment des avantages narratifs ressortissant à cette stratégie rhétorique –, c'est en raison de sa puissance à poser la question du sens: comment être un humain dans un tel univers? Qu'est-ce qui fait de nous des humains, si tout est réifié, instrumentalisé, réduit à la simple fonction de "moyens" en vue d'une "fin" inhumaine? Voilà le type de questions que les personnages de science-fiction critique se posent, mais ils ne sont pas les seuls. Et là, la matrice minimale d'intrigue, combinée avec le point de vue narratif en général utilisé, prouve sa véritable efficacité, puisqu'elle permet

[19] Ces mondes possibles sont, en règle générale, aliénants, car objectivés et objectivants : "objectivés", car les univers de la science-fiction critique sont construits sur des lois et des valeurs analogues à celles de notre réalité, en particulier sur la valeur technoscientifique du tout-objectivable; "objectivants", car ces mêmes univers mettent en scène des personnages à la recherche de toujours plus d'objectivité, attestant donc de la bénédiction, même inconsciente, que ces caractères témoignent aux propriétés de la société (néo)libérale et de la technoscience.

[20] Il est à noter que la science-fiction critique semble privilégier les narrations autodiégétiques qui ont entre autres pour vertus, (1) de favoriser l'immersion fictionnelle (le lecteur est celui-là même qui dit "je"), (2) d'induire chez le lecteur un malaise (ce qui est vécu par le personnage aliéné étant identique à ce qui est vécu par le lecteur, l'opposition de deux systèmes de valeurs n'en sera que plus grande) et (3) de prendre en charge subjectivement les questionnements produits par la subjectivité fictionnelle.

d'appréhender la pragmatique spécifique [21] d'un tel art de raconter. D'une part, la tension réflexive de la science-fiction critique autorise le lecteur à questionner les conséquences des progrès technoscientifiques grâce à l'articulation narrative des éléments suivants: narrateur-personnage aliéné pris dans son parcours de vie, mondes objectivés et objectivants, situations-limites. D'autre part, cette tension réflexive oriente le lecteur à se questionner sur le sens de son existence dans un monde technoscientifique et, si besoin est, à réévaluer la position qu'il a jusqu'alors adoptée face à celui-ci: la science-fiction critique ne dit pas ce qu'il faut faire ou ne pas faire, mais propose, grâce aux procédés formels mis au jour au fil de ce travail, de réfléchir à l'impensé qui, trop souvent, caractérise nos rapports à ce même monde. Pour le dire autrement, après tant d'années de désinvestissement théorique, il est temps de concevoir la science-fiction, en particulier dans sa veine "critique ", comme un "prisme" qui, en inversant la structure de l'imaginaire technoscientifique [22], accorde aux lecteurs de ne plus rêver à la gloire future des découvertes technoscientifiques, mais de penser, réflexivement, aux impacts socio-anthropologiques éventuels, ceux-là mêmes qu'imagine le "cœur" narratif représenté par la conjecture, qui pourraient venir ternir cette gloire supposée. En définitive, apprendre à se décentrer du projet technoscientifique, pourtant si séduisant, c'est apprendre à penser *autrement*: n'est-ce d'ailleurs pas ainsi qu'il nous faudrait, aujourd'hui plus que jamais, comprendre la science-fiction (critique)? Comme une littérature au service de la pensée?

## Références

Angenot, Marc. 2003. 'Le paradigme absent. Éléments d'une sémiotique de la science-fiction'. *Interventions critiques: Paralittératures, science-fiction, utopie.* 4:12. Montréal: Discours social/Social Discourse:193-214.

Atallah, Marc. 2008. Écrire demain, penser aujourd'hui. La Science-fiction à la croisée des disciplines: façonner une poétique, esquisser une pragmatique. Ph. D. Université de Lausanne.

[21] Je précise "spécifique" car, en leur qualité de fiction narrative, les récits de la science-fiction critique permettent aussi au lecteur, d'une part, de restructurer et re-décrire le réel, ses actions et son être-au-monde (Ricœur 2001, 2002) et, d'autre part, de vivre une autre vie dans un autre monde (Schaeffer 1999).

[22] En effet, l'imaginaire technoscientifique suit une direction prospective: présent → futur conjecturé. La science-fiction critique, quant à elle, parcourt le sens inverse: (présent →) futur conjecturé → présent.

Baroni, Raphael. 2007. *La Tension narrative. Suspense, curiosité et surprise*. Paris: Seuil.
Eschbach, Andreas. 2006. *Le Dernier de son espèce*. Nantes: L'Atalante.
Langlet, Irène. 2006. *La Science-fiction. Lecture et poétique d'un genre littéraire*. Paris: Armand Colin.
Ricœur, Paul. 1983. *Temps et récit. 1. L'intrigue et le récit historique*. Paris: Seuil.
Ricœur, Paul. 1975. *La Métaphore vive*. Paris: Seuil.
Saint-Gelais, Richard. 1999. *L'Empire du pseudo. Modernités de la science-fiction*. Québec: Nota Bene (Littérature(s)).
Sartre, Jean-Paul. 1946. "Forger des mythes". In Contat, Michel and Rybalka, Michel (eds). 1973. *Un théâtre de situations*. Paris: Gallimard.
Schaeffer, Jean-Marie. 1999. *Pourquoi la fiction ?* Paris: Seuil.
Snow, C. P. 1959. *The Two Cultures*. Cambridge/New York: Cambridge University Press.
Suvin, Darko. 1977. *Pour une poétique de la science-fiction*. Montréal: Les Presses de l'Université du Québec.
Versins, Pierre.1972. *Encyclopédie de l'utopie, des voyages extraordinaires et de la science-fiction*. Lausanne: L'Âge d'Homme.
Warwick, Kevin. 2002. *I, Cyborg*. London: Century.

# CHAPTER TWENTY

# TELLING NEW STORIES? *TWILIGHT* FAN FICTION PAIRING BELLA AND ALICE

MALIN ISAKSSON

Stephenie Meyer's *Twilight* saga about true and everlasting love between the college girl Bella and the beautiful vampire Edward has captured readers and film viewers all over the world. The commercial success of the *Twilight* saga is not the only sign of its popularity among readers and viewers. The large amount of fan fictions about the characters from the *Twilight* universe also show that readers and viewers not only appreciate the saga but also actively engage with the stories about the rather ordinary Bella and her extraordinary boyfriend with whom she eventually, once Edward has turned her into a vampire, shares a love that will literally never die.

Fan fiction authors develop aspects of an existing fictional universe, filling in the gaps of the narrative, rewriting plotlines or creating stories which focus on new couples, or new "pairings" to use established fanfic terminology. Twilight fan fictions inscribe themselves within the *Twilight* universe, which includes Meyer's four novels, *Twilight* (2005), *New Moon* (2006), *Eclipse* (2007) and *Breaking Dawn* (2008), as well as the film adaptations.[1] Two other texts by Meyer are a part of the Twilight universe, namely her unpublished novel *Midnight Sun* (accessible on her official website), in which the events from *New Moon* are related from Edward's point of view, and *The Short Second Life of Bree Tanner: An Eclipse Novella* (2010), about a peripheral character from the Twilight saga. This established fictional universe is referred to, both by fans and by fan studies scholars, as the "canon". Although fan fiction is a free text form, a general

---

[1] The Twilight Saga films are: *Twilight* (Hardwicke 2008), *New Moon* (Weitz 2009), *Eclipse* (Slade 2010), *Breaking Dawn Part I* (Condon 2011), and *Breaking Dawn Part 2* (Condon 2012).

"rule" stipulates that fanfic authors should respect the canon's internal logic and characterisations or clearly signal when they depart from it, for instance by indicating that a character in the fanfic is OOC ("out of character") or that a story is situated in an "alternative universe" (which is often a "what if"-scenario or narrative situated beyond the ending of the canon). By creating their own stories about characters from an already existing fictional world, fanfic writers are both producers and consumers within a "participatory culture" which, as Henry Jenkins writes, "contrasts with older notions of passive media spectatorship" (2006, 3).

Analyses of fanfic texts often show that the fan fiction authors are skilled close readers of the source texts they engage with. This suggests that fan fiction writing involves a mix of what Marie-Laure Ryan (2001) calls "immersion" in a fictional world on the one hand and, on the other, enough critical distance to analyse the source texts in order to create derivative works based on them. As Tzvetan Todorov argued in relation to the debate on the importance of emotionally engaged reading, being captivated by a story and its "péripéties" does not entail a passive reading:

> [...] les péripéties vécues par les personnages du roman ou les métaphores du poète se prêtent à des interprétations multiples. En figurant un objet, un événement, un caractère, l'écrivain n'assène pas une thèse, mais incite le lecteur à la formuler: il propose plutôt qu'il n'impose, il laisse donc son lecteur libre et en même temps l'incite à devenir plus actif. (Todorov 2007, 74)

This *incitation à l'interprétation* that an engaging story may inspire is aptly illustrated by the *Twilight* fan fictions discussed in this chapter. Even as they present new twists to some of the plots and the central characters, femslash texts still bear resemblances to the fictional universe that sparked their authors' imagination.

Fan fictions as rewritings follow a long tradition of derivative creations of various kinds and are thus by no means new phenomena *per se*. The novelty is connected to the medium: fan fictions are more easily and widely circulated than pre-internet productions. Most fanfic texts resemble word-processed texts in general, which is to say that their authors do not use the technological possibilities of the new, rhizomatic medium. The ways in which fanfic authors elaborate features of an existing fictional world also mirror well-known strategies of rewriting, such as the creation of prequels and sequels, shifting narrative perspectives or altered endings. The new mode of circulating these texts does however influence forms of writing. Specific fan fiction categories and a framework of writing conventions have been established, such as *femslash* and *slash*.[2] Femslash texts are homoerotic stories about female characters which do not have that kind of relationship in the canon, and slash designates fanfic about male couplings.

The questions I want to address are, firstly, to what extent the femslash fan fictions are telling *new* stories, both in relation to the *Twilight* saga and to popular romance. Secondly, I want to touch upon what the similarities and dissimilarities may say about the interpretation and reception of Meyer's stories. The three selected fan fictions are of different kinds and situate themselves at different points in relation to the *Twilight* canon. Unlike Meyer's novels, they are all third-person narratives with the shifting focalisation that is characteristic of romance stories. Meyer's four novels about Bella and Edward are first-person narratives related from Bella's point of view (with the exception of a number of chapters in the fourth novel, *Breaking Dawn*, narrated by Jacob). *The Edge* is a novel-length fan fiction in which the story "[t]akes place during the summer at the beginning of 'New Moon'" (the second novel of the Twilight quartet) according to the introductory note by the author, fembuck/Janine.[3] (Following established fan fiction conventions, the authors publish under pseudonyms, or user names.) *Destroy This*, by LostInTheWorld. ColdAndAlone, takes as its starting point the fourth novel, *Breaking Dawn*. *On y arrivera*, by Juline's, is an AU-all human fanfic, which means that the story is set in an alternative universe in which all the Twilight characters are human.

## Homoerotic Fan Fiction, Heteronormative Source Text

The selected fan fictions differ from the source texts in one rather fundamental way, since they are femslash texts. Femslash draws on a perceived homoerotic tension between characters in the canon, or "the sexually hypothetical", to use film theorist Chris Straayer's term (1996, 9-22).[4] To paraphrase Roland Barthes, one might talk about *les endroits où*

[2] The genre 'slash' takes its name from the sign "/" used by fan fiction writers to indicate which characters are paired (e.g. Edward/Jacob).

[3] The author uses both pseudonyms as author name(s) in links to and headings of this fan fiction. Henceforth, I will refer to her as 'fembuck', the name under which her fanfics are regrouped on fanfiction.net.

[4] Straayer uses this term to describe homoerotic inferences made about characters in films, but it applies to novels and other texts as well.

*le texte bâille*,[5] the appealing instances of "mise en scène d'une apparition-disparition" (Barthes 1973, 19). Femslash authors, then, develop stories which build on such "*entrebâillements*" in the canon. Meyer's novels revolve around the love between Bella, an ordinary and somewhat clumsy college girl, and the extraordinarily beautiful vampire Edward who tries to pass as human together with his coven of "vegetarian" vampires (feeding exclusively on animal blood) who call themselves a family: the Cullens.[6] Edward, who first meets Bella in the classroom, is drawn to her by her delicious scent which is repeatedly referred to as his "brand of heroin" (e.g. Meyer 2005, 234-5) although all other vampires are sensitive to it as well. They become a couple – a very chaste one, since Edward does not dare have sex with such a "breakable" creature for fear of losing control when aroused. While the literary vampire is traditionally portrayed as a threatening creature associated with dangerous or transgressive sexuality, Meyer's central vampire character, Edward, controls his sexual lust as well as his bloodlust and insists that Bella marries him before they have sexual intercourse. Bella spends a lot of time with Edward, unbeknownst to her at night, since he likes to watch over her as she sleeps, but also with his family, and particularly with Edward's sister Alice. Alice takes Bella shopping, buys her expensive designer clothes and takes her for joyrides in fast cars. Furthermore, Alice is frequently asked to "babysit" Bella, for instance by staging sleepovers, when Edward has to leave town in order to handle menacing creatures that threaten Bella or the town of Forks.

The femslash authors use a number of more or less open intertextual references to the canon in order to explain how Bella and Alice's friendship transforms into a romantic relationship. *The Edge* opens with a scene in Bella's bedroom at night. Alice suddenly climbs through the window to check on Bella since Edward is out of town. Alice thus functions as the "baby-sitter" she often is in the canon. At the same time, she takes on Edward's role as Bella's night watcher (using, like him, Bella's bedroom window as a discreet entrance). Furthermore, Bella's

---

[5] The quotation I am referring to reads: "L'endroit le plus érotique d'un corps n'est-il pas là où le vêtement bâille? [...] c'est ce scintillement même qui séduit, ou encore: la mise en scène d'une apparition-disparition" (Barthes 1973, 19).

[6] The Cullens are not biologically a family, but for mainstreaming reasons they present themselves as one. Carlisle and Esme, a couple of middle-aged looking vampires, pose as the adoptive parents of Rosalie, Alice and Edward. (Metaphorically, Carlisle is Rosalie's and Edward's father, or their "creator", since he is the one who turned them into vampires). Together with Rosalie's and Alice's partners, Emmett and Jasper, the Cullens form a coven which is protective of, rather than threatening to, the humans in the town of Forks.

compelling scent plays an important role in this fanfic, as it does in Meyer's novels. Since all vampires find Bella's scent extraordinary, it seems only logical that this is what attracts Alice in *The Edge*. As Alice gets physically very close to Bella during a playful wrestling-and-tickling game, she cannot restrain herself from briefly placing her mouth on Bella's throat. This proximity is too much for vampire Alice who has to catch a breath of fresh air by the window and eventually go hunting, that is, feed on animal blood. In this scene, Alice performs the same functions as Edward does in the canon, which creates a logical setting and atmosphere for the femslash story.

Bloodlust is closely connected to sexual lust in this fan fiction, as it is in the canon, but where the love scenes in Meyer's novels are rather elliptical, the sexual and vampiric desires in *The Edge* are related in graphic detail. Alice's self-control is in line both with Meyer's depiction of the Cullens as "vegetarians" and with Edward's self-restraint in erotically charged scenes with Bella. After the near-fatal scenario in Bella's bedroom, Alice tries to declare her feelings for Bella through a couple of embarrassed hints, one of which refers to Bella's special scent. Bella is confused and replies: "But you *all* want to bite me". Alice then provides a more specific explanation:

> "I wanted to bite you Bella, but I wanted to kiss you too," she said, the memory of her tongue licking Bella's throat causing her to turn her head away, in order to calm herself down. "I wanted you naked, and sweating, twisting underneath me, wet and desperate as your blood flowed into my mouth". (*The Edge*, Ch. 2)

The description of Alice's desires stands in contrast to that of Edward's corresponding desires in the canon not only because it is graphically sexual, but also because Alice here overtly expresses her desire to drink Bella's blood. Her pronouncement transgresses the "rules" of Meyer's romantic and chaste heteronormative universe, by being explicit, by illustrating a homoerotic desire and by depicting a "vegetarian" vampire wanting to drink human blood for the pleasure of it.

In the *Twilight* canon, Alice and Bella share a friendship which includes physical closeness, but they are also part of a heteronormative text world. The whole *Twilight* saga revolves around Bella and Edward's love and, although there is no explicit condemnation of same-sex love, no homosexual desires or couples are visible. Fembuck and LostInTheWorld. ColdAndAlone, who situate their stories within the canon, rather than in an alternative universe, acknowledge the canon's heteronormative framework even as they negotiate it. The "sexually hypothetical" which slash writers draw on to develop romantic relationships, are often homosocial bonds in the canon, or even "years of shared history and emotional entanglement", as Anne Kustritz states in her analysis of male slash (Kustritz 2003, 378). This statement is valid for femslash as well, but rather than years of shared history, femslash pairings of female characters may rely on depictions of friendships which include a physical proximity. Such friendships are easily read as ambiguous, or as "la mise en scène d'une apparition-disparition" to use Barthes' expression (1973, 19). In *Destroy This*, LostInTheWorld.ColdAndAlone refers to the close bond between Bella and Alice, as Bella thinks about Alice and "[a]ll the sleepovers, the hugs, kisses on my cheek" (Ch. 1). These events are described as "so normal and friendly". By contrast, the ambiguous *déclaration d'amour* "I love you", which Alice leaves on a hidden note for Bella, is somewhat disturbing for the latter. "I hoped I could assume that what she wrote was of that same friendly nature", she thinks (ibid.). From Bella's point of view in this fanfic, romantic love between women is clearly not normal which suggests that the character is immersed in the heteronormative framework that characterises the canon. Moreover, Bella's spontaneous reaction to Alice's expressed desire for her emphasizes the central part that her relationship with Edward plays in the canon: "Your note...you know I truly love Edward, right?" (ibid.). The initial attitude ascribed to Bella and Alice in this text is thus that heterosexual couplings are the normal state of love affairs. This norm is of course challenged, since femslash stories describe homosexual couples.

If Bella and Alice's initial hesitation regarding lesbian love is an attitude which reflects the framework of the *Twilight* saga, other traits from Meyer's text world serve to legitimate their new kind of relationship in the femslash texts. Fembuck refers to Bella's constantly restrained lust in erotic situations with Edward: "The truth was that she sometimes felt like an oversexed manic [sic] for touching his chest or tangling her fingers in his hair when they kissed" (*The Edge*, Ch. 2). This line underscores that Bella does not fit perfectly into the mould of appropriate sexual behaviour and desires which in the novels is shaped by Edward's standards. Fembuck draws on the "oversexed maniac" side of Bella, then, to explain why she feels aroused by Alice's wish to see her "naked, and sweating, twisting underneath [her]" rather than "scandalized and vaguely horrified", which Bella considers a more appropriate reaction (ibid.). Moreover, Bella is described as "overwhelmed and aroused" by Alice's words, because

> [s]he had never heard anything like that directed at her before (in fact, she'd never heard anything like that directed at *anyone* before). Edward

> had certainly never said anything remotely like that to her, and she had a hard time fathoming him ever doing so (*The Edge*, Ch. 2)

In this femslash, Alice responds to Bella's suppressed longing to express her desires physically, which Edward does not in the canon. Kustritz notes that an important theme of slash fan fiction is "an individual's desire to be recognized completely by another, to drop the pretense of an image, and to be accepted as a total human being, complete with imperfections and infractions" (Kustritz 2003, 379). Fembuck's portrayal of how Alice and Bella discover their mutual attraction is in line with Kustritz' observation regarding male/male slash: Alice accepts and welcomes Bella's wish to express her sexuality which, in the canon, is repressed by Edward.

Femslash, like its male counterpart slash, expresses resistance both to the heteronorm in today's popular culture in general and, in this case, to the very strong heteronorm in the *Twilight* universe. However, these text-types are not necessarily subversive, as Christine Scodari shows in her discussions of early fan scholars' slightly over-enthusiastic claims according to which slash as a genre is counter-hegemonic *per se* because it is "a way for female fans to envision an egalitarian romance" (Scodari 2003, 112).[7] In fact, a heteronormative canon may set certain limits to the fan production, as Maria Lindgren Leavenworth demonstrates in her analysis of slash about male characters from J.R. Ward's vampire romance novels *The Black Dagger Brotherhood.* In these fanfics, homoerotic encounters are relegated to "metaphorical spaces" (Lindgren Leavenworth 2009, 450), such as dreams or erasable moments, which allows for realization of homoerotic desires between characters that remain firmly heterosexual. By contrast, the femslash texts analysed here describe how the changes in Alice and Bella's relationship lead to a new lifestyle (with the exception of *On y arrivera* whose "alternative universe" posits both characters as lesbian from the outset) and, importantly, to the questioning of patriarchal ideals of love, as represented by the century-old vampire Edward. To a certain extent, love stories about female couples do encourage reworkings of conventional gender role patterns. Diana Holmes, discussing lesbian romance novels, points out that

> […] when the distribution of activity/passivity, or hardness/softness between two characters is no longer tied to gender, it can be deployed to

[7] The vast majority of fan fiction writers are women, according to studies of fan communities (e.g. Jenkins 1992, Bacon-Smith 1992, Pugh 2005).

> create a sense of complementarity in love without at the same time confirming deeply rooted social inequalities. (Holmes 2006, 128)

The femslash texts illustrate both "complementarity in love" and equality between the lovers. This combination is easier to play out within the female couple Bella and Alice than within the gender-power imbalanced couple Bella and Edward that readers know from the canon. This suggests that the femslash genre has a certain subversive potential regarding stories situated within a framework of conventional romance, although femslash authors also use formulaic patterns and stereotypical representations.

## Romance Respected and Revisited

A central element of the romance narrative, be it highbrow romance, Harlequin publications, or *Twilight* saga, is the presence of obstacles which the lovers have to overcome. In the femslash stories, one such obstacle is the fact that Alice and Bella are two women in love. This obstacle is easily overcome, despite initial hesitations, in the two fan fictions situated within the frame of the canon, *Destroy This* and *The Edge*. By contrast, the all-human fan fiction *On y arrivera* has a strong emphasis on lesbian identity, politics and the potentially problematic aspects of expressing same-sex desires. Placing Bella and human Alice in a contemporary, "realist" setting, without fantastic elements, the author thus addresses real-life issues. The difficulties of living in a same-sex relationship are alluded to already in the title, according to the résumé provided by the author: "Oui toutes les deux ensemble, on y arrivera. On se construira ensemble. Et on emmerdera ceux qui ne l'accepte [sic] pas ensemble". This "it" that others will or will not accept is of course the lesbian relationship. In this fanfic it is indirectly Bella's fear of being outed that constitutes the obstacle to a love story with Alice. Bella has left Forks for Port Angeles to be able to live openly as a lesbian which she cannot do in her hometown, for fear of being judged by her family and peers: "La peur du regard des autres, qu'ils changent d'attitude s'ils savaient. La peur de la réaction de mon père, des gens à la fac. Tout, je suis effrayée" (*On y arrivera*, Ch. 5). The ending of this fanfic shows how Bella is ready for true commitment with Alice rather than a brief relation, which is the kind of liaison she usually prefers since it is easier to hide from her parents. Bella's parents know nothing of Bella's new love, however, while Alice's parents, Carlisle and Esme, were already aware of Alice's lifestyle and seem happy that she and Bella have found each other. Whether the ending is "happy" or not is thus a matter of interpretation:

Bella does "get the girl" but it is an open question whether this true love will lead her out of the closet.

In contrast to the narrative patterns of conventional romance, the true love myth is used in the femslash texts to break the "rule" of heterosexual romance, and more specifically to criticize the values represented by Edward. Some critics have applauded Meyer's portrayal of a young adult couple where the woman is the one taking sexual initiatives while the male partner takes on the traditionally feminine role of being responsible for abstinence.[8] Feminist critic Christine Seifert (2008), on the other hand, argues that this allocation of roles diminishes Bella's agency and further stresses the unequal gender power balance between the two characters. The violent consummation of the young couple's love depicted in *Breaking Dawn* (Meyer 2008, 81-88) is particularly problematic, according to Seifert. The morning after the wedding night, Bella, still human, is described as sore and severely bruised, lying in the midst of torn-up pillows, trying to anticipate Edward's anger and frustration, for instance by concealing the worst bruises. In the femslash texts, sexual encounters between vampire Alice and human Bella are described as relatively unproblematic; despite the close connection between lust and bloodlust, which is at least as explicit here as it is in the canon, vampire Alice does not harm Bella. Hence, the sexual abstinence that Bella perceives as problematic in the canon, is unnecessary in the femslash stories. Alice is described as better for Bella in several other respects as well. LostInTheWorld.ColdAndAlone challenges the idea that Edward is "perfect" for Bella, by using two intertextual links to the canon: firstly, the fact that Edward leaves Bella for a longer period of time (in Meyer's novel *New Moon*) which sends Bella into a deep depression and, secondly, Edward's constant concern for Bella's safety, even in his company, since she is so "breakable", particularly in erotic situations. Alice, on the other hand, is "never questioning her ability to protect me", Bella says (*Destroy This,* Ch. 3), including in sexual situations. The author adds the interpretation that Alice's devotion "has *always* been more about [Bella's] feelings", which suggests that this is not true in Edward's case. Moreover, from a parental and rather humorous perspective, Bella's relationship with a girl means she does not run the risk of "end[ing] up knocked up", as her father Charlie puts it (*The Edge*, Ch. 24). By depicting Alice as Bella's *real* true love, the femslash authors criticise the values Edward represents, thus questioning core features of the *Twilight* universe (as well as of

---

[8] See e.g. Flanagan 2008.

traditional romance): heterosexual love and protective (or controlling) male partners.

The femslash authors recuperate some of the vampiric traits which are downplayed in the *Twilight* universe, where they are associated with evil vampires rather than with the good and de-fanged Cullens. Vampirism is closely connected to sexuality in the canon, but in a way which goes against previous vampire tropes since Edward's vampirism is a reason for abstinence rather than for the unbridled and dangerous sexuality traditionally associated with vampires. Alice is portrayed as even less vampiric than Edward in the *Twilight* novels and films. Her primary strength is her special "gift" of precognition. She remembers very little from her human life, having spent most of it in a mental institution. Fembuck elaborates on Alice's absence of memories to explain why she, unlike the rest of the Cullens, finds being a vampire rather unproblematic: "... when she had woken up a vampire she'd had very few hang ups. There were no lectures from mom, or the Reverend or a school teacher in her head telling her what was right and what was wrong, and what was normal and what was abnormal" (*The Edge*, Ch. 22). Here, this means that Alice can easily accept lesbian desires, and also that she has no moral objection to pre-marital sex, or to vampire-human sex, for that matter. The femslash author thus uses vampiric features in a more traditional way than Meyer, linking them to sexual practices that can be seen as "immoral", at least by *Twilight* canon standards. More importantly, Alice's lack of "hang ups" regarding her vampire state means that she can fulfil Bella's wish to be turned into a vampire: Alice does not believe that vampires are soulless creatures, as Edward does. The portrayal of Bella's transformation alludes to a marriage, Alice being escorted towards Bella by her father, Carlisle, and Bella feeling "like a bride on her wedding night" (Ch. 28). Alice's vampiric bite, then, is closely linked both to unrestrained sex and to strong, marriage-like bonds of love.[9] In these respects, the narrative patterns in the femslash text mirror those of traditional romance, where the heroine's sexual desires as well as her dreams of committed love are fulfilled by her true love.

---

[9] Alice and Bella do not consecrate their love by marriage in this story, although the similarities between their relationship and conventional marriage are further stressed by the ending of *The Edge* which shows Alice and Bella on their way to Esme Island, the place for Bella and Edward's honeymoon in Meyer's *Breaking Dawn*. Whether this suggests that certain rules are hard to transgress even in an alternative fanfic world or, on the contrary, that same-sex relationships should remain "alternative" rather than conform to the heteronorm that underpins marriage, is an open question.

## New stories?

The femslash authors discussed in this chapter are telling new stories in one rather crucial sense: they choose to break the very strong bond between Bella and Edward which constitutes the narrative centre of the whole *Twilight* saga, thus challenging its heteronormative framework. Various staples of the romance are used to renegotiate the heteronorm: as true love prevails in Alice/Bella femslash, same-sex love surmounts the obstacle of "compulsory heterosexuality", to use Adrienne Rich's expression, and furthermore questions the importance of marriage. Depicting the new lover as extraordinary also evokes romance tropes, but here, the trope serves to question features associated with traditional romance, and, more specifically, with Edward. The femslash texts can thus be read as a kind of feminist critique of the patriarchal values, including heteronormativity, which permeate the *Twilight* saga.

Explicit and graphically described sex scenes, including some kinky sex, are frequent in the femslash texts. In this respect, they bear more resemblance to popular romance and erotica than to the chaste *Twilight* novels which have been labelled "abstinence porn" (Seifert 2008). Perhaps such a text world is particularly inspiring for readings against the grain, as Barthes suggests:

> Plus une histoire est racontée d'une façon bienséante, bien disante, sans malice, sur un ton confit, plus il est facile de la retourner, de la noircir, de la lire à l'envers (Mme de Ségur lue par Sade). Ce renversement, étant une pure production, développe superbement le plaisir du texte. (Barthes 1973, 44)

The "renversement" in this case results in a concrete "production": a number of explicit sex scenes involving Bella and Alice. By spicing things up, yet remaining within a romance framework, the femslash authors grant Bella more agency than she has in the canon, while simultaneously emphasizing how perfect a partner her true love Alice is, since she fulfils Bella's wishes. The intimate connection between bloodlust and sexual lust is more explicit and, importantly, less problematic in the femslash stories than in the canon. Through the recuperation of the vampiric, bloodlust as well as unbridled sexuality are legitimised in ways that seem impossible in the canon, since the morally high-standing vampires in Meyer's novels do not want to harm "breakable" humans.

The all-human femslash *On y arrivera* turns away from the canon more radically than the other stories, not only because Meyer's already tamed vampires have been completely de-fanged, but also because the lesbian love story has clear political connotations. Furthermore, the all-human setting allows for a different allocation of roles in comparison to the vampire/human coupling in the other femslash texts. In *On y arrivera*, Bella is described as a sexually experienced young woman who is used to taking initiatives and also to being the active partner in sexual situations, while Fembuck and LostInTheWorld.ColdAndAlone portray her as something of a *oie blanche* compared to Alice who is much more knowledgeable (because of her hundred-or-so years of existence).

Fan fiction authors present variations on a theme, or new readings and interpretations of existing texts, thus adding associations and perspectives to the Derridean "archive" of possible texts, as fan fiction scholar Abigail Derecho suggests (2006, 64). The femslash authors discussed here have chosen to provide Bella with more agency, to criticize Edward's old-fashioned views on love, and to let Bella leave the limiting relationship with Edward for a romance with a female vampire capable of having (great) sex with the human girl Bella without hurting her and, furthermore, of respecting and fulfilling Bella's wish to be turned into a vampire. By their focus on a love story involving True Love, strong commitment, sexual and emotional fulfilment, the femslash stories evoke both old and new stories told and retold within the framework of formulaic romance as well as in more "literary" contexts. Compared to the *Twilight* saga, these fan-authored stories do however present new perspectives on the female characters – especially the central character Bella – as well as on romantic love. Perhaps these representations of a young woman and of romantic relationships correspond better to what the femslash authors appreciate in love stories than the traditional, gender-power unbalanced heterosexual romance in the *Twilight* canon.

## Works cited

Bacon-Smith, Camille. 1992. *Enterprising Women: Television Fandom and the Creation of Popular Myth.* Philadelphia: University of Pennsylvania Press.

Barthes, Roland. 1973. *Le Plaisir du texte*. Paris: Seuil. Derecho, Abigail. 2006. "Archontic Literature: A Definition, a History, and Several Theories of Fan Fiction". In *Fan Fiction and Fan Communities in the Age of the Internet*, edited by Karen Hellekson and Kristina Busse, 61-78. Jefferson: McFarland.fembuck. 2008. *The Edge*. Accessed 10 June 2012. http://fembuck.livejournal.com/204275.html?mode=reply

Flanagan, Caitlin. 2008. "What Girls Want". *Atlantic Monthly*, Dec., 108-120.

Holmes, Diana. 2006. *Romance and Readership in Twentieth-Century France: Love Stories*. Oxford: Oxford University Press.
Jenkins, Henry. 1992. *Textual Poachers: Television Fans and Participatory Culture.* New York: Routledge.
—. 2006. *Convergence Culture: Where Old and New Media Collide.* New York and London: New York University Press.
Juline's. 2010. *On y arrivera*. Accessed 10 June 2012. http://slayerstime.net/twilight/juline-s-on-y-arrivera-alice-bella-nc17-oui-toutes-les-deux-ensemble-on-y-arrivera-3011.html
Kustritz, Anne. 2003. "Slashing the Romance Narrative". *The Journal of American Culture* 26:3 (September): 371-84.
Lindgren Leavenworth, Maria. 2009. "Lover Revamped: Sexualities and Romance in the Black Dagger Brotherhood and Slash Fan Fiction". *Extrapolation* 50:3 (Fall): 442-62.
—. 2011. "Variations, Subversions and Endless Love: Fan Fiction and the *Twilight* Saga". In *Bringing Light to Twilight: Perspectives on a Pop Culture Phenomenon*, edited by Giselle Anatol, 69-81. Palgrave Macmillan.
LostInTheWorld.ColdAndAlone. 2008. *Destroy This*. Accessed 10 June 2012. http://www.fanfiction.net/s/4611262/1/Destroy_This_An_Alice_and_Bella_Fanfiction
Meyer, Stephenie. 2005.*Twilight*. New York: Little, Brown and Company.
—. 2006. *New Moon*. New York: Little, Brown and Company.
—. 2007. *Eclipse*. New York: Little, Brown and Company.
—. 2008. *Breaking Dawn*. New York: Little, Brown and Company.
—. 2008. *Midnight Sun*. Accessed 10 June 2012. http://www.stepheniemeyer.com/midnightsun.html
—. 2010. *The Short Second Life of Bree Tanner: An Eclipse Novella*. New York: Little, Brown and Company.
Pugh, Sheenagh. 2005. *The Democratic Genre: Fan Fiction in a Literary Context*. Bridgend: Seren.
Rich, Adrienne. 1980. "Compulsory Heterosexuality and Lesbian Existence". *Signs* 5:4 (Summer): 631-660.
Ryan, Marie-Laure. 2001. *Narrative as Virtual Reality: Immersion and Interactivity in Literature and Electronic Media*. Baltimore and London: Johns Hopkins University Press.
Scodari, Christine. 2003. "Resistance Re-Examined: Gender, Fan Practices, and Science Fiction Television". *Popular Communication: The International Journal of Media and Culture* 1:2, 111-130, doi: 10.1207/S15405710PC0102_3

Seifert, Christine. 2008. "Bite me! (Or Don't)". *Bitch Magazine*. Accessed 10 June 2012. http://bitchmagazine.org/article/bite-me-or-dont
Straayer, Chris. 1996. *Deviant Eyes, Deviant Bodies: Sexual Re-Orientation in Film and Video*. New York: Columbia University Press.
Todorov, Tzvetan. 2007. *La Littérature en péril*. Paris: Flammarion.

# CHAPTER TWENTY-ONE

# DAN BROWN, OR THE PARALITERARY AS THE GREAT CODE OF LITERATURE

ALEXANDRA IVANOVITCH

In the beginning of the *Da Vinci Code* were the apocryphal gospels of Philip and Mary. As Leigh Teabing, an expert on the Holy Grail consulted by the novel's two investigators, explains in the novel's central section at the Château de Villette, these texts narrate an incredible side of the gospel story that the Biblical canon and doctrinal orthodoxy have tried to occult: the alleged love story between Jesus and Mary Magdalen. In a seminal article, Tzvetan Todorov explains that the enigma novel, or to put it differently the "whodunit", is nothing but a long search for a lost text, a "pre-text" which tells of the crime motivating the investigation conducted in the actual novel (Todorov 1991: 11). So Dan Brown's novel is about apocryphal texts, in every sense of the word: in the Biblical sense, on the one hand, because according to Leigh Teabing's faulty exegesis, the ultimate revelation is kept in those two Gnostic gospels, and on the other hand, in the etymological sense of the term – "secret", "occult" – because it deals with a primitive narrative which is hidden and needs to be brought to light, thus corresponding to Todorov's analysis of the detective story and its variants. In the novel, the ultimate enigma associated with the Holy Grail, that is, Jesus's humanity, is everywhere to be seen: it is embodied in the work of the masters in literature and art in general, from Botticelli to Victor Hugo, through Mozart, but also in mass culture (Brown 2004, 270-71). Dan Brown's best-seller can be qualified as a "paraliterary masterpiece", paradoxical as this expression may be, because it offers an extensive rereading of "high" and "low" literature and art in its most accomplished forms, as well as in its most popular manifestations. The reader's pleasure comes from the reading grid of literature the thriller provides – a good illustration of what Daniel Couégnas terms the "profound superficiality" of the paraliterary (Couégnas 1991, 102). The mystery surrounding the success of the *Da Vinci Code* is associated with the mystery of the relationships between "low" and "high" art, between the queenly literary forms, and their bastard paraliterary siblings. Hence the question which will underlie our analysis: to borrow the words of Northrop Frye, which are themselves a reference to William Blake's famous sibylline aphorism[1], could the *Da Vinci Code* be the "Great Code" of Art?

Before developing this analysis, in a methodological aside, let us specify that we rely on Daniel Couégnas's critical works when using the terms "paraliterary" and "paraliterature", terms which Couégnas himself qualifies as a "Pandora's box" (Couégnas 1992, 11). Choosing this set of terms appears crucial, in spite of – or rather, because of – its assumptions, on which Dan Brown's novel plays, as we shall try to show. Far from seeing in this notion the paradigm of so-called "poor literature", Alain-Michel Boyer sees in it a "concept opératoire [...] grâce auquel, sans que l'on puisse accepter l'idée qu'une telle dichotomie reflète une distribution sociale des cultures, il devient possible de reconsidérer les deux ensembles littérature/paralittérature l'un en fonction de l'autre" (Boyer 1994, 131-132). Furthermore, thanks to this morphological parallelism, the term "paraliterature" allows us to confront two groups of texts which stand at the gates of both biblical and literary canons: the apocrypha and the so-called paraliterary novels. And the *Da Vinci Code* is precisely where the parabiblical and the paraliterary converge. In *La Séduction de la pseudo-vérité*, Friar Silouane Ponga asserts that "Le *Da Vinci Code* […] est donc une séduction romanesque porteuse d'une pseudo-vérité sur le Christ et sur l'Eglise, une anti-Bible qui est aussi anti-Christ" (Ponga 2006, 52-3). The major question our analysis will tackle is precisely the one that haunts all incredulous exegetes of this theological thriller, this best-seller of best-sellers: how can we explain the fact that the novel encountered such a massive success?

The *Da Vinci Code* narrates the investigation led by Professor Langdon and Sophie Neveu into a murder in the Louvre; the two quickly get involved in the battle opposing the Opus Dei and the Priory of Sion over the existence of the descendants of the hypothetical union between Jesus and Mary Magdalen. The different explanations given over time have mostly dealt with the novel's themes, and the polemic it engages against the Church. Dan Brown's best-seller is an anti-Bible in that it narrates a love story between Jesus Christ and Mary Magdalen, symbolising the ancient primacy of the Sacred Feminine, whose importance was supposedly

---

[1] Frye 1982. The "Great Code" of Frye's title is a reference to Blake's famous line in his *Laocoön*: "The Old and NewTestaments are the Great Code of Art".

repressed by the proto-orthodox Church. Some, like Friar Ponga, have argued that it is linked to the general decay of the Catholic Church as institution. The journalist Xavier Cheneseau, in *L'Anti-Da Vinci Code*, has even mentioned a form of "cathophobia". Another religious critic, Father Joseph-Marie Verlinde, connects the phenomenon with a perspective on the contemporary flowering of multiple forms of religiosity, in what Gérard Leclerc has termed "religious bricolage" (2002). Others like Gianluca Marletta in *La Riscoperta del Graal, dal fenomeno Dan Brown al ritorno dei miti* (2007) have shown how the novelist offers an intricately woven synthesis of different esoteric themes, such as the Grail, the Templars, the genesis of Christianity, thereby brewing a sort of alchemy between esotericism and paraliterature. All of these approaches rely more or less on the sociological study of literature, and more precisely on a sociological version of reception studies. Here, rather than relate the novel to external factors or the prevailing *Zeitgeist,* the aim is to tackle the question by looking more closely at the text itself.

If we tried to establish a typology of the commentaries on the *Da Vinci Code*, this would extend from Christian readings which react to the novel's polemical anti-Catholic charge, to ideologically neutral books published by writers unconcerned with the defence of their faith, but interested in trying to distinguish truth from fiction, from a purely historical perspective. Between these two poles, the faith-driven and the scientific, there lie multiple layers represented by books which bring forward both arguments appealing to believers and arguments appealing to specialists of the history of early Christianity. However divergent the ideological background of the studies may be, they all concur on one point: the *Da Vinci Code* contains unforgivable errors, of technique as well as fact, and whatever the paradigm adopted, all commentaries quickly come to resemble lists of howlers. We are not concerned here to synthesize the objections made by critical texts the quality of which is highly variable, but rather to encourage literary studies to deal in textual terms with a literary work, one that in terms of readership has also constituted a major literary event, whatever its accuracy in relation to the history of religions. The *Da Vinci Code* also tells us much about literature. As Daniel-Henri Pageaux writes: "...il n'y a pas de sujet pauvre, ou ingrat, il n'y a que des sujets mal poses" (2012).

According to one of the rare commentators who have discussed the novel not only in factual and historical but also in literary terms, the *Da Vinci Code* made one unforgivable error, as far the craft of thriller-writing is concerned: that of ruining the plot. Philippe Joret, in *Le "Da Vinci Code" et Jésus: les questions posées*, writes: 'Le mystère se dilue rapidement. A mi-course, Brown nous a déjà tout expliqué, ou presque [...] On sait tout tout de suite' (Joret 2006, 11). More precisely he argues that this occurs in the novel's central section, in both literal and figurative senses: the discussion at the château de Villette, when Leigh Teabing, with Robert Langdon's help, initiates Sophie Neveu into the mysteries of the Grail. The answer to the mysterious question *par excellence* - the nature of the Grail - is not given on the last page of the book, or suggested in what could have been an open ending, but on page 266 (Brown 2004). Let us start our analysis with this introductory paradox for such a successful best-seller: before being - and not being - the Great Code of Art, could the *Da Vinci Code* be, first and foremost, simply a bad thriller?

To use the typology of the detective novel offered by Tzvetan Todorov, Dan Brown's novel is certainly a thriller. Such a genre derives from the fusion of, on the one hand, the *roman d'énigme* which proceeds from consequence to cause, and strives to reconstitute the lost narrative of the crime motivating the investigation, and on the other hand, the *roman noir*, which proceeds from cause to consequence and which works through a succession of peripeteia. In short, the thriller mixes retrospection and prospection, and marries the two types of interest proper to the *roman d'énigme* and the *roman noir*: respectively, curiosity and suspense. Thus on the one hand the plot of the *Da Vinci Code* is about unveiling the fatal secret of the Louvre curator which motivated his assassination, the starting point of the narrative, and on the other it is about the investigation pursued by Robert Langdon, professor of symbology, investigator in his spare time, who is caught in a web of false appearances which triggers a series of unexpected turns. If we wanted to refine the description, the *Da Vinci Code* could be said to pertain to the sub-category of the theological thriller. Indeed, beneath the mystery of the assassination with which the novel begins lies a mystery of a theological kind: the presence of the Sacred Feminine occulted by the Church. The investigation reveals itself not only to be the quest for the lost narrative of the crime, but the quest *par excellence*, that of the Grail. Contrary to what some commentators have suggested, namely that the Grail is a literary motif amongst many others in the novel, it is in fact its principal subject theme. In the *Da Vinci Code*, Leigh Teabing describes the relic thus: "The quest for the Holy Grail is literally the quest to kneel before the bones of Mary Magdalene. A journey to pray at the feet of the outcast one, the lost sacred feminine" (Brown 2006, 266). And the novel ends precisely with Robert Langdon kneeling before the junction of the inverted pyramid and the miniature pyramid in the "Galerie du Carrousel du Louvre", next to the Louvre Museum.

Let us return now to the fundamental criticism made by Philippe Joret against this thriller which, he claims, reveals its code much too soon. What first appears as an anomaly, as far the thriller's plot is concerned, becomes fairly clear when we recall Todorov's discussion of the notion of the Grail novel, and notably the underlying opposition between two narrative schemes: the profane and the sacred. The profane is a narrative of contiguity, according to which the reader wants to know what comes next, whereas the sacred is one of substitution. The latter presupposes a series of paradigmatic variations which are aligned vertically; what the reader strives to know about each event is not what follows, but rather what it represents. This distinction casts this central, somewhat perplexing section of the novel, in which nothing happens and everything is revealed, in a different light. What occurs here is that the logic of Grail, the sacred narrative, momentarily prevails, supporting the claim that the *Da Vinci Code* is not, as some pretend, a poorly-written thriller, but rather, the avatar of a Grail novel.

In a famous article, Todorov comments on a passage of *La Queste del Saint Graal* where, at the threshold of a palace, Lancelot sees two lions standing guard. He unsheathes his sword, in accordance with a profane and chivalric code which is utterly inappropriate since this divine apparition pertains to a very different code. The critic comments, "Ignorer le code, c'est se voir refuser à jamais le Graal" then concludes:

> La Quête du Graal est la quête d'un code. Trouver le Graal, c'est apprendre à déchiffrer le langage divin, ce qui veut dire, nous l'avons vu, faire siens les a priori du système […].

Self-evidently, Dan Brown's novel has to do with codes, as the title itself announces. In the marginal notes he made on his novel *Il nome della rosa*, Umberto Eco attests to the significance of its title: "The title is already – unfortunately – a key for interpretation." But what sort of code are we dealing with? The Grail is partially a text, or more specifically, a group of texts which tell "the true story of Jesus": or to put it differently, a hidden Gospel. In the thriller, this group of revealing documents takes on many forms, the first of which are the Gnostic apocrypha. The term "gnostic" is generally used to designate a "specific assortment of religious systems or sects which are historically attested beginning in the second century C.E." (Williams 1999, 27). Here is the working definition produced at the famous international Congress held in Messina, Italy, in 1966, on the question of Gnosticism: "a coherent series of characteristics which can be summarized in the idea of a divine spark in man, deriving from the divine realm, fallen into this world of fate, birth and death, and needing to be awakened by the divine counterpart of the self in order to be finally re-integrated" (quoted in Williams 1999, 27). However, one needs to be very cautious when it comes to the definition of Gnosticism; Karen L. King, very much along the same lines as Williams, observes: "... the variety of phenomena classified as 'Gnostic' simply will not support a single, monolithic definition, and in fact, *none of the primary materials fits the standard typological definition*" (King 2003, 226).

Returning to the *Da Vinci Code*, Leigh Teabing extracts a volume of ancient apocrypha from one of the shelves in his library, which are misquoted in the novel. To this manifestation of the Grail texts, need to be added the hidden documents which supposedly lie in Mary Magdalen's tomb: they will never be found, but will forever stay "apocryphal", in the etymological sense of the word. But there remains yet another manifestation of this revealing text, and by no means the least significant. At the end of the novel, just before the epilogue, Robert Langdon asks Sophie's grand-mother, Marie Chauvel, why she does not care to reveal the mystery of the Grail, that is, the existence of the Sacred Feminine, which was occulted by Christian orthodoxy (Brown 2004, 444):

> "But if the Sangreal documents remain hidden, the story of Mary Magdalen will be lost forever", Langdon said.
> "Will it? Look around you. Her story is being told in art, music, and books. More so every day." (Brown 2004, 444)

In the central section of the novel there appears the same idea of a hidden revelation in the arts and literature; to borrow Barthes' expression, the "hermeneutic code" of the detective novel is indeed very peculiarly used in this best-seller. Sophie Neveu, who represents a figure of the reader in this scene of the initiation, remains stunned when faced with the importance of the revelation, and asks Robert Langdon for further explanations:

> "I know Leigh said the Grail story is all around us, but tonight is the first time I've ever heard any of this." [...]
>
> "You've heard her story before, Sophie. Everyone has. We just don't realize it when we hear it."
>
> "I don't understand."
>
> "The Grail story is everywhere, but it is hidden. When the Church outlawed speaking of the shunned Mary Magdalene, her story and importance has to be passed on through more discreet channels... channels that supported metaphor and symbolism."
>
> "Of course. The arts."

> Langdon motioned to the The Last Supper. "A perfect example. Some of today's most enduring art, literature, and music secretly tell the history of Mary Magdalene and Jesus."
>
> Langdon quickly told her about works by Da Vinci, Botticelli, Poussin, Bernini, Mozart, and Victor Hugo that all whispered of the quest to restore the banished sacred feminine. Enduring legends like Sir Gawain and the Green Knight, King Arthur, and Sleeping Beauty were Grail allegories. Victor Hugo's *Hunchback of Notre Dame* and Mozart's *Magic Flute* were filled with Masonic symbolism and Grail secrets.
>
> "Once you open your eyes to the Holy Grail", Langdon said, "you see her everywhere. Paintings. Music. Books. Even in cartoons, theme parks, and popular culture" (Brown 2004, 270-71).

In *Interpretation and Overinterpretation*, Umberto Eco reminds us that the secular poetry of Dante has built its own theory of interpretation on the foundations of biblical hermeneutics, and notably the theory of the four senses of scripture, be it in the *Convivio* or in the *Epistola XIII* (Eco 1992, 53). In the *Da Vinci Code*, literature opens itself to multiple layers of interpretation, not taking the Bible as a model, but intending to be its substitute. To the eyes of those initiated into the mysteries of the Grail, the Holy Scriptures are none other than literature and the arts. The Gnostic apocrypha, which are quoted for malign purposes, and totally rewritten by the thriller, become the sparse fragments of another Bible that would have been possible, of a "Great Code" of literature and the arts. Now the paradoxical expression mentioned in our introduction, that of the "paraliterary masterpiece", takes on a whole new dimension. As Daniel Couégnas shows, one of the criteria which were used to establish a "model of paraliterature", is the text's capacity "à imposer son propre code de lecture": "La paralittérature propose au lecteur un objet sémiotique accompagné, pourrait-on dire, de son mode d'emploi." *The Da Vinci Code* goes one step further by furnishing instructions for use concerning literature in general, from Hugo to the Sleeping Beauty, thus uniting, thanks to the same hermeneutic code, "high" and "low" literature: the winners and losers in the history of the literary canon. Dan Brown's best-seller fully belongs to "paraliterature", as we have decided to call popular fiction, but also positions itself above the fray of genres and categories: it is in a sense the Book of Books, if we borrow the well-known Hebraic superlative. In *S/Z*, when Roland Barthes comments on the following extract: "C'était plus qu'une femme, c'était un chef d'œuvre", he interprets the term "chef d'œuvre" as "l'origine (l'original) des copies", "la fondation du code dont seront issues les différentes répliques (de corps, en l'occurrence)" (Barthes 1970, 121). Or to put it differently, the code of codes.

This throws some light on the paradox which preoccupies many critics of the *Da Vinci Code*, this paraliterary Gnostic text, oxymoronic as the expression may appear to be. Indeed, an abyss separates what could be described as the extreme "readability" of a paraliterary text that is entirely transparent from the "unreadability" of Gnostic texts. Rémi Gounelle's commentary on the recently discovered Gospel of Judas could easily be extended to Gnostic texts in general:

> Ces développements, qui sont entrecoupés par de nombreuses lacunes, ne sont pas aisés à comprendre, et la recherche a à débattre encore de leur interprétation. Leur technicité n'est pas surprenante, et ne résulte pas d'une maladresse de l'auteur. Elle résulte de la complexité de la doctrine proposée, mais aussi de la volonté de ne pas la rendre accessible au grand nombre. (Gounelle 2007, 62)

What can be said of the relationship between paraliterature and Gnosticism? In the Château de Villette, the stunned Sophie Neveu asks Leigh Teabing how the secret attached to the descent of Jesus and Mary Magdalen could be hushed up for two millenia, and the latter stresses the paradox surrounding the mystery of the Grail. Avatar of Poe's "purloined letter", it is everywhere, but nobody can see it (Brown 2004, 261).

> "But how could a secret that big be kept quiet all of these years?"
>
> "Heavens!" Teabing said. "It has been anything but quiet! The royal bloodline of Jesus Christ is the source of the most enduring legend of all time – the Holy Grail. Magdalene's story has been shouted from the rooftops for centuries in all kinds of metaphors and languages. Her story is everywhere once you open your eyes."

The mystery, in other words, is everywhere around us. We just need to have the correct key to decipher it, or to put it differently, the right code to reveal it. The Gnostic and paraliterary logics can in some respects appear contradictory: Gnosticism addresses a handful of the chosen, whilst paraliterature by definition is aimed at the widest possible readership. Yet, Gnosticism and paraliterature converge, in that both are connected to the world outside by hermeneutic codes; both offer a vision of the world as a "boîte à double fond", to borrow the metaphor Couégnas uses, when he tackles the issue of the profound superficiality characterizing paraliterature:

> Il y a donc le plus souvent une espèce de superficialité du regard que le roman paralittéraire jette sur les êtres et les choses […] même si de manière faussement paradoxale, toute une rhétorique et une thématique du dévoilement, de l'élucidation, de la révélation au public, contribuent largement au succès d'une certaine paralittérature fondée sur les

> "mystères" (...de Paris), les "secrets", les "énigmes" [...]. Postuler que le monde ou la société fonctionnent comme des boîtes à double fond, c'est en limiter singulièrement le jeu, parce qu'une idéologie simpliste, éternelle et rassurante, très manichéenne – le "Mal" sous le "Bien" –, quelle que soit la thèse adoptée, se superpose à de telles investigations. (Couégnas 1992, 102)

Going from Gnosticism to paraliterature, we find the same binary obsession with the opposition between good and evil. It is not a mere coincidence from the point of view of the history of religions, that, to borrow Hans Jonas's expression in *The Gnostic Religion*, "the most important product of Gnosticism" precisely is Manichaeism (Jonas 1992, 208). Of course, this doctrine has been influenced by three religions - Christianity, Buddhism and Zoroastrianism - but it also re-interprets the fundamental Gnostic myth of cosmic exile and salvation.

The countless commentaries which have glossed the errors to be found in the *Da Vinci Code* have analyzed repeatedly Dan Brown's misrepresentation of the way Jesus is portrayed in Gnostic apocryphal gospels. Yet, beyond all of these mistakes, there subsists a kernel of truth about Gnosticism which the novel has faithfully represented: a hermeneutics of paranoia, as Umberto Eco analyzes it in *I limiti dell'interpretazione* (1990, 58). The Gnostic cosmology based on the duality between, on the one hand, the evil demiurge who created our world and, on the other, the *pleroma*, is after all nothing but a vast conspiracy theory. And it is ironic that behind this heterodox cosmology, we should find another use of the term "plot"! Gnosticism springs from "gnosis", or the knowledge one acquires of the mystery of the world, thanks to which the Gnostic reaches salvation:

> La gnosi non è, come il cristianesimo, una religione per gli schiavi, ma una religione per i signori. Lo gnostico si trova a disagio in un mondo che avverte estraneo e elabora un disprezzo aristocratico nei confronti della massa [...] A differenza della massa degli schiavi, solo il Superuomo gnostico capisce che il male non è un errore umano ma l'effetto di un complotto divino [...][2]

[2] "Gnosis is not, like Christianity, a religion for the slaves, but on the contrary, it is reserved to the masters. The Gnostic, who is not at ease in a world perceived as foreign, nourishes an aristocratic disdain towards the mass whom he reproaches for failing to recognize the world's negativity [...]. Contrary to the slaves, the Gnostic Übermensch understands that evil is not the result of a human mistake, but the consequence of a divine conspiracy [...]" (My translation)

As a Gnostic thriller, the *Da Vinci Code* stages the contradiction which lies at the heart of the paraliterary reading contract. Umberto Eco reminds us of the supreme paradox on which mass culture is based in his introduction to *Apocalittici e integrati*: mass culture gives its targeted public, the ordinary man, the illusion that he can become what the Italian critic, after Nietzsche, calls a "Superman":

> [...] si rifletta sul fatto che tipico della cultura di massa è stato sempre far balenare agli occhi dei propri lettori, cui viene richiesta una disciplinita "medietà", la possibilità che tuttavia – stanti le condizioni esistenti, e proprio grazie ad esse – possa un giorno fiorire dalla crisalide di ciascuno di noi uno *Űbermensch*. (Eco 2001, 5)[3]

To put it in a nutshell, from one "Superman" to another. In order to make sense of the *Da Vinci Code*, it is enlightening to link this paraliterary "Superman" to the Gnostic "Superman", as Umberto Eco defined him in *I limiti dell'interpretazione*. Dan Brown promises dozens of millions of readers a revelation which is reserved to few initiates. Thus, the paradoxical expression with which we started off, that of "a Gnostic, or more largely esoteric best-seller", expresses the truth underlying the whole of paraliterature.

Many commentators have spoken of "mystification" when describing the *Da Vinci Code*, notably when reflecting on the numerous *strata* of errors to be found in the novel. Jean-François Jeandillou, in his study entitled *Esthétique de la mystification,* reminds us that "to mystify" originally means "to initiate". The *Da Vinci Code* gives the reader the misleading impression of being fully initiated into the history of "high" art and literature, of being an *Űbermensch* of literary and artistic culture. Northrop Frye's study *The Great Code* focuses on that structuring element of Christian exegesis which is typology. Typology etymologically comes from "typos", which means mark or footprint: a typological reading of the Ancient Testament consists of examining it in order to discover the prefigurations of Christ's arrival. Just as the New Testament allows us to reread and understand the Old Testament in the light of the evangelical message, according to typology, so the *Da Vinci Code* claims to allow us to reread and understand literature in the light of the Grail secret, and thus to consider it as a whole entity, from popular fiction to masterpieces,

---

[3] "[...] we can see it by the fact that it is typical of mass culture to give... to its public, of whom is required a disciplined mediocrity, the possibility that in spite of all - those being the conditions, and precisely because of these conditions - one day from the chrysalis of each of one us will burst forth an Űbermensch." (My translation)

rather than as a field divided by splits – or, to maintain religious terminology, schisms –between "high" and "low".

Let us return to the initial scandal with which our analysis began, "scandal" in the sense of René Girard's term *skandalon*, which is generally translated as "scandale, obstacle, pierre d'achoppement, piège placée sur le chemin". Briefly put, the *Da Vinci Code* has been widely perceived as a scandalously ill-written thriller, because the plot and its corollary suspense are ruined from page 266 onwards. The reasons for the triumphant success of this thriller, though, are not to be found in the breath-taking peripeteia of a plot which, in the end, is caught between the contradictory imperatives of the thriller and the quest for the Grail. Rather, its appeal lies in its highly effective storytelling. Not only does Dan Brown offer us a labyrinthine plot, through the quests of his protagonists Langdon, Professor Teabing and Sophie Neveu (who in one of the final unexpected twists of the story discovers that she is actually a descendant of Christ). He goes even further: in this best-seller of best-sellers, he manages to retell the history of literature and the arts, casting these as the vectors of a hidden doctrine excluded from the Biblical canon. From this perspective, it can be argued that the *Da Vinci Code* enjoyed enormous success, in part because it is an avatar of a Grail quest novel where the reader, as seeker of the Grail, follows up clues and finally achieves a revelation, thereby validating the reading of the paraliterary text itself. The story that lies at the heart of the thriller is an effective "Storytelling" with a capital "S": it tells another Story of the way literature and the arts developed, from Arthurian romance to the novels of Hugo and beyond. Thanks to this last unexpected turn, the History of Literature has metamorphosed into a vast thriller made of pitfalls, shams and narratives, lost or occulted, which are yet to be revealed.

## Works Cited

Barthes, Roland. 1970. *S/Z*. Paris: Editions du Seuil, coll. Tel Quel.

Brown, Dan. 2004. *Da Vinci Code*. Special Illustrated Edition. London: Bantam Press.

Boyer, Alain-Michel. 1994. "Questions de paralittérature. La paralittérature face à la tradition orale et à l'ancienne rhétorique". *Poétique*, n°98, avril, 131-151.

Cheneseau, Xavier. 2006. *L'Anti "Da Vinci Code"*. Paris: Grancher, coll. Enigmes et polémiques.

Couégnas, Daniel. 1992. *Introduction à la paralittérature*. Paris: Editions du Seuil, coll. Poétique.

Eco, Umberto. 1993 (1964). *Apocalittici e integrati. Communicazioni di massa e teoria della communicazione di massa.* Milan: Bompiani, 21ème réédition.

—. 1993 (1978). *De Superman au surhomme*, trad. Myriem Bouzaher. Paris: Grasset.

—. 1987. *Apostille au Nom de la rose*, trad. Myriem Bouzaher. Paris: Librairie générale française, coll. Livre de poche.

—. 1996. *Interprétation et surinterprétation*, trad. Jean-Pierre Cometti. Paris: Presses Universitaires de France.

Frye, Northrop. 1981. *The Great Code. The Bible and Literature.* New York: Harcourt.

Girard, René. 1978. *Des choses cachées depuis la fondation du monde.* Paris: Librairie générale française, coll. Livre de poche.

—. 2001. *Celui par qui le scandale arrive.* Paris Desclée de Brouwer.

Gounelle, Rémi. 2007. "L'évangile de Judas ou comment devenir un bon gnostique?". Dans Jean-Daniel Kaestli et Daniel Marguerat dirs., *Le Mystère apocryphe, Introduction à une littérature méconnue.* Genève: Labor et fides, 2ème éd.

Jeandillou, Jean-François. 1994. *Esthétique de la mystification. Tactique et stratégie littéraires.* Paris: Les Editions de Minuit.

Jonas, Hans. 1978. *La Religion gnostique. Le message du Dieu étranger et les débuts du christianisme*, trad. Louis Evrard. Paris: Flammarion.

Joret, Philippe. 2006. *Le "Da Vinci Code" et Jésus: les questions posées.* Montpellier: P. Joret.

King, Karen L. 2003. *What is Gnosticism?* Cambridge, Mass./London: Harvard University Press.

Marletta, Gianluca. 2007. *La Riscoperta del Graal, dal fenomeno Dan Brown al ritorno dei miti.* Rome: Ed. Riuniti.

Pageaux, Daniel-Henri. 2005. "Littérature comparée et comparaisons" http://www.vox-poetica.org/sflgc/biblio/comparaisons.html

Ponga, Frère Silouane. 2006. *La Séduction de la pseudo-vérité: le "Da Vinci Code" de Dan Brown.* Nouan-le-Fuzelier: Ed. des Béatitudes.

Todorov, Tzvetan. 1991. *Poétique de la prose*, suivi *de Nouvelles recherches sur le récit.* Paris: Editions du Seuil, coll. Points.

Verlinde, Joseph-Marie. 2006. *Les Impostures antichrétiennes: des apocryphes au "Da Vinci Code".* Paris: Presses de la Renaissance.

Williams, Michael Allen. 1999 [1996]. *Rethinking Gnosticism: An Argument for Dismantling a Dubious Category.* Princeton, N.J.: Princeton University Press.

# POSTFACE

# *FINDING THE PLOT*: L'HISTOIRE N'EST PAS TERMINÉE …

## JACQUES MIGOZZI

"Finding the plot": par delà le jeu de mots, le titre de ce volume collectif vaut pour promesse, peut-être téméraire, d'éclairages nouveaux sur la force, les formes et les usages des fictions populaires d'hier, d'aujourd'hui et peut-être même de demain. Aussi faut-il se risquer, en guise d'ouverture conclusive à cet ouvrage, à faire saillir quelques points névralgiques du débat sur le *storytelling*, sa prégnance en régime médiatique et les plaisirs qu'il procure. Nous tenterons cette mise au point non pour asséner des vérités définitives mais bien au contraire en postulant que le renouvellement des perspectives, proposé par la polyphonie concertée des 21 contributions précédentes, appelle nécessairement des prolongements et des approfondissements, que la création récente, en mai 2011, de l'Association internationale des chercheurs en Littératures Populaires et Culture Médiatique devrait favoriser.

**1.** Toutes les contributions ici présentées plaident de facto ou explicitement pour un dépassement de l'opposition, trop commode pour être satisfaisante intellectuellement et pertinente sur le plan méthodologique, entre le "culturalisme" anglo-saxon, empirique et pragmatique, et la "pensée critique" européenne, conjuguant Ecole de Francfort et *french theory*, la seconde suspectant la première d'être complaisante à l'égard du pouvoir aliénant des industries culturelles, la première décelant dans les préventions antimédiatiques de la seconde et dans l'éloge de la *jouissance* du texte *scriptible* par opposition au plaisir plébéien du *lisible* – pour employer à dessein des notions barthésiennes évoquées dans l'Introduction – les symptômes d'un aristocratisme inavoué et bien peu progressiste. Les conditions semblent en effet désormais réunies sur le plan théorique pour penser la complexité du *storytelling* et de son impact sans céder à l'irénisme ou au catastrophisme, également réducteurs. Il peut paraître paradoxal d'affirmer cela alors que récemment l'essai de Christian Salmon a fait au contraire grand bruit en cultivant précisément un point de vue "apocalyptique" sur la question, démontrant encore une fois que, comme le rappelle l'Introduction du présent volume, la notion de *storytelling*, communément acceptée et approfondie théoriquement par les intellectuels anglophones, n'est apparue que rarement et le plus souvent dans des contextes polémiques dans les débats francophones. Mais c'est justement tout le mérite de plusieurs articles de démontrer que le succès médiatique de Salmon n'est possible qu'au prix de la méconnaissance des avancées de la recherche – y compris francophone, et peut-être même surtout francophone – depuis quinze ans sur les fictions et les pratiques des lecteurs-spectateurs au cœur de la culture médiatique moderne et contemporaine. Au sein du réseau des chercheurs scrutant de manière pluridisciplinaire ce qu'Eric Maigret et Eric Macé proposent de dénommer "médiacultures" (Maigret et Macé 2005), toute une salve de travaux se sont de fait efforcés récemment de prendre acte du rôle actif des individus dans l'appropriation des récits multimédiatiques, qu'ils ne se contentent pas seulement de "recevoir" mais métabolisent en quelque sorte dans une construction /renégociation constante de leur identité, au gré de pratiques éclectiques, volontiers ludiques, et de plus en plus interactives: il n'est que de se reporter par exemple aux contributions précédentes d'Anne Besson, Paul Bleton, Jacques Migozzi ou Malin Isaksson pour s'en convaincre. Le storytelling n'est donc désormais plus pensable, sauf à cultiver une certaine partialité pamphlétaire, comme une machinerie /machination nécessairement mystificatrice, qui dominerait ses lecteurs-spectateurs tout à la fois cibles et victimes: dès les années 1980, Michel de Certeau d'une part avec sa théorie des "usages" et sa vision de la lecture comme "braconnage", Paul Ricoeur d'autre part avec sa théorie du récit insistant sur l'étape décisive de la "reconfiguration" (*Mimesis III)* par le lecteur, avaient au demeurant forgé des outils pour dissiper cette légende noire de la fiction populaire comme opium du peuple, et l'influence séminale de ces deux philosophes est manifeste ici même dans plusieurs articles sous la plume de Marc Lits, Lise Dumasy, Jacques Migozzi, a fortiori Raphaël Baroni. Parallèlement aux échanges croissants des chercheurs spécialisés ès LPCM, des travaux majeurs, tels ceux du cognitiviste Jean-Marie Schaeffer ont en effet depuis quinze ans réhabilité l'importance anthropologique de la fiction en soulignant la complexité et la nécessité du jeu fabulatoire, et c'est en prolongeant ces travaux dans une perspective poéticienne nourrie de l'herméneutique ricoeurienne que Raphaël Baroni a pu éclairer de manière décisive la dynamique de la tension narrative fondatrice du storytelling, tension nécessaire et jubilatoire car nous avons foncièrement besoin d'être intrigués par des récits intriguants pour que "le vécu passionnel se converti[sse] en histoire passionnante" (Baroni 2007, 34). On trouvera ainsi dans la contribution de Baroni ici même une mise en perspective très suggestive sur le renouvellement du regard qu'autorise cette reconnaissance – sur tous les plans: cognitif, affectif, mais aussi symbolique – de la *discordance* éprouvée par le lecteur lors de la "lecture à l'endroit", i.e. celle de tous, alors que le regard savant – y compris celui de Paul Ricoeur ! – a jusqu'ici quasi exclusivement valorisé la saisie rétrospective et analytique d'une "lecture à l'envers", insistant ce faisant sur la *concordance* architecturée du récit, donc sur sa capacité à donner forme et sens à l'expérience humaine, mais hypertrophiant sans doute du même coup son pouvoir à modéliser les représentations de ses lecteurs... par le *storytelling.*

**2.** Or cette inflexion majeure du regard savant n'est possible, tant sur le plan théorique qu'au niveau des études de cas, qu'en se déprenant de l'ethnocentrisme de classe ou de caste qui a longtemps prédéterminé la conception lettrée de la lecture. Les clercs ont en effet, par une extrapolation qui tient du coup de force et de l'aveuglement volontaire sur ses propres pratiques, conçu le lecteur idéal à leur image, valorisant une posture de "coopération interprétative" distanciée de la fiction et de ses charmes, et ce bien sûr au détriment de l'"immersion mimétique" (Schaeffer) qu'active spontanément toute lecture consentant au romanesque. C'est donc au contraire du tête-à-tête intime du lecteur ordinaire avec le récit qu'il a toujours été question ici, ou plutôt de l'infinie variété *des* lecteur*s* et de*s* lecture*s* qui invalide certaines conjectures fondées sur l'artefact d'un "lecteur modèle". Ce lecteur ordinaire de fiction(s)– que j'ai même proposé de penser en *storyplayer* – pratique-t-il une lecture "populaire" de fictions "populaires"? Non si l'on entend par là une relation crédule d'un lecteur dominé à un *storytelling* dominant. Oui, si l'on désigne par "populaire" la part au cœur de toute lecture, donc chez tous et au sein de chacun, d'un engagement passionnel et passionnant dans la tension d'un récit. Au demeurant, il n'est que de lire les deux contributions de Richard Hibbitt et de Marc Lits pour se convaincre que le désir d'intrigue est irrépressible: Richard Hibbitt souligne d'une part que cette appétence pour une trame narrative organisatrice trouve à se satisfaire même à la lecture de textes expérimentaux, dont le roman symboliste *Bruges-la-morte* de Georges Rodenbach, dans ses raffinements stylistiques et son fragmentisme, offre un bel exemple; Marc Lits nous rappelle d'autre part avec netteté que dans notre société de "fabulation généralisée", selon la formule de Giorgio

Vattimo, le récit est partout et s'est même substitué à l'argumentation dans notre nouvel "espace public narratif symbolique".

**3.** Pour penser de manière renouvelée les plaisirs pris aux récits dont sont tissées nos vies, peut-être même faudrait-il alors se défier non seulement des connotations négatives de "*storytelling*" mais aussi de la charge sémantique négative qui leste en français le terme même d'"intrigue" – comme le rappelle judicieusement Paul Bleton – qui présuppose une domination par des manœuvres occultes. Plus neutre en apparence l'anglais "plot" n'en demeure pas moins lui aussi marqué par un imaginaire de la "machine à formater les esprits", car il est facilement assimilable à un "script" au sens qu'Yves Citton prête à ce terme dans son essai *Mythocratie. Storytelling et imaginaire de gauche* (Citton 2010, 78-81 et 104-5), c'est à dire à une forme narrative à fonction totalisatrice, capable d'orienter nos croyances et nos désirs par frayage neuronal. Que nous resterait-il alors à l'issue de cette table rase terminologique ? Peut-être, mais c'est peut-être beaucoup, "l'histoire"/ "the story", l'histoire/story qu'on habite, investit, métabolise par des usages ludiques et potentiellement libertaires, l'histoire/story qui permet au lecteur de s'évader, d'échapper aux assignations identitaires et d'explorer l'espace des possibles, l'histoire/*story* si vitale à notre "espèce fabulatrice" à écouter Nancy Huston…

**4.** Outre ces acquis d'ordre épistémologique, le présent volume offre par ailleurs nous semble-t-il des éclairages originaux sur les plaisirs de la lecture Romanesque.

**4.1.** Que la lecture des fictions de grande consommation, réputée divertissante et détendante, procure l'évasion dans le temps et dans l'espace, voilà qui n'est pas une révélation, d'autant que l'immersion dans les récits populaires a souvent été réduite – à tort – à un *escapisme* à fonction compensatoire et rassérénante. Mais à lire par exemple les contributions de Marc Guillaumie sur le genre du récit préhistorique ou de Diana Holmes sur les romans d'aventures historiques français à grand succès contant les tribulations d'une héroïne intrépide et libérée, on discerne mieux que ce dépaysement est d'autant plus piquant et prenant qu'il s'enlève sur un fond passionnel et pulsionnel, où le lecteur consent à une levée des normes sociales et morales, liée au libre exercice de la sexualité et/ou de la force. Matthieu Letourneux, dans sa synthèse de référence sur *Le Roman d'aventures. 1870-1930* (2010a), avait déjà souligné la "mauvaise foi" fondamentale du roman d'aventures, puisque le genre, s'il paraît condamner les valeurs de la sauvagerie, fonde sa séduction sur la mise en récit et en scène(s) de la violence transgressive, et parfois même sur les ambivalences d'un héros "roguish", au charme canaille, auquel il est moralement tentant de s'identifier… Cette thèse trouve ici confirmation et nous rappelle qu'au cœur de tout récit romanesque la catharsis – dont Natacha Levet repère l'importance au cœur du roman noir contemporain, d'essence tragique – joue sur la libido. Peter Brooks, significativement invoqué ici à la fois par Raphaël Baroni, Lise Dumasy ou Diana Holmes, avait pointé cette dimension libidinale essentielle du plaisir romanesque, et Michel Picard (1986) puis Vincent Jouve (1992), repris ici par Marc Lits, avaient insisté sur la projection du "lu", voyeuriste et désirant, au cœur de tout jeu lectoral. Le moment était probablement venu de rappeler cette évidence… mais sans assimiler, comme le faisait encore explicitement Michel Picard en 1986, ce plaisir indéniablement troublant à une satisfaction trouble et de bas étage que le lecteur supérieur devait dépasser pour atteindre à la dignité du "lectant".

**4.2**. Autre évidence ici revisitée et questionnée: celle du caractère foncièrement répétitif des fictions populaires et de leur plaisir fondé sur l'itération, tant de fois soulignée, depuis Umberto Eco parlant d'"orgie de redondance" "offrant au lecteur les joies de la reconnaissance du déjà connu", jusqu'au deuxième critère du "modèle paralittéraire" de Daniel Couégnas ("Une tendance à la reprise inlassable des mêmes procédés[… ]"), en passant par John Cawelti et sa notion de genres "formulaires". Personne ne disconvient ici de ce tropisme des formes et des genres populaires pour le retour du Même, le ressassement, le recyclage à tous niveaux, mais le plaisir pris par le lecteur à ces variations dans la répétition est saisi de manière neuve dans sa complexité, sans être réduit à "un plaisir régressif de retour à l'attendu" (Eco): de toute évidence, le regard dit savant sur les fictions dites populaires a changé de focale, depuis le cœur des années 1960 où de manière pionnière Umberto Eco s'intéressait à des objets *pop* comme James Bond et les structures narratives de la série de Ian Fleming, ou même depuis le début des années 1990 où Daniel Couégnas a bâti son modèle poéticien de la "lecture paralittéraire" selon des attendus encore très marqués par le textualisme dominant la "Nouvelle critique" française des années 1960-1980. Matthieu Letourneux, dont les travaux s'attachent à mieux cerner les enjeux de la sérialité narrative en matière de poétique des récits et de leurs usages, souligne par exemple avec subtilité que la prédictibilité de l'intrigue et de ses composants dramatiques et thématiques est au coeur du jeu lectoral: affranchi des pesanteurs de la réferentialité et de la relation à un auteur comme garant du texte, le *storytelling* sériel tire toute sa dynamique d'une intertextualité matricielle et procure au lecteur averti une "ivresse devant les infinies virtualités et l'arbitraire du conte". En scrutant les usages interactifs des fans, s'emparant de leurs récits-cultes, parfois de manière hétérodoxe par rapport au canon de l'auteur ou du producteur, et faisant ainsi proliférer une nébuleuse de fanfictions à partir d'un récit-source, on peut de même se convaincre avec Anne Besson que le *storytelling* des fictions visant le grand public, tout formulaire qu'il soit, fonctionne comme un incubateur de digressions. Anne Besson, lorsqu'elle considère la montée en puissance ces vingt dernières années, tant en littératures de genres qu'à la télévision, des récits cycliques à arc(s) narratif(s) long(s) au détriment des récits sériels fondés sur la duplication d'une formule à arc narratif court, affirme même que ce phénomène contemporain invalide la thèse désormais classique d'Umberto Eco selon laquelle "la narrativité de la redondance" des récits de grande consommation aurait pour fonction de rasséréner le lecteur accablé par l'opacité et la "surcharge informative" de "notre société industrielle contemporaine". Et pour faire bonne mesure, à croiser les conclusions de Natacha Levet sur le caractère foncièrement tragique du roman noir contemporain et celles de Diana Holmes sur la poétique picaresque de certaines sagas qui ne s'astreignent pas à un dénouement résolutif, on peut même affirmer que la vision d'un récit populaire clos, à la "narrativité non problématique", et dispensant par là même "espoir et consolation" au lecteur apaisé, vacille sérieusement sur ses bases…

**4.3**. L'intrigue ne saurait donc décidément plus longtemps être assimilée à un corset figeant le sens et menant le lecteur à la baguette, et il y aurait au contraire tout intérêt à mesurer à quel point le storytelling des récits multimédiatiques contemporains compose avec les usages ludiques des lecteurs-spectateurs-consomm*acteurs* d'aujourd'hui. La notion même d'intrigue est donc probablement à repenser dès lors qu'on tente de l'appliquer non à des textes clos et uniques, relevant – pour employer la terminologie de Richard Saint-Gelais – du "stade opéral" de la fiction, mais à des "polytextes" dont les avatars s'étoilent sur plusieurs supports et qui relèvent donc du "stade médiatique" de cette fiction désormais souvent gorgée de "transfictionnalité" (Saint Gelais 2011, 7).

N'assiste-t-on d'ailleurs pas avec l'avènement d'une seconde modernité que d'aucuns disent postmoderne à l'affaiblissement du rôle central de l'intrigue dans la séduction pourtant toujours aussi forte du récit? On sait qu'Alfred Hitchcock déclarait par boutade que "pour faire un bon film, vous avez besoin de trois choses: d'un bon scénario, d'un bon scénario, et d'un bon scénario", ce qui explique du même coup que le cinéma muet, pour prendre son essor, ait très pragmatiquement puisé à pleines mains dans le gisement des romans populaires à succès, à l'efficacité scénaristique éprouvée (pensons à la virtuosité d'Alexandre Dumas) et garantie par le succès. Pourtant, dès les années 1910 et 1920, sur les écrans européens le succès international de Fantômas, le "génie du crime",[1] ou de la cohorte des hommes forts, avec pour parangon l'italien Maciste (Dall'Asta, 1992), s'explique de toute évidence non pas tant par l'efficacité des intrigues que par le potentiel fantasmatique de ces figures héroïques érigées au rang d'icônes. Loïc Artiaga, lorsqu'il analyse ici même "les plaisirs mobiles" et très *pop* procurés par le polytexte se déployant autour de James Bond dans les *fifties* et les *sixties*, souligne également que 007, concentré de consumérisme, séduit avant tout en concentrant sur sa figure conquérante tous les hédonismes.

Un *storytelling* conquérant et séduisant ne serait donc pas nécessairement "*plotdriven*" avec fermeté mais peut se distinguer par sa force fantasmagorique. Cette hypothèse prend consistance si, comme le fait Matthieu Letourneux dans la revue *Strenae* (Letourneux, 2010b), on médite certaines conclusions de l'ouvrage d'Hiroki Azuma. Observant les pratiques des jeunes japonais immergés dans l'univers du manga, Azuma note que leur passion n'est pas soutenue par "l'unité de grands récits fictifs (logique architextuelle, univers transfictionnels, sérialité générique…) auxquels renverraient les œuvres" [car celle-ci] tend à disparaître; elle laisse alors place à des récits se contentant d'articuler des éléments d'attraction [personnages types, scènes de genres, détails fétichisés…] dont ils ne sont que les supports, sans renvoyer à d'autres cohérences que celle de l'accumulation des détails séducteurs". Azuma repère même

> une dernière tendance, caractéristique des décennies les plus récentes, et qui correspondrait à la disparition des récits eux-mêmes (y compris des "petits récits" de surface) au profit des seuls objets (figurines, images, jouets, cartes à jouer, etc.) qui seraient pour l'essentiel des composés de ces éléments d'attraction que l'amateur collectionnerait et déclinerait, repérant inlassablement les variations opérées à partir de cette "banque de données" implicite.

[1] Voir l'exposition virtuelle "Fantômas et l'Européenne du crime" du Musée virtuel "Popular Roots of European Culture": http://fantomas.popular-roots.eu/fr

Avec cet abandon de l'idée même de mise en intrigue ou de narration, irions-nous vers des fictions populaires sans *storytelling*, agrégeant des linéaments de narrativité portés par une nébuleuse d'images et d'objets?

**4.4**. Il serait toutefois bien téméraire de prophétiser l'effacement du récit et de son pouvoir intriguant, car Marc Lits comme Anne Besson, lorsqu'ils scrutent tous deux les pratiques contemporaines des réseaux sociaux organisés en "tribus" affinitaires, ou l'intense production de récits multimédiatiques par les *fandoms*, soulignent ici même tous deux la fonction cohésive des histoires sur le plan sociétal, au point qu'Anne Besson voit dans les récits fictionnels réappropriés par ces communautés de lecteurs partageant un même univers un substitut aux "grands récits", religieux ou politiques, de la première modernité. Restons plus prudents, et retenons a minima que l'un des charmes trop souvent méconnus du *storytelling* est qu'il crée des liens, en offrant en partage à des lecteurs un univers fabulatoire à investir, la jouissance d'une tension … et l'occasion d'échanger sur cette expérience.

**5.** Ce volume espère donc contribuer significativement à un renouvellement du regard savant sur l'intrigue, en la reliant systématiquement à "l'énergie cinétique d'une lecture passionnée", afin de la saisir "en mouvement et en puissance", pour employer deux formules de Raphaël Baroni. Le chantier ainsi balisé est aussi passionnant qu'immense. Nous n'avons pu en effet, dans les limites de ce volume, explorer les usages sociaux différents de cette aventure lectorale selon par exemple les variantes, absolument déterminantes, de la classe sociale du lecteur ou de son âge. Chaque lecteur le sait d'expérience, on n'habite pas un récit de la même manière – on ne lit d'ailleurs pas forcément le même type de récit – à 10, 15, 25, 40, ou 70 ans… Le sociologue Bernard Lahire (Lahire, 1993) a de même souligné de longue date à l'issue d'enquêtes approfondies, que les "lectures populaires" (en l'occurrence celles mises en œuvre par des lecteurs à capitaux social, scolaire et culturel modestes) se signalaient par des modes d'appropriation spécifiques de l'imprimé, qui se caractérisent fondamentalement par une volonté d'ancrage des textes dans une autre réalité que la seule réalité textuelle. Sans aucun doute donc cet ouvrage appelle des prolongements de sa réflexion sur une base résolument pluridisciplinaire.

Malgré les perspectives prometteuses ouvertes par certaines contributions, notamment celles questionnant le genre du *romance* et ses variantes transgressives, un dernier angle mort peut en particulier laisser le lecteur du présent livre sur sa faim: c'est celui du genre sexué (gender), dont la relation avec les plaisirs de lecture n'a pas ici fait l'objet d'investigations approfondies. Lit-on différemment selon son identité sexuée? Investit-on l'intrigue de manière genrée dans la tension d'une lecture immersive et "à l'endroit"? Certains genres fictionnels présenteraient-ils, par leurs thématiques ou leur poétique spécifiques, des affinités électives avec une lecture caractéristique du "deuxième sexe"?... Autant de questions légitimes et passionnantes, qui appellent plus que jamais les chercheurs à collaborer de manière interdisciplinaire et innovante, comme nous avons tenté ici de la faire.

## Références

Azuma, Hiroki. 2001. *Génération Otaku: les enfants de la post-modernité.* Paris: Hachette Littératures, Haute tension.

Baroni, Raphaël. 2007. *La Tension narrative. Suspense, curiosité et surprise*. Paris: Seuil, Poétique.

Citton, Yves. 2010. *Mythocratie. Storytelling et imaginaire de gauche.* Paris: Editions Amsterdam.

Couégnas, Daniel.1976. *Introduction à la paralittérature.* Paris: Presses Universitaires de France.

Dall'Asta, Monica. 1992. *Un cinéma musclé*. Crisnée: Yellow Now.

Frye, Northrop. 1982. *The Great Code: the Bible and Literature.* London: Routledge and Kegan Paul.

Jouve, Vincent. 1992. *L'Effet-personnage dans le roman*. Paris: PUF, Écriture.

Lahire, Bernard. 1993. "Lectures populaires: les modes d'appropriation des textes". *Revue française de pédagogie,* 104.

Letourneux, Matthieu. 2010a. *Le Roman d'aventure. 1870-1930*. Limoges: PULIM, coll. Médiatextes.

—. 2010b. Compte-rendu de Azuma 2001. *Strenae*, 1, 2010, http://strenae.revues.org/

Maigret, Eric et Macé, Eric, dirs. 2005. *Penser les médiacultures. Nouvelles pratiques et nouvelles approches de la représentation du monde*. Paris: Armand Colin et INA.

Picard, Michel. 1986. *La Littérature comme jeu*. Paris: Editions de Minuit, coll. Critique.

Ryan, Marie-Laure. 2001. *Narrative as Virtual Reality. Immersion and Interactivity in Literature and Electronic Media*. Baltimore & London: The John Hopkins University Press.

Saint-Gelais, Richard. 2011. *Fictions transfuges. La transfictionnalité et ses enjeux*. Paris: Poétique, Seuil.

# CONTRIBUTORS

## The Editors

**Loïc Artiaga** is **Assistant Professor** at the University of Limoges, and Associate Researcher of the *Centre d'histoire culturelle des sociétés contemporaines* (Université de Versailles Saint-Quentin-en-Yvelines). He is a member of the executive committee (Conseil d'Administration) of the LPCM (*Association internationale des chercheurs en Littératures Populaires et Cultures Médiatiques*). His publications include *Des Torrents de papier* (Limoges, Pulim, coll. « Médiatextes », 2007), and "James Bond: modes d'emploi (1965 – années 1990)", in *James Bond (2)007. Anatomie d'un mythe populaire* edited by Françoise Hache-Bissette, Fabien Boully and Vincent Chenille (Paris: Belin, 2007). His forthcoming book on Fantômas is due out in 2013: Loïc Artiaga and Matthieu Letourneux. *Fantômas. Figure mythique* (Paris: Autrement).

**Diana Holmes** is Professor of French at the University of Leeds. She is a founding member of the Leeds Popular Cultures Research network, and a member of the *Conseil d'Administration* of the LPCM. Her published work includes monographs on *Colette* (1991), *French Women Writers 1848-1994* (1996), *Rachilde – Decadence Gender and the Woman Writer* (2001), *Romance and Readership in Twentieth-Century France: Love Stories* (2006) and on the cinema of François Truffaut (1998) . She has recently co-edited a Special Issue of *French Cultural Studies* (with David Platten), *Story-Telling in Contemporary French Fiction: le 'prêt-à-penser' and Reading Pleasure*, 2010 (4), and a book on French popular culture (with David Looseley) forthcoming with Manchester University Press in 2013. Her current research is on the theory and practice of the middlebrow. She is a *Chevalier dans l'Ordre des Palmes Académiques.*

**Jacques Migozzi** is Professor of French Literature at the University of Limoges, and President of the *Association internationale des chercheurs en Littératures Populaires et Culture Médiatique* (LPCM). His more recent publications include *Boulevards du populaire* (Limoges, PULIM, coll. Médiatextes, 2005); two co-edited Special issues of journals :

"Récits journalistiques et culture médiatique", *A contrario* n° 12, 2009, http://www2.unil.ch/acontrario and "Roman populaire et idéologie", *Belphégor*, Volume 9, n° 2, janvier/février 2010, http://etc.dal.ca/belphegor/; "Storytelling: opium du peuple et / ou plaisirs du texte ?" in the Special Issue of *French Cultural Studies* referred to above; and "Cet obscur objet du désir universitaire: coup d'oeil dans le rétroviseur sur 15 ans de recherches sur les fictions populaires.", in *Fictions populaires*, edited by Nicolas Cremona, Bernard Gendrel and Patrick Moran (Classiques Garnier, 2011).

**David Platten** is Professor of Modern French Studies at the University of Leeds. He has published on a wide range of modern French writers, including Michel Tournier, Philippe Djian, Jorge Semprun and Jules Verne. His most recent book, published by Rodopi in 2011, is entitled *The Pleasures of Crime: Reading Modern French Crime Fiction.* A scholar and fan of detective and crime fiction, he has recently produced studies of the literary thriller and of the links between the media and politics in the contemporary crime novel. He is currently working on two projects: one on the aesthetics of popular fiction and the other on cultural representations of sport and sporting figures in France.

# Contributors

**Marc Atallah** holds the post of *Maître d'enseignement et de recherche* in the language and literature department of the University of Lausanne. His doctorate, awarded in 2008, was entitled "Écrire demain, penser aujourd'hui. La Science-fiction à la croisée des disciplines: façonner une poétique, esquisser une pragmatique". His current research is in the fields of science-fiction and theory of fiction and genres. In February 2011 he was also appointed Director of the *Maison d'Ailleurs*, a museum of science-fiction, utopias and 'voyages extrardinaires' in Yverdon-les-Bains. He has recently published *L'Homme-machine et ses avatars. Entre science, philosophie et littérature. XVIIe-XXIe siècles*, co-edited with D.Kunz Westerhoff (Paris: Vrin [Pour Demain]).

**Susan Bainbrigge** is Senior Lecturer in French at the University of Edinburgh. Her research focuses on twentieth-century and contemporary French literature and autobiography studies, especially in relation to Simone de Beauvoir. More recent research has taken her into the field of Belgian francophone literature. She is the author of *Writing against Death: the Autobiographies of Simone de Beauvoir* (2005), *Culture and Identity in*

*Belgian Francophone Writing: Dialogue, Diversity and Displacement* (2009), and co-editor, with Jeanette den Toonder, of *Amelie Nothomb: Authorship, Identity and Narrative Practice* (2003), and, with Joy Charnley and Caroline Verdier, of *Francographies: Identite et alterite dans les espaces francophones europeens* (2010).

**Raphaël Baroni** is Associate Professor of *didactique du français langue étrangère* at the University of Lausanne. In 2005 he established, with Thérèse Jeanneret, the *Groupe de recherche sur les biographies langagières*, and in 2010, with Françoise Revaz, the *Réseau romand de narratologie* (www.narratologie.ch). His work aims to develop general theories of narrative whilst exploring the implications of these for the teaching of literature and languages. He is the author of several books, including *La Tension narrative* (Seuil 2007), *L'Œuvre du temps* (Seuil 2009), *Le Savoir des genres* (PUR 2007, with Marielle Macé), and over fifty articles including "Rencontre de narrativités: perspectives sur l'intrigue musicale" (*Cahiers de narratologie*, n° 21, 2011, with Alain Corbellari).

**Anne Besson** is *maître de conférences* in general and comparative literature at the University of Artois (Arras). She specialises in novel series and cycles, particularly in the genres of science-fiction, fantasy and children's literature; her publications include *D'Asimov à Tolkien, cycles et séries dans la littérature de genre* (CNRS Editions, 2004), and *La Fantasy* (Klincksieck, collection « 50 questions », 2007). She is co-founder of the research association "Modernités médiévales", an executive member of the LPCM, and has edited several collaborative scholarly volumes. She is also a member of the jury for the book prize *Prix Imaginales*.

**Paul Bleton** is Professor of Literature at TELUQ, the distance-learning arm of the University of Quebec, and a longstanding and very active member of the LPCM. He has published extensively on modern and contemporary literature, particularly popular fiction; his recent books include *La Guerre fictive* (forthcoming 2012); *La Cristallisation de l'ombre* (Limoges: PULIM, 2011); with Désiré Nyela, *Lignes de front* (Montréal, PUM *espace littéraire*, 2009); with Mario Poirier, *Le Vagabond stoïque* (Montréal : PUM, 2004).

**Lise Dumasy-Queffélec** is Professor of French literature at the University Stendhal-Grenoble 3, and is also (since 2008) President of the University.

She is a specialist in the nineteenth-century *roman-feuilleton* : this was the subject of her doctoral thesis, and thereafter of two books *Le Roman-feuilleton français au XIXème siècle* (Paris: PUF, Que sais-je ?, 1989) and *La Querelle du roman-feuilleton* (Grenoble: ELLUG, coll. Archives critiques, 1999) as well as several further publications. Her research interests include the novel since the Revolution, and the relationship between imagination and ideology in literature.

**Tim Farrant** is Reader in Nineteenth-Century French Literature at the University of Oxford and Fellow and Tutor in French at Pembroke College Oxford. His publications include *Balzac's Shorter Fictions: Genesis and Genre* (Oxford: Oxford University Press, 2002) and *An Introduction to Nineteenth-Century French Literature* (London: Duckworth, 2007), as well as numerous articles on nineteenth-century French literature and culture. He is currently preparing two books on nineteenth-century short fiction, funded by the University of Oxford and the Arts and Humanities Research Council.

**Marc Guillaumie** teaches and researches at the University of Limoges. His specialist field is the prehistoric novel from the end of the nineteenth century to the present day: this has led him to explore the relationship between the modern imagination and prehistory, the popularisation of science in the arts, and the ideological uses to which prehistory lends itself. In 2006 he published *Le Roman préhistorique: essai de définition d'un genre, essai d'histoire d'un mythe*. (Limoges: PULIM, collection Médiatextes).

**Richard Hibbitt** is Senior Lecturer in French at the University of Leeds. His research interests are mainly in the field of late nineteenth-century French and comparative literature, but he also has wider interests in literature from the Renaissance to the present day. His publications include *Dilettantism and its Values: From Weimar Classicism to the Fin de Siècle* (2006), *Saturn's Moons: W. G Sebald – a Handbook* (2011, co-edited with Jo Catling), and essays on Paul Bourget, Jules Laforgue and Oscar Wilde. His current research is in the field of cosmopolitan and Decadence. He is member of the Executive Committee of the British Comparative Literature Association and Assistant Editor of its journal, *Comparative Critical Studies*.

**Brenda Hollweg** is a Visiting Research Fellow at the University of Leeds, School of Fine Art, History of Art & Cultural Studies. Her main research interests concern the interrelations of politics and aesthetics and the role experience and affect play in the production of knowledge. She is currently developing a new research project on the literary and visual personal essay, *Essaying Europe: New Subjectivities after 1989*. She is the co-editor (with Stephen Coleman) of a volume called *The Road to Voting* (with MUP, pending), following a larger interdisciplinary ARHC grant on the affective and aesthetic dimensions of voting. In 2010, she produced a 55min video essay also called *The Road to Voting* (accessible via LUTube, Uni Leeds). Brenda Hollweg has a PhD in English and American Studies; she has both worked inside and outside academia. She has taught at German and British universities on American literature and film, (Anglophone) cultural theory, feminist theory, the subject of collecting, exhibiting cultures and identity formation.

**Malin Isaksson** is Senior Lecturer in French at the Department of Language Studies, Umeå University, Sweden. Her research interests span reception studies, popular culture, contemporary French literature, gender and queer theory. She has published articles on femslash fanfic about 'tough girls' from popular culture, such as the vampire slayers Buffy and Faith from *Buffy the Vampire Slayer*. Together with Maria Lindgren Leavenworth she has co-authored essays about Twilight fan fiction, for instance in the anthologies *Fanpires: Audience Consumption of the Modern Vampire* (edited by Gareth Schott and Kirstine Moffat) and *Interdisciplinary Approaches to Twilight* (edited by Mariah Larsson and Ann Steiner). Isaksson is currently working on a book about vampire fan fiction (McFarland Publishers), also with Maria Lindgren Leavenworth, in a project funded by the Swedish Research Council.

**Alexandra Ivanovitch** is currently working on a PhD in Comparative Literature focusing on twentieth-century fictions of apocrypha (Borges, Bulgakov and Saramago) at the University of Paris-Sorbonne, where she also teaches. Her main research interests range from the relationship between the Bible and literature to translation studies and the works of Jorge Luis Borges. In 2009 she published an article in the *Revue de Littérature Comparée* on the poetry of Borges, notably on his poems which present themselves as fragments of apocryphal gospels; in 2010 her study of Goethe's reading of Johannes von Hildesheim's *Historia Trium Regum*: "Pour une poétique apocryphe" was published in the journal *Graphè*. Her 2011 article "Borges ¿profesor de literatura comparada ?", published in the 2011 collective volume *Borges y Francia,* deals with the courses in English Literature given by Borges in 1966 at the University of Buenos Aires.

**Matthieu Letourneux** is *maître de conférences* in French literature at the University of Paris Ouest Nanterre-La Défense. He specialises in nineteenth and twentieth-century literature and media culture, and in particular 'culture de jeunesse' or fictions designed for children. His publications include the edited works of Gustave Aimard, Gabriel Ferry, Emilio Salgari et Eugène Sue; he has also recently edited *Culture médiatique*, (*Compar(a)ison*, 2005), *L'Avenir du livre de jeunesse* (with Cécile Boulaire et Claudine Hervouet, BNF, 2010) and *Les Formes de la fiction dans la culture pour la jeunesse* (*Strenae*, 2011). With Pierre Brunel et Frédéric Mancier he co-edited the *Dictionnaire des mythes d'aujourd'hui* (éd. du Rocher, 1999). In 2010 he published his monograph *Roman d'aventures, 1870-1930* (PULIM, 2010), and in 2011, with Jean-Yves Mollier, *La Librairie Tallandier, Histoire d'une grande maison d'édition populaire (1870-2000)* (Nouveau Monde).

**Natacha Levet** is *maître de conférences* at the University of Limoges, and a member of the research team *Littératures populaires et culture médiatique* within the research institute *Espaces Humains et Interactions Culturelles*. Her principal research field is detective fiction, and in particular the *roman noir* from the late twentieth century to now, and the emergence of the figure of the investigator in European media culture at the end of the nineteenth century. Her post is in the *Institut Universitaire de Formation des Maîtres du Limousin*, where she collaborates on research into the cultural practices of teenagers. Her publications include *Sherlock Holmes. De Baker Street au grand écran* (Paris: Editions Autrement, 2012) and "Les engagements du polar pour la jeunesse" in *Contre l'innocence. Esthétique de l'engagement en littérature de jeunesse* (ed. B. Benert and P. Clermont, Oxford: Peter Lang, 2011).

**Marc Lits** is professor in the department of communication of the Catholic University of Louvain (Belgium) and dean of the faculty of economics, social and political science and communication. He is head of the *Observatoire du récit médiatique* (ORM), a research team specializing in the analysis of news media and popular or 'mass' cultural production. His most recent books are: *Du récit au récit médiatique* (2008), *Le Roman policier dans tous ses états* (2011) and *Communication politique et lobbying* (2011).

**Imogen Long** is Lecturer in French at the University of Hull. Having previously published several book chapters and articles on figures such as Simone de Beauvoir, Benoîte Groult, Danièle Sallenave and Françoise Parturier, she is currently preparing a research monograph on women intellectuals in France after May 68, forthcoming with Palgrave Macmillan. With Maggie Allison, she is also co-editor of *Women/Matter: French and Francophone Women and the Material World*, to be published with Peter Lang in 2012.

**David Looseley** is Emeritus Professor of Contemporary French Culture at the University of Leeds and, from April 2012 to 2013, honorary Research Fellow at the University of Bristol. He founded the Leeds-based Popular Cultures Research Network in 2005 and was its director until 2010. He has published extensively on contemporary French culture, including *Popular Music in Contemporary France: Authenticity, Politics, Debate* (Berg, 2003) and an edited special issue of *French Cultural Studies* on popular music (June 2005). He is co-editor with Diana Holmes of a monograph entitled *Imagining the Popular in Contemporary French Culture* (Manchester University Press, forthcoming 2013) and has begun researching a new monograph: *Édith Piaf: A Cultural History* (Liverpool University Press). In 2010, he was made Chevalier dans l'Ordre des Palmes Académiques by the French government for services to French culture.

# INDEX